PRAISE FOR OTHER AMERICA'S TEST KITCHEN TITLES

"*The Cook's Illustrated Cookbook* is the perfect kitchen home companion."
THE WALL STREET JOURNAL ON
THE COOK'S ILLUSTRATED COOKBOOK

"If this were the only cookbook you owned, you would cook well, be everyone's favorite host, have a well-run kitchen, and eat happily every day."
THECITYCOOK.COM ON *THE AMERICA'S TEST KITCHEN MENU COOKBOOK*

"This book upgrades slow cooking for discriminating, 21st-century palates—that is indeed revolutionary."
THE DALLAS MORNING NEWS ON
SLOW COOKER REVOLUTION

"Forget about marketing hype, designer labels and pretentious entrées: This is an unblinking, unbedazzled guide to the Beardian good-cooking ideal."
THE WALL STREET JOURNAL ON
THE BEST OF AMERICA'S TEST KITCHEN 2009

"Expert bakers and novices scared of baking's requisite exactitude can all learn something from this hefty, all-purpose home baking volume."
PUBLISHERS WEEKLY ON *THE AMERICA'S TEST KITCHEN FAMILY BAKING BOOK*

"If you're hankering for old-fashioned pleasures, look no further."
PEOPLE MAGAZINE ON *AMERICA'S BEST LOST RECIPES*

"This tome definitely raises the bar for all-in-one, basic, must-have cookbooks. . . . Kimball and his company have scored another hit."
PORTLAND OREGONIAN ON *THE AMERICA'S TEST KITCHEN FAMILY COOKBOOK*

"A foolproof, go-to resource for everyday cooking."
PUBLISHERS WEEKLY ON *THE AMERICA'S TEST KITCHEN FAMILY COOKBOOK*

"The strength of the Best Recipe series lies in the sheer thoughtfulness and details of the recipes."
PUBLISHERS WEEKLY ON *THE BEST RECIPE SERIES*

"These dishes taste as luxurious as their full-fat siblings. Even desserts are terrific."
PUBLISHERS WEEKLY ON *THE BEST LIGHT RECIPE*

"Further proof that practice makes perfect, if not transcendent. . . . If an intermediate cook follows the directions exactly, the results will be better than takeout or mom's."
NEW YORK TIMES ON *THE NEW BEST RECIPE*

"Like a mini-cooking school, the detailed instructions and illustrations ensure that even the most inexperienced cook can follow these recipes with success."
PUBLISHERS WEEKLY ON *BEST AMERICAN SIDE DISHES*

"Makes one-dish dinners a reality for average cooks, with honest ingredients and detailed make-ahead instructions."
NEW YORK TIMES ON *COVER & BAKE*

"Sturdy, stick-to-your-ribs fare that deserves a place at the table."
PORTLAND OREGONIAN ON *COOK'S COUNTRY BEST LOST SUPPERS*

"The best instructional book on baking this reviewer has seen."
LIBRARY JOURNAL (STARRED REVIEW) ON
BAKING ILLUSTRATED

"A must-have for anyone into our nation's cooking traditions—and a good reference, too."
LOS ANGELES DAILY NEWS ON *AMERICAN CLASSICS*

Pasta
REVOLUTION

200 FOOLPROOF RECIPES THAT GO BEYOND
SPAGHETTI AND MEATBALLS

BY THE EDITORS AT
America's Test Kitchen

PHOTOGRAPHY BY
Carl Tremblay and Daniel J. van Ackere

AMERICA'S TEST KITCHEN
17 Station Street, Brookline, MA 02445

Library of Congress
Cataloging-in-Publication Data

Pasta revolution : 200 foolproof recipes that go
beyond spaghetti and meatballs / by the editors
at America's Test Kitchen ; photography by
Carl Tremblay and Daniel J. van Ackere ;
additional photography by Keller + Keller.
— 1st ed.

  p. cm.

Includes index.

ISBN 978-1-936493-04-3

1. Cooking (Pasta) 2. Cooking, American.
3. Cookbooks.
I. Tremblay, Carl. II. Van Ackere, Daniel.
III. America's Test Kitchen (Firm)
IV. Keller + Keller.
TX809.M17P3655 2012
641.82'2--dc23
                    2011042335

Paperback: $26.95 US

Manufactured in the United States of America

10 9 8 7 6 5 4 3 2 1

Distributed by America's Test Kitchen
17 Station Street, Brookline, MA 02445

EDITORIAL DIRECTOR: Jack Bishop

EXECUTIVE EDITOR: Elizabeth Carduff

EXECUTIVE FOOD EDITOR: Julia Collin Davison

SENIOR EDITOR: Lori Galvin

ASSOCIATE EDITORS: Kate Hartke and Adelaide Parker

ASSISTANT TEST COOK: Ashley Wood

EDITORIAL ASSISTANT: Alyssa King

DESIGN DIRECTOR: Amy Klee

ART DIRECTOR: Greg Galvan

ASSOCIATE ART DIRECTOR: Erica Lee

PHOTOSHOOT KITCHEN TEAM:

  ASSOCIATE EDITOR: Chris O'Connor

  ASSISTANT TEST COOKS: Daniel Cellucci, Danielle DeSiato-
  Hallman, Sarah Mayer

FRONT COVER PHOTOGRAPH: Carl Tremblay

STAFF PHOTOGRAPHER: Daniel J. van Ackere

ADDITIONAL PHOTOGRAPHY: Keller + Keller, Kate Kelly, Steve Klise,
Anthony Tieuli, Carl Tremblay

FOOD STYLING: Marie Piraino, Kelly Upson

PRODUCTION DIRECTOR: Guy Rochford

SENIOR PRODUCTION MANAGER: Jessica Quirk

SENIOR PROJECT MANAGER: Alice Carpenter

PRODUCTION AND TRAFFIC COORDINATOR: Kate Hux

ASSET AND WORKFLOW MANAGER: Andrew Mannone

PRODUCTION AND IMAGING SPECIALISTS: Judy Blomquist, Heather Dube,
Lauren Pettapiece

COPYEDITOR: Jeffrey Schier

PROOFREADER: Debra Hudak

INDEXER: Elizabeth Parson

PICTURED ON FRONT COVER: Kale and Sunflower Seed Pesto (page 269)

PICTURED OPPOSITE TITLE PAGE: Super-Easy Spinach Lasagna (page 89)

PICTURED ON BACK OF JACKET: Penne with Sausage, Chickpeas, and
Broccoli Rabe (page 107), Ziti with Fire-Roasted Tomatoes, Pepperoni,
and Smoked Mozzarella (page 204), Skillet-Baked Ziti with Sausage
(page 43), Coconut Rice Noodles with Shrimp and Pineapple (page 156)

Contents

Welcome to America's Test Kitchen

This book has been tested, written, and edited by the folks at America's Test Kitchen, a very real 2,500-square-foot kitchen located just outside of Boston. It is the home of *Cook's Illustrated* magazine and *Cook's Country* magazine and is the Monday-through-Friday destination for more than three dozen test cooks, editors, food scientists, tasters, and cookware specialists. Our mission is to test recipes over and over again until we understand how and why they work and until we arrive at the "best" version.

We start the process of testing a recipe with a complete lack of conviction, which means that we accept no claim, no theory, no technique, and no recipe at face value. We simply assemble as many variations as possible, test a half-dozen of the most promising, and taste the results blind. We then construct our own hybrid recipe and continue to test it, varying ingredients, techniques, and cooking times until we reach a consensus. The result, we hope, is the best version of a particular recipe, but we realize that only you can be the final judge of our success

(or failure). As we like to say in the test kitchen, "We make the mistakes, so you don't have to."

All of this would not be possible without a belief that good cooking, much like good music, is indeed based on a foundation of objective technique. Some people like spicy foods and others don't, but there is a right way to sauté, there is a best way to cook a pot roast, and there are measurable scientific principles involved in producing perfectly beaten, stable egg whites. This is our ultimate goal: to investigate the fundamental principles of cooking so that you become a better cook. It is as simple as that.

You can watch us work (in our actual test kitchen) by tuning in to *America's Test Kitchen* (www.americastestkitchentv.com) or *Cook's Country from America's Test Kitchen* (www.cookscountrytv.com) on public television, or by subscribing to *Cook's Illustrated* magazine (www.cooksillustrated.com) or *Cook's Country* magazine (www.cookscountry.com). We welcome you into our kitchen, where you can stand by our side as we test our way to the "best" recipes in America.

Preface

Some folks are all for revolution whereas others, Vermonters, for example, don't take kindly to change. As one flatlander commented to a Vermonter, "I imagine you've seen a lot of great changes in your lifetime." "Yes," replied the older farmer, "sure have. And I've been against every darn one of them."

When it comes to the kitchen, many of us do have the urge to move forward, to find better ways of cooking familiar foods. A good example is pasta. In the days of Fannie Farmer, all pasta was referred to as "macaroni." It was boiled for 20 minutes, covered in cheese, and then baked in milk. In the 1950s and '60s, out came the ersatz pasta recipes, a shift that was closely followed by the reintroduction of authentic pasta dishes in the 1980s and '90s, and then food writers started looking farther afield, to Asian noodle recipes, for example. Still, all things considered, most of us depend much too heavily on a basic tomato sauce, butter and cheese, and olive oil and garlic.

So what is this pasta revolution about? We start by making pasta in a skillet, not just our classic Skillet Meaty Lasagna, but also Skillet Saltimbocca Spaghetti and Skillet-Baked Chicken Parmesan and Penne. Or, how about pasta casseroles that use uncooked pasta such as No-Prep Baked Spaghetti? Or, new ideas for whole-wheat pasta including Spaghetti with Lentils, Pancetta, and Escarole? Yes, we do have the greatest hits, carefully tested and updated for the 21st century, but we also offer Chilled Somen Noodles with Shrimp as well as Spaghetti with Lemon, Basil, and Scallops.

We also make good use of the slow cooker for a Big-Batch Marinara Sauce, get adventurous with a Green Olive and Orange Pesto, and offer a series of downsized pasta recipes for two including Mini Meat Lasagna.

Sure, many classic recipes are best left alone, at least in concept, but pasta, much like rice and potatoes, is such a foundation ingredient that it lends itself to endless variation. That can be a good thing if the recipes are well tested and vetted, or a bad thing if creativity runs amok. Hopefully, the rigor of our test kitchen offers the former, not the latter. The other type of recipes—they sound good but are a bit short in the taste department—is referred to in Vermont as "nothing I would run uphill after."

So, if you feel the time has come for a revolution in pasta cookery, join us for this well-tested group of recipes. I can promise that the recipes will work the first time, every time. And I would definitely run uphill after that!

CHRISTOPHER KIMBALL
Founder and Editor,
Cook's Illustrated and *Cook's Country*
Host, *America's Test Kitchen* and
Cook's Country from America's Test Kitchen

Pasta 101

Introduction

For many cooks, pasta is what you turn to when you don't have time to plan anything else. In other words, it's become a quick and filling but not terribly exciting dinner. With this book we aim to revolutionize not just how we cook pasta, but how we think about it.

The simplicity of preparing pasta has translated into complacency in the American kitchen. Most home cooks make the same tomato sauce over and over, occasionally "mixing up" the routine with some basil pesto or creamy Alfredo. But pasta for dinner doesn't have to mean a second-class supper. Take a look at the recipe on the cover of this book. It looks familiar, but that green pesto is actually made with kale and sunflower seeds along with a pinch of red pepper flakes. Because the kale and sunflower seeds are raw, the flavors are especially vibrant in this pesto, which takes just 10 minutes to prepare.

The biggest change in the pasta world has been the choice of noodles. Whole-wheat pasta was once sour, gritty, and downright awful, but new manufacturing processes have created firm, nutty noodles that will be a revelation to anyone who hasn't tried them recently. The quality of convenience products, such as shelf-stable gnocchi and frozen ravioli, has dramatically improved. And the influx of Asian noodles—everything from rice noodles to soba noodles—has opened up a whole new world of recipes to the American home cook. We hope this book will serve as your guide to this exciting new world of pasta. We guarantee that the 200 recipes you'll find here will offer plenty of inspiration.

It's worth noting that the media's obsession with counting carbs has obscured some basic facts about pasta. Pasta is an economical, nutritious, and almost infinitely variable ingredient. We have identified more than 50 recipes in this book as lighter choices,

all with no more than 600 calories and 14 grams of fat per serving. And because these dishes make a complete meal (perhaps with a simple leafy green salad added), they are an easy way to plan healthy meals everyone will eat. And more than a dozen recipes in this book show you how to turn nutritious whole-wheat pasta into satisfying dishes. In the test kitchen, we've found that whole-wheat pasta works best with hearty flavors, and so recipes like Penne with Sausage, Chickpeas, and Broccoli Rabe will teach you how to put this wholesome pasta to good use.

For the person who plans family meals, pasta is especially appealing because it is a blank canvas that can easily take on varied personalities. No one is going to complain about having Pad Thai with Shrimp one night, followed by Pasta with Garlicky Tuscan Chicken the next. But what many cooks might not realize is that pasta cooking techniques can be varied as well. We will teach you how to ditch that big pot of boiling water and cook a variety of pastas right in the sauce. How about Easiest-Ever Lasagna, which requires absolutely no prep or precooking? Have you ever toasted vermicelli in a hot pan to make Mexican-style sopa seca? And the slow cooker is a great tool for making big batches of sauce—that is, if you can figure out how to pump up the flavors and get sauces to simmer down to the proper consistency. (Don't worry, the test kitchen has.)

Use this book to reboot your view of pasta. Start by checking out the pasta myths on the opposite page. Make sure you have the right tools on hand and master our foolproof method for turning out perfectly al dente pasta every single time. Then dive into the recipes and start a revolution in your own kitchen. Keep the spaghetti and meatballs, but make room for some new favorites, too.

The Top Pasta Myths

We've been cooking pasta for a long time and have encountered numerous old wives' tales when it comes to the best way to do so. Here are the top myths we've encountered—and debunked.

MYTH: The best dried pastas come from Italy.
FACT: In taste tests, we've found that American spaghetti rivaled Italian pasta in terms of flavor and texture, and it costs much less.

MYTH: A pot of hot tap water will boil much more quickly than a pot of cold tap water.
FACT: Using hot tap water will save you only about 1½ minutes; we tested this using four quarts of water on an average stove. Also, the U.S. Environmental Protection Agency warns that hot tap water can contain higher levels of lead than cold tap water; they recommend running cold tap water (until the water is as cold as it can get) to ensure that any lead deposits are flushed out.

MYTH: Cooking the pasta in gently simmering water, rather than water at a rolling boil, will prevent boilovers after you add the pasta.
FACT: Boilovers happen not because of the water's temperature, but because of the size of the pot. So be sure to use a large pot (at least 6 quarts).

MYTH: Adding salt to the cooking water at the outset will make it come to a boil more quickly.
FACT: While salt will help the water boil more quickly, any undissolved grains may "pit" the pot, leaving marks that can't be washed away. The real reason to add salt is that it adds flavor—you should add at least a tablespoon of table salt for 4 quarts of water when cooking a pound of pasta. Add it with the pasta, not before, so it will dissolve and not stain the pot.

MYTH: Adding oil to the cooking water will keep pasta from sticking together as it cooks.
FACT: Don't waste your oil—it merely floats on top of the water, doing nothing for the pasta. The oil coats the pasta only when you drain it—and this prevents the sauce from sticking. To keep pasta from sticking, give the pot a stir several times while it's cooking.

MYTH: You should always follow the cooking times written on the pasta box.
FACT: While the cooking directions on the box will give you an idea of how long the pasta will take to cook, these times are usually too long and will result in mushy, overcooked pasta. Taste the pasta a few minutes ahead of time to determine the doneness; we prefer pasta cooked al dente, when it has a little bite left in the center.

MYTH: The best way to tell if pasta is cooked is to throw it against the wall to see if it sticks.
FACT: Throwing pasta at the wall only makes a mess. The best way to tell if your pasta is cooked perfectly—al dente—is to pluck a piece or two from the pot and taste it.

MYTH: When draining pasta, you should shake the colander to remove all the water you can.
FACT: When draining the pasta, leave it a little wet. The small amount of cooking water that remains on the pasta helps to spread the sauce and is especially useful when tossing pasta with relatively dry oil-based sauces. It's also a good idea to reserve a little pasta cooking water in case you need to thin out a thick sauce.

MYTH: You should rinse the pasta after draining it to wash away any excess starch.
FACT: Unless you're making a chilled pasta salad, leave the pasta hot and slightly starchy; the starch will help the sauce cling to the pasta.

How to Cook Pasta

Cooking pasta seems simple—just boil water and wait—but cooking perfect pasta takes some finesse. Here's how we do it in the test kitchen.

1. BRING PLENTY OF WATER TO A ROLLING BOIL
You'll need 4 quarts of water to cook 1 pound of dried pasta. Pasta leaches starch as it cooks; without plenty of water to dilute it, the starch will coat the noodles and they will stick. Use a pot with at least a 6-quart capacity.

2. SALT THE WATER, DON'T OIL IT
Adding oil to cooking water just creates a slick on the surface of the water, doing nothing for the pasta. And when you drain the pasta, the oil prevents the sauce from adhering. Adding salt to the water, however, is crucial, as it adds flavor. Add 1 tablespoon of salt per 4 quarts of water.

3. ADD PASTA, STIR IMMEDIATELY
Stirring the pasta for a minute or two when you add it to the boiling water, and occasionally while it's cooking, will prevent it from sticking together—and to the pot.

4. CHECK OFTEN FOR DONENESS
The timing instructions given on the box are almost always too long and will result in mushy, overcooked pasta. Tasting is the best way to check for doneness. We typically prefer pasta cooked al dente, when it still has a little bite left in the center.

5. RESERVE SOME COOKING WATER, THEN DRAIN THE PASTA
Reserve about ½ cup cooking water before draining the pasta—the water is flavorful and can help loosen a thick sauce. Drain the pasta in a colander, but don't rinse the pasta or shake the colander vigorously, since some water helps the sauce coat the pasta.

6. SAUCE, SEASON, AND SERVE
Return the drained pasta to the empty pot and add your sauce (usually about 3 to 4 cups per pound of pasta, depending on the sauce). To coat the noodles, toss them with a pasta fork or tongs, adding pasta cooking water as needed to get your sauce to the right consistency.

Pasta Equipment and Tools

Check out the cooking section at any retail shop or department store, and you'll be surprised by the amount of specialty pasta cooking equipment on display. But do you really need any of it? We don't think so. In fact, we think it's best to pass up the pasta-geared tools and gadgets (most of which just don't work) and instead invest in certain key pieces of equipment. You'll turn to these multitaskers again and again—and they are absolute must-haves when cooking pasta. Here are our pasta-making essentials, along with information on our recommended brands.

DUTCH OVEN

Though it doesn't really matter what kind of pot you use for boiling pasta, we prefer to use a Dutch oven, which is more compact and easier to maneuver than a big stockpot—especially when it's full of boiling water and a pound of pasta. In addition to cooking pasta in it, we also use this pot to make some pasta sauces and one-pot pasta suppers. When picking out a Dutch oven, look for one that's midweight—if it's too heavy, it'll be a pain to move when you need to drain your spaghetti, and if it's too light, it'll heat too quickly and could result in burnt sauces or other food. Also, it should have a capacity of at least 6 quarts—any smaller and you'll risk boil-overs. Our favorite brand is the **All-Clad Stainless 8-Quart Stockpot** ($294.95)

SKILLETS

In this book, we use skillets to cook both pasta sauces and one-pan pasta dishes (in which the pasta cooks directly in the sauce). When it comes to cooking sauces, the wide, flat surface of the skillet encourages evaporation, so liquids reduce and thicken quickly. We think every kitchen should be stocked with two kinds—traditional and nonstick. A traditional skillet lets you build pasta sauces with rich, deep, long-simmered flavor, even in quicker recipes, like our Campanelle with Sautéed Mushrooms and Thyme (page 17). How? It allows for the formation of fond, browned bits left behind after sautéing aromatics and vegetables or browning meats—these bits contribute flavor.

Our favorite brand is the **All-Clad Stainless 12-Inch Fry Pan** ($110; left). For recipes in which the pasta cooks right in the sauce, such as Skillet Meaty Lasagna (page 47), we like to use a nonstick skillet; its slick cooking surface means you don't have to worry about starchy noodles sticking to the pan while the pasta is simmering away. We like the **T-Fal Professional Total 12½-Inch Nonstick Fry Pan** ($34.99; right).

Pasta Equipment and Tools

COLANDER

Straining is obviously a big part of cooking pasta, and having a sturdy, heavy-duty colander is crucial and prevents a serious mishap with a huge pot of boiling water. The **RSVP International Endurance Precision Pierced 5-Quart Stainless Steel Colander** ($32.95) is a solidly constructed model that won't tip over, thanks to a metal ring on the bottom. This mega-perforated colander allows for quick draining, and the holes are small enough that pasta won't slip through.

FINE-MESH STRAINER

While a colander can tackle the bigger draining jobs, for smaller jobs you'll need a sturdy fine-mesh strainer. When it comes to pasta, we most often use this tool for draining canned tomatoes, but it is also useful for straining sauces. Our winner is the **CIA Masters Collection 6¾-Inch Fine-Mesh Strainer** ($27.50), which is durable and has a wide bowl rest so it will sit securely for straining.

LADLE

A ladle is the easiest way to sauce your pasta without making a huge mess on the counter. We prefer a stainless steel model; plastic can stain easily and melt on the stovetop. **The Rösle Ladle with Pouring Rim** ($36) has a deep bowl to hold a good amount of sauce and a spill-prevention rim for neat, tidy transport from pot to pasta bowl.

SPIDER SKIMMER

When we need to pull a piece of pasta out of a large pot of boiling water to test for doneness, or retrieve some quickly blanched vegetables from a big pot of water, we rely on a spider skimmer. Essentially a shallow basket at the end of a long handle, a spider is composed of wire mesh with wide openings that let the hot water drain away quickly and safely. We like the **WMF Profi Plus 13-Cm Wok Mesh Strainer** ($18); it has an angled handle, which keeps fingers far away from the sides of the pot.

WOODEN AND SLOTTED SPOONS

To stir aromatics, sauces, and pasta, you need a good, solid wooden spoon. Spoons that are too big, with long, hulking handles, will make extended stirring tiresome; on the other hand, spoons that are too light can snap or break easily. Aim for a midweight model with a broad bowl, which can cover a lot of surface area, and thin edges, which scrape more effectively than thick edges. We like the **Mario Batali 13-Inch Wooden Spoon** ($7.95; left); it has a form-fitting handle for comfortable stirring. Also, to pull a piece of small pasta from boiling water or to retrieve crisped pancetta or bacon from a pan, a slotted spoon is a must. The **OXO Good Grips Nylon Slotted Spoon** ($6.99; right) has a deep bowl to cradle food securely and holes that are small enough to allow liquid to drain quickly but not let anything else slip through.

Pasta Equipment and Tools

TONGS

Just as important as spoons and spatulas, tongs are a test kitchen staple and are pressed into service for many tasks. We utilize tongs to flip, lift, or turn any kind of food while it's cooking—and we also use them in less obvious ways, such as lifting pot lids when the potholder is out of reach. We also prefer tongs for handling and portioning spaghetti, linguine, or other kinds of long pasta. We like the **OXO Good Grips 12-Inch Locking Tongs** ($12.95). They open and close easily and have slightly concave pincers that grip food securely.

HEATPROOF RUBBER SPATULA

Heatproof spatulas aren't just for baking—they can be used for any number of pasta-related applications, from scraping up stuck-on bits from a pan's surface to folding delicate vegetables into a pot of pasta. Our favorite model is the **Rubbermaid Professional 13½-Inch High-Heat Scraper** ($15), which has a long, comfortable handle and a wide, stiff blade with a thin, flexible edge that makes getting into the corners of a pan easy.

GARLIC PRESS

If you're cooking a pasta dish, chances are that you'll need to mince some garlic—and using a garlic press is the easiest and fastest way to do that. We prefer presses that have a large chamber to hold multiple cloves of garlic. The test kitchen's favorite model is the **Kuhn Rikon Easy-Squeeze Garlic Press** ($20), which stays true to its name (it's really effortless to mince garlic) and has comfortable curved handles.

CHEESE GRATERS

What bowl of pasta is complete without a sprinkling of Parmesan? Not many. When we need a dish of Parmesan to pass at the table, we reach for our rasp-style grater or rotary grater. With its super-sharp teeth, the rasp grater can turn a hunk of hard cheese into ultra-fine shreds quickly. We like the **Microplane Classic 40200 Zester/Grater** ($14.95; left). We use a rotary grater when we want larger, more rustic shreds of cheese (it works with both hard and semisoft cheeses); it has a chamber that holds the food to be shredded and a crank handle that operates the grating mechanism. The easy-to-operate **Zyliss All Cheese Grater** ($19.95; center) is our winner. Though not ideal for tableside use, we find that a box grater is still an essential in the test kitchen. With its large shredding plane and holes in various sizes, it's the right tool for shredding both hard and soft cheeses—ideal when we need to blast through a big block of mozzarella for a casserole—plus onions and more. Our winner, the **OXO Good Grips Box Grater** ($17.95; right), has a snap-on container for easy cleanup.

PASTA CAPRESE

New Classics

Fusilli with Fresh Tomato Sauce

Serves 4 to 6

✔ WHY THIS RECIPE WORKS: Full, juicy, in-season tomatoes are a perfect match for pasta—if you know how to prepare them. For a sauce that makes the most of their bright, fresh flavor and meaty texture, we cooked the chopped tomatoes briefly in extra-virgin olive oil with a few cloves of garlic and a pinch of red pepper flakes. Peeling and seeding the tomatoes first gave us a more refined sauce, perfect for an elegant yet easy summer supper. Using a skillet promoted quick evaporation, and thinning out the sauce with a small amount of pasta cooking water brought it to just the right consistency to cling to the pasta. Chopped basil, saved for the end, contributed additional freshness and color, and a bit more olive oil enriched the sauce. The success of this dish depends on using ripe, flavorful tomatoes. For more information on peeling fresh tomatoes, see page 13. For the nutritional information for this recipe, see page 306.

2	pounds very ripe, in-season tomatoes
¼	cup extra-virgin olive oil
3	garlic cloves, minced
	Pinch red pepper flakes
	Salt and pepper
1	pound fusilli
2	tablespoons chopped fresh basil
	Grated Parmesan cheese

1. Bring 4 quarts water to boil in large pot. Using paring knife, cut out stem and core, then make small X in bottom of each tomato. Working with several tomatoes at a time, add them to boiling water and cook until skins begin to loosen, 15 to 45 seconds. Remove tomatoes from water (do not drain pot), let cool slightly, then remove loosened tomato skins with paring knife. Seed tomatoes, then cut them into ½-inch pieces.

2. Heat 2 tablespoons oil, garlic, and pepper flakes in 12-inch skillet over medium heat until garlic is fragrant but not browned, about 2 minutes. Stir in tomatoes and ¼ teaspoon salt, increase heat to medium-high, and cook until tomato pieces lose their shape and form chunky sauce, about 10 minutes.

3. Meanwhile, return pot of water to boil. Add pasta and 1 tablespoon salt and cook, stirring often, until al dente. Reserve ½ cup cooking water, then drain pasta and return it to pot. Add sauce, basil, ¼ cup reserved cooking water, and remaining 2 tablespoons oil and toss to combine. Season with salt and pepper to taste and add remaining reserved cooking water as needed to adjust consistency. Serve with Parmesan.

ON THE SIDE ROSEMARY-OLIVE FOCACCIA
Press 1 pound pizza dough into well-oiled 13 by 9-inch baking dish or 10-inch pie plate and dimple surface with fingers. Brush dough liberally with extra-virgin olive oil and sprinkle with ¼ cup chopped olives, ½ teaspoon minced fresh rosemary, ½ teaspoon kosher salt, and ½ teaspoon pepper. Bake in 400-degree oven until golden brown, about 30 minutes. Cool on wire rack and serve warm. Serves 6.

Summer Pasta with Corn, Cherry Tomatoes, and Ricotta Salata

Serves 4 to 6

✓ **WHY THIS RECIPE WORKS:** This fresh pasta dish features two farm stand favorites—sweet corn and tomatoes. To enhance the corn's natural sweetness, all we needed to do was sauté it briefly. For substantial bites of tomato, we selected cherry tomatoes and halved them. Adding them toward the end of cooking ensured they held their shape and didn't disintegrate; a few minutes was enough to soften them slightly and heat them through. To keep this dish fresh and light, we simply tossed the pasta with extra-virgin olive oil and a generous quantity of chopped basil and mint. Toasted pine nuts and shaved salty ricotta salata (a firm, tangy Italian sheep's-milk cheese) provided textural contrast and rounded out the dish. The fresh herbs are a major component rather than just a garnish in this dish, so we found it important to treat them with extra care. Both basil and mint have a tendency to discolor once chopped, so don't mince them too far ahead of time, and wait until just before serving to stir them into the pasta. We like the flavor of ricotta salata in this dish, but Pecorino Romano cheese can be substituted. Do not substitute frozen corn for the fresh corn here.

6	tablespoons extra-virgin olive oil
2	shallots, minced
3	ears corn, kernels cut from cobs
	Salt and pepper
6	garlic cloves, minced
⅛	teaspoon red pepper flakes
1	pound cherry tomatoes, halved
1	pound farfalle
¼	cup pine nuts, toasted
½	cup chopped fresh basil
½	cup chopped fresh mint
4	ounces ricotta salata, shaved

1. Heat 2 tablespoons oil in 12-inch nonstick skillet over medium-high heat until shimmering. Add shallots and cook until softened, about 2 minutes. Add 2 tablespoons more oil, corn, and ¼ teaspoon salt and cook until corn is tender and spotty brown, about 10 minutes. Stir in garlic and pepper flakes and cook until fragrant, about 1 minute. Stir in tomatoes and cook until they just begin to soften, about 3 minutes.

2. Meanwhile, bring 4 quarts water to boil in large pot. Add pasta and 1 tablespoon salt and cook, stirring often, until al dente. Reserve ½ cup cooking water, then drain pasta and return it to pot. Add sauce, pine nuts, and remaining 2 tablespoons oil and toss gently to combine. Season with salt and pepper to taste and add reserved cooking water as needed to adjust consistency. Before serving, stir in basil and mint. Sprinkle individual portions with ricotta salata and serve immediately.

QUICK PREP TIP PREPARING FRESH CORN
To remove kernels from an ear of corn, stand cob upright inside large bowl; this will help catch any flying kernels. Then, using paring knife, slice down along sides of cob to remove kernels.

Pasta Caprese

Serves 4 to 6

✓ **WHY THIS RECIPE WORKS:** Adding the popular Caprese trio of ripe tomatoes, fresh mozzarella, and fragrant basil to hot pasta ought to result in a satisfying, summery pasta dish. But usually the heat from the pasta makes the cheese clump in the bottom of the bowl. We found a solution: Freeze the cheese. Dicing the cheese and chilling it for a few minutes before adding it to the piping-hot pasta allowed the cheese to soften slightly but kept it from fully melting (and turning chewy). Basil and lemon juice, added just before serving, gives this dish a fresh, bright finish. The success of this recipe depends on high-quality ingredients, including ripe, in-season tomatoes and a fruity olive oil. Don't skip the step of freezing the mozzarella, or the cheese will become chewy in the finished dish.

¼	cup extra-virgin olive oil
2	teaspoons lemon juice, plus extra as needed
1	small shallot, minced
1	small garlic clove, minced
	Salt and pepper
1½	pounds vine-ripened tomatoes, cored, seeded, and cut into ½-inch pieces
12	ounces fresh mozzarella cheese, cut into ½-inch pieces and patted dry with paper towels
1	pound penne
¼	cup chopped fresh basil
	Sugar

1. Whisk oil, lemon juice, shallot, garlic, ½ teaspoon salt, and ¼ teaspoon pepper together in large serving bowl. Add tomatoes, toss gently to combine, and let marinate for 10 to 45 minutes (do not overmarinate). Place mozzarella on plate and freeze until slightly firm, about 10 minutes.

2. Meanwhile, bring 4 quarts water to boil in large pot. Add pasta and 1 tablespoon salt and cook, stirring often, until al dente. Drain pasta, then add to bowl of marinated tomatoes. Add frozen mozzarella, toss gently to combine, and let sit for 5 minutes. Stir in basil and season with salt, pepper, sugar, and extra lemon juice to taste. Serve immediately.

ON THE SIDE ARUGULA SALAD WITH FIGS AND PROSCIUTTO
Cook 2 ounces thinly sliced prosciutto, cut into ¼-inch-wide ribbons, in 1 tablespoon olive oil in small skillet over medium heat until crisp, about 7 minutes; drain on paper towels. Microwave ½ cup dried figs, stemmed and chopped, 3 tablespoons balsamic vinegar, and 1 tablespoon honey together in covered bowl until figs are plump, about 30 seconds. Stir in 3 tablespoons extra-virgin olive oil, 1 small minced shallot, ¼ teaspoon salt, and ⅛ teaspoon pepper and let cool. Toss fig dressing with 5 ounces arugula and sprinkle with crisped prosciutto and shaved Parmesan. Serves 6.

Fresh Tomatoes **101**

Nothing competes with the bright flavor and firm texture of fresh, ripe tomatoes. But, depending on the recipe, they might need some preparation. Here's how we get tomatoes ready for cooking, plus some tips on buying and storage.

Coring

Every part of the tomato is edible except the tough core and stem. To remove this inedible part, use the tip of a paring knife and cut around the stem, angling the tip of the knife slightly inward. When finished, you'll remove a cone-shaped piece of stem and hard core from the top.

Buying and Storing Tomatoes

If you can get your hands on in-season field-grown tomatoes, there is nothing better. But when the supermarket is your only option, be sure to buy vine-ripened tomatoes; they are juicier and more flavorful than the other beefsteak varieties that are ripened off the vine. At home, we've found the best way to prolong the shelf life of fresh tomatoes is to store them at room temperature, stem end down. The scar left on the tomato skin where the stem once grew provides both an escape for moisture and an entry point for mold and bacteria; placing a tomato stem end down blocks air from entering and moisture from exiting the scar.

Dicing

Tomatoes' shape and texture can make them hard to cut. Using a chef's knife or a serrated knife, after coring the tomato, cut it into round slices. Cut the slices into strips, then cut the strips into a dice. This works with both seeded and unseeded tomatoes.

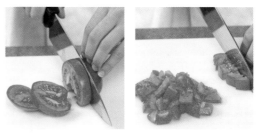

Seeding

Tomato seeds have great flavor, but they can be distracting if you want a smooth sauce. To seed a tomato, first cut it in half through the equator, then use your finger to pull out the seeds and the gel that surrounds them.

Peeling

The fibrous texture of tomato skins can be off-putting in some more refined pasta sauces, such as our Fusilli with Fresh Tomato Sauce (page 10), so we recommend peeling the tomatoes in these cases. To peel a tomato, first cut out the stem and core, then score a small X at the base. Lower the tomato into boiling water and simmer until the skin loosens, 15 to 45 seconds. Let cool slightly. Then, using a paring knife, remove the loosened tomato skin starting at the X at the base.

Spaghetti with Cherry Tomatoes, Olives, Capers, and Pine Nuts

Serves 4 to 6

✓ **WHY THIS RECIPE WORKS:** For an even-in-winter fresh tomato sauce with height-of-summer flavor, we turned to a supermarket staple, cherry tomatoes, and used heat to boost their flavor. Roasting them in a single layer cooked off extra moisture and produced a sweet and intensely flavored sauce in just over half an hour. Tossing them with a bit of sugar beforehand helped them develop a tasty, caramelized exterior and provided a bit more sweetness. Red pepper flakes, capers, and slivered garlic, roasted with the tomatoes, punched up the flavor of the sauce, while a final sprinkling of chopped kalamata olives amplified the bright and briny notes of the capers. A handful of toasted pine nuts introduced a welcome crunch factor.

2 **pounds cherry tomatoes, halved**
¼ **cup olive oil**
¼ **cup capers, rinsed**
3 **large garlic cloves, sliced thin**
1½ **teaspoons sugar, or to taste**
½ **teaspoon red pepper flakes**
  Salt and pepper
1 **pound spaghetti**
½ **cup pitted kalamata olives, chopped**
¼ **cup pine nuts, toasted**
3 **tablespoons chopped fresh oregano**
  Grated Pecorino Romano cheese

1. Adjust oven rack to middle position and heat oven to 350 degrees. Gently toss tomatoes with oil, capers, garlic, sugar, pepper flakes, ½ teaspoon salt, and ¼ teaspoon pepper, then spread into even layer on rimmed baking sheet. Roast tomatoes, without stirring, until their skins are slightly shriveled, 35 to 40 minutes. Let cool for 5 to 10 minutes.

2. Meanwhile, bring 4 quarts water to boil in large pot. Add pasta and 1 tablespoon salt and cook, stirring often, until al dente. Reserve ½ cup cooking water, then drain pasta and return it to pot. Scrape roasted tomato mixture into pasta using rubber spatula. Add olives, pine nuts, and oregano and toss to combine. Season with salt and pepper to taste and add reserved cooking water as needed to adjust consistency. Serve with Pecorino.

QUICK PREP TIP TOASTING NUTS AND SEEDS
Toasting nuts and seeds maximizes their flavor and takes only a few minutes. To toast a small amount (1 cup or less) of nuts or seeds, put them in a dry skillet over medium heat. Shake the skillet occasionally to prevent scorching and toast until they are lightly browned and fragrant, 3 to 8 minutes. Watch the nuts closely because they can go from golden to burnt very quickly. To toast a large quantity of nuts, spread the nuts in a single layer on a rimmed baking sheet and toast in a 350-degree oven. To promote even toasting, shake the baking sheet every few minutes, and toast until the nuts are lightly browned and fragrant, 5 to 10 minutes.

Ziti with Roasted Tomato Sauce and Goat Cheese

Serves 4 to 6

✔ WHY THIS RECIPE WORKS: Oven-roasted and slightly charred tomatoes make a great base for a vibrant, slightly smoky pasta sauce in this dish. To expose their juicy flesh, we halved our tomatoes, then spread them out on a baking sheet to roast. Unfortunately, they ended up stewing in their own juice. Upping the roasting time only led to dried-out tomatoes. Cooking them elevated—using a wire rack over the baking sheet—was the key. It allowed for maximum air circulation and promoted better charring, leading to a more concentrated roasted tomato flavor. Tossing the tomatoes with tomato paste prior to cooking gave the sauce a deep red color and another layer of tomato flavor. For some aromatic backbone, we used the open space on the rack to roast an onion and garlic cloves; setting them on a piece of aluminum foil in the center of the rack prevented them from falling through the wires or off the edge. A few crumbles of goat cheese provided a tangy richness, while woodsy fresh rosemary paired nicely with the roasted, smoky notes of the sauce. For the nutritional information for this recipe, see page 306.

2	tablespoons tomato paste
2	tablespoons extra-virgin olive oil
1	teaspoon minced fresh rosemary or ¼ teaspoon dried
	Salt and pepper
⅛	teaspoon red pepper flakes
3	pounds vine-ripened tomatoes, cored and halved pole to pole
1	small onion, sliced into ½-inch-thick rings
6	garlic cloves, peeled
1	teaspoon red wine vinegar
	Sugar, as needed
1	pound ziti
2	ounces goat cheese, crumbled (½ cup)

1. Adjust oven rack to middle position and heat oven to 475 degrees. Line rimmed baking sheet with aluminum foil, top with wire rack, and place 4-inch square of foil in center of rack. Combine tomato paste, 1 tablespoon oil, rosemary, ¾ teaspoon salt, ¼ teaspoon pepper, and pepper flakes in large bowl. Add tomatoes, onion, and garlic and toss to coat. Place onion rounds and garlic on foil square. Arrange tomatoes, cut side down, on rack around garlic and onions. Roast until vegetables are soft and tomato skins are well charred, 45 to 55 minutes.

2. Let roasted vegetables cool for 5 minutes. Pulse garlic and onion in food processor until finely chopped, about 5 pulses. Add tomatoes, vinegar, and remaining 1 tablespoon oil to processor and pulse until tomatoes are broken down but still chunky, about 5 pulses, scraping down bowl as needed. Season mixture with salt, pepper, and sugar to taste and pulse until sauce is slightly chunky, about 5 pulses.

3. Meanwhile, bring 4 quarts water to boil in large pot. Add pasta and 1 tablespoon salt and cook, stirring often, until al dente. Reserve ½ cup cooking water, then drain pasta and return it to pot. Add sauce and toss to combine. Season with salt and pepper to taste and add reserved cooking water as needed to adjust consistency. Sprinkle individual portions with goat cheese before serving.

QUICK PREP TIP ROASTING THE VEGETABLES
To maximize charring and flavor development, we elevated the vegetables on a rack set in an aluminum foil–lined rimmed baking sheet. The garlic and onion should be positioned on a small square of foil set in the center of the rack; the foil prevents them from slipping through the rack and drying out. Then the halved tomatoes can be placed, cut side down, around the edges of the rack.

Campanelle with Sautéed Mushrooms and Thyme

Serves 4 to 6

✓ **WHY THIS RECIPE WORKS:** For an effortless pasta and mushroom dish with bold, earthy flavor, we doubled-up on the mushrooms—cremini for their rich, meaty nature and shiitakes for their hearty flavor and chewy texture—and simply sautéed them with butter and oil. A bit of salt ensured they released their liquid and also encouraged browning. Because shiitakes contain more moisture, we gave them a head start in the pan. Minced thyme deepened the woodsy notes of the dish. Once the mushrooms had browned, we set them aside and built our sauce, scraping up the browned bits left in the pan to ensure that none of that meaty mushroom flavor went to waste. Chicken broth provided the backbone of the sauce, while heavy cream added a silky richness. So the sauce and pasta finish cooking at the same time, add the pasta to the boiling water just after adding the cremini to the skillet.

2	tablespoons unsalted butter
2	tablespoons extra-virgin olive oil
3	large shallots, minced
	Salt and pepper
3	garlic cloves, minced
10	ounces shiitake mushrooms, stemmed and sliced ¼ inch thick
10	ounces cremini mushrooms, trimmed and sliced ¼ inch thick
4	teaspoons minced fresh thyme
1¼	cups low-sodium chicken broth or vegetable broth
½	cup heavy cream
1	tablespoon lemon juice
1	pound campanelle
2	ounces Parmesan cheese, grated (1 cup)
2	tablespoons minced fresh parsley

1. Heat butter and oil in 12-inch skillet over medium heat until butter has melted. Add shallots and ½ teaspoon salt and cook until softened, about 4 minutes. Stir in garlic and cook until fragrant, about 30 seconds. Stir in shiitakes, increase heat to medium-high, and cook for 2 minutes. Stir in cremini mushrooms and cook, stirring occasionally, until golden brown, about 8 minutes. Stir in thyme and cook 30 seconds. Transfer mixture to bowl and cover to keep warm.

2. Add broth to now-empty skillet and bring to boil over high heat, scraping up any browned bits. Off heat, stir in cream and lemon juice. Season with salt and pepper to taste.

3. Meanwhile, bring 4 quarts water to boil in large pot. Add pasta and 1 tablespoon salt and cook, stirring often, until al dente. Reserve ½ cup cooking water, then drain pasta and return it to pot. Add mushroom mixture, cream sauce, Parmesan, and parsley and cook over medium heat, tossing to combine, until pasta absorbs some sauce, 1 to 2 minutes. Season with salt and pepper to taste and add reserved cooking water as needed to adjust consistency. Serve.

Pasta with Roasted Cauliflower, Garlic, and Walnuts

Serves 4 to 6

✔ **WHY THIS RECIPE WORKS:** High-heat roasting transforms cauliflower from a mild-mannered vegetable to an intensely flavored, sweet, nutty foil for pasta. To achieve a golden exterior, we sliced the cauliflower into wedges for maximum surface area while leaving the core and florets intact. Tossing the cauliflower with sugar jump-started the browning; preheating the baking sheet also helped. Cream-based sauces muted the nutty cauliflower flavor, and pestos overwhelmed it, so we focused on a simple lemony vinaigrette with roasted garlic.

2　garlic heads, top quarter cut off to expose garlic cloves

6　tablespoons plus 1 teaspoon extra-virgin olive oil

2　tablespoons lemon juice, plus extra as needed

¼　teaspoon red pepper flakes

1　head cauliflower (2 pounds)
　Salt and pepper

¼　teaspoon sugar

1　pound campanelle

1　ounce Parmesan cheese, grated (½ cup), plus extra for serving

1　tablespoon chopped fresh parsley

¼　cup walnuts, toasted and chopped coarse

1. Adjust oven rack to middle position, place large rimmed baking sheet on rack, and heat oven to 500 degrees. Place garlic heads, cut side up, in center of 12-inch square of aluminum foil. Drizzle each with ½ teaspoon oil and wrap securely. Place packet on oven rack and roast until garlic is very tender, about 40 minutes. Transfer packet to cutting board, let cool for 10 minutes, then unwrap garlic. Gently squeeze to remove cloves from skin, transfer to small bowl, and mash smooth with fork. Stir lemon juice and pepper flakes into mashed garlic, then slowly whisk in ¼ cup oil.

2. Meanwhile, remove outer leaves from cauliflower and cut stalk flush with bottom. Cut head from pole to pole into 8 equal wedges. Toss cauliflower with remaining 2 tablespoons oil, 1 teaspoon salt, ¼ teaspoon pepper, and sugar in bowl. Remove baking sheet from oven. Carefully lay cauliflower, cut sides down, on hot baking sheet in even layer. Roast cauliflower until well browned and tender, 20 to 25 minutes. Transfer cauliflower to cutting board, let cool slightly, then cut into ½-inch pieces.

3. Bring 4 quarts water to boil in large pot. Add pasta and 1 tablespoon salt and cook, stirring often, until al dente. Reserve 1 cup cooking water, then drain pasta and return it to pot. Add chopped cauliflower, garlic sauce, Parmesan, parsley, and ¼ cup reserved cooking water and toss to combine. Season with salt, pepper, and extra lemon juice to taste and add reserved cooking water as needed to adjust consistency. Sprinkle individual portions with walnuts and serve with extra Parmesan.

QUICK PREP TIP CUTTING CAULIFLOWER
To cut cauliflower into sizable pieces for roasting, first trim base of stalk. Then place head upside down and cut cauliflower crown in half through stalk. Cut each half of crown in half to make 4 wedges, and each of those in half again to make 8 equal wedges.

Pasta with Roasted Broccoli, Garlic, and Almonds

Serves 4 to 6

✔️ **WHY THIS RECIPE WORKS:** Inspired by our Pasta with Roasted Cauliflower, Garlic, and Walnuts (page 19), we decided to take a similar approach with broccoli. For intense browning, we prepared it the same way and tossed it with a little oil and sugar. For a nutty, crunchy finish, we sprinkled servings with toasted almonds.

2 garlic heads, top quarter cut off to expose garlic cloves

6 tablespoons plus 1 teaspoon extra-virgin olive oil

2 tablespoons lemon juice, plus extra as needed

¼ teaspoon red pepper flakes

1½ pounds broccoli
   Salt and pepper

¼ teaspoon sugar

1 pound campanelle

1 ounce Manchego cheese, grated (½ cup), plus extra for serving

¼ cup chopped fresh basil

¼ cup slivered almonds, toasted

1. Adjust oven rack to middle position, place large rimmed baking sheet on rack, and heat oven to 500 degrees. Place garlic heads, cut side up, in center of 12-inch square of aluminum foil. Drizzle each with ½ teaspoon oil and wrap securely. Place packet on oven rack and roast until garlic is very tender, about 40 minutes. Transfer packet to cutting board, let cool for 10 minutes, then unwrap garlic. Gently squeeze to remove cloves from skin, transfer to small bowl, and mash smooth with fork. Stir lemon juice and pepper flakes into mashed garlic, then slowly whisk in ¼ cup oil.

2. Meanwhile, cut broccoli crowns from large stems. Cut off tough outer layer on stems, then cut into 2- to 3-inch lengths about ½ inch thick. Cut smaller crowns (3 to 4 inches in diameter) into 4 wedges, and cut larger crowns (4 to 5 inches in diameter) into 6 wedges. Toss broccoli with remaining 2 tablespoons oil, 1 teaspoon salt, ¼ teaspoon pepper, and sugar in bowl. Remove baking sheet from oven. Carefully lay broccoli, cut sides down, on hot baking sheet in even layer. Roast broccoli until well browned and tender, 10 to 15 minutes. Transfer broccoli to cutting board, let cool slightly, then cut into ½-inch pieces.

3. Bring 4 quarts water to boil in large pot. Add pasta and 1 tablespoon salt and cook, stirring often, until al dente. Reserve 1 cup cooking water, then drain pasta and return it to pot. Add chopped broccoli, garlic sauce, ½ cup Manchego, basil, and ¼ cup reserved cooking water, and toss to combine. Season with salt, pepper, and extra lemon juice to taste and add reserved cooking water as needed to adjust consistency. Sprinkle individual portions with almonds and serve with extra Manchego.

QUICK PREP TIP
CUTTING BROCCOLI CROWNS
After cutting off stalk and setting it aside (do not discard it), place head upside down, then cut it in half through central stalk. Lay each half on its cut side. For each half, if it is 3 to 4 inches in diameter, cut it into 3 or 4 wedges, or into 6 wedges if 4 to 5 inches in diameter.

Penne with Pancetta, White Beans, and Rosemary

Serves 4 to 6

✓ **WHY THIS RECIPE WORKS:** Crispy pancetta, creamy cannellini beans, and earthy rosemary make up this humble yet satisfying pasta dish. Pancetta is cured with salt and spices, not smoked like bacon, so it has a more subtle, complex flavor. To infuse the whole dish with its richness, we browned the pancetta in the skillet first, then set it aside and sautéed the aromatics in the fat left behind. Adding chicken broth and white wine gave us the makings of a simple pan sauce, and two cans of cannellini beans added substance. Minced fresh rosemary contributed a woodsy, herbal background. To preserve the cooked pancetta's crispy texture, we added it just before serving. Though we prefer pancetta here, you can substitute prosciutto or bacon. For the nutritional information for this recipe, see page 306.

1	tablespoon olive oil
6	ounces thinly sliced pancetta, cut into ¼-inch-wide strips
1	onion, chopped fine
6	garlic cloves, minced
1	teaspoon minced fresh rosemary
⅛	teaspoon red pepper flakes
1½	cups low-sodium chicken broth
1	cup dry white wine
2	(15-ounce) cans cannellini beans, rinsed
1	pound penne
	Salt and pepper
2	ounces Parmesan cheese, grated (1 cup), plus extra for serving
¼	cup chopped fresh parsley

1. Cook oil and pancetta in 12-inch skillet over medium heat until pancetta is well browned and crisp, about 8 minutes. Using slotted spoon, transfer pancetta to paper towel–lined plate.

2. Add onion to fat left in pan and cook over medium heat until softened and golden brown, 10 to 12 minutes. Stir in garlic, rosemary, and pepper flakes and cook until fragrant, about 1 minute. Stir in chicken broth, wine, and beans, bring to simmer, and cook until sauce is slightly thickened, about 10 minutes.

3. Meanwhile, bring 4 quarts water to boil in large pot. Add pasta and 1 tablespoon salt and cook, stirring often, until al dente. Reserve ½ cup cooking water, then drain pasta and return it to pot. Add sauce, crisped pancetta, Parmesan, and parsley and toss to combine. Season with salt and pepper to taste and add reserved cooking water as needed to adjust consistency. Serve with extra Parmesan.

SMART SHOPPING **CANNED WHITE BEANS**

We sampled four brands of canned white beans in a side-by-side taste test in search of the best flavor and texture. Though we usually call for cannellini beans in our recipes, we found that very few brands of canned cannellini beans are distributed nationwide, so we broadened our taste test to include alternative white beans with widespread distribution, such as great Northern and navy beans. We tasted each contender twice: straight from the can (after being rinsed) and prepared in a simple soup where their flavor and texture really stood out. Tasters complained that most of the beans tasted "mealy," "bland," and "mushy," but loved the "creamy" but "firm" texture of **Progresso Cannellini Beans**.

Farfalle with Artichokes, Pancetta, and Spinach

Serves 4 to 6

✓ **WHY THIS RECIPE WORKS:** Artichokes boast a sweet, earthy, nutty flavor that pairs incredibly well with pasta, but fresh artichokes can be a pain to prep and cook. Enter frozen artichoke hearts—they simply need to be thawed and patted dry to remove excess moisture prior to cooking. For a bright, creamy sauce, shallots, garlic, lemon zest, lemon juice, plus cream and white wine did the trick. Pancetta, cooked at the outset and then set aside, provided crispy bites, and fresh tarragon contributed a hint of anise. This dish cried out for something green so we tossed in a hefty dose of baby spinach at the end of cooking. Farfalle, with its flat, wide surface, made the perfect cradle for the creamy sauce and wilted spinach. Though we prefer pancetta here, you can substitute prosciutto or bacon.

2	tablespoons unsalted butter
6	ounces thinly sliced pancetta, cut into ¼-inch-wide strips
2	shallots, minced
18	ounces frozen artichoke hearts, thawed and patted dry
3	garlic cloves, minced
2	teaspoons all-purpose flour
1	cup dry white wine
1	cup low-sodium chicken broth
1	cup heavy cream
1	teaspoon grated lemon zest plus 1 tablespoon juice
2	tablespoons minced fresh tarragon
1	pound farfalle
	Salt and pepper
1	ounce Parmesan cheese, grated (½ cup)
4	ounces (4 cups) baby spinach

1. Cook 1 tablespoon butter and pancetta in 12-inch skillet over medium heat until pancetta is well browned and crisp, about 8 minutes. Using slotted spoon, transfer pancetta to paper towel–lined plate.

2. Add remaining 1 tablespoon butter and shallots to fat left in pan and cook over medium heat until shallots are softened, about 3 minutes. Add artichoke hearts and cook until tender and beginning to brown, about 6 minutes. Stir in garlic and cook until fragrant, about 30 seconds. Stir in flour and cook for 1 minute. Whisk in wine, then broth and cream until smooth. Bring to simmer and cook until sauce is slightly thickened, 15 to 20 minutes. Off heat, stir in lemon zest, lemon juice, and tarragon.

3. Meanwhile, bring 4 quarts water to boil in large pot. Add pasta and 1 tablespoon salt and cook, stirring often, until al dente. Reserve ½ cup cooking water, then drain pasta and return it to pot. Add sauce, crisped pancetta, Parmesan, and spinach and toss until spinach is slightly wilted. Season with salt and pepper to taste and add reserved cooking water as needed to adjust consistency. Serve.

QUICK PREP TIP MINCING A SHALLOT

To mince a shallot, first make a number of closely spaced parallel cuts through peeled shallot, leaving root end intact. Next, make several cuts lengthwise through shallot. Finally, thinly slice shallot crosswise, creating a fine mince.

Penne with Sausage and Broccoli Rabe

Serves 4 to 6

✓ **WHY THIS RECIPE WORKS:** Pungent, earthy broccoli rabe pairs well with the savory meatiness of sausage in this dish. We gave this classic combination a lighter, fresher feel by adding red bell pepper for sweetness and crunch, and using Italian turkey sausage instead of pork sausage, which makes a lighter counterpart to the vegetable components. Blanching the broccoli rabe in the pasta cooking water helps curb its bitterness and cooks it quickly. Chicken broth, white wine, and sautéed onion and garlic create an uncomplicated sauce, and a little flour gives the sauce a nice clingy consistency. For the nutritional information for this recipe, see page 306.

2	tablespoons extra-virgin olive oil
1	onion, chopped fine
1	red bell pepper, stemmed, seeded, and cut into ½-inch pieces
6	garlic cloves, minced
⅛	teaspoon red pepper flakes
1	pound hot or sweet Italian turkey sausage, casings removed
1	tablespoon all-purpose flour
½	cup dry white wine
1	cup low-sodium chicken broth
1	pound broccoli rabe, trimmed and cut into 1½-inch pieces
	Salt and pepper
1	pound penne
¼	cup grated Parmesan cheese, plus extra for serving

1. Heat 1 tablespoon oil in 12-inch nonstick skillet over medium heat until shimmering. Add onion and bell pepper and cook until softened, about 5 minutes. Stir in garlic and pepper flakes and cook until fragrant, about 30 seconds. Add sausage and cook, breaking up meat with wooden spoon, until no longer pink, about 4 minutes. Stir in flour and cook for 1 minute. Stir in wine, scraping up any browned bits, and simmer until nearly evaporated, about 2 minutes. Stir in broth, return to simmer, and cook until slightly thickened, about 1 minute.

2. Meanwhile, bring 4 quarts water to boil in large pot. Add broccoli rabe and 1 tablespoon salt and cook, stirring often, until broccoli rabe is crisp-tender, 1 to 3 minutes. Using slotted spoon, transfer broccoli rabe to paper towel–lined plate.

3. Return pot of water to boil. Add pasta and cook, stirring often, until al dente. Reserve ½ cup cooking water, then drain pasta and return it to pot. Add sausage-broth mixture, broccoli rabe, remaining 1 tablespoon oil, and Parmesan and toss to combine. Season with salt and pepper to taste and add reserved cooking water as needed to adjust consistency. Serve with extra Parmesan.

QUICK PREP TIP
TRIMMING BROCCOLI RABE
Unlike broccoli, which has large florets, broccoli rabe consists mostly of stems and stalks. When prepping broccoli rabe, first trim off and discard very thick stalk ends, usually bottom 2 inches of each stalk. Then cut remaining stems and florets into 1½-inch pieces.

Pasta with Garlicky Tuscan Chicken

Serves 4 to 6

✓ **WHY THIS RECIPE WORKS:** Traditionally, Tuscan chicken combines mild, tender chicken with lots of garlic and lemon to create an intensely flavored dish. We decided to add penne to the mix for an easy weeknight supper. We started by coating boneless, skinless chicken breasts with flour, then we pan-fried them to golden perfection before setting them aside to build the garlic sauce. To infuse the sauce with intense garlic flavor that wasn't harsh, we sliced a whopping 12 cloves thin and sautéed them over moderate heat for a few minutes. This slow-and-low approach mellowed the garlic's harshness and drew out its sweet, nutty notes. Adding sliced shallot to the mix enhanced its sweetness and provided further insulation against burnt garlic. Red pepper flakes, white wine, and chicken broth serve as the base of the sauce, and a hefty amount of peppery arugula adds another flavor dimension and color. For the nutritional information for this recipe, see page 306.

3	(6- to 8-ounce) boneless, skinless chicken breasts, trimmed
	Salt and pepper
½	cup plus 1 tablespoon all-purpose flour
3	tablespoons olive oil
12	garlic cloves, sliced thin
3	shallots, sliced thin
	Pinch red pepper flakes
¾	cup dry white wine
3	cups low-sodium chicken broth
1	pound penne
5	ounces (5 cups) baby arugula
1½	ounces Parmesan cheese, grated (¾ cup), plus extra for serving
1	tablespoon lemon juice

1. Pat chicken dry with paper towels and season with salt and pepper. Place ½ cup flour in shallow dish. Working with one piece of chicken at a time, dredge in flour, shaking off excess.

2. Heat 2 tablespoons oil in 12-inch skillet over medium-high heat until just smoking. Carefully lay chicken in skillet and cook until well browned on first side, 6 to 8 minutes. Flip chicken over, reduce heat to medium, and continue to cook until chicken registers 160 degrees, 6 to 8 minutes longer; transfer to plate and tent loosely with aluminum foil.

3. Add remaining 1 tablespoon oil, garlic, and shallots to now-empty skillet and cook over medium-low heat until softened and beginning to brown, about 3 minutes. Stir in pepper flakes and remaining 1 tablespoon flour and cook for 30 seconds. Whisk in wine, then broth, until smooth. Increase heat to medium-high, bring to simmer, and cook until sauce is slightly thickened and measures 2½ cups, about 15 minutes; transfer to liquid measuring cup and cover to keep warm.

4. Meanwhile, bring 4 quarts water to boil in large pot. Add pasta and 1 tablespoon salt and cook, stirring often, until al dente. Reserve ½ cup cooking water, then drain pasta and return it to pot. Add 2 cups sauce, arugula, Parmesan, and lemon juice and toss until arugula is slightly wilted. Add reserved cooking water as needed to adjust consistency and season with salt and pepper to taste.

5. Slice chicken thinly on bias. Portion pasta into individual bowls, lay chicken over top, and drizzle remaining ½ cup sauce over chicken. Serve with extra Parmesan.

Pasta with Chicken Cacciatore Sauce

Serves 4 to 6

✔ **WHY THIS RECIPE WORKS:** Think about the rich, heady flavors of long-simmered tomato, mushroom, and onion, combined with tender chicken, and it's easy to see why chicken cacciatore is so popular. For a saucy yet speedy pasta dish inspired by these flavors, we turned to quick-cooking chicken breasts. Dried porcini added more mushroom-y depth. Woodsy herbs provide complexity in traditional recipes, but we found a shortcut in herbes de Provence, the dried herb mixture. For the nutritional information for this recipe, see page 306.

1	pound boneless, skinless chicken breasts, trimmed and sliced thin
	Salt and pepper
3	tablespoons olive oil
1	onion, chopped fine
10	ounces white mushrooms, trimmed and quartered
½	ounce dried porcini mushrooms, rinsed and minced
4	garlic cloves, minced
¾	teaspoon herbes de Provence
2	teaspoons all-purpose flour
½	cup dry red wine
1	cup low-sodium chicken broth
1	(28-ounce) can diced tomatoes
½	teaspoon sugar
1	pound penne
2	ounces Parmesan cheese, grated (1 cup), plus extra for serving
¼	cup chopped fresh parsley

1. Pat chicken dry with paper towels and season with salt and pepper. Heat 1 tablespoon oil in 12-inch nonstick skillet over high heat until just smoking. Add chicken in single layer and cook, without stirring, until beginning to brown, about 1 minute. Stir chicken and continue to cook until nearly cooked through, about 2 minutes; transfer to bowl and cover to keep warm.

2. Heat remaining 2 tablespoons oil in now-empty skillet over medium heat until shimmering. Add onion, white mushrooms, porcini, and ½ teaspoon salt, cover, and cook until mushrooms have released their liquid, about 5 minutes. Uncover and continue to cook until mushrooms are dry and browned, about 5 minutes.

3. Stir in garlic and herbes de Provence and cook until fragrant, about 30 seconds. Stir in flour and cook for 1 minute. Whisk in wine, then broth, until smooth. Add tomatoes and sugar, bring to simmer, and cook until sauce is thick, about 15 minutes.

4. Meanwhile, bring 4 quarts water to boil in large pot. Add pasta and 1 tablespoon salt; cook, stirring often, until al dente. Reserve ½ cup cooking water, then drain pasta and return it to pot. Add chicken along with any accumulated juice to sauce, bring to simmer, and cook until chicken is cooked through, about 1 minute. Add chicken-sauce mixture, Parmesan, and parsley to pasta and toss to combine. Season with salt and pepper to taste and add reserved cooking water as needed to adjust consistency. Serve with extra Parmesan.

QUICK PREP TIP
SLICING CHICKEN THINLY
To slice chicken breasts thinly, cut them across the grain into ¼-inch-wide strips that are 1½ to 2 inches long. Center pieces should be cut in half so that they are approximately the same length as the end pieces and will cook at the same rate. For tenderloins, cut them on the diagonal to produce pieces of meat that are roughly the same size.

Chicken Riggies

Serves 4 to 6

✔ **WHY THIS RECIPE WORKS:** This pasta dish from Utica, New York, matches rigatoni (aka "riggies") with tender chicken and vegetables in a spicy, creamy tomato sauce. Our version starts by sautéing mushrooms and bell peppers. Hot pickled cherry peppers give this dish its signature heat; we also use the brine for more tangy flavor. If you can find only sweet cherry peppers, add ¼ to ½ teaspoon red pepper flakes with the garlic. Parmesan cheese can be substituted for the Pecorino. For the nutritional information for this recipe, see page 306.

4   **(6-ounce) boneless, skinless chicken breasts, trimmed and cut into 1-inch pieces**

2   **tablespoons jarred sliced hot cherry peppers, chopped fine, plus 2 tablespoons brine**
    Salt and pepper

1   **tablespoon olive oil**

10 **ounces white mushrooms, trimmed and quartered**

2   **red bell peppers, stemmed, seeded, and cut into 1-inch pieces**

1   **onion, cut into 1-inch pieces**

5   **garlic cloves, minced**

1½ **teaspoons dried oregano**

1   **teaspoon cornstarch**

¾   **cup half-and-half**

1   **(28-ounce) can crushed tomatoes**

¼   **cup pitted kalamata olives, chopped**

1   **pound rigatoni**

1   **ounce Pecorino Romano cheese, grated (½ cup)**

1. Combine chicken, 2 tablespoons water, 1 tablespoon cherry pepper brine, and ⅛ teaspoon salt in bowl, cover, and refrigerate for 30 to 60 minutes.

2. Combine 1 teaspoon oil, mushrooms, and bell peppers in Dutch oven. Cover and cook over medium-low heat, stirring often, until softened, 8 to 10 minutes. Uncover, increase heat to medium, and continue to cook until well browned, 8 to 10 minutes; transfer to bowl.

3. Add remaining 2 teaspoons oil and onion to now-empty pot and cook over medium heat until softened, 5 to 7 minutes. Stir in cherry peppers, garlic, oregano, and ¼ teaspoon pepper and cook until fragrant, about 30 seconds. Whisk cornstarch into half-and-half, then stir into pot and bring to simmer. Add tomatoes and cook, stirring often, until sauce is very thick, 10 to 15 minutes.

4. Stir in cooked vegetables and chicken. Turn heat to medium-low, cover, and simmer gently, stirring often, until chicken is cooked through, 6 to 8 minutes. Off heat, stir in olives and remaining 1 tablespoon cherry pepper brine.

5. Meanwhile, bring 4 quarts water to boil in large pot. Add pasta and 1 tablespoon salt and cook, stirring often, until al dente. Reserve ½ cup cooking water, then drain pasta and return it to pot. Add sauce and Pecorino and toss to combine. Season with salt and pepper to taste and add reserved cooking water as needed to adjust consistency. Serve.

QUICK PREP TIP
CUTTING BELL PEPPERS
To cut bell pepper, slice top and bottom off, remove core, then slice down through side of pepper. Lay pepper flat on cutting board, cut away any remaining ribs, then cut pepper into pieces as directed in recipe.

Chicken Bolognese with Linguine

Serves 4 to 6

✔ **WHY THIS RECIPE WORKS:** Bolognese, traditionally made with ground beef, pork, and veal, achieves deep flavor from hours of simmering. We wanted a richly flavored Bolognese that relied on ground chicken in place of the three kinds of meat, and we wanted it on the table in a lot less time. To get rich flavor from lean ground chicken, we deployed two flavor powerhouses: pancetta and dried porcini mushrooms. The pancetta gave our sauce a hearty backbone, and the meaty mushrooms contributed depth. Sautéing our aromatics in butter imparted further richness, and tomato paste gave the sauce intensity. Simmering the meat in milk—a classic Bolognese method—kept the ground chicken from becoming tough and turning grainy while cooking. We found that sweet white wine tasted better than either a dry white or a dry red wine. Mincing the vegetables is important for the texture of the sauce; if desired, use a food processor and pulse each vegetable separately until finely minced. Also, be sure to break the chicken into small pieces in step 3, or the sauce will be too chunky.

1	**(28-ounce) can diced tomatoes**
1¼	**cups sweet white wine, such as Gewürztraminer, Riesling, or white Zinfandel**
4	**tablespoons unsalted butter**
4	**ounces pancetta, cut into ¼-inch pieces**
½	**carrot, peeled and minced**
½	**cup finely chopped onion**
½	**ounce dried porcini mushrooms, rinsed and minced**
	Salt and pepper
1	**garlic clove, minced**
1	**teaspoon sugar**
1¼	**pounds ground chicken**
1½	**cups whole milk**
2	**tablespoons tomato paste**
1	**pound linguine**
	Grated Parmesan cheese

1. Pulse tomatoes in food processor until finely chopped, about 8 pulses; set aside. Simmer wine in 10-inch nonstick skillet over medium-low heat until reduced to 2 tablespoons, about 20 minutes; set aside.

2. Cook butter and pancetta in 12-inch skillet over medium heat until pancetta is lightly browned, 3 to 5 minutes. Add carrot, onion, porcini, and ¼ teaspoon salt and cook, stirring often, until vegetables are softened, about 4 minutes. Stir in garlic and sugar and cook until fragrant, about 30 seconds.

3. Add chicken and cook, breaking up meat with wooden spoon, for 1 minute (chicken will still be pink). Stir in milk and simmer gently, breaking meat into small pieces, until most of liquid has evaporated and meat begins to sizzle, about 15 minutes. Stir in tomato paste and cook for 1 minute. Stir in processed tomatoes and simmer until sauce is thickened, 12 to 15 minutes. Stir in reduced wine and simmer until flavors are blended, about 5 minutes.

4. Meanwhile, bring 4 quarts water to boil in large pot. Add pasta and 1 tablespoon salt and cook, stirring often, until al dente. Reserve ½ cup cooking water, then drain pasta and return it to pot. Add sauce and toss to combine. Season with salt and pepper to taste and add reserved cooking water as needed to adjust consistency. Serve with Parmesan.

Spaghetti with Turkey-Pesto Meatballs

Serves 4 to 6

✔️ **WHY THIS RECIPE WORKS:** For an easy, family-friendly spin on the typical spaghetti-and-meatballs dinner, we replaced the beef with ground turkey and added fresh pesto to the meatballs for big flavor. The pesto replaces the need for garlic, cheese, and even the egg yolk in the standard meatball recipe, making these meatballs nearly prep-free—all they need is a sprinkling of salt, pepper, and bread crumbs (we like super-crisp panko). Chilling the meatballs in the fridge before sautéing ensured they didn't fall apart in the skillet. Processing a portion of the canned diced tomatoes in a food processor gave us a mostly smooth sauce with a few bigger bites of tomato. You can make your own pesto or use your favorite store-bought brand from the refrigerated section of the supermarket—they have a fresher flavor than the jarred pesto sold in the grocery aisles. Do not use ground turkey breast meat (sometimes also labeled as 99 percent fat-free); it will make meatballs that are dry and grainy. You can substitute ground chicken, pork, or 90 percent lean beef for the ground turkey if desired. You will need a 12-inch skillet with at least 2-inch sides to accommodate both the meatballs and the sauce; the skillet will be quite full.

1½	**pounds 93 percent lean ground turkey**
1	**(7-ounce) container basil pesto (⅔ cup)**
⅔	**cup panko bread crumbs**
	Salt and pepper
3	**(14.5-ounce) cans diced tomatoes**
1	**tablespoon olive oil**
1	**onion, chopped fine**
4	**garlic cloves, minced**
	Pinch red pepper flakes
1	**pound spaghetti**
3	**tablespoons chopped fresh basil**

1. Gently mix turkey, pesto, bread crumbs, ½ teaspoon salt, and ¼ teaspoon pepper in bowl using hands until uniform. Roll mixture into eighteen 1½-inch meatballs. Lay meatballs on large plate, cover, and refrigerate until firm, about 1 hour.

2. Pulse 2 cans diced tomatoes in food processor until mostly smooth, about 12 pulses; set aside. Heat oil in 12-inch nonstick skillet over medium heat until just smoking. Brown meatballs well on all sides, about 10 minutes; transfer to paper towel–lined plate.

3. Add onion and ⅛ teaspoon salt to fat left in skillet and cook over medium heat until softened, 5 to 7 minutes. Stir in garlic and pepper flakes and cook for 30 seconds. Stir in processed tomatoes and remaining 1 can diced tomatoes. Bring to simmer and cook for 10 minutes. Return meatballs to skillet, cover, and simmer gently until meatballs are cooked through, about 10 minutes.

4. Meanwhile, bring 4 quarts water to boil in large pot. Add pasta and 1 tablespoon salt and cook, stirring often, until al dente. Reserve 1 cup cooking water, then drain pasta and return it to pot. Add several large spoonfuls of tomato sauce (without meatballs) to pasta and toss to combine. Season with salt and pepper to taste and add reserved cooking water as needed to adjust consistency. Divide pasta among individual bowls. Top each bowl with remaining sauce and meatballs, sprinkle with basil, and serve.

QUICK PREP TIP **MAKING SMALL-BATCH PESTO**
Process 2 cups packed fresh basil leaves, 6 tablespoons extra-virgin olive oil, 2 tablespoons toasted pine nuts, and 1 small garlic clove, minced, in food processor until smooth, scraping down bowl as needed. Transfer pesto to bowl, stir in ¼ cup grated Parmesan cheese, and season with salt and pepper to taste. Makes about ⅔ cup.

Beef Ragu with Warm Spices

Serves 4 to 6

✓ **WHY THIS RECIPE WORKS:** Rustic Italian-style ragu is all about low-and-slow simmering—it relies on lots of time but minimal heat to turn the meat, cooked with tomatoes and red wine, fall-apart tender. For this recipe, we liked beef short ribs, which turned tender and moist during braising; they gave the sauce a truly meaty flavor. Processing whole and diced canned tomatoes made a sauce that was too smooth, while pulsing them briefly gave us a sauce that was too even in texture. Chopping whole canned tomatoes by hand was an easy fix—our sauce now had the perfect rustic texture and appearance. Cinnamon and cloves, while unexpected, offered a subtle warmth. To prevent the sauce from becoming greasy, trim as much fat as possible from the ribs.

1½	**pounds beef short ribs, trimmed**
	Salt and pepper
1	**tablespoon olive oil**
1	**onion, chopped fine**
2	**tablespoons minced fresh parsley**
½	**teaspoon ground cinnamon**
	Pinch ground cloves
½	**cup red wine**
1	**(28-ounce) can whole peeled tomatoes, drained with juice reserved, tomatoes chopped fine**
1	**pound rigatoni**
	Grated Parmesan cheese

1. Pat ribs dry with paper towels and season with salt and pepper. Heat oil in 12-inch skillet over medium-high heat until just smoking. Brown ribs well on all sides, 8 to 10 minutes; transfer to plate.

2. Pour off all but 1 teaspoon fat left in skillet, add onion, and cook over medium heat until softened, about 5 minutes. Stir in parsley, cinnamon, and cloves and cook until fragrant, about 30 seconds. Stir in wine, scraping up any browned bits, and simmer until nearly evaporated, about 2 minutes.

3. Stir in chopped tomatoes and reserved tomato juice. Nestle browned ribs into sauce, along with any accumulated juice, and bring to gentle simmer. Reduce heat to low, cover, and simmer gently, turning ribs occasionally, until meat is very tender and falling off bones, about 2 hours.

4. Transfer ribs to plate, let cool slightly, then shred meat into bite-size pieces, discarding fat and bones. Return shredded meat to sauce, bring to simmer, and cook until heated through and thickened slightly, about 5 minutes. Season with salt and pepper to taste.

5. Meanwhile, bring 4 quarts water to boil in large pot. Add pasta and 1 tablespoon salt and cook, stirring often, until al dente. Reserve ½ cup cooking water, then drain pasta and return it to pot. Add sauce and toss to combine. Season with salt and pepper to taste and add reserved cooking water as needed to adjust consistency. Serve with Parmesan.

Pasta with Weekday Meat Sauce

Serves 8 to 10

✔ **WHY THIS RECIPE WORKS:** In our quest for a quick yet richly flavored meat sauce that tasted like it had simmered all day, we discovered a few tricks. Browning the meat can dry it out and toughen it, so we skipped this step. Instead, we browned a small amount of white mushrooms, which we had spun through the food processor; cooking the mushrooms for just 10 minutes left browned bits on the bottom of the pan that instilled our sauce with deep, hearty flavor. To further keep the meat from becoming tough, we blended it with a panade (a mixture of bread and milk) before cooking it quickly, just until it lost its color; the bread's starches absorb liquid from the milk to form a gel that coats and lubricates the meat. Finally, for good tomato flavor, we added tomato paste to the browned vegetables and deglazed the pan with a little tomato juice before adding the canned tomatoes. Except for ground round (which tasters found spongy and bland), this recipe will work with most types of ground beef, as long as it is 85 percent lean. High-quality canned tomatoes will make a big difference in this sauce; see page 205 for information on our preferred brands. If using dried oregano, add the entire amount with the reserved tomato juice in step 2.

4 ounces white mushrooms, trimmed and halved if small or quartered if large

1 slice hearty white sandwich bread, torn into quarters

2 tablespoons whole milk
  Salt and pepper

1 pound 85 percent lean ground beef

1 tablespoon olive oil

1 large onion, chopped fine

6 garlic cloves, minced

¼ teaspoon red pepper flakes

1 tablespoon tomato paste

1 (14.5-ounce) can diced tomatoes, drained with ¼ cup juice reserved

1 tablespoon minced fresh oregano or 1 teaspoon dried

1 (28-ounce) can crushed tomatoes

¼ cup grated Parmesan cheese, plus extra for serving

2 pounds penne

1. Pulse mushrooms in food processor until finely chopped, about 8 pulses, scraping down bowl as needed; transfer to bowl. Add bread, milk, ½ teaspoon salt, and ½ teaspoon pepper to now-empty food processor and pulse until paste forms, about 8 pulses. Add ground beef and pulse until mixture is well combined, about 6 pulses.

2. Heat oil in large saucepan over medium-high heat until just smoking. Add processed mushrooms and onion and cook until vegetables are softened and well browned, 6 to 12 minutes. Stir in garlic, pepper flakes, and tomato paste and cook until fragrant, about 1 minute. Stir in ¼ cup reserved tomato juice and 2 teaspoons fresh oregano (if using dried, add full amount), scraping up any browned bits. Stir in meat mixture and cook, breaking up any large pieces with wooden spoon, until no longer pink, about 3 minutes (do not let meat brown).

3. Stir in diced tomatoes and crushed tomatoes, bring to gentle simmer, and cook until sauce has thickened and flavors meld, about 30 minutes. Stir in Parmesan and remaining 1 teaspoon fresh oregano and season with salt and pepper to taste.

4. Meanwhile, bring 8 quarts water to boil in 12-quart pot. Add pasta and 2 tablespoons salt and cook, stirring often, until al dente. Reserve 1 cup cooking water, then drain pasta and return it to pot. Add 1 cup sauce and reserved cooking water and toss to combine. Spoon remaining sauce over individual portions and serve with extra Parmesan.

Spaghetti with Lemon, Basil, and Scallops

Serves 4 to 6

✔ **WHY THIS RECIPE WORKS:** For a recipe with just a handful of ingredients, pasta with shellfish is awfully hard to get right. We love the combination of tender pasta and succulent, bite-size bay scallops, but all too often the scallops are overcooked and tough and the pasta is boring and flavorless. For an extraordinary but simple spaghetti dinner, we created a creamy vinaigrette packed with bright, lemony flavor and tossed it with tender scallops, hot pasta, butter, and shredded basil just before serving. Grated Parmesan ensured that our vinaigrette was perfectly clingy and hung on to the pasta and shellfish. Because this recipe is so simple, it is important to use high-quality extra-virgin olive oil, fresh-squeezed lemon juice, and fresh basil. For more information on mincing garlic to a paste, see page 237.

½ cup extra-virgin olive oil

2 teaspoons grated lemon zest plus ⅓ cup juice (2 lemons)

1 small garlic clove, minced to a paste
Salt and pepper

2 ounces Parmesan cheese, grated (1 cup)

1 pound small bay scallops

4 tablespoons unsalted butter, softened

1 pound spaghetti

¼ cup shredded fresh basil

1. Whisk oil, lemon zest, lemon juice, garlic, and ½ teaspoon salt together in small bowl, then stir in Parmesan cheese until thick and creamy; set aside.

2. Pat scallops dry with paper towels and season with salt and pepper. Melt 2 tablespoons butter in 12-inch nonstick skillet over medium heat. Add scallops and cook, stirring occasionally, until just cooked through, 3 to 4 minutes; transfer to bowl and cover to keep warm.

3. Meanwhile, bring 4 quarts water to boil in large pot. Add pasta and 1 tablespoon salt and cook, stirring often, until al dente. Reserve ½ cup cooking water, then drain pasta and return it to pot. Stir in olive oil mixture, cooked scallops, remaining 2 table-spoons butter, and basil and toss to combine. Season with salt and pepper to taste and add reserved cooking water as needed to adjust consistency. Serve.

QUICK PREP TIP JUICING A LEMON
How do you get the most juice from a lemon with the least amount of effort? First of all, choose your lemons wisely. We found that round lemons are slightly juicier than elliptical ones, and bigger lemons yield more juice than smaller ones. Also, be sure to squeeze them while you shop. Without fail, whole lemons that yielded under pressure contained more juice when compared to firm lemons that were nearly identical in size, shape, and weight. We've also tried countless methods and gizmos for juicing lemons and dismissed most of them. However, we do endorse rolling the lemon vigorously on a hard surface before slicing it open to be juiced. Once rolled, we recommend using either a citrus juicer or wooden reamer. However you squeeze it, we strongly recommend that you squeeze the lemon at the last minute; testing has proven that its flavor mellows quickly and will taste bland in a short time.

SKILLET PASTA WITH EGGPLANT AND ROASTED RED PEPPERS

Skillet Pastas

Bachelor Spaghetti with Sausage, Peppers, and Onions

Serves 4

WHY THIS RECIPE WORKS: You won't need to dirty even a knife to make this super-streamlined but surprisingly flavorful spaghetti dinner featuring the classic combination of sausage, peppers, and onions. We kept things simple by starting with frozen chopped onions and sliced bell peppers, and then relied on garlic powder, dried oregano, and red pepper flakes for seasoning. To draw out flavor from the dried herbs and spices, we sautéed them with the sausage and onions, which worked to deepen their flavor. Using canned tomato sauce and simmering it with the lid on provided rich, intense flavor in short order. For the pasta, we opted for thin spaghetti; we preferred its texture to that of traditional spaghetti for our one-pan pasta cooking method that cooks the pasta right in the sauce. We broke the spaghettini in half so that it would fit in the skillet, ensuring that the pasta cooked evenly. To make this dish even easier, you can use bulk Italian sausage or sausage patties, which can go directly into the skillet, saving the step of removing the sausage from its casings. See page 173 for tips on how to measure out long strands of pasta without using a scale. For the nutritional information for this recipe, see page 306.

1	tablespoon olive oil
2	cups frozen chopped onions, thawed (or 2 onions, chopped fine)
	Salt and pepper
1	pound hot or sweet Italian sausage, casings removed
1	teaspoon garlic powder (or 4 garlic cloves, minced)
1	teaspoon minced fresh oregano or ¼ teaspoon dried
¼	teaspoon red pepper flakes
3	cups water
1	(15-ounce) can tomato sauce
2½	cups (8 ounces) frozen sliced bell peppers (or 2 red bell peppers, stemmed, seeded, and sliced thin)
8	ounces thin spaghetti or spaghettini, broken in half
	Grated Parmesan cheese

1. Heat oil in 12-inch nonstick skillet over medium heat until shimmering. Add onions and ¼ teaspoon salt and cook until onions are softened and golden, about 12 minutes. Stir in sausage, garlic powder, oregano, and pepper flakes. Increase heat to medium-high and cook, breaking up meat with wooden spoon, until sausage is no longer pink, 7 to 10 minutes.

2. Stir in water, tomato sauce, bell peppers, and pasta. Cover and cook at vigorous simmer, stirring often, until pasta is tender, 12 to 15 minutes. Season with salt and pepper to taste. Serve with Parmesan.

SMART SHOPPING FROZEN CHOPPED ONIONS
Frozen chopped onions can be a convenient way to save a few minutes of prep time (as well as a few tears). Though we would never recommend them for salads or for recipes in which the onion flavor is particularly important, such as French onion soup, we think they work just fine in hearty, flavorful pasta dishes. You can swap one packed cup of frozen chopped onions for one medium finely chopped onion.

Skillet Pasta with Fresh Tomato Sauce

Serves 4

✔ **WHY THIS RECIPE WORKS:** For an effortless but delicious bright, fresh tomato sauce, we minimized tomato prep and cooked the pasta right in the sauce. We simply cored and chopped our tomatoes, then simmered them briefly, just until they started to break down and exude their juice. With the addition of a few cups of water, there was enough liquid in the pan to cook the pasta; by covering the pan, we ensured that the sauce didn't dry out. Starch released from the pasta helped thicken the sauce, making it nicely clingy. Although not traditional for tomato sauce, white wine enhanced the sauce's bright acidity. The curves of bell-shaped campanelle cradled the sauce perfectly and gave this rustic dish an elegant touch. Other pasta shapes can be substituted for the campanelle; however, their cup measurements may vary (see page 173). For the nutritional information for this recipe, see page 306.

2	tablespoons extra-virgin olive oil
1	onion, chopped fine
4	garlic cloves, minced
1	tablespoon tomato paste
2	pounds tomatoes, cored and cut into ½-inch pieces
	Salt and pepper
½	cup dry white wine
3½	cups water, plus extra as needed
12	ounces (3¾ cups) campanelle
¼	cup chopped fresh basil
	Grated Parmesan cheese

1. Heat oil in 12-inch nonstick skillet over medium heat until shimmering. Add onion and cook until softened, 5 to 7 minutes. Stir in garlic and tomato paste and cook until fragrant, about 1 minute. Stir in tomatoes, 1 teaspoon salt, and ½ teaspoon pepper and cook until tomato pieces lose their shape, 5 to 7 minutes. Stir in wine and simmer for 2 minutes.

2. Stir in water and pasta. Cover, increase heat to medium-high, and cook at vigorous simmer, stirring often, until pasta is nearly tender, about 12 minutes.

3. Uncover and continue to simmer, tossing pasta gently, until pasta is tender and sauce has thickened, 3 to 5 minutes; if sauce becomes too thick, add extra water as needed. Off heat, stir in basil and season with salt and pepper to taste. Serve with Parmesan.

ON THE SIDE HERBED RICOTTA BRUSCHETTA
Combine ½ cup whole-milk or part-skim ricotta, 2 tablespoons chopped fresh basil, 1 tablespoon olive oil, and 1 tablespoon lemon juice in bowl; season with salt and pepper to taste. Adjust oven rack 4 inches from broiler element and heat broiler. Place four (¾-inch-thick) large slices rustic bread on aluminum foil–lined baking sheet. Broil until bread is deep golden on both sides, 2 to 4 minutes, flipping as needed. Lightly rub 1 side of bread with raw, peeled garlic clove, season with salt and pepper, and spread ricotta mixture over top. Makes 4.

Skillet Pasta Puttanesca

Serves 4

✓ **WHY THIS RECIPE WORKS:** Puttanesca, a classic Italian sauce made with tomatoes, garlic, anchovies, capers, and olives, offers bold flavor and comes together fairly quickly. We sped up our recipe even more by cooking the tomato sauce in a skillet, then adding the pasta to the same pan. For a lightly thickened sauce, we used whole peeled tomatoes, pulsed in the food processor, which gave us more consistent results than canned crushed tomatoes. Sautéing the anchovies, garlic, and red pepper flakes at the outset provided a rich, savory foundation of flavor; finishing the dish with chopped kalamatas and capers preserved their briny notes and provided the big flavor we were after. Be sure to simmer the tomatoes gently in step 2 or the sauce will become too thick. See page 173 for tips on how to measure out long strands of pasta without using a scale. For the nutritional information for this recipe, see page 306.

3	(14.5-ounce) cans whole peeled tomatoes
3	tablespoons extra-virgin olive oil, plus extra for serving
6	anchovy fillets, rinsed and minced
6	garlic cloves, minced
½	teaspoon red pepper flakes
	Salt and pepper
2	cups water
12	ounces thin spaghetti or spaghettini, broken in half
¼	cup pitted kalamata olives, chopped coarse
¼	cup minced fresh parsley
3	tablespoons capers, rinsed
	Grated Parmesan cheese

1. Pulse tomatoes in food processor until coarsely ground and no large pieces remain, about 12 pulses.

2. Cook 2 tablespoons oil, anchovies, garlic, and pepper flakes together in 12-inch nonstick skillet over medium-low heat, stirring constantly, until garlic is fragrant, 1 to 2 minutes. Stir in processed tomatoes and ½ teaspoon salt. Simmer gently until tomatoes no longer taste raw, about 10 minutes.

3. Stir in water and pasta. Cover, increase heat to medium-high, and cook at vigorous simmer, stirring often, until pasta is tender, 12 to 15 minutes.

4. Stir in olives, parsley, capers, and remaining 1 tablespoon oil. Season with salt and pepper to taste. Serve with Parmesan and extra olive oil.

SMART SHOPPING CAPERS
Capers are sun-dried, pickled flower buds from the spiny shrub *Capparis spinosa*, and their unique pungent flavor is most commonly found in Mediterranean cooking. Capers range in size from tiny nonpareils to large caperberries, and they develop their flavor from being cured, either in a salty brine (sometimes with vinegar) or packed in salt. Brined capers are the most commonly available, and we've found that we prefer the smaller nonpareil capers for their compact size and slight crunch. We tasted six nationally available supermarket brands of brined nonpareil capers, evaluating them on their sharpness, saltiness, and overall appeal. Some brands we tasted were too salty and had unappealing "mothball" and "dirt" flavors, but tasters loved the bright, acidic punch and lingering sweetness of **Reese Non Pareil Capers**.

Skillet-Baked Ziti with Sausage

Serves 4

✓ **WHY THIS RECIPE WORKS:** An Italian-American classic, baked ziti is the ultimate in hearty, cheesy, satisfying fare. But what it's not is prep-free. Though not necessarily challenging to make, baked ziti takes some time—you have to boil the pasta, make the sauce and the filling (separately), then layer the whole thing together and bake. For a streamlined version, we ditched the baking dish in favor of a nonstick skillet. After building a simple tomato sauce—with crumbled Italian sausage for meaty flavor—and stirring in enough water so we could cook the pasta, we added the ziti and let it simmer. Cream added some richness, and stirring in Parmesan and topping it all off with mozzarella before a quick stint in the oven gave our skillet casserole plenty of cheesy appeal. Be sure to simmer the tomatoes gently in step 2 or the sauce will become too thick. Other pasta shapes can be substituted for the ziti; however, their cup measurements may vary (see page 173).

1	**(28-ounce) can whole peeled tomatoes**
1	**pound sweet or hot Italian sausage, casings removed**
6	**garlic cloves, minced**
¼	**teaspoon red pepper flakes**
	Salt and pepper
3	**cups water**
12	**ounces (3¾ cups) ziti**
½	**cup heavy cream**
1	**ounce Parmesan cheese, grated (½ cup)**
¼	**cup chopped fresh basil**
4	**ounces mozzarella cheese, shredded (1 cup)**

1. Adjust oven rack to middle position and heat oven to 475 degrees. Pulse tomatoes in food processor until coarsely ground and no large pieces remain, about 12 pulses.

2. Cook sausage in 12-inch ovensafe nonstick skillet over medium-high heat, breaking up meat with wooden spoon, until no longer pink, about 4 minutes. Stir in garlic and pepper flakes and cook until fragrant, about 1 minute. Stir in processed tomatoes and ½ teaspoon salt. Reduce heat to medium-low and simmer gently until tomatoes no longer taste raw, about 10 minutes.

3. Stir in water and pasta. Cover, increase heat to medium-high, and cook at vigorous simmer, stirring often, until pasta is tender, 15 to 18 minutes.

4. Stir in cream, Parmesan, and basil and season with salt and pepper to taste. Sprinkle mozzarella evenly over top. Transfer skillet to oven and bake until cheese has melted and browned, 10 to 15 minutes. Serve.

ON THE SIDE CAESAR SALAD
Whisk ¾ teaspoon garlic paste (see page 237) with 2 tablespoons lemon juice in large bowl; let stand for 10 minutes. Whisk in ½ teaspoon Worcestershire sauce, 6 anchovy fillets, patted dry and mashed to paste, and 2 large egg yolks. Whisking constantly, slowly add 5 tablespoons canola oil and 5 teaspoons extra-virgin olive oil. Whisk in ½ cup grated Parmesan and season with pepper to taste. Toss with 2 romaine lettuce hearts, sliced ¾ inch thick, and serve with extra grated Parmesan. Serves 4 to 6.

Skillet-Baked Chicken Parmesan and Penne

Serves 4

✔ **WHY THIS RECIPE WORKS:** Chicken Parmesan is a bona fide crowd-pleaser, but it is more work (and dirties more pans) than we want to tackle on a weeknight. For a chicken Parmesan dinner—pasta and sauce included—that takes less than 30 minutes and requires only a skillet, we started with frozen breaded chicken cutlets, which bake in the oven while everything else is being prepped. Canned fire-roasted tomatoes gave the sauce a smoky complexity in no time. We usually add water to the sauce when cooking pasta in a skillet, but for savory depth we swapped some of the water for chicken broth. Once the pasta was tender, we sliced the baked chicken into strips and placed them on top. We found it best to stir the Parmesan into the pasta, then sprinkle the mozzarella over the chicken before tossing the pan into a hot oven to melt the cheese. Other pasta shapes can be substituted for the penne; however, their cup measurements may vary (see page 173).

1   **pound frozen breaded boneless chicken breasts**

1   **(28-ounce) can whole peeled fire-roasted tomatoes**

1   **tablespoon olive oil**

6   **garlic cloves, minced**

1   **teaspoon minced fresh oregano or ¼ teaspoon dried**

¼   **teaspoon red pepper flakes**
    Salt and pepper

2   **cups water**

1½ **cups low-sodium chicken broth**

12 **ounces (3¾ cups) penne**

2   **ounces Parmesan cheese, grated (1 cup)**

4   **ounces mozzarella cheese, shredded (1 cup)**

¼   **cup chopped fresh basil**

1. Bake chicken according to package instructions. Let chicken cool slightly, then slice into ½-inch-thick strips. Adjust oven rack to middle position and heat oven to 475 degrees. Meanwhile, pulse tomatoes in food processor until coarsely ground and no large pieces remain, about 12 pulses.

2. Cook oil, garlic, oregano, pepper flakes, and ¼ teaspoon salt in 12-inch ovensafe nonstick skillet over medium-high heat until fragrant, about 1 minute. Stir in processed tomatoes, water, 1 cup broth, and pasta. Cover and cook at vigorous simmer, stirring often, until pasta is tender, 15 to 18 minutes.

3. Stir in remaining ½ cup broth and Parmesan. Season with salt and pepper to taste. Scatter sliced chicken evenly over top and sprinkle with mozzarella. Transfer skillet to oven and bake until cheese has melted and chicken is crisp, 5 to 10 minutes. Sprinkle with basil and serve.

QUICK PREP TIP MAKING BREADED CHICKEN CUTLETS
Place ½ cup flour in shallow dish or pie plate. Whisk 1 large egg with 1 tablespoon vegetable oil in second shallow dish. Combine 2 cups panko bread crumbs, ½ teaspoon salt, and ¼ teaspoon pepper in third shallow dish. Pat 3 (6-ounce) chicken cutlets, trimmed, ½ inch thick, dry with paper towels and season with salt and pepper. Coat chicken with flour, then dip in egg, and finally coat with panko. Heat ⅓ cup vegetable oil in 12-inch nonstick skillet over medium-high heat until shimmering; add chicken. Cook until well browned on both sides and chicken registers 160 degrees, about 8 minutes, flipping as needed; transfer to paper towel–lined plate. Makes about 1 pound.

Skillet Pasta with Eggplant and Roasted Red Peppers

Serves 4

✔ **WHY THIS RECIPE WORKS:** This one-pan dinner features the same satisfying flavors and textures as eggplant Parmesan but with a lighter, fresher angle—and it requires a fraction of the work. In lieu of the deep flavor of a long-simmered sauce, we infused our sauce with the bold, sweet, slightly smoky flavor of roasted red peppers; a can of fire-roasted tomatoes contributed additional smokiness. Microwaving cubed, salted eggplant quickly drew out its moisture; after sautéing it, we set it aside while we built our sauce so it wouldn't turn to mush. We cooked the pasta right in the sauce, then stirred in the eggplant and topped everything with thinly sliced fresh mozzarella, which melted into a gooey layer in the oven. A sprinkling of toasted panko bread crumbs provided a nutty, crunchy finish. We prefer to use kosher salt in this recipe because it clings best to the eggplant in step 3; if using table salt, reduce all salt amounts by half. Other pasta shapes can be substituted for the ziti; however, their cup measurements may vary (see page 173).

¾	cup panko bread crumbs
¼	cup olive oil
	Kosher salt and pepper
3	ounces Parmesan cheese, grated (1½ cups)
1	(14.5-ounce) can diced fire-roasted tomatoes
3	cups jarred roasted red peppers, rinsed, patted dry, and chopped coarse
1½	pounds eggplant, cut into 1-inch pieces
6	garlic cloves, minced
1	teaspoon minced fresh oregano or ¼ teaspoon dried
4	cups water
12	ounces (3¾ cups) ziti
6	ounces fresh mozzarella cheese, sliced thin
¼	cup chopped fresh basil

1. Adjust oven rack to middle position and heat oven to 475 degrees. Toss panko with 1 tablespoon oil and season with salt and pepper to taste. Spread on rimmed baking sheet and bake, stirring often, until golden, about 10 minutes. Let cool slightly, transfer to bowl, and toss with ½ cup Parmesan.

2. Meanwhile, pulse tomatoes and red peppers in food processor until coarsely ground and no large pieces remain, about 12 pulses.

3. Line large plate with double layer of coffee filters and lightly spray with vegetable oil spray. Toss eggplant with 1 teaspoon salt, then spread out over coffee filters. Microwave eggplant, uncovered, until dry and slightly shriveled, about 10 minutes, tossing halfway through cooking. Let eggplant cool slightly, then toss with 1 tablespoon oil in bowl.

4. Heat 1 tablespoon oil in 12-inch ovensafe nonstick skillet over medium-high heat until shimmering. Add eggplant and cook, stirring occasionally, until well browned and tender, about 10 minutes; transfer to plate.

5. Let now-empty skillet cool slightly. Add remaining 1 tablespoon oil, garlic, and oregano and cook over medium heat until fragrant, about 1 minute. Stir in processed tomato mixture and 1 teaspoon salt and cook for 1 minute. Stir in 3½ cups water and pasta. Cover, increase heat to medium-high, and cook at vigorous simmer, stirring often, until pasta is tender, 15 to 18 minutes.

6. Stir in remaining ½ cup water, remaining 1 cup Parmesan, and eggplant. Season with salt and pepper to taste. Layer on mozzarella, then sprinkle panko mixture evenly over top. Transfer skillet to oven and bake until topping is well browned, 5 to 10 minutes. Sprinkle with basil and serve.

Skillet Meaty Lasagna

Serves 4

✔ **WHY THIS RECIPE WORKS:** Lasagna is one of our favorite casseroles here in the test kitchen. That's why we decided to come up with a streamlined skillet version. To start, we created a richly flavored, yet quickly simmered, tomato sauce with canned whole tomatoes, which we pulsed in the food processor; these gave us more reliable results than crushed tomatoes, which we found to vary in texture and thickness from brand to brand. Meatloaf mix, which we browned first, contributed deep, meaty flavor but kept our shopping list short (it's a mix of ground beef, pork, and veal). To fit the lasagna noodles in the pan, we broke them into short lengths. Finally, for the cheesy layer, we not only stirred in some shredded mozzarella, but we also sprinkled more mozzarella and dropped big dollops of ricotta on top before serving; covering the pan briefly provided enough residual heat to melt them into a creamy topping. Do not substitute no-boil lasagna noodles for the traditional, curly-edged lasagna noodles here. Meatloaf mix is sold prepackaged in many supermarkets; if it's unavailable, use 8 ounces each ground pork and 85 percent lean ground beef. You can substitute part-skim ricotta if desired, but do not use nonfat ricotta, which has a very dry texture and bland flavor.

3	**(14.5-ounce) cans whole peeled tomatoes**
1	**tablespoon olive oil**
1	**onion, chopped fine**
	Salt and pepper
3	**garlic cloves, minced**
⅛	**teaspoon red pepper flakes**
1	**pound meatloaf mix**
10	**curly-edged lasagna noodles, broken into 1½- to 2-inch lengths**
2	**ounces mozzarella cheese, shredded (½ cup)**
¼	**cup grated Parmesan cheese**
6	**ounces (¾ cup) whole-milk ricotta cheese**
3	**tablespoons chopped fresh basil**

1. Pulse tomatoes in food processor until coarsely ground and no large pieces remain, about 12 pulses.

2. Heat oil in 12-inch nonstick skillet over medium heat until shimmering. Add onion and ½ teaspoon salt and cook, stirring often, until softened, 5 to 7 minutes. Stir in garlic and pepper flakes and cook until fragrant, about 30 seconds. Add ground meat and cook, breaking up meat with wooden spoon, until no longer pink, 3 to 5 minutes.

3. Scatter pasta in skillet, then pour processed tomatoes over top. Cover, increase heat to medium-high, and cook at vigorous simmer, stirring often, until pasta is tender, about 20 minutes.

4. Off heat, stir in half of mozzarella and half of Parmesan. Season with salt and pepper to taste. Dot heaping tablespoons of ricotta over noodles, then sprinkle with remaining mozzarella and Parmesan. Cover and let stand off heat until cheese melts, 2 to 4 minutes. Sprinkle with basil and serve.

QUICK PREP TIP BREAKING LASAGNA NOODLES

To make sure that the lasagna noodles cook through evenly in the skillet and are easier to eat, we break them into 1½- to 2-inch pieces. Simply snap the noodles crosswise using your hands. Be sure to use traditional, not no-boil, lasagna noodles here.

Skillet Penne with Chicken and Broccoli

Serves 4

WHY THIS RECIPE WORKS: Though there's no red sauce in it, pasta with chicken and broccoli is on the menu at just about every Italian restaurant. And with good reason—the trio of tender pasta, fresh, bright broccoli, and mild chicken draped in a garlicky, velvety sauce is hard to beat. To move this multiple-pot recipe to a single skillet, we browned the chicken, then set it aside while we sautéed aromatics and built the sauce (we'd add it back later to finish cooking). Chicken broth and water, with a pile of minced garlic, red pepper flakes, and white wine, formed the base of the sauce and provided enough liquid to cook the pasta; leaving the pan uncovered allowed the broth and water to reduce and everything to intensify in flavor. Stirring Parmesan in at the end gave it a slightly creamy consistency that wasn't too rich. For bright green yet tender broccoli, we added it to the pan when the pasta was almost ready; in mere minutes, both were perfectly done and ready to be joined by the chicken. Other pasta shapes can be substituted for the penne; however, their cup measurements may vary (see page 173).

1	pound boneless, skinless chicken breasts, trimmed and sliced thin (see page 26)
	Salt and pepper
¼	cup olive oil
1	onion, chopped fine
	Salt and pepper
6	garlic cloves, minced
¼	teaspoon red pepper flakes
¼	teaspoon dried oregano
½	cup dry white wine
2½	cups water
2	cups low-sodium chicken broth
8	ounces (2½ cups) penne
8	ounces broccoli florets, cut into bite-size pieces
2	ounces Parmesan cheese, grated (1 cup), plus extra for serving

1. Pat chicken dry with paper towels and season with salt and pepper. Heat 1 tablespoon oil in 12-inch nonstick skillet over medium-high heat until just smoking. Add chicken in single layer and cook, without stirring, until beginning to brown, about 1 minute. Stir chicken and continue to cook until nearly cooked through, about 2 minutes; transfer to bowl and cover to keep warm.

2. Add 1 tablespoon oil to now-empty skillet and heat over medium heat until shimmering. Add onion and ½ teaspoon salt and cook until softened, 5 to 7 minutes. Stir in garlic, pepper flakes, and oregano and cook until fragrant, about 30 seconds. Stir in wine and simmer until nearly evaporated, 1 to 2 minutes.

3. Stir in water, broth, and pasta. Increase heat to medium-high and cook at vigorous simmer, stirring often, until pasta is nearly tender, about 12 minutes.

4. Stir in broccoli and cook until pasta and broccoli are tender and sauce has thickened, 3 to 5 minutes. Stir in chicken, along with any accumulated juice, and cook until warmed through, about 1 minute. Off heat, stir in remaining 2 tablespoons oil and Parmesan and season with salt and pepper to taste. Serve with extra Parmesan.

SMART SHOPPING CHICKEN BROTH
When buying chicken broth, you should look for a few things. First, it should have a lower sodium content—less than 700 milligrams per serving—since the reduction of a higher-sodium broth can make a skillet pasta dish taste inedibly salty. Also, pick a mass-produced broth. We tasted several broths with rancid and off-flavors—which are caused by fat oxidation—and the worst were those made by smaller companies. Last, look for a short ingredient list that includes vegetables like carrots, celery, and onions. Our pick? **Swanson Certified Organic Free Range Chicken Broth**.

Skillet Spicy Chicken Abruzzo

Serves 4

✓ **WHY THIS RECIPE WORKS:** The Abruzzo region in Italy, well known for its spicy cuisine and liberal use of hot peppers, is the inspiration for this lively dish, which gets its flavor from three kinds of peppers. Pickled pepperoncini and pickled hot cherry peppers provide a complex heat and tang, while fresh red bell peppers add sweetness and a slight crunch; if you can't find jarred sliced peppers, you can simply buy jarred whole peppers and slice them yourself. We reinforced the hot peppers' flavor by adding some of their vinegary brine to the cooking liquid for the pasta; we also stirred a little more fresh brine in at the end for a bright, bracing punch. Other pasta shapes can be substituted for the fusilli; however, their cup measurements may vary (see page 173). For the nutritional information for this recipe, see page 306.

1	pound boneless, skinless chicken breasts, trimmed and sliced thin (see page 26)
	Salt and pepper
2	tablespoons olive oil, plus extra for serving
1	onion, halved and sliced ¼ inch thick
2	red bell peppers, stemmed, seeded, and cut into ¼-inch strips
¼	cup jarred sliced hot cherry peppers, plus 2 tablespoons brine
¼	cup jarred sliced pepperoncini peppers, plus 2 tablespoons brine
3	garlic cloves, minced
2½	cups low-sodium chicken broth
2	cups water
2	teaspoons sugar
8	ounces (3 cups) fusilli
¼	cup minced fresh basil and/or parsley

1. Pat chicken dry with paper towels and season with salt and pepper. Heat 1 tablespoon oil in 12-inch nonstick skillet over medium-high heat until just smoking. Add chicken in single layer and cook, without stirring, until beginning to brown, about 1 minute. Stir chicken and continue to cook until nearly cooked through, about 2 minutes; transfer to bowl and cover to keep warm.

2. Add remaining 1 tablespoon oil and onion to now-empty skillet and cook over medium-high heat until onion begins to soften, about 3 minutes. Stir in bell peppers, cherry peppers, and pepperoncini peppers and cook until bell peppers begin to soften, about 5 minutes. Stir in garlic and cook until fragrant, about 30 seconds.

3. Stir in broth, water, 1 tablespoon cherry pepper brine, 1 tablespoon pepperoncini pepper brine, sugar, ¼ teaspoon salt, and pasta and cook at vigorous simmer, stirring often, until pasta is tender and sauce has thickened, 15 to 18 minutes.

4. Stir in chicken, along with any accumulated juice, and cook until warmed through, about 1 minute. Off heat, stir in basil and season with remaining pepper brines, salt, and pepper to taste. Serve with extra olive oil.

ON THE SIDE EASY DINNER ROLLS
Cut 8 ounces pizza dough into 4 even pieces and roll into balls. Arrange on well-oiled baking sheet, brush lightly with olive oil, and sprinkle with salt and pepper. Bake in 400-degree oven until golden, about 20 minutes. Let cool for 5 minutes before serving. Makes 4.

Skillet Saltimbocca Spaghetti

Serves 4

✓ **WHY THIS RECIPE WORKS:** For a deconstructed chicken saltimbocca, we kept the key elements in place—crisp prosciutto, browned chicken, and fried sage—but changed things up a bit. First, saving the fried prosciutto and sage for a garnish, rather than layering them on the chicken, ensured a dish permeated with meaty crunch and woodsy sweetness. Slicing the chicken breasts into strips, instead of leaving them whole, promised more bites of tender chicken throughout; browning the strips in the rendered fat left behind from the prosciutto gave the chicken rich, meaty flavor. Building our sauce in the pan with plenty of chicken broth, water, and wine provided enough volume to cook our pasta. At the end, our saltimbocca spaghetti was flavored through and through with the rich, savory notes of sage, prosciutto, and chicken. Fresh sage is important to the flavor of this dish; do not substitute dried sage. See page 173 for tips on how to measure out long strands of pasta without using a scale.

3	tablespoons olive oil
4	ounces thinly sliced prosciutto, sliced crosswise ⅓ inch thick
8	large fresh sage leaves plus 3 tablespoons minced
1	pound boneless, skinless chicken breasts, trimmed and sliced thin (see page 26)
	Salt and pepper
1	onion, chopped fine
4	garlic cloves, minced
2	teaspoons all-purpose flour
1	cup dry white wine
3	cups low-sodium chicken broth
1½	cups water
12	ounces thin spaghetti or spaghettini, broken in half
3	tablespoons capers, rinsed
2	tablespoons unsalted butter
½	teaspoon lemon zest plus 3 tablespoons juice

1. Heat 2 tablespoons oil in 12-inch nonstick skillet over medium-high heat until shimmering. Add prosciutto and cook until crisp, about 5 minutes. Add sage leaves and continue to cook until leaves are crisp, about 20 seconds. Using slotted spoon, transfer prosciutto and sage to paper towel–lined plate.

2. Pat chicken dry with paper towels and season with salt and pepper. Heat remaining 1 tablespoon oil in now-empty skillet over medium-high heat until just smoking. Add chicken in single layer and cook, without stirring, until beginning to brown, about 1 minute. Stir chicken and continue to cook until nearly cooked through, about 2 minutes; transfer to bowl and cover to keep warm.

3. Add onion to fat left in skillet and cook over medium heat until softened and golden, 7 to 10 minutes. Stir in garlic and minced sage and cook until fragrant, about 30 seconds. Stir in flour and cook for 1 minute. Stir in wine and simmer until reduced by half, about 1 minute.

4. Stir in broth, water, and pasta. Increase heat to medium-high and cook at vigorous simmer, stirring often, until pasta is tender and sauce has thickened, 12 to 15 minutes.

5. Stir in chicken, along with any accumulated juice, and capers, butter, lemon zest, and lemon juice and cook until chicken is warmed through, about 1 minute. Off heat, season with salt and pepper to taste. Sprinkle individual portions with crisped prosciutto and sage and serve.

Skillet Penne with Chicken Sausage, Sun-Dried Tomatoes, and Spinach

Serves 4

✔ **WHY THIS RECIPE WORKS:** For a super-speedy yet exciting weeknight meal, we combined penne with chicken sausage and a good amount of greens (baby spinach). Chopped sun-dried tomatoes provided big, bold flavor in quick order. Saving the spinach until the end kept this dish both bright in color and flavor. The spinach may seem like a lot at first, but it wilts down substantially. Other pasta shapes can be substituted for the penne; however, their cup measurements may vary (see page 173). For the nutritional information for this recipe, see page 306.

2	teaspoons olive oil
1	pound sweet or hot Italian chicken sausage, casings removed
3	garlic cloves, minced
2½	cups low-sodium chicken broth
2	cups water
½	cup oil-packed sun-dried tomatoes, rinsed and chopped fine
	Salt and pepper
8	ounces (2½ cups) penne
6	ounces (6 cups) baby spinach
	Grated Parmesan cheese

1. Heat oil in 12-inch nonstick skillet over medium-high heat until just smoking. Add sausage and cook, breaking up meat with wooden spoon, until no longer pink, about 4 minutes. Stir in garlic and cook until fragrant, about 30 seconds.

2. Stir in broth, water, sun-dried tomatoes, ½ teaspoon salt, and pasta. Cook at vigorous simmer, stirring often, until pasta is tender and sauce has thickened, 15 to 18 minutes.

3. Stir in spinach, one handful at a time, and cook until wilted. Season with salt and pepper to taste and serve with Parmesan.

SMART SHOPPING SUN-DRIED TOMATOES
Here in the test kitchen, we prefer oil-packed sun-dried tomatoes to their leatherlike counterparts. Because the packing oil can impart a musty, herbal flavor to the tomatoes, we recommend rinsing them before using them in any recipe. We've found that washing away excess herbs and spices improves their taste.

Skillet-Baked Tex-Mex Macaroni

Serves 4

✔️ **WHY THIS RECIPE WORKS:** For this jazzed-up macaroni dinner, we headed south of the border. We started by sautéing an onion and garlic with bell pepper, chili powder, and cayenne; this helped bloom the spices' flavors and took down their raw, harsh notes. Next, we added ground beef to the pan to jump-start its cooking. A can of tomato sauce and some water made our meat sauce saucier, and provided ample liquid to cook the pasta. Because this wouldn't be a Tex-Mex dish without corn and green chiles, we stirred in both once the pasta was done, along with a cup of shredded Mexican cheese blend. After sprinkling more cheese on top, we slid the pan in the oven just long enough for it to melt into an ooey, gooey layer. If you can't find shredded Mexican cheese blend, substitute 1 cup each shredded Monterey Jack cheese and shredded cheddar cheese.

1 tablespoon vegetable oil

1 onion, chopped fine

1 green bell pepper, stemmed, seeded, and cut into ½-inch pieces

3 garlic cloves, minced

2 tablespoons chili powder

⅛ teaspoon cayenne pepper

1 pound 90 percent lean ground beef

2 cups water

1 (15-ounce) can tomato sauce

8 ounces (2 cups) elbow macaroni

1 cup frozen corn

1 (4.5-ounce) can chopped green chiles

8 ounces shredded Mexican cheese blend (2 cups)
Salt and pepper

2 tablespoons minced fresh cilantro

1. Adjust oven rack to middle position and heat oven to 475 degrees. Heat oil in 12-inch ovensafe nonstick skillet over medium heat until shimmering. Add onion and bell pepper and cook until softened, 5 to 7 minutes.

2. Stir in garlic, chili powder, and cayenne and cook until fragrant, about 30 seconds. Stir in beef, breaking up meat with wooden spoon, and cook until no longer pink, about 1 minute.

3. Stir in water, tomato sauce, and pasta. Cover, increase heat to medium-high, and cook at vigorous simmer, stirring often, until pasta is tender, 9 to 12 minutes.

4. Off heat, stir in corn, chiles, and 1 cup cheese and season with salt and pepper to taste. Sprinkle remaining 1 cup cheese evenly over top. Transfer skillet to oven and bake until cheese has melted and browned, 10 to 15 minutes. Sprinkle with cilantro and serve.

ON THE SIDE SWEET AND CAKEY CORNBREAD
Whisk 1½ cups all-purpose flour, 1 cup yellow cornmeal, 2 teaspoons baking powder, ¾ teaspoon salt, and ¼ teaspoon baking soda together in medium bowl. Process 1 cup buttermilk, ¾ cup thawed frozen corn kernels, and ¼ cup packed light brown sugar in food processor until combined, about 5 seconds. Add 2 large eggs and process until well combined (batter will be lumpy), about 5 seconds. Fold buttermilk mixture into flour mixture, then fold in 8 tablespoons melted unsalted butter. Scrape batter into greased 8-inch square pan. Bake in 400-degree oven until golden brown, 25 to 35 minutes. Let cool for 15 minutes before serving. Serves 8.

Skillet Macaroni and Cheese with Broccoli

Serves 4

✓ **WHY THIS RECIPE WORKS:** Packaged mac and cheese might be easy, but that's about all it has going for it. We wanted mac and cheese enrobed in a smooth, silky sauce that *really* tasted like cheese—and we wanted to use just one pan to get there. Many recipes start with a béchamel sauce, made with butter, milk, and flour, but that seemed a bit fussy for our skillet mac and cheese, so we began with a mixture of butter, evaporated milk (which kept the sauce smooth), and water—just enough to cook the pasta. Cornstarch, mixed with more evaporated milk, provided thickening power, and dry mustard, garlic, and hot sauce gave the sauce a piquant backbone. When it came to the cheese, a hefty three cups gave us the uber-cheesy flavor and creaminess we were after; cheddar gave our dish good cheesy flavor, while Monterey Jack ensured a smooth texture. A final pat of butter enriched the sauce, and broccoli florets, blanched in the pan beforehand, added a splash of color and ensured that everyone got their veggies in.

4	cups water, plus extra as needed
8	ounces broccoli florets, cut into bite-size pieces
	Salt and pepper
3	tablespoons unsalted butter
3	garlic cloves, minced
¼	teaspoon red pepper flakes
1	(12-ounce) can evaporated milk
12	ounces (3 cups) elbow macaroni
1	teaspoon cornstarch
½	teaspoon dry mustard
¼	teaspoon hot sauce
6	ounces cheddar cheese, shredded (1½ cups)
6	ounces Monterey Jack cheese, shredded (1½ cups)

1. Bring ½ cup water to boil in 12-inch nonstick skillet over high heat. Add broccoli and pinch salt, cover, and cook until broccoli is just tender, about 5 minutes. Drain broccoli and set aside.

2. Wipe now-empty skillet dry, add 1 tablespoon butter, and melt over medium-high heat. Add garlic and pepper flakes and cook until fragrant, about 1 minute. Stir in remaining 3½ cups water, 1 cup evaporated milk, ½ teaspoon salt, and pasta. Cook at vigorous simmer, stirring often, until pasta is tender and sauce has thickened, 9 to 12 minutes.

3. Whisk remaining ½ cup evaporated milk, cornstarch, mustard, and hot sauce together in bowl, then stir into skillet. Continue to simmer until slightly thickened, about 1 minute.

4. Off heat, stir in cheddar and Monterey Jack, one handful at a time, until melted. Add extra water as needed to adjust consistency. Stir in remaining 2 tablespoons butter and cooked broccoli. Season with salt and pepper to taste and serve.

SMART SHOPPING MACARONI

With so many brands of elbow macaroni on the market, which one should you buy? Are they all the same? To find out, we rounded up eight contenders and tasted them simply dressed with vegetable oil and in a macaroni and cheese recipe. What we found is that an Italian brand (which makes pasta for the American market domestically) won our tasting by a large margin. Our tasters praised **Barilla Elbows** for their "wheaty," "buttery" flavor and "firm texture," and they especially liked that these elbows have small ridges and a slight twist that "holds sauce well."

Skillet Macaroni and Cheese with Ham and Peas

Serves 4

✔ **WHY THIS RECIPE WORKS:** Hot on the heels of our Skillet Macaroni and Cheese with Broccoli (page 56), we decided to create another one-pan mac and cheese supper. This time, we set our sights on a dish that combined salty, meaty ham and tender peas. We took the same approach—we simmered water and evaporated milk to cook the pasta, then added cornstarch for thickening and stirred in the cheese—but this time, we added our ham and peas, too. The ham (a small steak) simply needed to be cut into pieces, while the peas needed zero prep—they went directly from freezer to skillet. Not only was our one-pan mac and cheese incredibly flavorful, it was also unbelievably easy.

3½   cups water, plus extra as needed
1   (12-ounce) can evaporated milk
     Salt and pepper
12   ounces (3 cups) elbow macaroni
1   teaspoon cornstarch
½   teaspoon dry mustard
¼   teaspoon hot sauce
8   ounces ham steak, rind removed, diced
½   cup frozen peas
6   ounces cheddar cheese, shredded (1½ cups)
6   ounces Monterey Jack cheese, shredded (1½ cups)
2   tablespoons unsalted butter

1. Bring water, 1 cup evaporated milk, ½ teaspoon salt, and pasta to simmer in 12-inch nonstick skillet over high heat. Cook at vigorous simmer, stirring often, until pasta is tender and sauce has thickened, 9 to 12 minutes.

2. Whisk remaining ½ cup evaporated milk, cornstarch, mustard, and hot sauce together in bowl, then stir into skillet. Stir in ham and peas and continue to simmer until slightly thickened, about 2 minutes.

3. Off heat, stir in cheddar and Monterey Jack, one handful at a time, until melted. Add extra water as needed to adjust consistency. Stir in butter, season with salt and pepper to taste, and serve.

SMART SHOPPING **SHARP CHEDDAR CHEESE**
Since our Skillet Macaroni and Cheese dinners call on a cup and a half of grated cheddar for ultra-cheesy flavor, we wanted to know which brand of cheddar to use. In a side-by-side taste test of sharp cheddars, three supermarket brands topped our list. We were surprised to find that modestly priced Cracker Barrel, which ended up in third place, outranked other cheddars that cost over twice as much. It was bested, however, by Vermont-made **Cabot Sharp Cheddar Cheese**, which sells for about $5 a pound, and Oregon-made Tillamook, which sells for about $10 a pound. All three possessed rich, tangy flavor and melted smoothly.

Skillet Wagon Wheel Pasta with Turkey Sausage

Serves 4

✓ **WHY THIS RECIPE WORKS:** For a family-friendly pasta supper that would appeal to diners of all ages, we picked a fun pasta shape—wagon wheels—and added sausage for heartiness. Turkey sausage won us over for its meaty but not overpowering flavor. For the backbone of our sauce, we sautéed an onion and garlic with the sausage; a small amount of flour worked well as the thickener, and adding it before the cooking liquid (a mix of chicken broth and water) and pasta enabled its raw flavor to cook off. We simmered the pasta uncovered so the sauce could reduce and thicken; grated Parmesan gave it a velvety sheen. Baby spinach and peas, stirred in at the end, lightened the dish, while a handful of chopped tarragon added a bit of interest for the adults in the crowd. The spinach may look like too much at first but it wilts down substantially as it cooks. Italian chicken sausage can be substituted for the turkey sausage. Other pasta shapes can be substituted for the wagon wheels; however, their cup measurements may vary (see page 173). For the nutritional information for this recipe, see page 306.

1	tablespoon olive oil
1	onion, chopped fine
8	ounces sweet or hot Italian turkey sausage, casings removed
3	garlic cloves, minced
2	teaspoons all-purpose flour
2½	cups low-sodium chicken broth
2	cups water
8	ounces (3 cups) wagon wheel (or rotelle) pasta
5	ounces (5 cups) baby spinach
2	ounces Parmesan cheese, grated (1 cup), plus extra for serving
½	cup frozen peas, thawed
1	tablespoon minced fresh tarragon (optional)
	Salt and pepper

1. Heat oil in 12-inch nonstick skillet over medium heat until shimmering. Add onion and cook until softened, about 5 minutes. Stir in sausage and cook, breaking up meat with wooden spoon, until no longer pink, about 4 minutes. Stir in garlic and cook until fragrant, about 30 seconds. Stir in flour and cook for 1 minute.

2. Stir in broth, water, and pasta. Increase heat to medium-high and cook at vigorous simmer, stirring often, until pasta is tender and sauce has thickened, 15 to 18 minutes.

3. Stir in spinach, one handful at a time, until wilted, about 2 minutes. Off heat, stir in Parmesan, peas, and tarragon, if using. Season with salt and pepper to taste and serve with extra Parmesan.

QUICK PREP TIP **REMOVING SAUSAGE FROM ITS CASING**
Italian sausage is sold in several forms, including links (which is most common), bulk-style tubes, and patties. If using links, remove the meat from the casing before cooking so that it can crumble into small, bite-size pieces. To remove sausage from its casing, hold the sausage firmly on one end, and squeeze the sausage out of the opposite end.

Skillet Penne with Cherry Tomatoes, White Beans, and Olives

Serves 4

✔ **WHY THIS RECIPE WORKS:** This dish is all about taking a few humble ingredients and turning them into something extraordinary. To start, we added penne to the pan with a good amount of water and chicken broth for decent but not overwhelming savory flavor (vegetable broth works well, too). Once the sauce had reduced and the pasta was cooked, we added a can of creamy white beans, juicy halved cherry tomatoes, and some chopped kalamatas for a briny punch. Grated Parmesan cheese gave the sauce an underlying richness, while fresh basil and high-quality extra-virgin olive oil, stirred in last, elevated our simple supper to new heights. Other pasta shapes can be substituted for the penne; however, their cup measurements may vary (see page 173). For the nutritional information for this recipe, see page 306.

2½ cups water

2 cups low-sodium chicken or vegetable broth

    Salt and pepper

8 ounces (2½ cups) penne

1 (15-ounce) can cannellini beans, rinsed

12 ounces cherry tomatoes, halved

½ cup pitted kalamata olives, chopped

1 ounce Parmesan cheese, grated (½ cup), plus extra for serving

½ cup chopped fresh basil

2 tablespoons extra-virgin olive oil

1 tablespoon lemon juice

1. Bring water, broth, ½ teaspoon salt, and pasta to simmer in 12-inch nonstick skillet over high heat. Cook at vigorous simmer, stirring often, until pasta is tender and sauce has thickened, 15 to 18 minutes.

2. Stir in beans, tomatoes, and olives and continue to cook until warmed through, about 1 minute. Off heat, stir in Parmesan, basil, oil, and lemon juice. Season with salt and pepper to taste and serve with extra Parmesan.

SMART SHOPPING PENNE
Curious if there was any difference between the various brands of penne you find at the supermarket—from fancy imported brands to inexpensive domestic brands—we pitted eight brands against each other in a taste-off. Though the fancier brands from Italy boasted traditional techniques and ingredients (such as slow kneading, mixing cold mountain spring water with hard durum semolina, and extruding the dough through traditional bronze cast dies for a coarse texture), we found they didn't necessarily translate into better-tasting pasta. In fact, the three most expensive imports landed at the bottom of our rankings. Though none were so bad that they were deemed unacceptable, there were significant differences among the brands we tasted. In the end, tasters rated **Mueller's Penne Rigate** the highest for "hearty," "wheaty" flavor.

Skillet Turkey Tetrazzini

Serves 4

✔ **WHY THIS RECIPE WORKS:** Rumored to have been named for an opera singer, turkey tetrazzini is one rich dish. This classic casserole pairs turkey with sautéed mushrooms and drapes them in a butter- and cream-laden Parmesan sauce flavored with sherry. For our skillet version, we traded the usual spaghetti found in tetrazzini for egg noodles, which have a wider surface area—perfect for cradling that creamy sauce. After browning thin slices of turkey, we sautéed the mushrooms in butter until lightly browned. A mixture of chicken broth, heavy cream, and sherry provided the best flavor, richness, and volume to cook our egg noodles. When the noodles were done, we added frozen peas for a splash of green, and a pile of shredded Gruyère. Finally, to gild the lily, we sprinkled Ritz cracker crumbs over the top and baked the casserole until it was hot and bubbling. Do not substitute other types of noodles for the wide egg noodles here.

1	**pound thin turkey cutlets, trimmed and sliced thin**
	Salt and pepper
3	**tablespoons unsalted butter**
10	**ounces white mushrooms, trimmed and sliced thin**
1	**onion, chopped fine**
3½	**cups low-sodium chicken broth**
1	**cup heavy cream**
2	**tablespoons dry sherry**
8	**ounces (3 cups) wide egg noodles**
1	**cup frozen peas**
4	**ounces Gruyère cheese, shredded (1 cup)**
2	**tablespoons minced fresh parsley**
20	**Ritz crackers, crushed to coarse crumbs (1 cup)**

1. Adjust oven rack to middle position and heat oven to 475 degrees. Pat turkey dry with paper towels and season with salt and pepper. Melt 1 tablespoon butter in 12-inch ovensafe nonstick skillet over high heat. Add turkey in single layer and cook, without stirring, until beginning to brown, about 1 minute. Stir turkey and continue to cook until nearly cooked through, about 2 minutes; transfer to bowl and cover to keep warm.

2. Melt remaining 2 tablespoons butter in now-empty skillet over medium-high heat. Add mushrooms, onion, and ½ teaspoon salt and cook until mushrooms have released their moisture and are golden, 7 to 10 minutes.

3. Stir in broth, cream, sherry, and noodles and cook at vigorous simmer, stirring often, until pasta is tender and sauce has slightly thickened, about 8 minutes.

4. Off heat, stir in turkey, along with any accumulated juice, and peas, Gruyère, and parsley. Season with salt and pepper to taste. Sprinkle Ritz crumbs over top, transfer skillet to oven, and bake until topping is crisp and casserole is bubbling lightly around edges, about 8 minutes. Serve.

SMART SHOPPING EGG NOODLES
Classic egg noodles are thick, wide ribbons of pasta with a fat content that's slightly higher than that of other kinds of pasta because of their high percentage of eggs. We tasted several brands, and our favorite is **Light 'n Fluffy**, which tasters praised for its clean, slightly buttery flavor and a firm yet yielding texture.

Skillet-Baked Shrimp and Orzo

Serves 4

✔ **WHY THIS RECIPE WORKS:** For a satisfying dish of creamy orzo and moist, tender shrimp, a common pairing in Greek cuisine, we settled on a stovetop-to-oven cooking method to guarantee perfectly cooked shrimp and pasta. After briefly sautéing the orzo to bring out its flavor, we cooked it in broth and tomato juice until it was al dente and had released its starch, creating a creamy sauce. Then we added the shrimp and moved the pan to the oven so the shrimp could cook through in its gentle, even heat. Stirring the shrimp into the orzo—versus scattering them on top—shielded the shrimp so they didn't dry out. Bell pepper, red onion, diced tomatoes, and peas provided the vegetable components. Oregano and garlic were a nod to this pairing's Greek heritage; a pinch of saffron, though not traditional, gave the dish a bright, sunny hue and warm flavor. Salty bites of feta and fresh scallions made the perfect finishing touches. Make sure that the orzo is al dente, or slightly firm to the bite; otherwise it may overcook in the oven. If using smaller or larger shrimp, the cooking times may vary accordingly. You can leave the shrimp tails on, if desired. The small amount of saffron makes a big difference to the flavor and look of the dish, so be sure to include it. For the nutritional information for this recipe, see page 306.

1	**pound extra-large shrimp (21 to 25 per pound), peeled, deveined, and tails removed**
	Salt and pepper
1	**tablespoon olive oil**
1	**red onion, chopped fine**
1	**red bell pepper, stemmed, seeded, and cut into ½-inch pieces**
4	**garlic cloves, minced**
2	**teaspoons minced fresh oregano or ½ teaspoon dried**
2	**cups orzo (12 ounces)**
	Pinch saffron threads, crumbled
3	**cups low-sodium chicken broth**
1	**(14.5-ounce) can diced tomatoes, drained with juice reserved**
½	**cup frozen peas**
3	**ounces feta cheese, crumbled (¾ cup)**
2	**scallions, sliced thin**
	Lemon wedges

1. Adjust oven rack to middle position and heat oven to 400 degrees. Pat shrimp dry with paper towels and season with salt and pepper; transfer to bowl, cover, and refrigerate until needed.

2. Heat oil in 12-inch ovensafe nonstick skillet over medium heat until shimmering. Add onion and bell pepper and cook until vegetables are softened, 5 to 7 minutes. Stir in garlic and oregano and cook until fragrant, about 30 seconds. Stir in orzo and saffron and cook, stirring frequently, until orzo is coated with oil and lightly browned, about 4 minutes.

3. Stir in broth and reserved tomato juice, bring to simmer, and cook, stirring occasionally, until orzo is al dente, 10 to 12 minutes. Stir in shrimp, tomatoes, and peas, then sprinkle feta evenly over top. Transfer skillet to oven and bake until shrimp are cooked through and cheese is lightly browned, about 20 minutes. Sprinkle with scallions and serve with lemon wedges.

SMART SHOPPING **FETA**
Within the European Union, only cheese made in Greece from a mixture of sheep's and goat's milk can be legally called feta, but most of the feta in American supermarkets is made from pasteurized cow's milk that has been curdled, shaped into blocks, sliced (*feta* is Greek for "slice"), and steeped in brine. Feta dries out quickly when removed from its brine, so always store it in the brine it's packed in (we do not recommend buying precrumbled feta, which not only is more expensive, but is also lacking in flavor and texture). Our favorite brand is **Mt. Vikos Traditional Feta**, which tasters found to be flavorful yet mild and to have a pleasing "creamy, crumbly" texture.

Skillet Paella Pasta

Serves 4

✓ **WHY THIS RECIPE WORKS:** For this speedy, one-pan version of paella, we swapped pasta for the rice and pared down the extensive ingredient list. Most paella recipes sauté the rice, and we followed suit, toasting the pasta to give it a nutty flavor. We liked the classic feel of spaghetti, which we broke into pieces so it would be easy to toast. Instead of a laundry list of meat and seafood, we winnowed down the options: Chorizo added deep flavor, while shrimp and mussels were crowd-pleasers and low-maintenance (they could be stirred in for the last few minutes of cooking). Chicken broth, white wine, saffron, and canned diced tomatoes added flavor to the sauce. Frozen peas and minced parsley round out this streamlined yet flavorful homage to Spain's most popular dish. See page 173 for tips on how to measure out long strands of pasta without using a scale.

8 **ounces spaghetti, broken into 2-inch lengths**

3 **tablespoons olive oil**

1 **onion, chopped fine**
  Salt and pepper

4 **ounces chorizo, halved length-wise and sliced ¼ inch thick**

6 **garlic cloves, minced**

¼ **teaspoon saffron threads, crumbled**

½ **cup dry white wine**

1 **(14.5-ounce) can diced tomatoes**

2 **cups water**

1 **cup low-sodium chicken broth**

8 **ounces extra-large shrimp (21 to 25 per pound), peeled and deveined**

½ **cup frozen peas**

1 **pound mussels, scrubbed and debearded**

2 **tablespoons minced fresh parsley**

1. Toast spaghetti in 2 tablespoons oil in 12-inch nonstick skillet over medium-high heat, tossing frequently with tongs, until golden, about 4 minutes; transfer to paper towel–lined plate.

2. Add remaining 1 tablespoon oil, onion, and ¼ teaspoon salt to now-empty skillet and cook over medium heat until softened, 5 to 7 minutes. Stir in chorizo, garlic, and saffron and cook until fragrant, about 1 minute. Stir in wine and simmer until nearly evaporated, 1 to 2 minutes.

3. Stir in tomatoes, water, broth, and toasted pasta. Cover, increase heat to medium-high, and cook at vigorous simmer, stirring often, until pasta is nearly tender, about 12 minutes.

4. Pat shrimp dry with paper towels and season with salt and pepper. Stir in shrimp and peas. Nestle mussels, hinge side down, into pasta. Cover and continue to cook until pasta is tender, mussels have opened, and shrimp are cooked through, 2 to 4 minutes. Off heat, season with salt and pepper to taste. Sprinkle with parsley and serve.

QUICK PREP TIP TOASTING NOODLES
To develop a deep, nutty flavor in some pasta dishes, we first toast the noodles in the skillet with a little oil until golden before adding the liquid. Be sure to toss and stir noodles often as they toast so they don't burn. We find it easiest to use tongs to stir the noodles, but they should be nonstick tongs so as not to mar the surface of a nonstick skillet.

Skillet Sopa Seca with Chorizo and Black Beans

Serves 4

✔ **WHY THIS RECIPE WORKS:** Its name might mean "dry soup," but sopa seca is really a saucy pasta dish. In this enticing Mexican specialty, fideos—thin, coiled strands of pasta toasted until golden—are baked in a flavorful broth studded with tomatoes and capped with melted cheese. When we couldn't find fideos at our local supermarket, we turned to vermicelli and just toasted it ourselves. Most sopa seca recipes call for a variety of dried chiles that must be rehydrated before being used. To keep things streamlined, we reached for canned, smoky chipotle chiles, which delivered serious flavor and ample heat with minimum work. Chicken broth provided the "soupy" portion of the dish and offered a savory backbone. To make our skillet sopa seca a complete meal, we added chorizo and black beans, which stayed true to the dish's Mexican roots. To make the dish spicier, increase the amount of chipotle chiles to 1 tablespoon. Serve with sour cream, diced avocado, and thinly sliced scallions. See page 173 for tips on how to measure out long strands of pasta without using a scale.

8	ounces vermicelli, broken in half
2	tablespoons vegetable oil
1	onion, chopped fine
4	ounces chorizo, halved lengthwise and sliced ¼ inch thick
2	garlic cloves, minced
2	teaspoons minced canned chipotle chile in adobo sauce
2	cups low-sodium chicken broth
1	(15-ounce) can black beans, rinsed
1	(14.5-ounce) can diced tomatoes
	Salt and pepper
2	ounces Monterey Jack cheese, shredded (½ cup)
¼	cup minced fresh cilantro

1. Toast vermicelli in 1 tablespoon oil in 12-inch nonstick skillet over medium-high heat, tossing frequently with tongs, until golden, about 4 minutes; transfer to paper towel–lined plate.

2. Add remaining 1 tablespoon oil and onion to skillet and cook over medium heat until softened, 5 to 7 minutes. Stir in chorizo, garlic, and chipotle and cook until fragrant, about 30 seconds.

3. Stir in broth, beans, tomatoes, and toasted vermicelli. Cover, increase heat to medium-high, and cook at vigorous simmer, stirring often, until pasta is tender, about 10 minutes.

4. Off heat, season with salt and pepper to taste and sprinkle Monterey Jack over top. Cover and let stand until cheese melts, 2 to 4 minutes. Sprinkle with cilantro and serve.

QUICK PREP TIP BREAKING LONG-STRAND PASTA IN HALF
To neatly snap noodles in half without having them fly every which way, put them in a zipper-lock bag (or wrap them in a clean kitchen towel), then press against the corner of the counter.

SUPER-EASY SPINACH LASAGNA

Casseroles

No-Prep Baked Spaghetti

Serves 4

✔ **WHY THIS RECIPE WORKS:** For the ultimate, easiest-ever, prep-free spaghetti dinner, we cooked both pasta and sauce together in the oven, combining canned tomatoes, beef, and spaghetti in a baking dish—with no precooking whatsoever. Breaking the spaghetti strands in half ensured they would fit in the baking dish, and crumbling the beef into bite-size pieces promised a hearty dish with meaty bites throughout. Crushed tomatoes gave our no-prep sauce a fresh tomato flavor, while a small can of tomato sauce provided body and smooth texture. Adding water upped the volume of our sauce and provided enough liquid to cook the pasta. Dried porcini, garlic powder, oregano, and red pepper flakes offered a savory foundation. Baking our pasta dinner covered ensured that the spaghetti was perfectly al dente, and uncovering the dish for the last few minutes helped to create a nicely thickened sauce. Make sure to crumble the beef into pieces that measure ½ inch or smaller in step 1. See page 173 for tips on how to measure out long strands of pasta without using a scale. For the nutritional information for this recipe, see page 306.

12	**ounces spaghetti, broken in half**
1	**pound 90 percent lean ground beef**
	Salt and pepper
1	**(28-ounce) can crushed tomatoes**
2¼	**cups water**
1	**(8-ounce) can tomato sauce**
⅛	**ounce dried porcini mushrooms, rinsed and minced**
½	**teaspoon garlic powder (or 2 garlic cloves, minced)**
½	**teaspoon minced fresh oregano or ⅛ teaspoon dried**
⅛	**teaspoon red pepper flakes**
	Grated Parmesan cheese

1. Adjust oven rack to middle position and heat oven to 475 degrees. Grease 13 by 9-inch baking dish with vegetable oil spray. Spread pasta into prepared dish, crumble beef into ½-inch pieces over top, and season with salt and pepper.

2. Whisk crushed tomatoes, water, tomato sauce, porcini, garlic powder, oregano, pepper flakes, ¾ teaspoon salt, and ½ teaspoon pepper together in bowl. Pour into baking dish and toss gently with tongs to combine. Cover dish tightly with aluminum foil and bake for 30 minutes.

3. Remove baking dish from oven and stir pasta thoroughly, scraping sides and bottom of dish. Return uncovered dish to oven and continue to bake until pasta is al dente and sauce is thickened, 5 to 8 minutes. Toss pasta to coat with sauce, season with salt and pepper to taste, and serve with Parmesan.

SMART SHOPPING SPAGHETTI

Spaghetti makes a versatile partner for just about any type of sauce. Plus, it promises a cheap dinner—or, at least, it used to. When we recently checked out brands at the supermarket, we saw a few boxes priced around a dollar, while others cost four times that. We recently sampled eight brands of spaghetti to find out if we had to spend more money for great pasta. After cooking and tasting six Italian imports and two domestic brands dressed simply with olive oil and tossed with a tomato sauce, we found our winner. Our favorite spaghetti—and also one of the two cheapest brands we tasted (less than $2 a pound)—was an Italian import. Tasters preferred **De Cecco Spaghetti no. 12** for its "clean wheat flavor" and "firm" strands with "good chew."

ALL ABOUT Italian Cheese

Cheese is as integral as the tomatoes to many pasta dishes—even if it's just being used to sprinkle over a plate of finished pasta. Here are the cheeses we call for most often in this book, along with a few tips on properly grating and storing cheese.

Parmesan Cheese

Genuine Italian Parmigiano-Reggiano cheese offers a buttery, nutty taste and crystalline crunch. Produced for the past 800 years in northern Italy using traditional methods, this hard cow's-milk cheese has a distinctive flavor, but it comes at a steep price. Our top-rated brand, chosen from a lineup of supermarket cheeses, is **Boar's Head Parmigiano-Reggiano**; this Italian import costs about $18 per pound, and our tasters say it offers a "good crunch" and "nice tangy, nutty" flavor. For a more affordable option, they also liked Belgioioso Parmesan, which costs about half the price.

Storing Parmesan Cheese

After conducting a number of tests to find the best storage method for Parmesan wedges, we found that the best way to preserve its flavor and texture is to wrap it in parchment paper, then aluminum foil. However, if you're hanging on to just a small piece of cheese, tossing it in a zipper-lock bag works almost as well; just be sure to squeeze out as much air as possible before fastening the seal. Note these methods also work for Pecorino Romano.

Pecorino Romano

Pecorino Romano is an aged sheep's-milk cheese from Rome, hence its name. It has a rich, salty, grassy flavor, and it's often paired with Parmesan to moderate its sharp saltiness. Pecorino is traditional in many pasta dishes, such as Spaghetti with Pecorino Romano and Black Pepper (Cacio e Pepe, page 175) and Pasta all'Amatriciana (page 167). When shopping, look for imported Pecorino Romano— not the bland domestic cheese that's labeled simply "Romano."

Shredding Semisoft Cheese

Semisoft cheese, such as mozzarella, can be tough to shred because it can clog the holes on a box grater. To prevent this from happening, simply spray the grater lightly with vegetable oil spray, then shred the cheese as usual. The cooking spray will keep the cheese from sticking to the grater.

Mozzarella

Most supermarkets offer two kinds of mozzarella: high-moisture (or fresh) and low-moisture. Fresh mozzarella is sold in spheres and usually packed in brine. We usually reserve fresh mozzarella for eating raw or mixing into dishes like our Pasta Caprese (page 12), in which it's tossed with hot pasta. Low-moisture mozzarella typically comes shrink-wrapped in a block or preshredded in a bag. This cheese is less perishable and melts into beautifully gooey strands. Our favorite brand is **Sorrento Whole Milk Mozzarella** (sold as Precious on the West Coast), which is sold block-style.

Ricotta Cheese

Originally crafted from the whey by-product of Romano cheese-making (its name means "recooked"), ricotta cheese is used in many baked pasta dishes. Nowadays, ricotta is made from milk, not whey. We like **Calabro Ricotta Cheese**, which is made of milk, a starter, and salt. (Note that Calabro makes both part-skim and whole-milk ricotta.) If you can't find this brand, look for one without gums or stabilizers.

Bacon-Cheeseburger Pasta Bake

Serves 4

✔ **WHY THIS RECIPE WORKS:** For another (practically) prep-free pasta bake, we added ground beef, pickles, American cheese, bacon, and chopped onion to macaroni for a casserole with all the bright, tangy, meaty flavors of our favorite burger. Tomato sauce, with its smooth texture and long-cooked flavor, provided the perfect base for our sauce, which we seasoned with Worcestershire sauce and dry mustard. Combining chopped dill pickles with brown sugar gave the sauce the same sweetly pungent flavor of pickle relish but with more crunch. Slices of American cheese, bits of crispy bacon (precooked in the microwave), and a sprinkling of chopped onion made the perfect toppings; to preserve their flavor and texture (save for the cheese, which turned creamy as it melted), we didn't add the cheese, bacon, and onion until the very end. Make sure to crumble the beef into pieces that measure ½ inch or smaller in step 1.

12	ounces (3 cups) elbow macaroni
1	pound 85 percent lean ground beef
	Salt and pepper
3	cups water
1	(15-ounce) can tomato sauce
⅓	cup chopped dill pickles
2	teaspoons Worcestershire sauce
2	teaspoons dry mustard
1	teaspoon brown sugar
½	teaspoon garlic powder (or 2 garlic cloves, minced)
4	slices bacon
6	slices American cheese
½	cup finely chopped onion (optional)

1. Adjust oven rack to middle position and heat oven to 475 degrees. Grease 13 by 9-inch baking dish with vegetable oil spray. Spread pasta into prepared dish, crumble beef into ½-inch pieces over top, and season with salt and pepper.

2. Whisk water, tomato sauce, pickles, Worcestershire, mustard, sugar, garlic powder, ½ teaspoon salt, and ½ teaspoon pepper together in bowl. Pour into baking dish and toss gently with tongs to combine. Cover dish tightly with aluminum foil and bake for 25 minutes.

3. Meanwhile, microwave bacon on plate until crisp, about 5 minutes. Transfer to paper towel–lined plate to drain, then crumble into ½-inch pieces.

4. Remove baking dish from oven and stir pasta thoroughly, scraping sides and bottom of dish. Lay cheese slices over top and sprinkle with crisped bacon. Return uncovered dish to oven and continue to bake until pasta is al dente and cheese is melted, 5 to 8 minutes. Let cool for 10 to 15 minutes, sprinkle with onion, if using, and serve.

ON THE SIDE SESAME ROLLS
Cut 1 pound pizza dough into 4 equal pieces, pat gently into balls, and arrange on parchment paper–lined baking sheet. Brush rolls with beaten egg, season with salt, and sprinkle with sesame seeds. Bake in 350-degree oven until golden, 25 to 30 minutes. Makes 4.

Pizza Pasta Bake

Serves 4

✔ **WHY THIS RECIPE WORKS:** Tired of having to choose between pasta night and pizza night, we decided to combine the two and add the salty, meaty flavors of our favorite pie to a simple pasta bake. For a smooth-textured, but slightly thickened, sauce—just like pizza sauce—we combined crushed tomatoes with tomato sauce. Sausage and pepperoni were a given, and adding the sausage at the outset ensured that the whole dish absorbed its spicy, rich flavor. Reserving the pepperoni until the end and layering it on top of the pasta with shredded mozzarella gave our pasta bake a real "pizza" look. Another popular pizza topping, sliced mushrooms, balanced the meatiness of our pasta bake; parcooking them beforehand in the microwave prevented them from releasing too much liquid in the oven. Make sure to crumble the sausage into pieces that measure ½ inch or smaller in step 2. If using hot Italian sausage, omit the red pepper flakes.

12	ounces white mushrooms, trimmed and sliced thin
1	tablespoon extra-virgin olive oil
	Salt and pepper
12	ounces (3 cups) macaroni
1	pound hot or sweet Italian sausage, casings removed
1	(28-ounce) can crushed tomatoes
2	cups water
1	(8-ounce) can tomato sauce
1	teaspoon minced fresh oregano or ¼ teaspoon dried
½	teaspoon garlic powder (or 2 garlic cloves, minced)
¼	teaspoon red pepper flakes
8	ounces mozzarella cheese, shredded (2 cups)
2	ounces thinly sliced deli pepperoni

1. Adjust oven rack to middle position and heat oven to 475 degrees. Toss mushrooms with oil in bowl and season with salt and pepper. Microwave, uncovered, until mushrooms are softened and release liquid, 2 to 3 minutes. Drain mushrooms and let cool slightly.

2. Grease 13 by 9-inch baking dish with vegetable oil spray. Spread pasta into prepared dish, crumble sausage into ½-inch pieces over top, and sprinkle with mushrooms.

3. Whisk crushed tomatoes, water, tomato sauce, oregano, garlic powder, pepper flakes, ½ teaspoon salt, and ¼ teaspoon pepper together in bowl. Pour into baking dish and toss gently with tongs to combine. Cover dish tightly with aluminum foil and bake for 25 minutes.

4. Remove baking dish from oven and stir pasta thoroughly, scraping sides and bottom of dish. Sprinkle with cheese, then pepperoni. Return uncovered dish to oven and continue to bake until pasta is al dente and cheese is melted, 5 to 8 minutes. Let cool for 10 to 15 minutes and serve.

SMART SHOPPING PEPPERONI
More than just a pizza topping, pepperoni provides meaty, savory depth in a few of our casseroles. To find the best one, we gathered six national brands of sliced pepperoni and called tasters to the table. Sampling them all straight from the package as well as baked on a pizza, we preferred those that tasted meaty, spicy, and chewy. The winning pepperoni, **Margherita Italian Style Pepperoni**, was praised for its balance of "meatiness and spice" as well as its "tangy and fresh" flavor. Some tasters even picked up hints of "fruity licorice and peppery fennel."

Tex-Mex Pasta Casserole

Serves 4

✔ **WHY THIS RECIPE WORKS:** For a Tex-Mex spin on a pasta casserole, we took our inspiration from King Ranch Casserole, a chicken and tortilla casserole with spicy tomatoes and a rich, cheesy sauce. First, we built a sauce with sautéed onion, jalapeño, cumin, and spicy Ro-Tel tomatoes (a hallmark of the original recipe). Cream and chicken broth added richness and flavor, while flour worked as a thickener. For convenience, we folded in cooked, shredded chicken. Egg noodles took the place of the tortilla layers, but a crunchy topping of corn chips paid homage to the original Lone Star State dish. To make this dish spicier, add the reserved chile seeds. You can either use leftover cooked chicken here, or quickly cook chicken following the instructions on page 80. Monterey Jack cheese can be substituted for the Colby Jack. The casserole can be assembled, cooled, covered with plastic wrap, and refrigerated for up to 2 days. To bake, remove the plastic and cover with aluminum foil; bake in a 450-degree oven until hot, about 20 minutes, then remove the foil and bake until the corn chips are crisp, 10 to 12 minutes.

6	ounces (2¼ cups) wide egg noodles
	Salt and pepper
1	tablespoon unsalted butter
1	onion, chopped fine
1	jalapeño chile, stemmed, seeded, and minced
1	teaspoon ground cumin
1	(10-ounce) can Ro-Tel tomatoes
3	tablespoons all-purpose flour
2¼	cups low-sodium chicken broth
¼	cup heavy cream
8	ounces Colby Jack cheese, shredded (2 cups)
2	tablespoons minced fresh cilantro
2	cups cooked, shredded chicken
1	cup Fritos corn chips, crushed

1. Adjust oven rack to middle position and heat oven to 450 degrees. Bring 4 quarts water to boil in large Dutch oven. Add pasta and 1 tablespoon salt and cook, stirring often, until nearly al dente. Drain pasta and set aside.

2. Dry now-empty pot, add butter, and melt over medium heat. Add onion, jalapeño, and cumin and cook until vegetables are softened and lightly browned, 8 to 10 minutes. Stir in tomatoes and cook until most of liquid has evaporated, about 8 minutes.

3. Stir in flour and cook for 1 minute. Slowly whisk in broth and cream until smooth, bring to simmer, and cook until thickened, about 2 minutes. Stir in cheese until melted. Off heat, stir in cilantro and season with salt and pepper to taste. Fold in cooked pasta and shredded chicken, breaking up any clumps of pasta.

4. Pour mixture into 8-inch square baking dish and sprinkle corn chips evenly over top. Bake until bubbling around edges and corn chips are toasted, 10 to 12 minutes. Let cool for 10 to 15 minutes and serve.

SMART SHOPPING RO-TEL TOMATOES

This blend of tomatoes, green chiles, and spices was created by Carl Roettele in Elsa, Texas, in the early 1940s. By the 1950s, Ro-Tel tomatoes had become popular in the Lone Star State and beyond. The spicy, tangy tomatoes add just the right flavor to countless local recipes, like King Ranch Casserole and Ro-Tel Dip (aka chili con queso). We call on Ro-Tel tomatoes when we need an extra flavor boost, often in Southwest- and Texas-inspired recipes. If you can't find them, substitute 1¼ cups diced tomatoes plus a minced jalapeño per 10-ounce can of Ro-Tel tomatoes.

Spicy Spaghetti Pie

Serves 4

✔ **WHY THIS RECIPE WORKS:** This pasta dish takes the classic flavors of spaghetti and tomato sauce and turns them into a kid-friendly, sliceable pie. Thinner versions of spaghetti (vermicelli or thin spaghetti) proved a better choice than spaghetti itself, which didn't stick together well when we cut into the pie. For bold flavor, we swapped in easy-to-find shredded Mexican cheese blend (a combination of Monterey Jack, cheddar, and asadero cheeses) for the mozzarella and spicy pepperoni for plain ground beef. Heavy cream added an underlying richness that countered the acidity of the tomatoes. Using a spatula to press the pasta into the pie plate ensured that the finished pie sliced neatly. In order to make the pie sliceable, we folded just a portion of the sauce in with the pasta and then served the pie topped with a little extra sauce, passing the remainder at the table. See page 173 for tips on how to measure out long strands of pasta without using a scale.

12 ounces vermicelli or
    thin spaghetti
    Salt and pepper
 4 ounces sliced deli pepperoni,
    chopped fine
 1 onion, chopped fine
 ½ teaspoon red pepper flakes
 3 (14.5-ounce) cans diced
    tomatoes
 8 ounces (2 cups) shredded
    Mexican cheese blend
 ¾ cup heavy cream
 ½ cup chopped fresh basil
1½ cups water, plus extra as needed

1. Adjust oven rack to upper-middle position and heat oven to 475 degrees. Grease 9-inch pie plate with vegetable oil spray. Bring 4 quarts water to boil in large pot. Add pasta and 1 tablespoon salt and cook, stirring often, until nearly al dente. Drain pasta and return it to pot.

2. Meanwhile, cook pepperoni in 12-inch skillet over medium-high heat until crisp, about 2 minutes. Stir in onion and cook until softened, about 5 minutes. Stir in pepper flakes and cook for 30 seconds. Stir in tomatoes and simmer until sauce is thickened and reduced to 4 cups, about 10 minutes. Season with salt and pepper to taste.

3. Add 2 cups tomato sauce, cheese, cream, and basil to pasta and toss to combine. Transfer pasta to prepared pie plate and press with a spatula to flatten surface. Bake until golden and bubbling around edges, about 15 minutes. Let cool for 10 to 15 minutes.

4. While pasta bakes and cools, add water to remaining sauce in skillet and simmer, mashing tomatoes with back of spoon, until sauce is smooth and thickened, about 25 minutes. Add extra water as needed to adjust sauce consistency. To serve, slice pie into wedges and top with sauce.

SMART SHOPPING PRESHREDDED MEXICAN CHEESE BLEND
The refrigerated section of our local supermarket practically overflows with varieties of preshredded cheese, but the flavorful combination known as "Mexican cheese blend" (a mix of three or four cheeses, often Monterey Jack, cheddar, queso quesadilla, and asadero) is both authentic and convenient. It's a great choice for myriad dishes, including our Spicy Spaghetti Pie, where you are looking for a flavorful cheese combination but don't want to spend time shredding multiple types of cheese.

Baked Macaroni and Cheese

Serves 6

✔ **WHY THIS RECIPE WORKS:** For a classic, home-style macaroni and cheese that would appeal to adults and kids alike, we kept things simple, staying away from pungent cheeses and an overly rich sauce made with eggs and cream. Instead, we started with a béchamel sauce—butter, flour, and milk, with some chicken broth for savory flavor—and added the cheese. Using a combination of sharp cheddar and Colby gave us both ultra-cheesy flavor and an incredibly creamy texture. Once the cheese was incorporated, we stirred in our macaroni (cooked until nearly tender) and moved it all to a baking dish. For a crunchy topping, we tossed homemade bread crumbs with melted butter, sprinkled them over the casserole, and baked the dish until it was bubbling and golden on top. The casserole can be assembled, cooled, covered with plastic wrap, and refrigerated for up to 2 days. To bake, remove the plastic and cover with aluminum foil; bake in a 400-degree oven until hot, 40 to 45 minutes, then remove the foil and bake until the crumbs are crisp, 15 to 20 minutes.

8   **tablespoons unsalted butter**
2   **cups fresh bread crumbs**
     Salt and pepper
1   **pound elbow macaroni or small shells**
1   **garlic clove, minced**
1   **teaspoon dry mustard**
¼   **teaspoon cayenne pepper**
6   **tablespoons all-purpose flour**
3½   **cups whole milk**
2¼   **cups low-sodium chicken broth**
1   **pound Colby cheese, shredded (4 cups)**
8   **ounces extra-sharp cheddar cheese, shredded (2 cups)**

1. Adjust oven rack to middle position and heat oven to 400 degrees. Melt 2 tablespoons butter, toss with bread crumbs, and season with salt and pepper. Spread crumbs onto rimmed baking sheet and bake until golden, about 8 minutes.

2. Meanwhile, bring 4 quarts water to boil in large Dutch oven. Add pasta and 1 tablespoon salt and cook, stirring often, until nearly al dente. Drain pasta and set aside.

3. Dry now-empty pot, add remaining 6 tablespoons butter, and melt over medium heat. Stir in garlic, mustard, and cayenne and cook until fragrant, about 30 seconds. Stir in flour and cook until golden, about 1 minute. Slowly whisk in milk and broth until smooth. Simmer, whisking often, until thickened, about 15 minutes.

4. Off heat, gradually whisk in Colby and cheddar until melted. Season with salt and pepper to taste. Stir in cooked pasta, breaking up any clumps. Pour into 13 by 9-inch baking dish and sprinkle with toasted bread crumbs. Bake until golden and bubbling around edges, 25 to 35 minutes. Let cool for 10 to 15 minutes and serve.

QUICK PREP TIP   **MAKING FRESH BREAD CRUMBS**
Making fresh bread crumbs is as easy as pulsing pieces of bread in the food processor. In the test kitchen, we make fresh bread crumbs from slices of white sandwich bread. At home, however, it makes sense to make crumbs out of any white bread you have around (even if it's stale). In general, a slice of white sandwich bread makes about ¾ cup of fresh bread crumbs. Bread crumbs can be frozen in a zipper-lock bag for up to 1 month.

Ultimate Chili Mac

Serves 6

WHY THIS RECIPE WORKS: Sure, it's a kid favorite, but chili mac is a dish with a huge adult following, too. For the ultimate chili mac, we started by combining browned ground beef with sautéed onion, bell pepper, and garlic. In lieu of fresh chiles (jalapeños added too much heat for this family-friendly supper), we added chili powder and cumin. A mix of tomato products—puree and diced—created a thick sauce to ensure that the pasta stayed tender in the oven. Stirring some of the shredded cheese into the chili mac also helped. Colby Jack gave us a creamy, flavorful, cheesy topping, but if you can't find it, Monterey Jack cheese can be substituted. Ground turkey can be substituted for the ground beef. Don't forget to reserve ¾ cup of the pasta cooking water in step 1; the water is used to thin out the chili base of the casserole. The casserole can be assembled, cooled (add the cheese topping when cool), covered with plastic wrap, and refrigerated for up to 2 days. To bake, remove the plastic and cover with aluminum foil; bake in a 400-degree oven until hot, 40 to 45 minutes, then remove the foil and bake until the cheese begins to brown, 5 to 10 minutes.

8	ounces (2 cups) elbow macaroni
	Salt and pepper
2	tablespoons vegetable oil
2	onions, chopped fine
1	red bell pepper, stemmed, seeded, and chopped fine
6	garlic cloves, minced
2	tablespoons chili powder
1	tablespoon ground cumin
1½	pounds 85 percent lean ground beef
1	(28-ounce) can tomato puree
1	(14.5-ounce) can diced tomatoes
1	tablespoon brown sugar
10	ounces Colby Jack cheese, shredded (2½ cups)

1. Adjust oven rack to middle position and heat oven to 400 degrees. Bring 4 quarts water to boil in large Dutch oven. Add pasta and 1 tablespoon salt and cook, stirring often, until nearly al dente. Reserve ¾ cup cooking water, then drain pasta and set aside.

2. Dry now-empty pot, add oil, and heat over medium heat until shimmering. Add onions, bell pepper, and ¾ teaspoon salt and cook until softened, 8 to 10 minutes. Stir in garlic, chili powder, and cumin and cook until fragrant, about 1 minute. Stir in beef and cook, breaking up meat with wooden spoon, until no longer pink, 5 to 8 minutes.

3. Stir in tomato puree, diced tomatoes, sugar, and ¾ cup reserved cooking water. Cover pot partially (leaving about 1 inch of pot open) and simmer, stirring occasionally, until flavors have blended, about 20 minutes.

4. Off heat, season with salt and pepper to taste. Stir in cooked pasta, breaking up any clumps, then stir in 1 cup cheese. Pour into 13 by 9-inch baking dish. Sprinkle remaining 1½ cups cheese over top. Bake until bubbling around edges and cheese is spotty brown, about 15 minutes. Let cool for 10 to 15 minutes and serve.

SMART SHOPPING CHILI POWDER
To see what the difference was between the various brands of chili powder found at the market, we gathered up as many brands as possible and pitted them against one another in a taste-off. To focus on the flavor of the chili powder, we made a basic, bare-bones version of chili and then rated each chili powder for aroma, depth of flavor, and level of spiciness. Tasters concluded that **Spice Islands Chili Powder** was the clear winner. This well-known supermarket brand was noted by one taster as having "a big flavor that stands out among the others."

Baked Penne with Roasted Red Peppers, Chicken, and Goat Cheese

Serves 4

✔ **WHY THIS RECIPE WORKS:** In this effortless weeknight casserole, the only thing we precooked was the pasta. Jarred roasted red peppers provided the perfect big, bold flavor base for a simple no-cook sauce. All we had to do was rinse them first to wash away any off-flavors from the brining liquid before chopping them. For a bright, balanced sauce, we processed the peppers with plenty of fresh parsley, Parmesan, shallot, thyme, and garlic, along with a good amount of extra-virgin olive oil. After combining our richly flavored (and colored) sauce with the cooked pasta, we stirred in shredded chicken so we'd have a filling dinner. Dollops of ricotta made for a creamy topping; for more flavor, we paired it with tangy goat cheese. Do not use nonfat ricotta here. You can either use leftover cooked chicken here, or quickly cook chicken following the instructions on page 80.

8   **ounces (2½ cups) penne**
     Salt and pepper
4   **ounces (½ cup) whole-milk ricotta cheese**
4   **ounces goat cheese, softened**
6   **tablespoons extra-virgin olive oil**
3   **cups jarred roasted red peppers, rinsed, patted dry, and chopped coarse**
2   **ounces Parmesan cheese, grated (1 cup)**
⅓   **cup fresh parsley leaves**
1   **shallot, minced**
2   **teaspoons minced fresh thyme**
1   **garlic clove, minced**
2   **cups shredded cooked chicken**

1. Adjust oven rack to middle position and heat oven to 450 degrees. Bring 4 quarts water to boil in large pot. Add pasta and 1 tablespoon salt and cook, stirring often, until nearly al dente. Drain pasta, then return it to pot.

2. Meanwhile, mix ricotta, goat cheese, 1 tablespoon oil, ¼ teaspoon salt, and ¼ teaspoon pepper together in bowl; set aside. Process peppers, Parmesan, remaining 5 tablespoons oil, parsley, shallot, thyme, garlic, ¼ teaspoon salt, and ¼ teaspoon pepper in food processor until smooth, about 25 seconds, scraping down sides of bowl as needed.

3. Add processed pepper sauce to pasta and toss to coat. Season with salt and pepper to taste and fold in shredded chicken. Pour mixture into 8-inch square baking dish. Dollop ricotta mixture evenly over top. Bake until bubbling around edges and cheese is spotty brown, about 15 minutes. Let cool for 10 to 15 minutes and serve.

SMART SHOPPING GOAT CHEESE
We conducted a tasting of three domestic and four readily available imported fresh goat cheeses, and our tasters concluded that American producers have mastered the craft of making goat cheese. The clear favorite was **Vermont Chèvre**, from the Vermont Butter & Cheese Company. It was creamy and tangy but not overpowering. Meanwhile, reviews of the imported cheeses were mixed. Tasters were enthusiastic about Le Biquet from Canada, but the French cheeses were for the most part described as gamy or muttony, with a chalky, Spacklelike texture. A few adventurous tasters appreciated the assertive flavors of the imported cheeses, but the overall feeling was that the domestic cheeses were cleaner-tasting and more balanced.

Baked Penne with Spinach, Artichokes, and Chicken

Serves 4 to 6

✔ **WHY THIS RECIPE WORKS:** To transform a happy-hour favorite—spinach and artichoke dip—into an easy pasta dinner, we created a casserole using frozen spinach and frozen artichoke hearts. First, we built a simple cream sauce, then stirred in the star vegetables, which simply needed to be thawed, dried, and cut into smaller pieces. So our baked pasta dish offered the same cheesy appeal as the appetizer version, we stirred in a hefty amount of mozzarella and Parmesan. Shredded cooked chicken elevated our appetizer to main-dish status, and lemon juice perked up the flavors of the sauce. Penne worked well for the pasta; its short, tubular shape ensured that every forkful held an even mix of pasta, vegetables, and chicken. Do not use fat-free mozzarella here. You can either use leftover cooked chicken here, or quickly cook chicken following the instructions below. The casserole can be assembled, cooled (add the cheese topping when cool), covered with plastic wrap, and refrigerated for up to 2 days. To bake, remove the plastic and cover with aluminum foil; bake in a 450-degree oven until hot, about 20 minutes, then remove the foil and bake until the cheese is spotty brown, about 15 minutes.

12	ounces (3¾ cups) penne
	Salt and pepper
3	tablespoons unsalted butter
1	onion, chopped fine
3	garlic cloves, minced
3	tablespoons all-purpose flour
2½	cups low-sodium chicken broth
1	cup heavy cream
18	ounces frozen artichoke hearts, thawed, patted dry, and quartered
10	ounces frozen spinach, thawed, squeezed dry (see page 89), and chopped fine
10	ounces mozzarella cheese, shredded (2½ cups)
2	ounces Parmesan cheese, grated (1 cup)
2	tablespoons lemon juice
4	cups shredded cooked chicken

1. Adjust oven rack to middle position and heat oven to 450 degrees. Bring 4 quarts water to boil in large Dutch oven. Add pasta and 1 tablespoon salt and cook, stirring often, until nearly al dente. Drain pasta and set aside.

2. Dry now-empty pot, add butter, and melt over medium heat. Add onion and ¼ teaspoon salt and cook until softened, about 5 minutes. Stir in garlic and cook until fragrant, about 30 seconds. Stir in flour and cook for 1 minute. Slowly whisk in broth and cream until smooth and bring to simmer. Stir in artichokes and spinach and continue to simmer until vegetables are heated through, about 1 minute.

3. Stir in 1½ cups mozzarella and ½ cup Parmesan until melted. Off heat, stir in lemon juice and season with salt and pepper to taste. Fold in cooked pasta and shredded chicken, breaking up any clumps of pasta. Pour into 13 by 9-inch baking dish and sprinkle with remaining 1 cup mozzarella and remaining ½ cup Parmesan. Bake until bubbling around edges and cheese is spotty brown, 12 to 15 minutes. Let cool for 10 to 15 minutes and serve.

QUICK PREP TIP EASY POACHED CHICKEN
Pat 12 ounces boneless, skinless chicken breasts dry with paper towels and season with salt and pepper. Heat 1 tablespoon vegetable oil in 12-inch skillet over medium-high heat until just smoking. Carefully lay chicken in skillet and cook until well browned on first side, 6 to 8 minutes. Flip chicken, add ½ cup water, and cover. Reduce heat to medium-low and continue to cook until chicken registers 160 degrees, 5 to 7 minutes. Transfer chicken to cutting board, let cool slightly, then shred into bite-size pieces (see page 289). Makes about 2 cups. (This recipe can be doubled to make 4 cups, or halved to make 1 cup.)

21st-Century Tuna Noodle Casserole

Serves 4

✔ **WHY THIS RECIPE WORKS:** Once an immensely appealing family favorite, tuna noodle casserole nowadays tends to be a dense, gloppy letdown, thanks to shortcut ingredients like cream of mushroom soup and a heavy hand with the dairy. We decided it was time for a makeover. For a lighter, fresher tuna noodle casserole, we ditched the usual canned soup and went with a Mediterranean flavor profile instead. To start, we swapped most of the heavy cream in the sauce for chicken broth, which we thickened with a little flour. Cherry tomatoes took the place of the mushrooms, and tangy feta cheese jumped in for the standard mozzarella and cheddar. In addition to a generous quantity of garlic and a pinch of red pepper flakes, we rounded out the sauce with briny olives, sliced scallions, and fragrant lemon zest. Stirring the tuna and egg noodles into the sauce before baking protected them from the heat and ensured moist tuna and tender noodles. As for the topping, we took the classic route and stuck with bread crumbs, but instead of grinding and pretoasting our own, we relied on store-bought, super-crisp panko.

6	ounces (2¼ cups) wide egg noodles
	Salt and pepper
3	tablespoons extra-virgin olive oil
1	onion, chopped fine
6	garlic cloves, minced
⅛	teaspoon red pepper flakes
2	tablespoons all-purpose flour
1¾	cups low-sodium chicken broth
½	cup heavy cream
2	(5-ounce) cans solid white tuna, drained well and flaked
12	ounces cherry tomatoes, halved
3	ounces feta cheese, crumbled (¾ cup)
¼	cup pitted kalamata olives, chopped
2	scallions, sliced thin
1	teaspoon grated lemon zest
¾	cup panko bread crumbs
	Lemon wedges

1. Adjust oven rack to middle position and heat oven to 475 degrees. Bring 4 quarts water to boil in large Dutch oven. Add pasta and 1 tablespoon salt and cook, stirring often, until nearly al dente. Drain pasta and set aside.

2. Dry now-empty pot, add 2 tablespoons oil, and heat over medium heat until shimmering. Add onion and ¼ teaspoon salt and cook until softened, 5 to 7 minutes. Stir in garlic and pepper flakes and cook until fragrant, about 30 seconds. Stir in flour and cook for 1 minute. Slowly whisk in broth and cream until smooth and simmer until slightly thickened, about 2 minutes.

3. Off heat, stir in cooked pasta, tuna, tomatoes, feta, olives, scallions, and lemon zest, breaking up any clumps of pasta. Season with salt and pepper to taste. Pour into 8-inch square baking dish. Toss panko with remaining 1 tablespoon oil, season with salt and pepper, and sprinkle over top. Bake until bubbling around edges and topping is crisp, 8 to 10 minutes. Let cool for 10 to 15 minutes and serve with lemon wedges.

Stuffed Shells with Meat Sauce

Serves 6

✔ **WHY THIS RECIPE WORKS:** A plate of stuffed shells might be incredibly tempting, but who can ever finish a serving? It makes sense, considering that a typical plate clocks in at around 800 calories and 50 grams of fat. For a lighter version, we started by focusing on the cheese. Nonfat ricotta gave the filling a grainy texture, but fat-free cottage cheese made the filling smooth and clean-tasting. Part-skim mozzarella, in lieu of the full-fat stuff, offered plenty of flavor. To bind the filling, which was a bit thin, we added saltines (crushed in the food processor). Lean ground beef worked well for the sauce; an unusual ingredient, soy sauce, provided ultra-savory notes and boosted the overall beefy flavor of the sauce. With these changes, we'd easily lopped 36 grams of fat off our shells, which were still rich and decadent. Do not use fat-free mozzarella or whipped cottage cheese here. If the cottage cheese appears watery, drain it through a fine-mesh strainer for 15 minutes before using. Separate the shells after draining them to keep them from sticking together. The casserole can be assembled, cooled, covered with plastic wrap, and refrigerated for up to 2 days. To bake, remove the plastic, cover with aluminum foil, and increase the covered baking time to 45 to 50 minutes. For the nutritional information for this recipe, see page 306.

SAUCE

- 6 ounces 95 percent lean ground beef
- 1 tablespoon soy sauce
- 3 (14.5-ounce) cans diced tomatoes
- 1 tablespoon olive oil
- 1 onion, chopped fine
- 2 tablespoons tomato paste
- 3 garlic cloves, minced
- ¼ teaspoon red pepper flakes
- ½ teaspoon salt
- ¼ cup finely chopped fresh basil

SHELLS

- 12 ounces jumbo pasta shells
  Salt
- 12 saltines, broken into pieces
- 20 ounces (2½ cups) fat-free cottage cheese, drained if necessary
- 8 ounces part-skim mozzarella cheese, shredded (2 cups)
- 1 ounce Parmesan cheese, grated (½ cup)
- 2 tablespoons chopped fresh basil
- 2 garlic cloves, minced

1. FOR THE SAUCE: Adjust oven rack to upper-middle position and heat oven to 375 degrees. Pulse beef and soy sauce in food processor until well combined; transfer to bowl. Add tomatoes to processor and pulse until coarsely ground.

2. Heat oil in large saucepan over medium heat until shimmering. Add onion and cook until softened, about 5 minutes. Stir in beef mixture and cook, breaking up meat with wooden spoon, until no longer pink, about 3 minutes. Stir in tomato paste, garlic, and pepper flakes and cook until fragrant, about 1 minute. Stir in processed tomatoes and salt and simmer until slightly thickened, about 25 minutes. Off heat, stir in basil.

3. FOR THE SHELLS: Meanwhile, bring 4 quarts water to boil in large pot. Add pasta and 1 tablespoon salt and cook, stirring often, until nearly al dente. Drain pasta and transfer to kitchen towel–lined baking sheet. Reserve 24 shells, discarding any that have broken.

4. Pulse crackers in clean food processor bowl until finely ground. Add cottage cheese, 1½ cups mozzarella, Parmesan, basil, garlic, and ½ teaspoon salt and process until smooth; transfer to large zipper-lock bag. Using scissors, cut off one corner of bag and pipe 2 tablespoons filling into each shell.

5. Spread half of sauce into 13 by 9-inch baking dish. Arrange filled shells, seam side up, over sauce in dish. Spread remaining sauce over shells. Cover with aluminum foil and bake until bubbling around edges, 35 to 40 minutes. Remove foil and sprinkle with remaining ½ cup mozzarella. Bake until cheese is melted, about 5 minutes. Let cool for 10 to 15 minutes and serve.

Pastitsio

Serves 8

✔ **WHY THIS RECIPE WORKS:** The Greek take on lasagna, pastitsio is a rich casserole made up of pasta (usually macaroni), a tomatoey meat sauce, plenty of cheese, and a rich white sauce, all baked to golden perfection. But the creamy white sauce—a béchamel that's used to both coat the pasta and create the top layer of the dish—can weigh it down. For a brighter yet still rich Greek lasagna, we swapped out the usual heavy cream in favor of whole milk. Upping the cheese and garlic amounts and adding tangy, creamy Greek yogurt to the mix ensured that the béchamel had plenty of flavor. For the meat sauce, we traded the traditional lamb for leaner ground beef, which kept the grease factor to a minimum. Plain tomato sauce, with a few spoonfuls of tomato paste for extra punch, gave our sauce the perfect texture. As for the pasta, we'd taken enough liberties with our recipe that we opted to stick with tradition—plus, the elbow macaroni formed a nice, tidy layer that tasters appreciated. Do not use 2 percent or nonfat Greek yogurt here.

MEAT SAUCE

- 1 tablespoon olive oil
- 1 onion, chopped fine
- 3 tablespoons tomato paste
- 6 garlic cloves, minced
- 2 teaspoons dried oregano
- 2 teaspoons ground cinnamon
- 1½ pounds 95 percent lean ground beef
  Salt and pepper
- ½ cup red wine
- 1 (15-ounce) can tomato sauce
- 1 ounce Pecorino Romano cheese, grated (½ cup)

PASTA AND BÉCHAMEL SAUCE

- 8 ounces (2 cups) elbow macaroni
  Salt and pepper
- 5 tablespoons unsalted butter
- ½ cup all-purpose flour
- 3 garlic cloves, minced
- 5 cups whole milk
- 3 ounces Pecorino Romano cheese, grated (1½ cups)
- 3 large eggs
- ⅓ cup whole-milk Greek yogurt

1. FOR THE MEAT SAUCE: Adjust oven rack to middle position; heat oven to 425 degrees. Heat oil in 12-inch skillet over medium heat until shimmering. Add onion; cook until softened, about 5 minutes. Stir in tomato paste, garlic, oregano, and cinnamon and cook until paste begins to darken, 1 to 2 minutes. Stir in beef and 1 teaspoon salt and cook, breaking up meat with wooden spoon, until no longer pink, about 5 minutes. Stir in wine and cook until reduced to about 1 tablespoon, 2 to 4 minutes. Stir in tomato sauce and simmer until slightly thickened, about 10 minutes. Off heat, stir in Pecorino and season with salt and pepper to taste; set aside. (Sauce can be refrigerated in airtight container for up to 3 days; before assembling casserole, reheat in microwave, covered, until hot, about 1 minute.)

2. FOR THE PASTA AND BÉCHAMEL SAUCE: Meanwhile, bring 4 quarts water to boil in large Dutch oven. Add pasta and 1 tablespoon salt and cook, stirring often, until nearly al dente. Drain pasta, rinse with cold water until cool, and drain again; transfer to large bowl.

3. Dry now-empty pot, add butter, and melt over medium heat. Stir in flour and garlic and cook until golden and fragrant, about 1 minute. Slowly whisk in milk until smooth, then simmer until thickened and reduced to 4 cups, about 12 minutes. Off heat, whisk in 1 cup Pecorino until melted. Season with salt and pepper to taste.

4. Stir 2 cups béchamel into pasta until combined, then transfer to 13 by 9-inch baking dish. Beat eggs in now-empty pasta bowl until combined, then whisk in 1 cup béchamel to temper. Slowly whisk tempered egg mixture into remaining béchamel. Whisk in yogurt.

5. Spread meat sauce over macaroni; top with egg-béchamel mixture. Sprinkle with remaining Pecorino. Bake until golden brown, 35 to 40 minutes. Let cool for 10 to 15 minutes and serve.

Manicotti Puttanesca

Serves 6 to 8

✔ **WHY THIS RECIPE WORKS:** True, manicotti is an Italian-American classic, but it's also a labor of love. First there's the sauce to make, then the filling, then the manicotti tubes need to be cooked and cooled, and finally they are filled, topped with sauce, and baked. For a baked manicotti with all of the comforting, rich, cheesy flavor but none of the fuss, we did away with the slippery pasta tubes and instead spread the filling onto no-boil lasagna noodles. Briefly soaking the noodles in hot water made them pliable enough to roll up easily. Adding the bright, zesty notes of puttanesca—anchovies, garlic, olives, and capers—to the sauce and filling ensured that each bite of our hassle-free manicotti offered big, bold flavor. Sprinkling Parmesan on at the end of baking and broiling the dish for a few minutes gave it a nicely bronzed crown. Do not use nonfat ricotta or fat-free mozzarella here. Note that you will need 16 no-boil lasagna noodles to make this dish; our favorite brand of noodles, Barilla, has 16 noodles per box, but other brands may contain fewer. The casserole can be assembled, cooled, covered with plastic wrap, and refrigerated for up to 2 days. To bake, remove the plastic, cover with aluminum foil, and increase the covered baking time to 1 hour.

SAUCE

- 2 tablespoons olive oil
- 3 garlic cloves, minced
- 3 anchovy fillets, rinsed and minced
- ½ teaspoon red pepper flakes (optional)
- 2 (28-ounce) cans crushed tomatoes
- 2 tablespoons chopped fresh basil
  Salt and pepper

FILLING AND NOODLES

- 1½ pounds (3 cups) whole-milk ricotta cheese
- 8 ounces mozzarella cheese, shredded (2 cups)
- 4 ounces Parmesan cheese, grated (2 cups)
- 2 large eggs, lightly beaten
- ¼ cup pitted kalamata olives, quartered
- 2 tablespoons capers, rinsed
- 2 tablespoons chopped fresh basil
- ¾ teaspoon salt
- ½ teaspoon pepper
- 16 no-boil lasagna noodles

1. FOR THE SAUCE: Adjust oven rack to middle position and heat oven to 375 degrees. Heat oil, garlic, anchovies, and pepper flakes, if using, in large saucepan over medium heat until fragrant but not brown, about 1 minute. Stir in tomatoes and simmer until slightly thickened, about 15 minutes. Off heat, stir in basil and season with salt and pepper to taste.

2. FOR THE FILLING AND NOODLES: Mix ricotta, mozzarella, 1 cup Parmesan, eggs, olives, capers, basil, salt, and pepper together in bowl.

3. Pour 1 inch boiling water into 13 by 9-inch broiler-safe baking dish and slip noodles into water, one at a time. Let noodles soak until pliable, about 5 minutes, separating noodles with tip of knife to prevent sticking. Remove noodles from water and place in single layer on clean kitchen towels; discard water and dry baking dish.

4. Spread 1½ cups sauce into baking dish. Spread ¼ cup ricotta mixture evenly over bottom three-quarters of each noodle. Roll noodles up around filling and lay them, seam side down, in baking dish. Spoon remaining sauce over top to cover pasta completely.

5. Cover dish tightly with aluminum foil and bake until bubbling around edges, about 40 minutes. Remove baking dish from oven, adjust oven rack 6 inches from broiler element, and heat broiler. Remove foil, sprinkle with remaining 1 cup Parmesan, and broil until cheese is spotty brown, 4 to 6 minutes. Let cool for 10 to 15 minutes and serve.

Meaty Manicotti

Serves 6 to 8

✔ **WHY THIS RECIPE WORKS:** Hot on the heels of our successfully streamlined Manicotti Puttanesca (page 85), we decided a meatlovers' manicotti was in order. First, we employed our established manicotti time-saving trick: swapping the pasta tubes for no-boil lasagna noodles that simply had to be hydrated until they were pliable. Next, we turned to building a flavorful sauce. Using the food processor to break down ground meat allowed its flavor to permeate the sauce quickly. For even more meaty flavor, we added a popular pizza topping—pepperoni—which gave the sauce a spicy backbone. To liven up the filling, we included assertive provolone, plus a portion of the processed ground beef and pepperoni; a single egg helped to bind it all together. Note that you will need 16 no-boil lasagna noodles to make this dish; our favorite brand of noodles, Barilla, has 16 noodles per box, but other brands may contain fewer. Do not use nonfat ricotta or fat-free mozzarella here. The casserole can be assembled, cooled, covered with plastic wrap, and refrigerated for up to 2 days. To bake, remove the plastic, cover with aluminum foil, and increase the covered baking time to 1 hour.

SAUCE

- 1   onion, chopped
- 6   ounces sliced deli pepperoni
- 1   pound 85 percent lean ground beef
- 1   tablespoon tomato paste
- 5   garlic cloves, minced
- ¼   teaspoon red pepper flakes
- 2   (28-ounce) cans crushed tomatoes
    Salt and pepper

FILLING AND NOODLES

- 1½ pounds (3 cups) whole-milk ricotta cheese
- 10 ounces mozzarella cheese, shredded (2½ cups)
- 6   ounces provolone cheese, shredded (1½ cups)
- 1   large egg, lightly beaten
- ¼   cup chopped fresh basil
- ½   teaspoon salt
- ½   teaspoon pepper
- 16 no-boil lasagna noodles

1. FOR THE SAUCE: Adjust oven rack to upper-middle position and heat oven to 375 degrees. Pulse onion and pepperoni in food processor until coarsely ground. Add beef and pulse until thoroughly combined. Transfer mixture to large saucepan and cook over medium heat, breaking up meat with wooden spoon, until no longer pink, about 5 minutes. Using slotted spoon, transfer 1 cup meat mixture to paper towel–lined plate and reserve.

2. Add tomato paste, garlic, and pepper flakes to pot and cook until fragrant, about 1 minute. Stir in tomatoes and simmer until sauce is slightly thickened, about 20 minutes. Season with salt and pepper to taste.

3. FOR THE FILLING AND NOODLES: Combine ricotta, 2 cups mozzarella, 1 cup provolone, egg, basil, salt, pepper, and 1 cup reserved meat mixture in bowl.

4. Pour 1 inch boiling water into 13 by 9-inch baking dish and slip noodles into water, one at a time. Let noodles soak until pliable, about 5 minutes, separating noodles with tip of knife to prevent sticking. Remove noodles from water and place in single layer on clean kitchen towels; discard water and dry baking dish.

5. Spread half of sauce into baking dish. Spread ¼ cup ricotta mixture evenly over bottom three-quarters of each noodle. Roll noodles up around filling and lay them, seam side down, in baking dish. Spoon remaining sauce over top to cover pasta completely.

6. Cover dish tightly with aluminum foil and bake until bubbling around edges, about 40 minutes. Remove foil, sprinkle with remaining ½ cup mozzarella and ½ cup provolone, and continue to bake until cheese is melted, about 5 minutes. Let cool for 10 to 15 minutes and serve.

Easiest-Ever Lasagna

Serves 4

✓ **WHY THIS RECIPE WORKS:** A prep-free (no chopping required) lasagna—with rich, meaty flavor and a bubbling, cheesy topping? No problem. We developed a scaled-down weeknight lasagna so this classic doesn't have to be relegated to Sunday-only status, and it's easy enough that even beginners can tackle it. We relied on convenient store-bought pasta sauce to take the place of simmered-all-day sauce and added spiced Italian sausage to give it deep flavor. We didn't even have to get out a pan to cook the sausage—we just crumbled it into small pieces and added it to the dish raw. Instead of the traditional time-consuming layering of individual ingredients, we devised a smart, streamlined assembly that takes mere minutes—we simply stirred the sauce, cheeses, and sausage together, then added the mixture to the baking dish, alternating it with no-boil noodles. A sprinkling of extra mozzarella on top gives the lasagna that picture-perfect browned cheesy blanket that everyone wants. Do not use nonfat ricotta or fat-free mozzarella here.

- 8 **ounces hot or sweet Italian sausage, casings removed**
- 1 **(25-ounce) jar pasta sauce**
- 8 **ounces mozzarella cheese, shredded (2 cups)**
- 1 **ounce Parmesan cheese, grated (½ cup)**
- 8 **ounces (1 cup) whole-milk ricotta cheese**
- 6 **no-boil lasagna noodles**

1. Adjust oven rack to middle position and heat oven to 375 degrees. Crumble sausage into ½-inch pieces in large bowl and add sauce, 1½ cups mozzarella, and Parmesan. Gently fold in ricotta, leaving some clumps.

2. Spread ½ cup sauce into 8-inch square baking dish. Lay 2 noodles in dish and top with 1½ cups sauce. Repeat layering of noodles and sauce two more times. Top with remaining ½ cup mozzarella.

3. Cover dish tightly with aluminum foil and bake until bubbling around edges, about 20 minutes. Remove foil and continue to bake until cheese is spotty brown, about 35 minutes. Let cool for 10 to 15 minutes and serve.

SMART SHOPPING **JARRED PASTA SAUCE**

We lean on jarred pasta sauce to help us reduce the prep work in our Easiest-Ever Lasagna. But with so many options on supermarket shelves—from the standard, everyday jarred marinara sauces to fancy, upscale sauces that advertise imported olive oil or special herb blends—what should you buy? We have a few favorites in the test kitchen. **Victoria Marinara Sauce** is our favorite premium brand; it has a short ingredient list (just tomatoes, olive oil, fresh onions, fresh basil, fresh garlic, salt, and spices) and, accordingly, boasts a "robust" flavor that tastes like "homemade" and fresh tomatoes. For a runner-up to our favorite premium sauce, we also like Classico Marinara with Plum Tomatoes and Olive Oil, which tasters found to have a "great texture" that they described as "chunky" and "hearty." For a traditional, everyday sauce, we prefer Bertolli Tomato and Basil Sauce. Though not as fresh-tasting as the top-rated premium brand, this sauce offers a "good balance of flavors," "a nice, chunky texture."

Super-Easy Spinach Lasagna

Serves 4

✔ WHY THIS RECIPE WORKS: Having already figured out an effortless meaty lasagna (see page 88), we decided to add a creamy, veggie-laden version to our lineup. Looking for ingredients that would require little prep, we hit on frozen spinach, which simply needed a good thaw and squeeze until it was dry. A single chopped tomato provided brightness and some acidity. For the sauce, we combined store-bought Alfredo sauce, thinned with a bit of water, with ricotta cheese. To amp up its flavor, we added nutty, buttery fontina. For further complexity, we turned to dried porcini mushrooms, which became hydrated in the oven alongside the no-boil noodles. Instead of following an intricate layering procedure, we simply stirred the sauce, water, cheeses, and vegetables together and alternated this mixture with the no-boil noodles. A relatively high oven temperature shortened the lasagna's cooking time, ensuring perfectly cooked pasta and spinach that maintained its bright green hue. Do not use nonfat ricotta here.

1	**(15-ounce) jar Alfredo sauce**
1	**cup water**
10	**ounces frozen spinach, thawed, squeezed dry, and chopped fine**
1	**tomato, cored and cut into ½-inch pieces**
4	**ounces fontina cheese, shredded (1 cup)**
⅛	**ounce dried porcini mushrooms, rinsed and minced**
4	**ounces (½ cup) whole-milk ricotta cheese**
6	**no-boil lasagna noodles**

1. Adjust oven rack to middle position and heat oven to 425 degrees. Grease 8-inch square baking dish with vegetable oil spray. Combine Alfredo sauce, water, spinach, tomato, ½ cup fontina, and porcini in bowl until uniform. Gently fold in ricotta, leaving some clumps.

2. Spread ½ cup sauce into prepared baking dish. Lay 2 noodles in dish and top with 1⅓ cups sauce. Repeat layering of noodles and sauce two more times. Top with remaining ½ cup fontina.

3. Cover dish tightly with aluminum foil and bake until bubbling around edges, about 25 minutes. Remove foil and continue to bake until cheese is just beginning to brown, about 10 minutes. Let cool for 10 to 15 minutes and serve.

QUICK PREP TIP SQUEEZING FROZEN SPINACH
To rid thawed spinach of excess water before adding it to a casserole or other recipes, simply wrap it in cheesecloth and squeeze it firmly.

Classic Lasagna with Hearty Meat Sauce

Serves 6 to 8

✔ **WHY THIS RECIPE WORKS:** We wanted a rich, ultra-meaty lasagna that would impress the whole family at the next get-together—but we didn't want to spend all day making it. Determined to create a flavorful lasagna in two hours or less, we came up with several shortcuts. First, we made a quick meat sauce by cooking onion, garlic, and meatloaf mix (ground beef, pork, and veal) and then adding tomatoes and cream. For the cheese layer, we stuck with tradition and combined ricotta, mozzarella, Parmesan, fresh basil, and an egg to help thicken and bind the mixture. No-boil lasagna noodles eliminated the process of boiling and draining conventional lasagna noodles. Covering the lasagna with aluminum foil before baking helped the noodles soften; removing the foil for the last 25 minutes guaranteed a perfect, golden-brown, cheesy layer on top. Meatloaf mix is sold prepackaged in many supermarkets. If it's unavailable, you can substitute 8 ounces each 85 percent lean ground beef and sweet Italian sausage, casings removed. Do not use nonfat ricotta or fat-free mozzarella here. The lasagna can be assembled, covered with plastic wrap, and refrigerated for up to 2 days. To bake, remove the plastic, cover with aluminum foil, and increase the covered baking time to 25 minutes.

SAUCE

- 1   **tablespoon olive oil**
- 1   **onion, chopped fine**
- 6   **garlic cloves, minced**
- 1   **pound meatloaf mix**
- ¼   **cup heavy cream**
- 1   **(28-ounce) can tomato puree**
- 1   **(28-ounce) can diced tomatoes, drained**
-   **Salt and pepper**

FILLING AND NOODLES

- 1   **pound (2 cups) whole-milk ricotta cheese**
- 2½   **ounces Parmesan cheese, grated (1¼ cups)**
- ½   **cup chopped fresh basil**
- 1   **large egg, lightly beaten**
- ½   **teaspoon salt**
- ½   **teaspoon pepper**
- 12   **no-boil lasagna noodles**
- 1   **pound mozzarella cheese, shredded (4 cups)**

1. FOR THE SAUCE: Adjust oven rack to middle position and heat oven to 375 degrees. Heat oil in large Dutch oven over medium heat until shimmering. Add onion and cook until softened, 5 to 7 minutes. Stir in garlic and cook until fragrant, about 30 seconds. Stir in meatloaf mix and cook, breaking up meat with wooden spoon, until no longer pink, about 4 minutes.

2. Stir in cream and simmer until liquid evaporates and only fat remains, about 4 minutes. Stir in tomato puree and diced tomatoes and simmer until flavors are blended, about 3 minutes. Off heat, season with salt and pepper to taste.

3. FOR THE FILLING AND NOODLES: Combine ricotta, 1 cup Parmesan, basil, egg, salt, and pepper together in bowl.

4. Spread ¼ cup sauce into 13 by 9-inch baking dish. Lay 3 noodles in dish, spread 3 tablespoons ricotta mixture over each noodle, sprinkle with 1 cup mozzarella, and top with 1½ cups sauce; repeat layering two more times. Lay remaining 3 noodles in dish and top with remaining sauce, remaining mozzarella, and remaining Parmesan.

5. Cover dish tightly with aluminum foil that has been sprayed with vegetable oil spray; bake for 15 minutes. Remove foil and continue to bake until bubbling around edges and cheese is spotty brown, about 25 minutes. Let cool for 10 to 15 minutes and serve.

SMART SHOPPING BROILER-SAFE CASSEROLE DISH
Here in the test kitchen, we're big fans of the classic, clear Pyrex Bakeware 13 by 9-Inch Baking Dish ($8.95), which we find to be perfect for most casseroles, except that it's not broiler-safe. For casseroles that require the broiler, we like the **HIC Porcelain Lasagna Baking Dish** ($37.49), which has large handles for secure gripping and straight sides for easy serving.

Roasted Eggplant and Zucchini Lasagna

Serves 6 to 8

WHY THIS RECIPE WORKS: Though easy in theory, creating a lighter lasagna starring vegetables, not meat, can be tough. Vegetables release a lot of liquid in the oven, making for a waterlogged casserole, and cutting the meat can cut richness and flavor. Our first step was roasting the veggies to drive off excess moisture; tasters liked eggplant and zucchini, which cooked at the same rate in a 400-degree oven. Part-skim mozzarella kept our lasagna rich and cheesy; Parmesan offered a salty, nutty punch. For even more creamy appeal, we deployed a trick from our Stuffed Shells with Meat Sauce (page 82), adding a layer of fat-free cottage cheese thickened with saltines. Do not use fat-free mozzarella or whipped cottage cheese here. This lasagna cannot be assembled ahead of time, but the sauce, roasted vegetables, and cottage cheese mixture can be prepared and refrigerated separately in airtight containers for up to 1 day. Before assembling the lasagna, reheat the sauce in the microwave, covered, until hot, about 1 minute. For the nutritional information for this recipe, see page 306.

Olive oil spray
2 pounds zucchini, cut into ½-inch pieces
2 pounds eggplant, cut into ½-inch pieces
Salt and pepper
4 garlic cloves, minced
1 tablespoon olive oil
1 (28-ounce) can crushed tomatoes
2 tablespoons chopped fresh basil
Water, as needed
5 saltines, broken into pieces
8 ounces (1 cup) fat-free cottage cheese, drained if necessary
12 no-boil lasagna noodles
12 ounces part-skim mozzarella cheese, shredded (3 cups)
1½ ounces Parmesan cheese, grated (¾ cups)

1. Adjust two oven racks to upper-middle and lower-middle positions and heat oven to 400 degrees. Spray two rimmed baking sheets with olive oil spray. Spread zucchini and eggplant on prepared baking sheets, spray with olive oil spray, and season with salt and pepper. Roast, stirring occasionally, until golden, about 35 minutes.

2. Meanwhile, cook garlic and oil in small saucepan over medium heat until fragrant but not browned, about 30 seconds. Stir in tomatoes and simmer until slightly thickened, about 5 minutes. Stir in basil and season with salt and pepper to taste. Pour sauce into large measuring cup and add enough water to make 3½ cups.

3. Pulse crackers in food processor until finely ground. Add cottage cheese and ½ teaspoon salt and process until smooth.

4. Spread ½ cup sauce into 13 by 9-inch baking dish. Lay 3 noodles in dish and top with one-third of roasted vegetables, ½ cup sauce, ½ cup mozzarella, and ¼ cup Parmesan; repeat layering two more times. Dollop cottage cheese mixture on top, then top with remaining 3 noodles, remaining sauce, and remaining mozzarella.

5. Cover dish tightly with aluminum foil that has been sprayed with vegetable oil spray and bake for 25 minutes. Remove foil and continue to bake until top turns golden brown in spots, about 15 minutes. Let cool for 10 to 15 minutes and serve.

SMART SHOPPING NO-BOIL NOODLES
No-boil (also called oven-ready) lasagna noodles are precooked at the factory; during baking, the moisture from the sauce softens, or rehydrates, them. The most common no-boil noodle is a rectangle, measuring 7 inches long and 3½ inches wide; 3 noodles fit perfectly in a 13 by 9-inch pan, and 2 noodles fit nicely in an 8-inch square pan. Our favorite brand is **Barilla No-Boil Lasagne**; we found these delicate, flat noodles closely resembled fresh pasta in texture.

Baked Ziti

Serves 6 to 8

✔ **WHY THIS RECIPE WORKS:** For an inspired—not tired—baked ziti, we kept things simple and focused on perfecting every element of this family favorite. Cooking the pasta to al dente ensured that it was tender, but not overcooked, in the finished dish. Sautéed garlic and red pepper flakes provided a savory foundation to our easy sauce, and two big cans of crushed tomatoes added rich, long-simmered flavor in short order while keeping the casserole moist. Stirring some of the pasta cooking water into the briefly simmered sauce provided further insurance against a dry baked ziti. A middle layer of ricotta promised creamy, tomatoey forkfuls of pasta, while a topping of shredded mozzarella and grated Parmesan gave us a nicely browned crust. Finishing with chopped basil kept our perfect baked ziti fresh-looking and bright-tasting. Do not use nonfat ricotta or fat-free mozzarella here. The casserole can be assembled, cooled (add the cheese topping when cool), covered with plastic wrap, and refrigerated for up to 2 days. To bake, remove the plastic and cover with aluminum foil. Bake in a 400-degree oven until bubbling, 30 to 40 minutes, then remove the foil and bake until the cheese is well browned, 15 to 20 minutes.

1	pound ziti
	Salt and pepper
2	tablespoons olive oil
3	garlic cloves, minced
¼	teaspoon red pepper flakes
2	(28-ounce) cans crushed tomatoes
8	ounces (1 cup) whole-milk ricotta cheese
6	ounces mozzarella cheese, shredded (1½ cups)
2	ounces Parmesan cheese, grated (1 cup)
¼	cup chopped fresh basil

1. Adjust oven rack to middle position and heat oven to 400 degrees. Bring 4 quarts water to boil in large Dutch oven. Add pasta and 1 tablespoon salt and cook, stirring often, until nearly al dente. Reserve ¾ cup cooking water, then drain pasta and set aside.

2. Dry now-empty pot, add 1 tablespoon oil, garlic, and pepper flakes, and cook over medium heat until fragrant but not brown, about 1 minute. Stir in tomatoes and simmer until slightly thickened, about 10 minutes. Off heat, season with salt and pepper to taste, then stir in cooked pasta and reserved cooking water, breaking up any clumps.

3. Mix ricotta, remaining 1 tablespoon oil, ¼ teaspoon salt, and ¼ teaspoon pepper together in bowl.

4. Pour half of pasta mixture into 13 by 9-inch baking dish. Dollop large spoonfuls of ricotta mixture evenly into dish, then spread remaining pasta over ricotta. Sprinkle with mozzarella and Parmesan. Bake until bubbling around edges and cheese is spotty brown, about 25 minutes. Let cool for 10 to 15 minutes, then sprinkle with basil and serve.

ON THE SIDE **TRICOLOR SALAD WITH BALSAMIC VINAIGRETTE**

Whisk 7 teaspoons balsamic vinegar, 2 teaspoons red wine vinegar, ¼ teaspoon salt, and ⅛ teaspoon pepper together in small bowl. Whisking constantly, drizzle in 6 tablespoons extra-virgin olive oil. In large bowl, toss 5 ounces (5 cups) baby arugula with 1 head radicchio and 2 heads Belgian endive, both torn into bite-size pieces. Just before serving, whisk dressing to re-emulsify, then drizzle over salad and toss gently to coat. Serves 8.

FUSILLI WITH ASPARAGUS, PEAS, AND ARUGULA

Whole-Wheat Pasta

Fusilli with Asparagus, Peas, and Arugula

Serves 4

✔ **WHY THIS RECIPE WORKS:** For a bright and light springtime sauce that would contrast nicely with the hearty, earthy flavors of whole-wheat pasta, we focused on the classic duo of asparagus and green peas. Leeks and garlic contributed aromatic depth and sweetness, and baby arugula added a slightly spicy bite. To stream-line our recipe and keep the asparagus brightly colored and crisp-tender in the finished dish, we blanched it right in the water we then used to cook the pasta. For a creamy sauce, we added tangy, bold goat cheese, which stood up well to the whole-wheat pasta. Finishing the dish with a drizzle of extra-virgin olive oil added even more richness. Baby spinach can be substituted for the arugula. For the nutritional information for this recipe, see page 306.

4	teaspoons extra-virgin olive oil
1	pound leeks, white and light green parts only, halved lengthwise, sliced thin, and washed thoroughly
2	garlic cloves, minced
2	teaspoons minced fresh thyme
1¼	cups low-sodium chicken broth
¾	cup frozen peas, thawed
3	tablespoons lemon juice
	Salt and pepper
1	pound asparagus, trimmed and cut on bias into 1-inch lengths
12	ounces (5 cups) whole-wheat fusilli
4	ounces (4 cups) baby arugula
2	ounces goat cheese, crumbled (½ cup)
¼	cup shredded fresh basil

1. Heat 2 teaspoons oil in 12-inch nonstick skillet over medium heat until shimmering. Add leeks and cook until softened and beginning to brown, 5 to 7 minutes. Stir in garlic and thyme and cook until fragrant, about 30 seconds. Stir in broth and bring to brief simmer. Off heat, stir in peas and lemon juice, cover, and let sit until peas are heated through, about 2 minutes. Season with salt and pepper to taste.

2. Meanwhile, bring 4 quarts water to boil in large pot. Add asparagus and 1 tablespoon salt and cook until asparagus is crisp-tender, about 2 minutes. Using slotted spoon, transfer asparagus to paper towel–lined plate.

3. Return pot of water to boil. Add pasta and cook, stirring often, until al dente. Reserve ½ cup cooking water, then drain pasta and return it to pot. Add arugula, one handful at a time, and toss to wilt. Add leek mixture, asparagus, goat cheese, basil, and remaining 2 teaspoons oil and toss to combine. Season with salt and pepper to taste and add reserved cooking water as needed to adjust consistency. Serve.

QUICK PREP TIP PREPARING LEEKS

Trim and discard root and dark green leaves. Cut trimmed leek in half lengthwise, then slice it crosswise into thin pieces. Rinse cut leeks thoroughly to remove all dirt and sand using either a salad spinner or bowl of water.

In recent years, whole-wheat pasta has become increasingly popular, practically giving white pasta a run for its money. With its health benefits—whole-wheat pasta delivers up to three times more dietary fiber than white pasta—it's no wonder. But because of its chewy texture and nutty flavor, it doesn't work with just any sauce. Here are our tips for buying and cooking whole-wheat pasta, and pairing it with the right ingredients and flavors.

The Best Whole-Wheat Spaghetti

In accordance with the U.S. Food and Drug Administration laws, in order to carry the "100 percent whole-wheat" label on a package of pasta, brands must contain 100 percent whole durum wheat; brands simply tagged "whole-wheat" or "multigrain" have no minimum requirement of whole or alternative flours (made from wheat and a hodgepodge of grains like barley, flaxseed, oats, and spelt) to earn the healthy-sounding label, so what they are composed of can vary wildly. We recently sampled 18 brands of whole-wheat spaghetti, including a few multigrain brands as well, tasting them with olive oil and with sauces. Two were whole-grain imposters, with refined wheat as their first ingredient. Most 100 percent whole-wheat and 100 percent whole-grain pastas fell to the bottom of the rankings, with "mushy" or "doughy" textures and "sour," "fishy" flavors. However, one boasted a good chewy and firm texture, making it our top pick. **Bionaturae Organic 100% Whole Wheat Spaghetti** was praised for its "earthy," "wheaty," "nutty" flavor and "pleasantly chewy," "firm" texture. Three things put this spaghetti ahead of the rest: It's custom-milled for good flavor, extruded through a bronze, not Teflon, die to build gluten in the dough, and slowly dried for a sturdier texture.

The Best Whole-Wheat Lasagna

To find the best whole-wheat lasagna, we sampled four brands—three made from 100 percent whole-wheat flour and one a whole-wheat–white flour blend—plain and baked in a vegetable lasagna. While texture was important, tasters' likes and dislikes were mainly centered around wheat flavor. Noodles that were too gritty and cardboard-y fell to the bottom of the heap. But pasta that too closely resembled the white kind wasn't their top pick either. Our champ turned out to be the same brand that took top honors in our whole-wheat spaghetti tasting. **Bionaturae Organic 100% Whole Wheat Lasagne** won us over with its "nutty," "rich" wheat flavor and a texture that was pleasantly "chewy."

Pair with Hearty Sauce

Whole-wheat pasta offers a nutty, hearty flavor very different from the mild flavor that defines traditional white pasta. For this reason, we prefer to pair whole-wheat pasta with ingredients and sauces that match its robust flavor profile. That's why you'll see a number of recipes in this chapter that call upon hearty, assertive vegetables, such as kale, Brussels sprouts, broccoli rabe, and cauliflower. Also, because whole-wheat pasta is quite sturdy, it stands up well to chunky sauces, so the sauces we've included here include bigger pieces of vegetables and crumbled sausage or chunks of chicken.

Check the Label

Unlike traditional white pasta, which generally comes in 1-pound boxes or sleeves, whole-wheat pasta is often packaged in odd amounts, such as 13.25 ounces or 14.5 ounces. So before you head to the supermarket, it's worth double-checking what your recipe calls for so you can be sure that you have the right amount on hand when you start cooking.

Test for Doneness

Everyone knows when white pasta is done—it's tender, or what we refer to as "al dente"—but because of whole-wheat pasta's composition, its texture is slightly firmer when it's fully cooked and ready to be removed from the heat. Keep this in mind as you're sampling the pasta during cooking, and aim for a slightly firmer bite than you would with white pasta.

Spaghetti with Zucchini and Sun-Dried Tomatoes

Serves 4

✔ **WHY THIS RECIPE WORKS:** Here we paired piquant sun-dried tomatoes with sautéed zucchini to make a bright and bold sauce perfect for whole-wheat pasta. Garlic and red pepper flakes added the perfect backdrop to this lively, fresh-tasting sauce. Starch from reserved pasta cooking water thickened the sauce nicely and helped it cling to the spaghetti. A sprinkling of freshly grated Pecorino Romano, which tasters preferred to the more subtle Parmesan, added a salty tang. Chopped fresh basil and toasted pine nuts contributed color and crunch. See page 173 for tips on how to measure out long strands of pasta without using a scale.

¼ cup extra-virgin olive oil

4 garlic cloves, minced

½ teaspoon red pepper flakes
  Salt

1 zucchini, quartered lengthwise and cut into ½-inch pieces

⅓ cup pine nuts, toasted and coarsely chopped

⅓ cup oil-packed sun-dried tomatoes, rinsed, patted dry, and chopped coarse

⅓ cup coarsely chopped fresh basil

12 ounces whole-wheat spaghetti
  Grated Pecorino Romano cheese

1. Combine 3 tablespoons oil, garlic, pepper flakes, and ½ teaspoon salt in small bowl. Heat remaining 1 tablespoon oil in 12-inch nonstick skillet over medium-high heat until shimmering. Add zucchini and ¼ teaspoon salt and cook, stirring often, until tender, about 5 minutes.

2. Clear center of skillet, add garlic mixture, and cook, mashing mixture into pan, until fragrant, about 1 minute. Stir garlic mixture into zucchini and cook for 1 minute longer. Off heat, stir in pine nuts, sun-dried tomatoes, and basil.

3. Meanwhile, bring 4 quarts water to boil in large pot. Add pasta and 1 tablespoon salt and cook, stirring often, until al dente. Reserve ¾ cup cooking water, then drain pasta and return it to pot.

4. Add zucchini mixture and ½ cup reserved cooking water to pasta and toss to combine. Season with salt to taste and add remaining reserved cooking water as needed to adjust consistency. Serve with Pecorino.

SMART SHOPPING BUYING ZUCCHINI
We've found that smaller zucchini (measuring 8 ounces or smaller) are the best choice for adding to pasta. By comparison, larger zucchini (larger than 8 ounces) have a softer, spongier texture and are loaded with seeds.

TOO BIG   JUST RIGHT

Spaghetti with Cauliflower and Raisins

Serves 4

✓ **WHY THIS RECIPE WORKS:** When sautéed or roasted, cauliflower takes on a whole new dimension—earthy, nutty, sweet, and altogether delicious. We thought these flavors would match perfectly with a tangle of whole-wheat spaghetti, but for ease, we kept the dish out of the oven and on the stovetop. Golden raisins and pine nuts amped up the sweet and crunchy textures, and a secret ingredient—anchovies—added potent, savory flavor without imparting any fishiness. The anchovies may seem like an unusual ingredient here, but they add tremendous flavor; do not omit them. Adjust the amount of lemon juice to suit your taste. See page 173 for tips on how to measure out long strands of pasta without using a scale.

5	tablespoons extra-virgin olive oil
4	garlic cloves, minced
4	anchovy fillets, rinsed and minced
¼	teaspoon red pepper flakes
	Salt
½	head cauliflower (1 pound), cored and cut into 1-inch florets
⅓	cup golden raisins, coarsely chopped
⅓	cup pine nuts, toasted and coarsely chopped
3	tablespoons coarsely chopped fresh parsley
1	tablespoon lemon juice, plus extra to taste
12	ounces whole-wheat spaghetti
	Grated Pecorino Romano cheese

1. Combine 3 tablespoons oil, garlic, anchovies, pepper flakes, and ¼ teaspoon salt in bowl. Heat remaining 2 tablespoons oil in 12-inch nonstick skillet over medium-high heat until shimmering. Add cauliflower and ¼ teaspoon salt and cook, stirring occasionally, until well browned and tender, 10 to 12 minutes.

2. Clear center of skillet, add garlic mixture, and cook, mashing mixture into pan, until fragrant, about 1 minute. Stir garlic mixture into cauliflower and cook for 1 minute longer. Off heat, stir in raisins, pine nuts, parsley, and lemon juice.

3. Meanwhile, bring 4 quarts water to boil in large pot. Add pasta and 1 tablespoon salt and cook, stirring often, until al dente. Reserve ¾ cup cooking water, then drain pasta and return it to pot.

4. Add cauliflower mixture and ½ cup reserved cooking water to pasta and toss to combine. Season with salt and additional lemon juice to taste. Add remaining reserved cooking water as needed to adjust consistency. Serve with Pecorino.

ON THE SIDE ROMAINE AND ENDIVE SALAD WITH PEAR
Whisk 1 tablespoon minced fresh mint, ¾ teaspoon grated lemon zest, 1 tablespoon lemon juice, ¼ teaspoon salt, and ⅛ teaspoon pepper together in large bowl. Whisking constantly, drizzle in 2 tablespoons extra-virgin olive oil. Add 1 romaine lettuce heart, torn into bite-size pieces, and 1 head Belgian endive, leaves separated and cut into 1-inch pieces; toss to combine. Garnish with 1 very ripe pear, peeled, cored, and sliced thin, before serving. Serves 4.

Penne with Butternut Squash and Sage

Serves 4

✔ **WHY THIS RECIPE WORKS:** We wanted a pasta dish in which butternut squash took center stage—and not just as a ravioli filling. Sautéing the squash first amplified its mild flavor and ensured that it took on rich, caramelized flavor. We then built a sauce in the same pan we used to brown the squash, and after a short braise we had perfectly cooked and deeply flavorful squash with a silky texture. Mascarpone gave the sauce a velvety texture, and scallions provided a pungent note that contrasted nicely with the sweet earthiness of the squash. A final sprinkling of sliced almonds added some crunch. Fresh sage is a natural pairing with squash, and crucial to the flavor of this dish; don't substitute dried sage. You can substitute cream cheese for the mascarpone. When simmering the squash in step 3, do not stir too frequently or the squash will begin to fall apart.

2	tablespoons olive oil
2	pounds butternut squash, peeled, seeded, and cut into ½-inch pieces (4 cups)
6	scallions, sliced thin
3	garlic cloves, minced
¼	teaspoon ground nutmeg
2	teaspoons all-purpose flour
1½	cups low-sodium chicken broth
¾	cup dry white wine
1	ounce Parmesan cheese, grated (½ cup), plus extra for serving
1	ounce (2 tablespoons) mascarpone cheese
2	tablespoons minced fresh sage
4	teaspoons lemon juice
	Salt and pepper
12	ounces (4 cups) whole-wheat penne
¼	cup sliced almonds, toasted

1. Heat 1 tablespoon oil in 12-inch nonstick skillet over medium heat until shimmering. Add squash and cook, stirring occasionally, until spotty brown, 15 to 20 minutes; transfer to bowl.

2. Add remaining 1 tablespoon oil, scallions, garlic, and nutmeg to now-empty skillet and cook over medium heat until scallions are softened, 1 to 2 minutes. Stir in flour and cook for 1 minute. Slowly whisk in broth and wine, scraping up any browned bits.

3. Stir in browned squash and simmer until squash is tender and sauce has thickened slightly, 10 to 15 minutes. Off heat, gently stir in Parmesan, mascarpone, sage, and lemon juice. Season with salt and pepper to taste.

4. Meanwhile, bring 4 quarts water to boil in large pot. Add pasta and 1 tablespoon salt and cook, stirring often, until al dente. Reserve ½ cup cooking water, then drain pasta and return it to pot.

5. Add squash and sauce to pasta and gently toss to combine. Season with salt and pepper to taste and add reserved cooking water as needed to adjust consistency. Sprinkle individual portions with almonds and serve with extra Parmesan.

QUICK PREP TIP
CUTTING UP BUTTERNUT SQUASH
Peel away tough outer skin with peeler, then trim off top and bottom of squash. Using chef's knife, slice squash in half to separate solid neck piece from bottom. Slice neck piece crosswise into rounds, then cut into pieces as directed. Slice bottom in half, remove seeds with spoon, then cut into pieces as directed.

Rotini with Brussels Sprouts, Bacon, and Peas

Serves 4

✓ **WHY THIS RECIPE WORKS:** Earthy Brussels sprouts and nutty whole-wheat pasta add depth to this slightly unusual—but incredibly satisfying—pasta dish. After frying bacon until crisp, we sautéed sliced Brussels sprouts with shallots in the rendered fat, which promised smoky bacon flavor throughout the whole dish. To make sure the sprouts were evenly cooked, we simmered them in a combination of chicken broth and cream, which also provided the base of our sauce. Parmesan imparted a tangy note and gave the sauce some clinginess, while toasted walnuts provided further rich flavor and an appealing crunch that played nicely against sweet peas. Small, firm Brussels sprouts (about 1 inch in diameter) work best here. Slicing the sprouts in a food processor cuts down on prep time and ensures that the sprouts integrate well with the pasta.

4	slices bacon, chopped
10	ounces Brussels sprouts, trimmed and sliced thin
2	shallots, sliced thin
	Salt and pepper
½	cup low-sodium chicken broth
½	cup heavy cream
½	cup frozen peas, thawed
12	ounces (4½ cups) whole-wheat rotini
⅓	cup walnuts, toasted and chopped
1	ounce Parmesan cheese, grated (½ cup), plus extra for serving

1. Cook bacon in 12-inch skillet over medium-high heat until crisp, about 5 minutes; transfer to paper towel–lined plate. Pour off all but 2 tablespoons fat from skillet.

2. Add Brussels sprouts, shallots, ½ teaspoon salt, and ¼ teaspoon pepper to fat left in skillet and cook over medium-high heat until sprouts begin to soften, about 5 minutes. Stir in broth and cream, cover, and simmer until sprouts are tender, about 3 minutes. Off heat, stir in peas, cover, and let sit until heated through, about 2 minutes.

3. Meanwhile, bring 4 quarts water to boil in large pot. Add pasta and 1 tablespoon salt and cook, stirring often, until al dente. Reserve ½ cup cooking water, then drain pasta and return it to pot. Stir in Brussels sprouts mixture, crisped bacon, walnuts, and Parmesan and toss to combine. Season with salt and pepper to taste and add reserved cooking water as needed to adjust consistency. Serve with extra Parmesan.

QUICK PREP TIP SLICING BRUSSELS SPROUTS
While you could slice the Brussels sprouts for this recipe by hand, using a food processor fitted with the slicing disk makes quick work of the task and ensures even slices. First, trim the stem ends from the Brussels sprouts. Then, working in batches, fill the feed tube with sprouts and press them through with the feed tube plunger.

Spaghetti with Greens, Beans, Pancetta, and Garlic Bread Crumbs

Serves 4

✔ **WHY THIS RECIPE WORKS:** Pasta, hearty greens, and beans can make for a sublime experience, but these humble ingredients traditionally take time—like an hours-long simmer—to make the transition to full-flavored entrée. To turn this Italian classic into an easy and quick weeknight supper, we kept our greens to a minimum, choosing just kale or collards, which needed but a quick braise. Onion, garlic, red pepper flakes, and chicken broth provided a savory backbone. Using canned, not dried, beans saved on time, and pancetta and fontina cheese added hearty depth in the absence of a long simmer. Cooking the pasta with the greens, beans, and sauce for a few moments created a gutsy, harmonious flavor. Prosciutto can be substituted for the pancetta. See page 173 for tips on how to measure out long strands of pasta without using a scale.

3	tablespoons olive oil
1½	cups fresh bread crumbs (see page 76)
6	garlic cloves, minced
	Salt and pepper
3	ounces pancetta, cut into ½-inch pieces
1	onion, chopped fine
¼	teaspoon red pepper flakes
1-1½	pounds kale or collard greens, stemmed and chopped into 1-inch pieces
1½	cups low-sodium chicken broth
1	(15-ounce) can cannellini beans, rinsed
12	ounces whole-wheat spaghetti
4	ounces fontina cheese, shredded (1 cup)

1. Heat 2 tablespoons oil in 12-inch skillet over medium heat until shimmering. Add bread crumbs and cook, stirring often, until beginning to brown, 4 to 6 minutes. Stir in half of garlic and ¼ teaspoon salt and continue to cook until garlic is fragrant and crumbs are golden brown, 1 to 2 minutes; transfer to bowl.

2. Wipe now-empty skillet clean with paper towels. Add remaining 1 tablespoon oil and pancetta and cook over medium heat until pancetta is crisp, 5 to 7 minutes; transfer to paper towel–lined plate.

3. Add onion to fat left in pan and cook over medium heat until softened and lightly browned, 5 to 7 minutes. Stir in remaining garlic and pepper flakes and cook until fragrant, about 30 seconds. Add half of kale and cook, tossing occasionally, until it begins to wilt, about 2 minutes. Add remaining kale, broth, and ¾ teaspoon salt and bring to simmer. Reduce heat to medium, cover (pan will be very full), and cook, tossing occasionally, until greens are tender, about 15 minutes (mixture will be somewhat soupy). Stir in beans and crisped pancetta.

4. Meanwhile, bring 4 quarts water to boil in large pot. Add pasta and 1 tablespoon salt and cook, stirring often, until al dente. Reserve ½ cup cooking water, then drain pasta and return it to pot. Stir in greens mixture and cook over medium heat, tossing to combine, until sauce thickens, about 2 minutes.

5. Off heat, stir in fontina. Season with salt and pepper to taste and add reserved cooking water as needed to adjust consistency. Sprinkle individual portions with toasted crumbs and serve.

Spaghetti with Lentils, Pancetta, and Escarole

Serves 4

✔ **WHY THIS RECIPE WORKS:** An earthy, hearty, soul-satisfying dish, pasta with lentils has long been a tradition in Italy. But when we developed our own version, we ended up going with a nontraditional choice for the main ingredient: French green lentils, or lentils du Puy, which retained a firm yet tender texture after the long simmering time. Using a combination of water and chicken broth as the cooking liquid imparted a savory backbone without obscuring the lentils' earthy notes. White wine provided a bright punch of acidity, but we couldn't add it until the lentils were softened, lest it prevent them from cooking through. Pancetta, carrots, and spicy escarole rounded out the flavors of this rustic dish. You can substitute brown or green lentils for the lentils du Puy, but they will produce a thicker, starchier sauce. Do not substitute red or yellow lentils. See page 173 for tips on how to measure out long strands of pasta without using a scale.

¼ **cup extra-virgin olive oil**
4 **ounces pancetta, cut into ¼-inch pieces**
1 **onion, chopped fine**
2 **carrots, peeled, halved lengthwise, and sliced ¼ inch thick**
2 **garlic cloves, minced**
¾ **cup lentils du Puy, picked over and rinsed**
3 **cups water**
2 **cups low-sodium chicken broth**
¼ **cup dry white wine**
1 **head escarole (1 pound), trimmed and sliced ½ inch thick**
12 **ounces whole-wheat spaghetti Salt and pepper**
¼ **cup chopped fresh parsley Grated Parmesan cheese**

1. Cook 2 tablespoons oil and pancetta in large saucepan over medium heat until pancetta is lightly browned, 3 to 5 minutes. Add onion and carrots and cook until vegetables are softened, 5 to 7 minutes. Stir in garlic and cook until fragrant, about 30 seconds. Add lentils, water, and broth, cover, and simmer until lentils are fully cooked and tender, 40 to 50 minutes.

2. Uncover, stir in wine, and simmer for 2 minutes. Add escarole, one handful at a time, and cook until completely wilted, about 5 minutes.

3. Meanwhile, bring 4 quarts water to boil in large pot. Add pasta and 1 tablespoon salt and cook, stirring often, until al dente. Reserve ¾ cup cooking water, then drain pasta and return it to pot. Stir in lentil mixture, ½ cup reserved cooking water, remaining 2 tablespoons oil, and parsley and toss to combine. Season with salt and pepper to taste and add remaining reserved cooking water as needed to adjust consistency. Serve with Parmesan.

SMART SHOPPING LENTILS
Lentils come in various sizes and colors, and the differences in flavor and texture are surprisingly distinct. Lentils du Puy are smaller than the more common brown and green varieties and take their name from the city of Puy in central France. They are dark olive-green, almost black, in color, and are praised for their "rich, earthy, complex flavor" and "firm yet tender texture." Brown lentils are larger in size and have a uniform brown color and a "mild yet light and earthy flavor"; green lentils are similar in size to the brown but are greenish-brown in color and have a very "mild flavor." Red lentils are very small, have an orange-red hue, and disintegrate completely when cooked; yellow lentils are also small and brightly colored and break down completely when cooked. Red and yellow lentils are most frequently used in Indian and Middle Eastern cuisines.

Penne with Sausage, Chickpeas, and Broccoli Rabe

Serves 4

✓ **WHY THIS RECIPE WORKS:** Whole-wheat pasta meets its match in this recipe, which features equally assertive broccoli rabe. Blanching the broccoli rabe tamed its bitterness, and using the same water for cooking the pasta kept things streamlined and our pile of dirty pots to a minimum. Italian sausage gave the dish meaty substance, and mild, creamy chickpeas reinforced the nutty flavor of the whole-wheat penne. Slices of red bell pepper added a pop of color and sweetness.

2	tablespoons extra-virgin olive oil
1	onion, chopped fine
1	red bell pepper, stemmed, seeded, and cut into ¼-inch-wide strips
6	garlic cloves, minced
⅛	teaspoon red pepper flakes
8	ounces hot or sweet Italian sausage, casings removed
1	(15-ounce) can chickpeas, rinsed
¾	cup low-sodium chicken broth
	Salt and pepper
1	pound broccoli rabe, trimmed (see page 23) and cut into 1½-inch pieces
12	ounces (4 cups) whole-wheat penne
¼	cup grated Parmesan cheese, plus extra for serving

1. Heat 1 tablespoon oil in 12-inch nonstick skillet over medium heat until shimmering. Add onion and bell pepper and cook until softened, about 5 minutes. Stir in garlic and pepper flakes and cook until fragrant, about 30 seconds. Add sausage and cook, breaking up meat with wooden spoon, until no longer pink, about 4 minutes. Stir in chickpeas and broth. Bring to simmer and cook until chickpeas are heated through, about 2 minutes. Season with salt and pepper to taste.

2. Meanwhile, bring 4 quarts water to boil in large pot. Add broccoli rabe and 1 tablespoon salt and cook, stirring often, until broccoli rabe is crisp-tender, 1 to 3 minutes. Using slotted spoon, transfer broccoli rabe to paper towel–lined plate.

3. Return pot of water to boil. Add pasta and cook, stirring often, until al dente. Reserve ½ cup cooking water, then drain pasta and return it to pot. Add sausage-broth mixture, broccoli rabe, remaining 1 tablespoon oil, and Parmesan and toss to combine. Season with salt and pepper to taste and add reserved cooking water as needed to adjust consistency. Serve with extra Parmesan.

SMART SHOPPING CANNED CHICKPEAS
Think all brands of canned chickpeas taste the same? So did we until we tried six brands of them in a side-by-side taste test. Once we peeled back the can lids and drained and rinsed the beans, we found that many of them were incredibly bland or, worse yet, had bitter and metallic flavors. Tasters preferred those that were well seasoned and had a creamy yet "al dente" texture. **Pastene Chickpeas** came out on top for their clean flavor and firm yet tender texture.

Penne with Turkey Sausage, Fennel, and Spinach

Serves 4

✔ **WHY THIS RECIPE WORKS:** To lighten up the well-loved duo of pasta and sausage, we swapped Italian pork sausage for Italian turkey sausage. Though lighter in fat, the turkey sausage still provides meaty flavor and is a hearty foil to the whole-wheat pasta. Since fennel seeds are commonly used to season Italian sausages, we added sliced fennel to the dish for even deeper flavor, and a few handfuls of spinach, stirred in at the end, contributed color and freshness. Italian chicken sausage can be substituted for the turkey sausage. The spinach may look like a lot at first, but it wilts down substantially as it cooks. For the nutritional information for this recipe, see page 306.

1 tablespoon olive oil

1 pound hot or sweet Italian turkey sausage, casings removed

1 fennel bulb, stalks discarded, bulb halved, cored, and sliced thin (see page 248)

1 onion, chopped fine

3 garlic cloves, minced

2 teaspoons all-purpose flour

2 cups low-sodium chicken broth

1 cup dry white wine
Salt and pepper

12 ounces (4 cups) whole-wheat penne

6 ounces (6 cups) baby spinach
Grated Parmesan cheese

1. Heat 1½ teaspoons oil in 12-inch nonstick skillet over medium-high heat until just smoking. Add sausage and cook, breaking up meat with wooden spoon, until browned, about 5 minutes; transfer to paper towel–lined plate.

2. Add remaining 1½ teaspoons oil, fennel, and onion to now-empty skillet and cook over medium heat until softened and lightly browned, about 10 minutes. Stir in garlic and cook until fragrant, about 30 seconds. Stir in flour and cook for 1 minute. Slowly whisk in broth and wine, scraping up any browned bits, and simmer until slightly thickened, about 15 minutes. Return sausage to skillet and cook until sausage is heated through, about 1 minute. Season with salt and pepper to taste.

3. Meanwhile, bring 4 quarts water to boil in large pot. Add pasta and 1 tablespoon salt and cook, stirring often, until al dente. Reserve ½ cup of cooking water, then drain pasta and return it to pot. Stir in spinach, one handful at a time, and toss to wilt. Add sausage-broth mixture and toss to combine. Season with salt and pepper to taste and add reserved cooking water as needed to adjust consistency. Serve with Parmesan.

SMART SHOPPING NONSTICK-FRIENDLY WHISKS

Whisks coated with silicone are an essential tool when cooking in a nonstick skillet or else you risk scratching and ruining the pan's slick surface. We tested six brands in a variety of shapes, and quickly found that design often trumped efficiency. In one model, only the tip of the whisk was covered in silicone, leaving unprotected wire portions free to scratch the pan near the rim. Others had overly thick coatings, so that the fat wires were difficult to move through food. In the end, we found a lightweight, comfortable whisk with wires that were fully but thinly coated. Our winner, the **Cuisipro Silicone Egg Whisk** ($13), whipped the rest of the field by being flexible yet resistant enough to make roux for gravy and pastry cream that didn't curdle or stick, all without damaging our nonstick pan.

Penne with Chicken, Caramelized Onions, and Red Peppers

Serves 4

✔ **WHY THIS RECIPE WORKS:** Sweet, rich, caramelized onions add a bit of flair and sophistication to this whole-wheat pasta dish. Adding sugar when we sautéed our onions helped to draw out their moisture, enhancing caramelization. Sliced red peppers played up the underlying sweetness of the sauce. Thinly sliced chicken, which cooked in minutes, transformed this simple dish to a satisfying supper with some oomph. Parmesan cheese can be substituted for the Asiago. For the nutritional information for this recipe, see page 306.

5	teaspoons olive oil
3	onions, halved and sliced thin
¾	teaspoon packed light brown sugar
2	red bell peppers, stemmed, seeded, and cut into ¼-inch-wide strips
1	pound boneless, skinless chicken breasts, trimmed and sliced thin (see page 26)
	Salt and pepper
6	garlic cloves, minced
2	teaspoons minced fresh thyme
⅛	teaspoon red pepper flakes
2	teaspoons all-purpose flour
2	cups low-sodium chicken broth
1	cup dry white wine
1	ounce Asiago cheese, grated (½ cup)
12	ounces (4 cups) whole-wheat penne
½	cup shredded fresh basil

1. Heat 2 teaspoons oil in 12-inch nonstick skillet over medium-high heat until shimmering. Add onions and sugar and cook until softened, about 5 minutes. Reduce heat to medium-low and continue to cook, stirring often, until onions are dark golden and caramelized, 20 to 25 minutes. Stir in bell peppers and cook until softened, about 5 minutes; transfer to bowl.

2. Pat chicken dry with paper towels and season with salt and pepper. Heat 2 teaspoons oil in now-empty skillet over high heat until just smoking. Add chicken in single layer and cook, without stirring, until beginning to brown, about 1 minute. Stir chicken and continue to cook until nearly cooked through, about 2 minutes; transfer to bowl with vegetables.

3. Add remaining 1 teaspoon oil, garlic, thyme, and pepper flakes to now-empty skillet and cook over medium heat until fragrant, about 1 minute. Stir in flour and cook for 1 minute. Slowly whisk in broth and wine, scraping up any browned bits, and simmer until thickened, about 15 minutes. Return chicken and vegetables with any accumulated juice to skillet and simmer until chicken is cooked through, about 1 minute. Off heat, stir in Asiago and season with salt and pepper to taste.

4. Meanwhile, bring 4 quarts water to boil in large pot. Add pasta and 1 tablespoon salt and cook, stirring often, until al dente. Reserve ½ cup cooking water, then drain pasta and return it to pot. Stir in chicken mixture and basil and toss to combine. Season with salt and pepper to taste and add reserved cooking water as needed to adjust consistency. Serve.

QUICK PREP TIP **NO-TEARS ONION SLICING**

When an onion is cut, the cells that are damaged in the process release sulfuric compounds as well as various enzymes that mix to form a new compound that evaporates in the air and irritates the eyes, causing us to cry. Of all the suggested ways to lessen this teary effect, we've found that the best options are to protect the eyes by covering them with goggles or contact lenses, or to introduce a flame (from a candle or gas burner) near the cut onions. The flame changes the activity of the compound that causes the tearing, while contact lenses and goggles simply form a physical barrier that the compound cannot penetrate. So if you want to keep tears at bay when handling onions, light a candle or gas burner. Or, if you don't mind looking a little silly, put on some ski goggles.

Creamy Chicken and Spinach Pasta Casserole

Serves 4

✔ **WHY THIS RECIPE WORKS:** For a rich, creamy casserole starring whole-wheat penne, we kept the supporting flavors simple and straightforward. We created a basic sauce with sautéed aromatics, a bit of flour for thickening, milk and Parmesan for creaminess and savory flavor, and lemon juice for bright, clean notes. Sliced chicken, sautéed to golden perfection, amped up the heartiness of our casserole, and frozen spinach was a convenient way to get our vegetables in. To prevent the pasta from becoming mushy and overdone in the finished dish, we undercooked it slightly. This way, the pasta could finish cooking in the sauce as the casserole baked in the oven; stirring in some of the pasta cooking water ensured that it stayed moist. Shredded mozzarella, sprinkled over the top, gave our casserole a bubbling, golden crown when we pulled it from the oven. Be sure to squeeze the spinach thoroughly so it is as dry as possible.

12 **ounces boneless, skinless chicken breasts, trimmed and sliced thin (see page 26)**
   Salt and pepper
1½ **tablespoons olive oil**
1 **onion, chopped fine**
3 **garlic cloves, minced**
⅛ **teaspoon red pepper flakes**
2 **tablespoons all-purpose flour**
4 **cups 1 percent low-fat milk**
1 **bay leaf**
1 **ounce Parmesan cheese, grated (½ cup)**
2 **teaspoons lemon juice**
10 **ounces frozen spinach, thawed, squeezed dry (see page 89), and chopped coarse**
8 **ounces (2⅔ cups) whole-wheat penne**
2 **ounces part-skim mozzarella cheese, shredded (½ cup)**

1. Adjust oven rack to middle position and heat oven to 425 degrees. Grease 8-inch square baking dish with vegetable oil spray.

2. Pat chicken dry with paper towels and season with salt and pepper. Heat 1½ teaspoons oil in 12-inch nonstick skillet over high heat until just smoking. Add chicken in single layer and cook, without stirring, until beginning to brown, about 1 minute. Stir chicken and continue to cook until nearly cooked through, about 2 minutes; transfer to bowl.

3. Add remaining 1 tablespoon oil and onion to now-empty skillet and cook over medium heat until softened, about 5 minutes. Stir in garlic and pepper flakes and cook until fragrant, about 30 seconds. Stir in flour and cook for 1 minute. Slowly whisk in milk, add bay leaf, and simmer, stirring occasionally, until slightly thickened, about 10 minutes.

4. Return chicken with any accumulated juice to skillet and simmer until chicken is cooked through, about 1 minute. Off heat, remove bay leaf and stir in Parmesan and lemon juice. Stir in spinach, breaking up any clumps. Season with salt and pepper to taste.

5. Meanwhile, bring 4 quarts water to boil in large pot. Add pasta and 1 tablespoon salt and cook, stirring often, until nearly al dente. Reserve ¼ cup cooking water, then drain pasta and return it to pot. Stir in chicken-spinach mixture and reserved cooking water and toss to combine. Transfer to prepared baking dish and sprinkle with mozzarella. Bake until sauce is bubbling and cheese is lightly browned, about 15 minutes. Let cool for 10 to 15 minutes and serve.

Baked Penne and Sausage with Bell Pepper and Onion

Serves 4

✔ **WHY THIS RECIPE WORKS:** Sausage, peppers, and onions are one of the best flavor combinations we can think of. For an effortless casserole that marries these big, hearty flavors with whole-wheat penne, we created a simple sauce with sautéed red bell pepper and onion and crumbled, browned Italian sausage. Processed diced tomatoes contributed a bright, flavorful backbone. Slightly undercooking the pasta guaranteed that it didn't dry out in the oven. We kept casserole assembly easy, alternating the pasta and sauce with shredded mozzarella, which melted into a cheesy, gooey middle layer and topping. If you prefer a chunkier sauce, pulse the tomatoes just two or three times in the food processor in step 1.

1   **(14.5-ounce) can diced tomatoes**
1   **tablespoon olive oil**
1   **onion, halved and sliced thin**
1   **red bell pepper, stemmed, seeded, and cut into ¼-inch-wide strips**
3   **garlic cloves, minced**
⅛   **teaspoon red pepper flakes**
8   **ounces hot or sweet Italian sausage, casings removed**
     Salt and pepper
8   **ounces (2⅔ cups) whole-wheat penne**
4   **ounces part-skim mozzarella cheese, shredded (1 cup)**

1. Adjust oven rack to middle position and heat oven to 425 degrees. Grease 8-inch square baking dish with vegetable oil spray. Pulse tomatoes in food processor until mostly smooth, about 5 pulses.

2. Heat oil in 12-inch nonstick skillet over medium heat until shimmering. Add onion and bell pepper and cook until softened, about 5 minutes. Stir in garlic and pepper flakes and cook until fragrant, about 30 seconds. Stir in sausage and cook, breaking up meat with wooden spoon until no longer pink, about 4 minutes. Stir in processed tomatoes and simmer until slightly thickened, 6 to 8 minutes. Season with salt and pepper to taste.

3. Meanwhile, bring 4 quarts water to boil in large pot. Add pasta and 1 tablespoon salt and cook, stirring often, until nearly al dente. Reserve ¼ cup cooking water, then drain pasta and return it to pot. Stir in meat sauce and reserved cooking water and toss to combine.

4. Spread half of pasta mixture into prepared baking dish and sprinkle with ½ cup mozzarella; repeat with remaining pasta and mozzarella. Bake until sauce is bubbling and cheese is lightly browned, about 15 minutes. Let cool for 10 to 15 minutes and serve.

ON THE SIDE SPINACH SALAD WITH SHERRY VINAIGRETTE
Whisk 1 tablespoon sherry vinegar, ½ minced shallot, ½ teaspoon Dijon mustard, ¼ teaspoon salt, and pinch pepper together in large bowl. Whisking constantly, drizzle in 2 tablespoons extra-virgin olive oil. Add 6 ounces (6 cups) baby spinach and 1 small red bell pepper, stemmed, seeded, and cut into ½-inch pieces; toss to coat. Serves 4.

Spinach Lasagna

Serves 10

✓ **WHY THIS RECIPE WORKS:** Nutty whole-wheat lasagna noodles boost the flavor and bump up the healthy quotient in this spinach lasagna recipe. In place of a tomato-based sauce, we preferred a béchamel, a simple white sauce made with flour and butter (also known as a roux) and milk. Low-fat milk kept the béchamel lean but creamy, and swapping the butter for a small amount of olive oil further lightened it while delivering plenty of richness. For the cheesy layer, nonfat ricotta imparted a grainy texture, but fat-free cottage cheese, pulsed in a food processor until smooth, made a great substitute, with both its creamy, rich texture and great, tangy flavor. Part-skim mozzarella offered plenty of flavor and was better for the waistline than the full-fat version. To thicken our low-fat cheese mixture, we turned to ground-up crackers, which bound our mixture together perfectly without adding extra fat or noticeable flavor. You'll need a 16-ounce container of fat-free cottage cheese; do not use whipped cottage cheese. If the cottage cheese appears watery, drain it through a fine-mesh strainer for 15 minutes before using. For the nutritional information for this recipe, see page 306.

10	saltines, broken into pieces
1	pound (2 cups) fat-free cottage cheese, drained if necessary
10	ounces part-skim mozzarella cheese, shredded (2½ cups)
2	ounces Parmesan cheese, grated (1 cup)
	Salt and pepper
2	tablespoons olive oil
1	onion, chopped fine
8	garlic cloves, minced
¼	cup all-purpose flour
5	cups 1 percent low-fat milk
2	bay leaves
½	teaspoon ground nutmeg
30	ounces frozen spinach, thawed, squeezed dry (see page 89), and chopped coarse
16	whole-wheat lasagna noodles

1. Adjust oven rack to middle position and heat oven to 375 degrees. Grease 13 by 9-inch baking dish with vegetable oil spray. Pulse crackers in food processor until finely ground. Add cottage cheese, 1½ cups mozzarella, ½ cup Parmesan, ½ teaspoon salt, and ½ teaspoon pepper and process until smooth. Transfer to bowl, cover, and refrigerate until needed.

2. Heat oil in large saucepan over medium heat until shimmering. Add onion and cook until softened, about 5 minutes. Stir in garlic and cook until fragrant, about 30 seconds. Stir in flour and cook for 1 minute. Slowly whisk in milk and add bay leaves. Bring to simmer and cook, stirring occasionally, until slightly thickened, about 10 minutes.

3. Off heat, remove bay leaves; whisk in nutmeg and remaining Parmesan. Stir in spinach, breaking up any clumps, until well combined. Season with salt and pepper to taste; cover until needed.

4. Meanwhile, bring 6 quarts water to boil in large pot. Stir in pasta and 1 tablespoon salt and cook, stirring often, until nearly al dente. Drain and rinse pasta under cold water until cool. Lay pasta out over clean kitchen towels.

5. Spread 1 cup spinach sauce into prepared baking dish. Place 4 noodles into dish, spread ¼ cup cottage cheese mixture over each noodle, and top with 1 cup sauce; repeat layering two more times. Lay remaining 4 noodles into dish, and top with remaining sauce and remaining mozzarella.

6. Cover dish tightly with aluminum foil that has been sprayed with vegetable oil spray. Place lasagna on foil-lined rimmed baking sheet and bake until bubbling, 40 to 45 minutes. Remove foil and continue to bake until cheese is melted and beginning to brown, about 20 minutes. Let cool for 10 to 15 minutes and serve.

GARLICKY TORTELLINI WITH SHRIMP AND ARUGULA

Ravioli, Tortellini, and Gnocchi

Ravioli with Creamy Tomato Sauce

Serves 4

✔ **WHY THIS RECIPE WORKS:** Store-bought ravioli and jarred pasta sauce sure make for a dinner that's easy. But flavorful? We'd have to say no. For a weeknight supper that's both, we kept the store-bought ravioli, but made our own quick tomato sauce using diced tomatoes. Chicken broth provided savory flavor, and a bit of heavy cream added richness. Cooking the pasta right in the sauce helped to thicken it in record time (the liquid reduces as the pasta cooks, and the pasta releases its starch into the sauce). Chopped basil completed this dish with its freshness and bright, herbal flavor. This recipe works with two 9-ounce packages or one 20-ounce package of fresh cheese ravioli. Do not substitute frozen ravioli. If necessary, add hot water, 1 tablespoon at a time, to adjust the consistency of the sauce before serving.

3	tablespoons unsalted butter
1	onion, chopped fine
3	garlic cloves, minced
2	cups low-sodium chicken broth
1	(14.5-ounce) can diced tomatoes
⅓	cup heavy cream
18–20	ounces fresh cheese ravioli
1	ounce Parmesan cheese, grated (½ cup)
¼	cup chopped fresh basil
	Salt and pepper

1. Melt butter in Dutch oven over medium heat. Add onion and cook until softened and golden brown, 10 to 12 minutes.

2. Stir in garlic and cook until fragrant, about 30 seconds. Stir in broth, tomatoes, cream, and ravioli. Increase heat to medium-high and cook at vigorous simmer, stirring often, until ravioli is tender and sauce is thickened, 6 to 9 minutes.

3. Off heat, stir in Parmesan and basil. Season with salt and pepper to taste and serve.

SMART SHOPPING RAVIOLI

For an easier, more practical alternative to homemade ravioli, we looked for a supermarket brand that would pass muster with our discriminating tasters. We sampled five brands—four frozen and one refrigerated—cooked and tossed with neutral-tasting plain olive oil, looking for ravioli with a flavorful, cheesy filling. The best ravioli had the most filling per pasta square or round (at least a gram of filling for every 2 grams of pasta), and its filling tasted really cheesy, with the favored brands including Parmesan or Romano cheese along with the usual ricotta. The better samples also used a light hand when it came to spices, herbs, and additional fillers (like cracker meal), but were more generous with the salt (though brands with too much salt were downgraded). Overall, our favorite was a frozen brand, **Rosetto Cheese Ravioli**, which boasted a

"creamy, plush, rich" blend of ricotta, Romano, and Parmesan that provided "a burst of creamy cheese" in every bite. As for fresh ravioli, which are essential for recipes where the pasta cooks in the sauce, tasters praised **Buitoni Four Cheese Ravioli** for its "nutty cheese flavor" that came from a blend of mozzarella, Parmesan, and ricotta, and for "great" pasta texture that offered "good bite."

Ravioli with Meat Sauce

Serves 4

✔ **WHY THIS RECIPE WORKS:** For an effortless take on the classic duo of cheese ravioli and meat sauce, we cooked fresh ravioli in a quick sauce that we enhanced with a couple of key ingredients. Instead of using ground beef, we turned to meatloaf mix, which is a combination of ground beef, pork, and veal; it didn't need a long simmering time before it was both tender and flavorful. To further bump up the flavor of our sauce, we called upon a powerhouse ingredient, dried porcini mushrooms, for savory depth. For the tomatoes, we liked the canned, crushed variety—they thickened to the perfect consistency. Because we cooked the ravioli right in the sauce, it absorbed the rich, meaty flavors as it simmered—and there's just one pot to clean. This recipe works with two 9-ounce packages or one 20-ounce package of fresh cheese ravioli. Do not substitute frozen ravioli. If necessary, add hot water, 1 tablespoon at a time, to adjust the consistency of the sauce before serving.

2	tablespoons olive oil
1	onion, chopped fine
3	garlic cloves, minced
⅛	ounce dried porcini mushrooms, rinsed and minced
1	pound meatloaf mix
1	(28-ounce) can crushed tomatoes
	Salt and pepper
1½	cups water
18–20	ounces fresh cheese ravioli
¼	cup chopped fresh basil
	Grated Parmesan cheese

1. Heat oil in Dutch oven over medium heat until shimmering. Add onion and cook until softened and lightly browned, 8 to 10 minutes. Stir in garlic and porcini and cook until fragrant, about 1 minute.

2. Stir in meatloaf mix, breaking up meat with wooden spoon, and cook for 1 minute. Stir in tomatoes, ¼ teaspoon salt, and ¼ teaspoon pepper and simmer until sauce is slightly thickened, 8 to 10 minutes.

3. Stir in water and ravioli. Increase heat to medium-high and cook at vigorous simmer, stirring often, until ravioli is tender and sauce is thickened, 6 to 9 minutes. Off heat, stir in basil and season with salt and pepper to taste. Serve with Parmesan.

ON THE SIDE ARUGULA AND FENNEL SALAD WITH SHAVED PARMESAN
Whisk 1 tablespoon lemon juice, 1 small minced shallot, ½ teaspoon Dijon mustard, ½ teaspoon minced fresh thyme, 1 small minced garlic clove, ⅛ teaspoon salt, and pinch pepper together in large bowl. Add 1 thinly sliced fennel bulb and 6 ounces (6 cups) baby arugula; toss to combine. Garnish with Parmesan shavings and serve. Serves 4.

Ravioli with Squash and Pancetta

Serves 4

✔ **WHY THIS RECIPE WORKS:** Homemade butternut squash ravioli is more effort than we care to expend on an average weeknight, so we decided to put a new spin on this bistro classic by tossing store-bought cheese ravioli with tender bites of squash. We started by sautéing some pancetta and using the rendered fat to cook the squash. A little butter and sugar brought out the squash's sweet, nutty notes. Chicken broth alone proved too overpowering for the sauce, so we combined it with water; thyme and nutmeg rounded out the flavors of the dish. Just before serving, we stirred in the crisped pancetta, a pile of grated Parmesan, and a spritz of lemon juice. Chopped walnuts, sprinkled over individual servings, offered even more crunch and textural interest to the pillowy ravioli, tender squash, and velvety sauce. This recipe works with two 9-ounce packages or one 20-ounce package of fresh cheese ravioli. Do not substitute frozen ravioli. If necessary, add hot water, 1 tablespoon at a time, to adjust the consistency of the sauce before serving.

1	tablespoon unsalted butter
4	ounces pancetta, cut into ¼-inch pieces
2	pounds butternut squash, peeled, seeded, and cut into ¾-inch pieces (6 cups)
1	shallot, minced
1	teaspoon minced fresh thyme
1	teaspoon sugar
¼	teaspoon ground nutmeg
	Salt and pepper
2	cups low-sodium chicken broth
1½	cups water
18–20	ounces fresh cheese ravioli
¼	cup grated Parmesan cheese, plus extra for serving
1	tablespoon lemon juice
¼	cup walnuts, toasted and chopped (optional)

1. Cook butter and pancetta in Dutch oven over medium heat until pancetta is well browned and crisp, about 8 minutes. Using slotted spoon, transfer pancetta to paper towel–lined plate.

2. Add squash to fat left in pan, spread into even layer, and cook over medium-high heat, without stirring, until golden brown on first side, 5 to 7 minutes. Stir squash and continue to cook, stirring occasionally, until spotty brown, about 3 minutes.

3. Stir in shallot, thyme, sugar, nutmeg, and ½ teaspoon pepper and cook until shallot is softened, about 2 minutes. Stir in broth, water, and ravioli, bring to vigorous simmer, and cook, stirring often, until squash and ravioli are tender and sauce is thickened, 6 to 9 minutes.

4. Off heat, gently stir in Parmesan, lemon juice, and crisped pancetta. Season with salt and pepper to taste. Before serving, sprinkle individual portions with extra Parmesan and walnuts, if using.

SMART SHOPPING BUTTERNUT SQUASH
It certainly saves prep time to buy precut, peeled butternut squash, but how does the flavor and texture of this timesaving squash stand up to a whole squash you cut up yourself? The test kitchen has found that whole squash that you peel and cube yourself can't be beat in terms of flavor or texture, but when you are trying to make the most of every minute, the peeled, halved squash is perfectly acceptable. Avoid the precut chunks; test kitchen tasters agree they are dry and stringy, with barely any squash flavor.

Baked Ravioli with Sausage

Serves 4

✔ **WHY THIS RECIPE WORKS:** For a lasagna-like casserole that's also a snap to prepare, we started with store-bought ravioli. Italian sausage, sautéed in a skillet, gave our speedy sauce deep flavor. Cooking a spoonful of tomato paste with the sausage provided further depth, and a can of crushed tomatoes made for a smooth sauce with real clinginess. A small amount of heavy cream provided some underlying richness. Tossing the cooked ravioli in the sauce, then pouring the mixture into a baking dish and sprinkling it with mozzarella, made for a casserole that practically assembled itself. After five minutes in the oven, the cheese had melted into a perfect, lightly browned, gooey layer. This recipe calls for frozen ravioli, but you can substitute two 9-ounce packages or one 20-ounce package of fresh cheese ravioli.

25 ounces frozen cheese ravioli
Salt and pepper
1 pound sweet or hot Italian sausage, casings removed
3 garlic cloves, minced
1 tablespoon tomato paste
1 (28-ounce) can crushed tomatoes
¼ cup heavy cream
3 tablespoons chopped fresh basil
Salt and pepper
4 ounces mozzarella cheese, shredded (1 cup)

1. Adjust oven rack to middle position and heat oven to 475 degrees. Bring 4 quarts water to boil in large pot. Add ravioli and 1 tablespoon salt and cook, stirring often, until tender. Drain ravioli and return it to pot.

2. Meanwhile, cook sausage in 12-inch nonstick skillet over medium-high heat, breaking meat up with wooden spoon, until no longer pink, about 5 minutes. Stir in garlic and tomato paste and cook until fragrant, about 1 minute. Stir in tomatoes and cook until slightly thickened, 5 to 7 minutes. Off heat, stir in cream and basil.

3. Stir sauce into ravioli and season with salt and pepper to taste. Spread mixture into 13 by 9-inch baking dish and sprinkle evenly with mozzarella. Bake until cheese is melted and lightly browned, about 5 minutes. Let cool slightly and serve.

ON THE SIDE ARUGULA SALAD WITH BALSAMIC-MUSTARD VINAIGRETTE
Whisk 2 tablespoons balsamic vinegar, 1½ teaspoons Dijon mustard, ½ teaspoon finely minced shallot, ⅛ teaspoon salt, and pinch pepper together in large bowl. Whisking constantly, drizzle in 2 tablespoons extra-virgin olive oil. Add 6 ounces (6 cups) baby arugula and toss to combine. Serves 4.

Baked Ravioli with Fennel, Olives, and Feta

Serves 4

✔ **WHY THIS RECIPE WORKS:** Hot on the heels of our Baked Ravioli with Sausage (page 120), we looked to create a vegetable-rich ravioli casserole that was every bit as easy and satisfying. Inspired by the bright flavors of Mediterranean cuisine, we built a sauce with crushed tomatoes, anise-scented fennel, and briny kalamatas. Heavy cream brought richness, while crumbled feta contributed a salty, creamy tang. For a fresh note, we stirred in a bit of chopped basil. Drizzling a spoonful of olive oil over the assembled casserole further enriched our vegetarian ravioli bake. This recipe calls for frozen ravioli, but you can substitute two 9-ounce packages or one 20-ounce package of fresh cheese ravioli.

25	ounces frozen cheese ravioli
	Salt and pepper
3	tablespoons olive oil
1	fennel bulb, stalks discarded, bulb halved, cored, and sliced thin (see page 248)
3	garlic cloves, minced
1	(28-ounce) can crushed tomatoes
½	cup pitted kalamata olives, chopped coarse
¼	cup heavy cream
3	tablespoons chopped fresh basil
4	ounces feta cheese, crumbled (1 cup)

1. Adjust oven rack to middle position and heat oven to 475 degrees. Bring 4 quarts water to boil in large pot. Add ravioli and 1 tablespoon salt and cook, stirring often, until tender. Drain ravioli and return it to pot.

2. Meanwhile, heat 2 tablespoons oil in 12-inch nonstick skillet over medium-high heat until shimmering. Add fennel and ¼ teaspoon salt and cook until lightly browned, about 6 minutes. Stir in garlic and cook until fragrant, about 30 seconds. Stir in tomatoes and cook until slightly thickened, 5 to 7 minutes. Off heat, stir in olives, cream, and basil.

3. Stir sauce into ravioli and season with salt and pepper to taste. Spread mixture into 13 by 9-inch baking dish, sprinkle evenly with feta, and drizzle with remaining 1 tablespoon oil. Bake until cheese is melted and lightly browned, about 5 minutes. Let cool slightly and serve.

SMART SHOPPING KALAMATA OLIVES
Although kalamata olives are often packed in olive oil in their native Greece, on American soil we almost always find them swimming in a vinegary brine. We prefer the fresher kalamatas from the refrigerated section of the supermarket (also packed in brine), as the jarred, shelf-stable ones are bland and mushy in comparison. If you can't find kalamatas in the refrigerated section of your market, look for them at the salad bar.

Creamy Baked Tortellini with Radicchio, Peas, and Bacon

Serves 6 to 8

✓ **WHY THIS RECIPE WORKS:** For a restaurant-worthy take on baked tortellini, we turned to slightly bitter radicchio and sweet peas—both of which could be simply tossed in with our cooked tortellini and sauce. A combination of chicken broth, heavy cream, and white wine, thickened with a bit of flour, produced a rich, savory sauce that was balanced in flavor and neither too rich nor too lean. Cooking a few slices of bacon, then using the rendered fat to sauté our aromatics, provided a flavorful backbone and added meaty depth to the sauce. Before baking, we sprinkled our casserole with a topping of buttery bread crumbs and walnuts for a crunchy finish. You can substitute three 9-ounce packages of fresh cheese tortellini for the dried tortellini; increase the chicken broth to 2 cups and omit the water in step 4.

½	**cup walnuts**
4	**slices hearty white sandwich bread, torn into quarters**
2	**tablespoons unsalted butter, melted**
1	**pound dried cheese tortellini**
	Salt and pepper
1	**tablespoon olive oil**
4	**slices bacon, chopped fine**
1	**onion, chopped fine**
6	**garlic cloves, minced**
2	**teaspoons minced fresh thyme**
¼	**cup all-purpose flour**
1	**cup dry white wine**
1	**cup low-sodium chicken broth**
1	**cup water**
1	**cup heavy cream**
2	**ounces Parmesan cheese, grated (1 cup)**
1	**medium head radicchio (10 ounces), cored and chopped medium**
1	**cup frozen peas**

1. Adjust oven rack to middle position and heat oven to 400 degrees. Process walnuts in food processor until coarsely chopped, about 5 seconds. Add bread and melted butter and continue to process to create uniformly coarse crumbs, about 6 pulses.

2. Bring 6 quarts water to boil in Dutch oven over high heat. Add tortellini and 1½ tablespoons salt and cook, stirring often, until tender. Drain tortellini, then transfer to large bowl and toss with oil. Cover to keep warm; set aside.

3. Wipe now-empty pot dry, add bacon, and cook over medium heat until brown and crisp, about 5 minutes. Stir in onion and cook until softened, 5 to 7 minutes. Stir in garlic and thyme and cook until fragrant, about 30 seconds. Stir in flour and cook for 1 minute.

4. Slowly whisk in wine, scraping up any browned bits, and cook until nearly evaporated, about 1 minute. Gradually whisk in broth, water, and cream, smoothing out any lumps, and bring to simmer.

5. Off heat, stir in Parmesan and season with salt and pepper to taste. Stir in tortellini, radicchio, and peas. Pour into 13 by 9-inch baking dish and sprinkle with processed walnut mixture. Bake until topping is brown and crisp, about 15 minutes. Let cool slightly and serve.

SMART SHOPPING WHITE WINE FOR COOKING
When a recipe calls for dry white wine, it's tempting to grab whatever open bottle is in the fridge. Chardonnay and Pinot Grigio may taste different straight from the glass, but how much do those distinctive flavor profiles really come through in a cooked dish? To find out, we tried four varietals and a supermarket "cooking wine" in five different recipes. Only Sauvignon Blanc consistently boiled down to a "clean" yet sufficiently acidic flavor that played nicely with the rest of the ingredients. Vermouth can be an acceptable substitute in certain recipes, but because its flavor is stronger, we don't recommend using vermouth unless it is listed as an option in the recipe. Never buy supermarket "cooking wine," which has a significant amount of added sodium and an unappealing vinegary flavor.

Garlicky Tortellini with Shrimp and Arugula

Serves 4

✔ **WHY THIS RECIPE WORKS:** With the bold but simple flavors of shrimp scampi in mind, we created a dish that combines tortellini with tender shrimp and a garlicky, lemony sauce. Best of all, everything—sauce, pasta, and shrimp—is cooked in a single pot. For intense but balanced garlic flavor, we cooked a generous nine cloves of garlic with olive oil and red pepper flakes slowly over low heat, which gave our sauce a deep, garlicky flavor and subtle sweetness. A paste of raw garlic and olive oil, added at the end of cooking, contributed a punch of fresh garlic flavor and heat. Though chicken broth might seem unusual here, we preferred its flavor, when combined with white wine and water, over clam juice for the sauce (the clam juice masked the subtle complexity of the shrimp). Poaching the shrimp right in the sauce was both easy and ensured a moist and tender texture. Wilted baby arugula added color and a hint of spiciness, while lemon zest, lemon juice, and parsley, stirred in at the end, contributed brightness and reinforced the traditional scampi feel. You can substitute two 9-ounce packages or one 20-ounce package of fresh cheese tortellini for the dried tortellini; increase the broth to 1½ cups and reduce the water to 1 cup. If necessary, add hot water, 1 tablespoon at a time, to adjust the consistency of the sauce before serving.

1	pound extra-large shrimp (21 to 25 per pound), peeled, deveined, and tails removed
	Salt and pepper
11	garlic cloves, peeled, 2 minced to a paste (see page 237) and 9 minced
¼	cup extra-virgin olive oil
¼	teaspoon red pepper flakes
½	cup white wine
2½	cups water
1	cup low-sodium chicken broth
12	ounces dried cheese tortellini
5	ounces (5 cups) baby arugula
2	tablespoons minced fresh parsley
½	teaspoon grated lemon zest plus 2 tablespoons juice

1. Season shrimp with salt and pepper in bowl, cover, and refrigerate until needed. In separate bowl, combine garlic paste and 2 tablespoons oil.

2. Cook remaining 2 tablespoons oil, minced garlic, and pepper flakes in Dutch oven over low heat, stirring constantly, until garlic is sticky and golden, about 4 minutes. Add wine, increase heat to medium-high, and simmer until nearly evaporated, about 2 minutes.

3. Stir in water, broth, and tortellini and cook at vigorous simmer, stirring often, until tortellini are tender and sauce is thickened, 6 to 9 minutes.

4. Gently fold in shrimp and continue to cook until shrimp are cooked through, about 3 minutes. Off heat, stir in garlic-oil mixture, arugula, parsley, lemon zest, and lemon juice. Season with salt and pepper to taste and serve.

SMART SHOPPING TORTELLINI

Handmade tortellini is a rich-tasting, albeit time-consuming, kitchen project. Store-bought tortellini makes a great runner-up, offering both good flavor and tender texture in a fraction of the time. To find the best one, we recently sampled seven supermarket brands of cheese tortellini, including two refrigerated, two dried, and three frozen. Our winner, surprisingly, was a dried brand, **Barilla Tortellini Three Cheese**. It was praised for a filling that tasters called "creamy," "pungent," and "tangy," thanks to its bold mixture of ricotta, Emmentaler, and Grana Padano cheeses. Another factor in Barilla's win was the texture of the pasta: The delicate wrapper of these petite tortellini was strong enough to contain the filling during boiling, but not overly gummy or prone to blowouts like other brands.

Tortellini with Fennel, Peas, and Spinach

Serves 4

✔ **WHY THIS RECIPE WORKS:** We wanted an elegant yet uncomplicated recipe for tender tortellini combined with a melange of spring vegetables in a luxurious (but not overly rich) sauce. Fennel, peas, and spinach proved the perfect trio of vegetables, providing sweetness, freshness, and a variety of textures. Slicing the fennel thin and browning it in butter before adding the cooking liquid (chicken broth alone worked well here) and pasta deepened its flavor immensely. Once the tortellini were tender and the sauce was nicely thickened from the released starches, we added the spinach, peas, and some cream for richness and body. Grated Parmesan also helped to thicken the sauce and contributed a nutty flavor, while a splash of lemon juice added brightness. To top it all off, we added a garnish of crisped prosciutto, which we cooked first before setting it aside—this enabled us to incorporate its rendered fat into the dish, adding another layer of flavor and balancing the sweetness of the fennel, peas, and cream. You can substitute two 9-ounce packages or one 20-ounce package of fresh cheese tortellini for the dried tortellini; increase the broth to 2¾ cups and omit the water in step 2. If necessary, add hot water, 1 tablespoon at a time, to adjust the consistency of the sauce before serving.

2	ounces thinly sliced prosciutto, cut into ¼-inch pieces
1	tablespoon unsalted butter
1	fennel bulb, stalks discarded, bulb halved, cored, and cut into ½-inch pieces (see page 248)
3	garlic cloves, minced
2	cups water
1	cup low-sodium chicken broth
12	ounces dried cheese tortellini
½	cup heavy cream
5	ounces (5 cups) baby spinach
1	cup frozen peas
1	ounce Parmesan cheese, grated (½ cup), plus extra for serving
1	tablespoon lemon juice
	Salt and pepper

1. Cook prosciutto in Dutch oven over medium heat until browned and crisp, 5 to 7 minutes. Using slotted spoon, transfer prosciutto to paper towel–lined plate.

2. Add butter to now-empty pot and melt over medium heat. Add fennel and cook until lightly browned, 6 to 9 minutes. Stir in garlic and cook until fragrant, about 30 seconds. Stir in water, broth, and tortellini. Increase heat to medium-high and cook at vigorous simmer, stirring often, until tortellini are tender and sauce is thickened, 6 to 9 minutes.

3. Reduce heat to low and stir in cream, spinach, and peas. Cook, stirring gently, until spinach is wilted and tortellini are coated in sauce, 2 to 3 minutes.

4. Off heat, stir in Parmesan and lemon juice and season with salt and pepper to taste. Serve, sprinkling individual portions with crisped prosciutto and extra Parmesan.

QUICK PREP TIP STORING BABY SPINACH

Baby spinach is sold in bags and plastic containers of various sizes. If you happen to have leftover spinach, store it either in its original bag with the open end folded over and taped shut, or in its original plastic container, as long as it has holes that allow air to pass through. These specially designed breathable bags and containers keep the spinach fresh as long as possible; if you transfer the spinach to a sealed airtight bag or container, it will spoil prematurely.

Gnocchi with Mushrooms and Cream Sauce

Serves 4

✔ **WHY THIS RECIPE WORKS:** Homemade gnocchi can be quite the laborious undertaking—so we looked to the next best thing: store-bought gnocchi. To give it a flavorful, browned exterior, we sautéed our cooked gnocchi in butter. We found the velvety texture of a cream sauce to be the best complement for our gnocchi, especially when paired with meaty cremini mushrooms. Covering the cremini until they released their liquid sped up the cooking process, and the addition of some dried porcini really amped up their meaty flavor. For aromatics, we added minced shallots, garlic, and fresh thyme. To thicken the sauce, we added a little flour, which we cooked briefly to rid it of its raw flavor. Chicken broth and a splash of white wine cut the richness of the cream while frozen peas, stirred into the sauce with the browned gnocchi, added color and a fresh, vegetal element. For optimal texture, be sure to brown the gnocchi shortly after draining them, while they are still warm. We strongly prefer the flavor and texture of vacuum-packed gnocchi found in the pasta aisle; we don't recommend substituting refrigerated or frozen gnocchi.

1	pound vacuum-packed gnocchi
	Salt and pepper
4	tablespoons unsalted butter
12	ounces cremini mushrooms, trimmed and sliced thin
2	shallots, minced
¼	ounce dried porcini mushrooms, rinsed and minced
2	garlic cloves, minced
2	teaspoons all-purpose flour
1	teaspoon minced fresh thyme
2	cups low-sodium chicken broth
½	cup heavy cream
¼	cup dry white wine
¾	cup frozen peas, thawed
2	tablespoons minced fresh parsley

1. Bring 4 quarts water to boil in large pot. Add gnocchi and 1 tablespoon salt and cook until gnocchi are just tender and floating, about 2 minutes. Drain gnocchi.

2. Melt 2 tablespoons butter in 12-inch nonstick skillet over medium-high heat. Add gnocchi and cook, stirring occasionally, until golden brown, 5 to 7 minutes; transfer to plate.

3. Melt remaining 2 tablespoons butter in now-empty skillet over medium heat. Add cremini mushrooms, shallots, and porcini, cover, and cook until cremini mushrooms have released their liquid, about 4 minutes. Uncover and continue to cook, stirring often, until cremini mushrooms are well browned, 5 to 7 minutes.

4. Stir in garlic, flour, and thyme and cook until fragrant, about 30 seconds. Stir in broth, cream, and wine and simmer until sauce has thickened slightly and reduced to 2 cups, 8 to 10 minutes.

5. Fold in gnocchi and peas and cook until gnocchi are well coated and peas are heated through, about 1 minute. Season with salt and pepper to taste, sprinkle with parsley, and serve.

QUICK PREP TIP STORING MUSHROOMS

Curious as to the best way to store mushrooms once you get them home from the market, we pitted several storing methods against each other over a five-day period to see what worked and what didn't. Among the things we tried were leaving them in their original box and covering them with plastic wrap or a damp paper towel, wrapping them in aluminum foil, storing them in a paper bag, storing them in a paper bag cut with airholes, storing them in an airtight zipper-lock bag, and simply leaving them uncovered. The winners turned out to be either the original packaging (if purchased in a tray wrapped in plastic), or in a simple paper bag (if purchased loose). The other methods were flat-out losers, and turned the mushrooms either slimy or dried-out in just a couple days.

Tomato-Basil Gnocchi Gratin

Serves 4

✓ **WHY THIS RECIPE WORKS:** We wanted to turn our store-bought gnocchi into a satisfying dinner with ultra-cheesy appeal and from-scratch flavor—all in under a half-hour. While we waited for the water to boil to cook the gnocchi, we made a simple tomato sauce in a skillet. For deep flavor, we sautéed a chopped onion until it was nearly caramelized, then added garlic and a can of tomato sauce. Next, we stirred in the cooked gnocchi and finished the sauce with chopped fresh basil before transferring it all to a gratin dish and sprinkling the top with mozzarella and Parmesan. After a few minutes under the broiler, a perfect golden, cheesy crust had formed—and our rich, deeply flavorful gnocchi dinner was on the table in about 20 minutes. We strongly prefer the flavor and texture of vacuum-packed gnocchi found in the pasta aisle; we don't recommend substituting refrigerated or frozen gnocchi.

1	**pound vacuum-packed gnocchi**
	Salt and pepper
3	**tablespoons extra-virgin olive oil**
1	**onion, chopped fine**
3	**garlic cloves, minced**
1	**(15-ounce) can tomato sauce**
¼	**cup chopped fresh basil**
2	**ounces mozzarella cheese, shredded (½ cup)**
1	**ounce Parmesan cheese, grated (½ cup)**

1. Adjust oven rack 6 inches from broiler element and heat broiler. Bring 4 quarts water to boil in large pot. Add gnocchi and 1 tablespoon salt and cook until gnocchi are tender and floating, about 4 minutes. Drain gnocchi.

2. Meanwhile, heat oil in 12-inch skillet over medium heat until shimmering. Add onion and pinch salt and cook until well browned, about 15 minutes. Stir in garlic and cook until fragrant, about 1 minute. Stir in tomato sauce and bring to simmer. Stir in gnocchi and simmer until gnocchi are heated through, about 1 minute. Stir in basil and season with salt and pepper to taste.

3. Transfer to 3-quart broiler-safe baking dish and sprinkle with mozzarella and Parmesan. Broil until cheese is well browned, 3 to 5 minutes. Let cool slightly and serve.

SMART SHOPPING GNOCCHI

Without a doubt, fresh homemade gnocchi is more tender and delicately flavorful than any store-bought option, but there isn't always time to make your own. When time is short, should you reach for vacuum-packed, shelf-stable gnocchi, which can be ready in less than five minutes? We recently tasted four nationally available brands, sampling them plain, then sautéed in brown butter, and finally in our Tomato-Basil Gnocchi Gratin. Plain and in the brown butter, all of the gnocchi had a distinct acidic "sourdough" flavor due to preservatives that help keep the product shelf-stable. However, when covered in tomato sauce and cheese in the gratin, this flavor was less noticeable in three brands, and disappeared altogether in our winner, **Gia Russa Gnocchi with Potato**. This gnocchi was praised for having the best flavor and texture of the bunch. Tasters described it as having a "nice potato flavor and tender pillow-y texture."

Gnocchi, Cauliflower, and Gorgonzola Gratin

Serves 4

WHY THIS RECIPE WORKS: For a more sophisticated take on our Tomato-Basil Gnocchi Gratin (page 128), we reached for pungent blue cheese and nutty, sweet cauliflower. Gorgonzola had just the right boldness for the job, while the cauliflower provided the perfect contrast in texture. Cutting the cauliflower into florets ensured that our dish was fork-friendly, and browning it before building the sauce jump-started its cooking. Instead of reserving the cheese for the topping, we added it to the sauce, and used bread crumbs for the crust. A combination of chicken broth and heavy cream gave us a velvety sauce that wasn't overly rich. Fresh thyme and sherry added depth, while a little cornstarch gave the sauce body without adding any cooking time. For a bright note to offset the rich flavors, we added baby spinach; stirring it in at the end preserved its green hue and fresh texture. We strongly prefer the flavor and texture of vacuum-packed gnocchi found in the pasta aisle; we don't recommend substituting refrigerated or frozen gnocchi.

4	tablespoons unsalted butter
2	slices hearty white sandwich bread, torn into large pieces
	Salt and pepper
1	pound vacuum-packed gnocchi
½	large head cauliflower (1½ pounds), cored and cut into 1-inch florets
1½	cups low-sodium chicken broth
2	ounces Gorgonzola cheese, crumbled (½ cup)
4	teaspoons dry sherry
1	tablespoon minced fresh thyme
½	cup heavy cream
1	tablespoon cornstarch
2	ounces (2 cups) baby spinach

1. Adjust oven rack 6 inches from broiler element and heat broiler. Melt 2 tablespoons butter in bowl in microwave. Pulse bread, melted butter, ¼ teaspoon salt, and ⅛ teaspoon pepper in food processor to form coarse crumbs, about 6 pulses. Set aside.

2. Bring 4 quarts water to boil in large pot. Add gnocchi and 1 tablespoon salt and cook until gnocchi are tender and floating, about 4 minutes. Drain gnocchi.

3. Meanwhile, melt remaining 2 tablespoons butter in 12-inch skillet over medium-high heat. Add cauliflower and cook until lightly browned, about 7 minutes. Stir in broth, Gorgonzola, sherry, and thyme. Whisk cream and cornstarch together, then stir into skillet and simmer until cheese is melted and sauce is thickened, about 5 minutes. Stir in gnocchi and simmer until gnocchi are heated through, about 1 minute. Stir in spinach and season with salt and pepper to taste.

4. Transfer mixture to 3-quart broiler-safe baking dish. Sprinkle bread crumbs evenly over top and broil until they are lightly browned, 3 to 5 minutes. Let cool slightly and serve.

SMART SHOPPING GORGONZOLA

Gorgonzola is a veined Italian cow's-milk blue cheese produced in the regions of Piedmont and Lombardy. There are two types: Gorgonzola naturale, a crumbly, firm, and salty blue cheese, and Gorgonzola dolce, a soft, creamy, milder blue cheese. Either version will work here. Tubs of precrumbled Gorgonzola, however, often taste dry and are of poor quality, so try to avoid them.

Homemade Ricotta Gnocchi with Browned Butter and Sage

Serves 4

✔ **WHY THIS RECIPE WORKS:** Not only are ricotta gnocchi lighter in texture and more delicate in flavor, making them from scratch is relatively easy compared to making potato gnocchi. And while you might not want to tackle them on a weeknight, they're not difficult to make. We started by draining ricotta cheese in coffee filters to help ensure light, not heavy, gnocchi. To further ensure delicate gnocchi, we relied on both bread crumbs and flour in the dough. We also let the dough chill slightly before cutting it into small pillows. Simmering, not boiling, the dumplings was essential to preventing them from breaking apart during cooking. A simple browned butter and sage sauce made the perfect complement to our featherlight, delicate ricotta gnocchi. The trays of uncooked gnocchi can be wrapped with plastic wrap and refrigerated for up to 24 hours.

GNOCCHI

- 1 **pound (2 cups) whole-milk ricotta cheese**
- 2 **slices hearty white sandwich bread, crusts removed, torn into quarters**
- 1 **ounce Parmesan cheese, grated (½ cup)**
- 6 **tablespoons all-purpose flour, plus extra as needed**
- 1 **large egg**
- 2 **tablespoons chopped fresh basil**
- 2 **tablespoons minced fresh parsley**
  Salt and pepper

SAUCE

- 4 **tablespoons unsalted butter, cut into 4 pieces**
- 1 **small shallot, minced**
- 2 **teaspoons minced fresh sage**
- 1 **teaspoon lemon juice**
- ⅛ **teaspoon salt**

1. FOR THE GNOCCHI: Set fine-mesh strainer over bowl; line with 3 coffee filters. Place ricotta in strainer, cover, and refrigerate for 1 hour. Adjust oven rack to middle position and heat oven to 300 degrees.

2. Pulse bread in food processor to fine crumbs, about 15 pulses. Spread crumbs on rimmed baking sheet and bake, stirring often, until dry and lightly golden, about 10 minutes. Transfer to bowl, let cool, and stir in Parmesan and flour.

3. Transfer drained ricotta to now-empty food processor and pulse to fine, grainy consistency, about 8 pulses. Transfer to large bowl and stir in egg, basil, parsley, ½ teaspoon salt, and ¼ teaspoon pepper. Stir in bread-crumb mixture. Refrigerate until slightly tacky and few crumbs stick to fingers when touched, about 15 minutes. (If dough is too wet and several crumbs stick to fingers, stir in additional flour, 1 tablespoon at a time, until dough is slightly tacky.)

4. Line 2 rimmed baking sheets with parchment paper. Lightly dust baking sheets and counter with flour. Cut dough into 8 pieces and gently shape each into ¾-inch-thick rope. Cut each rope into ¾-inch lengths and transfer to prepared sheets.

5. FOR THE SAUCE: Melt butter in 12-inch skillet over medium-high heat, swirling occasionally, until butter is browned and has nutty aroma, about 1½ minutes. Off heat, stir in shallot and sage and cook until fragrant, about 1 minute. Stir in lemon juice and salt; cover to keep warm.

6. Bring 4 quarts water to gentle simmer in large pot. Add 1 tablespoon salt. Using parchment paper as sling, add half of gnocchi and simmer until firm, about 3 minutes (gnocchi will float after 1 minute). Using slotted spoon, transfer gnocchi to sauce; cover to keep warm. Simmer remaining gnocchi and transfer to sauce. Serve.

SPICY BASIL NOODLES WITH CRISPY TOFU, SNAP PEAS, AND BELL PEPPERS

Asian Noodles and Dumplings

Beef Lo Mein with Broccoli and Bell Pepper

Serves 4

✓ **WHY THIS RECIPE WORKS:** For a full-flavored, better-than-takeout beef lo mein, we started with the sauce—oyster sauce, soy sauce, hoisin sauce, toasted sesame oil, and five-spice powder infused our dish with bold, complex flavor. Marinating the meat in this mixture briefly, prior to stir-frying it, ensured well-seasoned beef. To guarantee crisp-tender broccoli, we steamed it first, then cooked it uncovered so it could brown. Our red bell pepper strips simply needed to be sautéed for a couple of minutes until they were the perfect texture. A generous amount of scallions added a sweet, grassy pungency, ginger and garlic contributed some punch, and sweet-and-spicy Asian chili-garlic sauce, stirred in at the end, completed the dish. Fresh Chinese noodles provided the perfect chewy texture, although we found that dried linguine worked well as a substitute.

3	tablespoons soy sauce
2	tablespoons oyster sauce
2	tablespoons hoisin sauce
1	tablespoon toasted sesame oil
¼	teaspoon five-spice powder
1	pound flank steak, trimmed and sliced thin across grain on bias (see page 141)
½	cup low-sodium chicken broth
1	teaspoon cornstarch
2	garlic cloves, minced
2	teaspoons grated fresh ginger
1½	tablespoons vegetable oil
12	ounces broccoli florets, cut into 1-inch pieces
⅓	cup water
1	red bell pepper, stemmed, seeded, sliced into ½-inch-wide strips, and halved crosswise
2	bunches scallions, white parts sliced thin, greens parts cut into 1-inch pieces
12	ounces fresh Chinese noodles or 8 ounces dried linguine
1	tablespoon Asian chili-garlic sauce

1. Whisk soy sauce, oyster sauce, hoisin sauce, sesame oil, and five-spice powder together in medium bowl. Measure 3 tablespoons of mixture into separate bowl and stir in beef; cover and refrigerate for at least 15 minutes or up to 1 hour. Whisk broth and cornstarch into remaining mixture. In separate small bowl, combine garlic, ginger, and ½ teaspoon vegetable oil.

2. Heat 1 teaspoon vegetable oil in 12-inch nonstick skillet over high heat until just smoking. Add half of beef in single layer and cook without stirring for 1 minute. Stir beef and continue to cook until browned, about 1 minute; transfer to bowl. Repeat with 1 teaspoon vegetable oil and remaining beef; transfer to bowl.

3. Wipe now-empty skillet clean with paper towels, add 1 teaspoon vegetable oil, and heat over high heat until just smoking. Add broccoli and cook for 30 seconds. Add water, cover, and steam until broccoli is bright green and begins to soften, about 2 minutes. Uncover and continue to cook until water has evaporated and broccoli begins to brown, about 2 minutes; transfer to bowl with beef.

4. Add remaining 1 teaspoon oil and bell pepper to now-empty skillet and cook over high heat until crisp-tender and spotty brown, about 2 minutes. Add scallions and continue to cook until wilted, 2 to 3 minutes. Clear center of skillet, add garlic-ginger mixture, and mash into pan until fragrant, about 30 seconds; stir into vegetables. Stir in cooked beef and vegetables with any accumulated juices. Stir in broth mixture and simmer until sauce has thickened, 1 to 2 minutes. Remove from heat and cover to keep warm.

5. Meanwhile, bring 4 quarts water to boil in large pot. Add noodles and cook, stirring often, until tender. Drain noodles and return them to pot. Add beef mixture and chili-garlic sauce and toss to combine. Serve.

ALL ABOUT Asian Noodles

While Italian pasta is typically made from durum wheat flour, Asian noodles can be made from a variety of grains and even rice. We use several types of Asian noodles in this chapter; here's some additional information on what they're made from and the types of dishes we use them in.

Fresh Chinese Noodles

Fresh Chinese noodles are a bit more starchy and chewy than dried noodles. Though they are made from wheat flour, their flavor is less wheaty than Italian pasta, making them an excellent match for potent, highly seasoned sauces, as in our Beef Lo Mein with Broccoli and Bell Pepper (page 134) and Spicy Sichuan Noodles (page 138). If you can't find them, you can substitute dried Italian pasta, such as linguine or spaghetti.

Rice Noodles

This delicate pasta, made from rice flour and water, is used in a variety of dishes in Southeast Asia and southern China. These noodles should be steeped in hot water to soften them; they overcook quickly, so boiling tends to make them mushy. Flat rice noodles (shown) come in several widths; we use a medium width noodle in Pad Thai with Shrimp (page 152), but like a larger noodle for our Drunken Noodles with Chicken (page 160). Round rice noodles, also called vermicelli, come in a variety of sizes, but we prefer the thinner kind (see pages 156 and 158).

Ramen Noodles

Ramen noodles were introduced to Japan by China and India in the 17th century, but the Japanese have taken ramen noodles to another level and made them distinctly their own. Ramen noodles are traditionally made from wheat flour and eggs, but for our recipes we rely on the easier-to-find instant variety, which doesn't contain eggs, and just discard the dusty seasoning packet found in the package in favor of our own sauce or broth (see our Hot and Sour Ramen with Tofu, Shiitakes, and Spinach on page 144).

Soba Noodles

Soba noodles possess a rich, nutty flavor and delicate texture. They get their unusual flavor from buckwheat flour, which contains no gluten so a binder, usually wheat, is added to give the noodles structure and hold them together during cooking. The Japanese agricultural department requires that all noodles labeled as soba contain a minimum of 30 percent buckwheat flour, and the higher the percentage of buckwheat flour, the higher the price. Soba noodles are traditionally served chilled with a dipping sauce (see our adaptation of this dish, Cold Soba Noodle Salad, on page 148), but we also like them warm and accompanied by a simple sauce (see pages 150–151).

Somen Noodles

Also popular in Japan, somen noodles are made from high-gluten wheat flour, and the dough is stretched rather than cut. They are sold only in their dry form, and many believe that their flavor improves after aging over one to two years. Somen are eaten in much the same way as soba noodles, accompanied by a dipping sauce (see our Chilled Somen Noodles with Shrimp on page 147).

Udon Noodles

Another popular Japanese noodle, udon noodles are made with all-purpose flour, water, and salt. The result is a highly elastic dough that yields thick, chewy noodles. Udon dough was originally kneaded by placing it between two towels and stepping on it. Today, machines do much of the work. Udon noodles can be purchased both fresh and dried. We think their chewy, hearty texture works especially well in ultra-rich, savory dishes, such as our Udon Noodles with Pork, Shiitakes, and Miso (page 145).

Pork Lo Mein with Shiitakes and Napa Cabbage

Serves 4

✔ **WHY THIS RECIPE WORKS:** For another satisfying lo mein, this time starring tender pork, meaty mushrooms, and still-crisp cabbage, we started by searing strips of meat from country-style pork ribs (which we like for their tenderness and rich flavor) over high heat. We used our meat marinade as a sauce base—adding chicken broth and a spoonful of cornstarch gave it some body. Shiitakes contributed rich, meaty flavor, and strips of napa cabbage added textural intrigue. Fresh Chinese noodles provided the perfect chewy texture, although we found that dried linguine worked well as a substitute.

3	tablespoons soy sauce
2	tablespoons oyster sauce
2	tablespoons hoisin sauce
1	tablespoon toasted sesame oil
¼	teaspoon five-spice powder
1	pound boneless country-style pork ribs, trimmed and sliced crosswise into ⅛-inch-thick pieces
½	cup low-sodium chicken broth
1	teaspoon cornstarch
2	garlic cloves, minced
2	teaspoons grated fresh ginger
1½	tablespoons vegetable oil
¼	cup Chinese rice wine or dry sherry
8	ounces shiitake mushrooms, stemmed and halved if small or quartered if large
2	bunches scallions, white parts sliced thin, greens parts cut into 1-inch pieces
½	small head napa cabbage, cored and sliced crosswise ½ inch thick (4 cups)
12	ounces fresh Chinese noodles or 8 ounces dried linguine
1	tablespoon Asian chili-garlic sauce

1. Whisk soy sauce, oyster sauce, hoisin sauce, sesame oil, and five-spice powder together in medium bowl. Measure 3 tablespoons of mixture into separate bowl and stir in pork; cover and refrigerate for at least 15 minutes or up to 1 hour. Whisk broth and cornstarch into remaining mixture. In separate small bowl, combine garlic, ginger, and ½ teaspoon vegetable oil.

2. Heat 1 teaspoon vegetable oil in 12-inch nonstick skillet over high heat until just smoking. Add half of pork in single layer and cook, without stirring, until beginning to brown, about 1 minute. Stir pork and continue to cook until browned, about 2 minutes. Stir in 2 tablespoons wine and cook until nearly evaporated, 30 to 60 seconds; transfer to bowl. Repeat with 1 teaspoon vegetable oil, remaining pork, and remaining 2 tablespoons wine; transfer to bowl.

3. Wipe now-empty skillet clean with paper towels, add 1 teaspoon vegetable oil, and heat over high heat until just smoking. Add mushrooms and cook until browned, 4 to 6 minutes. Stir in scallions and cook until wilted, 2 to 3 minutes; transfer to bowl with pork.

4. Add remaining 1 teaspoon vegetable oil and cabbage to now-empty skillet and cook over high heat until spotty brown, 3 to 5 minutes. Clear center of skillet, add garlic-ginger mixture, and mash into pan until fragrant, about 30 seconds; stir into cabbage. Stir in cooked pork and vegetables with any accumulated juices. Stir in broth mixture and simmer until sauce has thickened, 1 to 2 minutes. Remove from heat and cover to keep warm.

5. Meanwhile, bring 4 quarts water to boil in large pot. Add noodles and cook, stirring often, until tender. Drain noodles and return them to pot. Add pork mixture and garlic-chili sauce and toss to combine. Serve.

Spicy Sichuan Noodles

Serves 4

✔ **WHY THIS RECIPE WORKS:** Spicy Sichuan noodles, or *dan dan mian*, offer a lively mix of flavors and textures: Chinese noodles are topped with a rich, savory sauce of browned ground pork seasoned with garlic, ginger, Asian sesame paste, and chiles and finished with sliced scallions and bean sprouts. We amped up the flavor on our streamlined version from the get-go by browning the pork with rice wine, soy sauce, and white pepper. Sautéed garlic, ginger, and red pepper flakes (our stand-in for the fresh chiles) provided a potent aromatic background. Chicken broth, spiked with more soy sauce and rice vinegar, oyster sauce, and peanut butter, added a depth and richness similar to that of traditional but hard-to-find Asian sesame paste. A spoonful of toasted sesame oil and a bit of ground Sichuan peppercorns added even more complexity and heat. Dried linguine can be substituted for the fresh Chinese noodles.

8	ounces ground pork
3	tablespoons soy sauce
2	tablespoons Chinese rice wine or dry sherry
	White pepper
¼	cup smooth peanut butter
2	tablespoons oyster sauce
1	tablespoon rice vinegar
1¼	cups low-sodium chicken broth
1	tablespoon vegetable oil
6	garlic cloves, minced
1	tablespoon grated fresh ginger
¾	teaspoon red pepper flakes
1	tablespoon toasted sesame oil
1	pound fresh Chinese noodles or 12 ounces dried linguine
3	scallions, sliced thin on bias
4	ounces (2 cups) bean sprouts
1	tablespoon Sichuan peppercorns, toasted and ground (optional)

1. Toss pork, 1 tablespoon soy sauce, wine, and pinch white pepper together with fork in bowl. In separate bowl, whisk remaining 2 tablespoons soy sauce, peanut butter, oyster sauce, vinegar, and pinch white pepper together, then whisk in broth.

2. Heat vegetable oil in 12-inch skillet over high heat until just smoking. Add pork and cook, breaking meat into very fine bits, until well browned, about 5 minutes. Stir in garlic, ginger, and pepper flakes and cook until fragrant, about 1 minute. Stir in broth mixture and bring to boil, whisking often. Reduce heat to medium-low and simmer, stirring occasionally, until flavors have blended, about 3 minutes. Off heat, stir in sesame oil.

3. Meanwhile, bring 4 quarts water to boil in large pot. Add noodles and cook, stirring often, until tender. Drain noodles and divide among individual bowls. Ladle pork sauce over top and sprinkle with scallions, bean sprouts, and ground Sichuan peppercorns, if using. Serve.

SMART SHOPPING **SICHUAN PEPPERCORNS**
Sichuan peppercorns are berries from a spiny shrub indigenous to the Sichuan province of China. Banned in the United States from 1968 until 2005 (they were thought to be potential carriers of a tree disease that could harm citrus crops), they have since been appearing more and more frequently in authentic Sichuan recipes in the States. The peppercorns have purplish-red husks and shiny black seeds. It is preferable to buy Sichuan peppercorns with the shiny black seeds removed, as it's the reddish-brown husks that are used for their aromatic, gently floral fragrance and their telltale numbing effect on the tongue.

Sesame Noodles with Shredded Chicken

Serves 4

✓ **WHY THIS RECIPE WORKS:** Our recipe for easy but authentic-tasting sesame noodles relies on everyday pantry staples to deliver the same sweet, nutty, addictive flavor. Chunky peanut butter and toasted sesame seeds, ground together in the blender, made the perfect stand-in for hard-to-find Asian sesame paste. Fresh garlic and ginger, as well as soy sauce, rice vinegar, hot sauce, and brown sugar, rounded out the sauce. After tossing our cooked Chinese noodles with the sauce, shredded chicken (which we simply broiled), sliced scallions, and grated carrot, we sprinkled on another spoonful of sesame seeds for more crunch and nutty flavor. Creamy peanut butter can be substituted for the chunky peanut butter if necessary. Dried spaghetti or linguine can be substituted for the fresh Chinese noodles.

¼   **cup chunky peanut butter**

¼   **cup sesame seeds, toasted**

2   **garlic cloves, minced**

1   **tablespoon grated fresh ginger**

5   **tablespoons soy sauce**

2   **tablespoons rice vinegar**

2   **tablespoons light brown sugar**

1   **teaspoon hot sauce**

½   **cup hot water**

4   **(6-ounce) boneless, skinless chicken breasts, trimmed Salt and pepper**

1   **pound fresh Chinese noodles or 12 ounces dried spaghetti or linguine**

2   **tablespoons toasted sesame oil**

4   **scallions, sliced thin on bias**

1   **carrot, peeled and grated**

1. Process peanut butter, 3 tablespoons sesame seeds, garlic, ginger, soy sauce, vinegar, sugar, and hot sauce in blender until smooth, about 30 seconds. With blender running, add hot water, 1 tablespoon at a time, until sauce has consistency of heavy cream (you may not need all of water).

2. Adjust oven rack 6 inches from broiler element and heat broiler. Spray broiler pan top with vegetable oil spray. Pat chicken dry with paper towels, season with salt and pepper, and lay on prepared pan. Broil chicken until lightly browned and it registers 160 degrees, 10 to 15 minutes, flipping chicken halfway through broiling. Transfer chicken to cutting board, let cool slightly, then shred into bite-size pieces.

3. Meanwhile, bring 4 quarts water to boil in large pot. Add noodles and cook, stirring often, until tender. Drain noodles, rinse with cold water, and drain again, leaving noodles slightly wet. Transfer to large bowl and toss with sesame oil. Add shredded chicken, scallions, carrot, and sauce and toss to combine. Sprinkle individual portions with remaining 1 tablespoon sesame seeds and serve.

SMART SHOPPING SESAME OIL
Raw sesame oil, which is very mild and light in color, is used mostly for cooking, while toasted sesame oil, which has a deep amber color, is primarily used for seasoning because of its intense, nutty flavor. For the biggest hit of sesame flavor, we prefer to use toasted sesame oil. Just a few drops will give dishes a deep, rich flavor. Sesame oil stored at room temperature will turn rancid if not used within a few months. Refrigeration will extend its shelf life.

Ramen with Beef, Shiitakes, and Spinach

Serves 4

✔ **WHY THIS RECIPE WORKS:** In Japan, ramen shops line the streets, offering piping-hot bowls of noodles paired with meat and vegetables for a rich, hearty pick-me-up any time of day. For our own flavorful take on this Japanese staple, we started with instant ramen noodles but ditched the uber-salty seasoning packet in favor of building our own sauce. After stir-frying flank steak strips, which we'd marinated in soy sauce, and shiitake mushrooms, we added garlic, ginger, and chicken broth to the pan. Next, we stirred in the ramen and simmered it just until tender and the sauce was nicely thickened. Soy sauce, rice wine, and a bit of sugar added savory, sweet flavor to the velvety sauce, and spinach, stirred in at the end, added freshness and color. Freezing the beef for 15 minutes before slicing makes it easier to slice thin. Do not substitute other types of noodles for the ramen noodles here. The sauce in this dish will seem a bit brothy when finished, but the liquid will be absorbed quickly by the noodles when serving.

1	pound flank steak, trimmed and sliced thin across grain on bias
8	teaspoons soy sauce
2	tablespoons vegetable oil
8	ounces shiitake mushrooms, stemmed and sliced thin
3	garlic cloves, minced
1	tablespoon grated fresh ginger
3½	cups low-sodium chicken broth
4	(3-ounce) packages ramen noodles, seasoning packets discarded
3	tablespoons Chinese rice wine or dry sherry
2	teaspoons sugar
6	ounces (6 cups) baby spinach

1. Toss beef with 2 teaspoons soy sauce in small bowl. Heat 1 tablespoon oil in 12-inch nonstick skillet over high heat until just smoking. Add beef in single layer and cook without stirring for 1 minute. Stir and continue to cook until browned, about 1 minute; transfer to bowl.

2. Wipe now-empty skillet clean with paper towels, add remaining 1 tablespoon oil, and heat over medium-high heat until shimmering. Add mushrooms and cook until browned, about 4 minutes. Stir in garlic and ginger and cook until fragrant, about 30 seconds. Stir in broth.

3. Break ramen into chunks and add to skillet. Bring to simmer and cook, tossing ramen constantly with tongs to separate, until it is just tender but there is still liquid in pan, about 2 minutes.

4. Stir in remaining 2 tablespoons soy sauce, wine, and sugar. Stir in spinach, one handful at a time, until it is wilted and sauce is thickened. Add cooked beef with any accumulated juice and heat until warmed through, about 30 seconds. Serve.

QUICK PREP TIP
SLICING FLANK STEAK THINLY
To make it easier to slice beef thinly, place it in freezer for 15 minutes. Slice partially frozen steak lengthwise, with grain, into 2-inch-wide pieces. Then, cut each piece crosswise, across grain, into very thin slices.

Ramen with Crispy Chicken and Kimchi

Serves 4

✓ **WHY THIS RECIPE WORKS:** Crispy, golden chicken is served with tender ramen simmered in a kimchi-spiked broth in this lively dish that combines elements of Japanese and Korean cuisine. To ensure deeply browned chicken thighs with ultra-crisp skin, we placed a heavy weight on top as they cooked (a Dutch oven worked well)—this guaranteed that more of the skin came in contact with the pan. Seasoning the chicken first with five-spice powder promised warm spice notes in every bite. To infuse our dish with spicy-hot flavor, we added kimchi (spicy Korean pickled vegetables) to the dish. When that wasn't enough, we added its pickling liquid, too. Minced cilantro made for a fresh finish. Look for kimchi in the refrigerated section of the market. Do not substitute other types of noodles for the ramen noodles here.

½	**teaspoon five-spice powder**
¼	**teaspoon salt**
8	**(6- to 8-ounce) bone-in, skin-on chicken thighs, trimmed**
2	**teaspoons vegetable oil**
2	**cups cabbage kimchi, drained with ⅓ cup pickling liquid reserved**
3	**garlic cloves, minced**
2	**cups low-sodium chicken broth**
1½	**cups water**
4	**(3-ounce) packages ramen noodles, seasoning packets discarded**
3	**tablespoons Chinese rice wine or dry sherry**
1	**tablespoon soy sauce**
2	**teaspoons sugar**
⅓	**cup minced fresh cilantro**

1. Combine five-spice powder and salt in bowl. Pat chicken dry with paper towels and season with spice mixture. Heat oil in 12-inch nonstick skillet over medium-high heat until just smoking. Add chicken, skin side down, and weight with heavy pot. Cook until skin is deep mahogany brown and very crisp, 15 to 20 minutes. (Chicken should be moderately brown after 10 minutes; adjust heat as necessary.)

2. Remove pot, flip chicken over, and reduce heat to medium. Continue to cook chicken, without weight, until it registers 175 degrees, about 10 minutes; transfer to plate.

3. Discard all but 1 tablespoon fat left in skillet. Add drained kimchi and garlic and cook over medium heat until fragrant, about 1 minute. Stir in broth, water, and reserved kimchi liquid. Break ramen into chunks and add to skillet. Bring to simmer and cook, tossing ramen constantly with tongs to separate, until it is just tender but there is still liquid in pan, about 2 minutes.

4. Stir in wine, soy sauce, and sugar until incorporated. Off heat, stir in cilantro. Serve with chicken.

QUICK PREP TIP
MAKING CRISPY CHICKEN
To ensure super-crisp skin on the chicken thighs, we set a heavy pot on top as they cook skin side down. After the skin has browned nicely, remove the pot, flip the chicken over, and continue to cook the second side (without the weight) until browned.

Hot and Sour Ramen with Tofu, Shiitakes, and Spinach

Serves 4

✓ **WHY THIS RECIPE WORKS:** Inspired by our Ramen with Beef, Shiitakes, and Spinach (page 141), we wanted another dish starring the same crinkly noodles but that traded the beef for tofu. We started by browning the tofu (we selected extra-firm tofu, which held up in the pan) and mushrooms, then turned to the sauce. To infuse our dish with a hot-and-sour flavor profile, we included Asian chili-garlic sauce, cider vinegar, and a bit of sugar. Vegetable broth contributed to the sweetness and vegetal notes of our ramen dish, but low-sodium chicken broth makes a fine substitute. To make the dish spicier, add extra Asian chili-garlic sauce. Do not substitute other types of noodles for the ramen noodles here. The sauce in this dish will seem a bit brothy when finished, but the liquid will be absorbed quickly by the noodles when serving. For the nutritional information for this recipe, see page 306.

14 **ounces extra-firm tofu, cut into 1-inch cubes**

8 **teaspoons soy sauce**

5 **teaspoons vegetable oil**

8 **ounces shiitake mushrooms, stemmed and sliced thin**

2 **teaspoons Asian chili-garlic sauce**

3 **garlic cloves, minced**

1 **tablespoon grated fresh ginger**

3½ **cups vegetable broth or low-sodium chicken broth**

4 **(3-ounce) packages ramen noodles, seasoning packets discarded**

3 **tablespoons cider vinegar**

2 **teaspoons sugar**

6 **ounces (6 cups) baby spinach**

1. Spread tofu over paper towel–lined baking sheet, let drain for 20 minutes, then gently press dry with paper towels. Toss tofu with 2 teaspoons soy sauce. Heat 2 teaspoons oil in 12-inch nonstick skillet over high heat until just smoking. Add tofu and cook, turning occasionally, until browned on all sides, 8 to 10 minutes; transfer to bowl.

2. Add remaining 1 tablespoon oil to now-empty skillet and heat over medium-high heat until shimmering. Add mushrooms and cook until browned, about 4 minutes. Stir in chili-garlic sauce, garlic, and ginger and cook until fragrant, about 30 seconds. Stir in broth.

3. Break ramen into chunks and add to skillet. Bring to simmer and cook, tossing ramen constantly with tongs to separate, until it is just tender but there is still liquid in pan, about 2 minutes.

4. Stir in remaining 2 tablespoons soy sauce, vinegar, and sugar. Stir in spinach, one handful at a time, until spinach is wilted and sauce is thickened. Return tofu to skillet and heat until warmed through, about 30 seconds. Serve.

SMART SHOPPING BUYING TOFU

Tofu is made from the curds of soy milk. Although freshly made tofu is common across the Pacific, in the United States tofu is typically sold in refrigerated blocks packed in water. Tofu is available in a variety of textures, including silken, soft, medium-firm, firm, and extra-firm. We prefer to use extra-firm for noodle dishes, because it holds its shape well when cooked and tossed with the pasta. Tofu is perishable and should be kept well chilled. If you want to keep an open package of tofu fresh for several days, cover the tofu with fresh water in an airtight container and store it in the refrigerator, changing the water daily. Any hint of sourness means the tofu is past its prime (we prefer to use it within a few days of opening).

Udon Noodles with Pork, Shiitakes, and Miso

Serves 4

✓ **WHY THIS RECIPE WORKS:** Udon noodles in a miso-flavored broth is a tempting noodle bar dish—the thick, chewy noodles matched with the potent miso make for an otherworldly experience. For a sweet yet savory backbone, we wanted a richly flavored pork broth—but we didn't want to spend all day making it. Browned country-style pork ribs (finely chopped in the food processor to create more flavor-releasing surface area), combined with water and store-bought chicken broth, gave us deep, savory flavor in record time. Ginger, garlic, onion, mirin, soy sauce, and, of course, miso (we prefer bolder red miso, although milder white miso can be substituted) amped up our broth quickly; adding the miso at the last minute prevented its flavor from becoming dulled over the heat. Cooking sliced shiitake mushrooms, fresh udon noodles, and more pork (thin slices of the country-style ribs) right in our strained broth infused them with flavor—and kept this easy dish contained to just one pot. Do not trim the excess fat from the ribs, as the fat contributes flavor and moistness. Do not substitute other types of noodles for the udon noodles here.

1½	pounds boneless country-style pork ribs
1	tablespoon vegetable oil
1	onion, chopped medium
6	garlic cloves, peeled and smashed
1	(1-inch) piece ginger, peeled, sliced thin, and smashed
3	cups low-sodium chicken broth
2	cups water
¼	cup red miso
8	ounces shiitake mushrooms, stemmed and sliced thin
1	pound fresh udon noodles
2	tablespoons mirin
1	tablespoon soy sauce
½	teaspoon toasted sesame oil
2	scallions, sliced thin on bias
1	tablespoon sesame seeds, toasted

1. Slice 8 ounces of pork crosswise into ⅛-inch-thick pieces; refrigerate until needed. Cut remaining 1 pound pork into 1-inch chunks, then pulse in food processor to coarsely chopped texture, 10 to 12 pulses.

2. Heat vegetable oil in Dutch oven over medium heat until shimmering. Add processed pork and cook, breaking up meat with wooden spoon, until well browned, about 10 minutes. Stir in onion, garlic, and ginger and cook until onion begins to soften, about 2 minutes. Stir in broth and water and bring to boil. Reduce to gentle simmer, cover partially (leaving about 1 inch of pot open), and cook until broth is flavorful, about 40 minutes.

3. Strain broth through fine-mesh strainer, gently pressing on solids to extract as much liquid as possible. Return strained broth to clean Dutch oven and bring to simmer. In small bowl, whisk ½ cup hot broth with miso until dissolved and smooth; set aside. Stir shiitakes into pot and simmer until nearly tender, about 2 minutes. Add noodles and cook, stirring often, until noodles and mushrooms are tender, about 3 minutes.

4. Stir in miso mixture and return to brief simmer. Stir in sliced pork, mirin, soy sauce, and sesame oil, then immediately remove pot from heat. Cover and let stand off heat until pork is cooked through, 2 to 3 minutes. Sprinkle individual portions with scallions and sesame seeds and serve.

Chilled Somen Noodles with Shrimp

Serves 4

✔ **WHY THIS RECIPE WORKS:** Served in ice water with a bowl of dipping sauce and pickled ginger, iced somen noodles are just the thing to help cool off when it's a scorcher outside. For our modern-day version, we tossed our somen with the sauce—which was much easier than dipping it in the sauce. For a rich, savory sauce, we made a simple dashi (a sweet, fishy broth) from simmered kombu (dried seaweed) and dried bonito flakes (bonito is a kind of fish). Soy sauce, mirin, and sugar helped to season it. After cooking the somen, we rinsed them in cold water to remove extra starch that would make them gummy. We tossed the somen with the sauce, then topped individual bowls with poached shrimp, sliced cucumber, pickled ginger, and fresh cilantro and scallions for an exotic, refreshing dish—no matter the weather outside. Do not substitute other types of noodles for the somen noodles here.

1½ cups water

1 (2-inch) piece kombu

¼ cup dried bonito flakes

½ cup soy sauce

¼ cup mirin

1 teaspoon sugar

1 pound medium-large shrimp (31 to 40 per pound), peeled, deveined, tails removed, and sliced in half lengthwise

12 ounces somen noodles

½ cucumber, halved lengthwise and sliced thin

¼ cup pickled ginger, chopped coarse

¼ cup fresh cilantro leaves

2 scallions, sliced thin on bias

1. Bring water and kombu to boil in large saucepan over medium-low heat. Remove from heat, stir in bonito flakes, and let sit for 3 minutes. Strain broth through fine-mesh strainer into large bowl, pressing on solids to extract as much broth as possible. Whisk in soy sauce, mirin, and sugar until sugar is dissolved. Cover and refrigerate until well chilled, about 3 hours.

2. Bring 4 quarts water to boil in large pot. Fill large bowl with ice water. Add shrimp to boiling water, remove from heat, and cover; let sit until shrimp are just cooked through, about 1 minute. Using slotted spoon, transfer shrimp to ice water and let chill; drain and pat dry with paper towels.

3. Return water to boil, add noodles, and cook, stirring often, until tender. Drain noodles, rinse with cold water, and drain again, leaving noodles slightly wet. Toss noodles with chilled broth in large bowl. Top individual portions with shrimp, cucumber, pickled ginger, cilantro, and scallions. Serve.

SMART SHOPPING KOMBU AND BONITO FLAKES
Kombu and bonito flakes give our Chilled Somen Noodles with Shrimp its authentic and distinctive flavor. You can usually find both ingredients in the international aisle at the supermarket, or at an Asian market or a natural foods market. Kombu is a type of seaweed sold in dried, whole sheets that are quite thick and often have a chalky, white powder on the exterior. Bonito flakes are dried fish flakes; they have a distinct, smoky flavor.

KOMBU   BONITO FLAKES

Cold Soba Noodle Salad

Serves 4

✔ **WHY THIS RECIPE WORKS:** Just like chilled somen, cold soba noodles are traditionally served with a dipping sauce that offers a delicate balance of Japanese flavors. For a fork-friendly take on this simple yet satisfying dish, we decided to turn the dipping sauce into a dressing. Soy sauce, mirin, and wasabi provided a flavorful base. Ginger added some heat, and thin slices of nori (dried seaweed), sprinkled over the top, offered slightly briny, grassy notes. Peppery radishes and thinly sliced scallion added freshness and crunch. To prevent the cooked soba noodles from sticking together while we prepped the dressing, we tossed them with vegetable oil. To give this salad more heat, add additional wasabi paste to taste. Nori and bonito flakes can be found in the international aisle at the supermarket, or at an Asian market or a natural foods market; bonito flakes add a distinct, smoky flavor to this dish, but they can be omitted if desired. Do not substitute other types of noodles for the soba noodles here.

14	ounces dried soba noodles
1	tablespoon salt
1	tablespoon vegetable oil
¼	cup soy sauce
3	tablespoons mirin
½	teaspoon sugar
½	teaspoon grated fresh ginger
¼	teaspoon wasabi paste or powder
4	large red radishes, trimmed and shredded
2	scallions, sliced thin on bias
1	(8 by 2½-inch) piece nori, cut into matchsticks with scissors
¼	cup dried bonito flakes (optional)

1. Bring 4 quarts water to boil in large pot. Add noodles and salt and cook, stirring often, until tender. Drain noodles, rinse with cold water, and drain again, leaving noodles slightly wet. Transfer to large bowl and toss with oil.

2. Whisk soy sauce, mirin, sugar, ginger, and wasabi together in small bowl, then pour over noodles. Add radishes and scallions and toss until well combined. Sprinkle individual portions with nori and bonito flakes, if using, and serve.

SMART SHOPPING WASABI

Hot and pungent, wasabi is commonly used as a condiment for sushi and sashimi but is also useful as an ingredient in other Japanese dishes. Fresh wasabi root (also known as Japanese horseradish) is hard to find and expensive (about $8 per ounce). More widely available is wasabi that is sold in paste or powder form (the powder is mixed with water to form a paste). Because fresh wasabi root is so expensive, most pastes and all powders contain no wasabi at all, but instead a mixture of garden-variety horseradish, mustard, and cornstarch, plus food coloring. We advise seeking out wasabi paste made from real wasabi root for its complex flavor.

Soba Noodles with Roasted Eggplant and Sesame

Serves 4

✔️ **WHY THIS RECIPE WORKS:** The creamy texture and mild flavor of cooked eggplant make the perfect foil to rich, nutty soba noodles in this recipe. Roasting proved an easy, hands-off way to cook the eggplant; tossing it with soy sauce and vegetable oil beforehand helped to season the vegetable and draw out its moisture. For the sauce, we started with more soy sauce for savory richness. Oyster sauce, sugar, Asian chili-garlic sauce, and toasted sesame oil provided a nice balance of sweet and spicy flavors, while a bit of sake contributed clean, ricelike notes that bolstered the complexity of the sauce. Vermouth can be substituted for the sake if necessary. Do not substitute other types of noodles for the soba noodles here.

¼	cup vegetable oil
2	pounds eggplant, cut into 1-inch pieces
¼	cup soy sauce
¼	cup sugar
2	tablespoons oyster sauce
1	tablespoon Asian chili-garlic sauce
2	tablespoons toasted sesame oil
4	teaspoons sake (Japanese rice wine)
8	ounces dried soba noodles
¾	cup fresh cilantro leaves
2	teaspoons sesame seeds, toasted

1. Adjust oven rack to middle position and heat oven to 450 degrees. Line large rimmed baking sheet with aluminum foil and brush with 1 tablespoon vegetable oil. Toss eggplant with remaining 3 tablespoons vegetable oil and 1 tablespoon soy sauce, then spread onto prepared baking sheet. Roast until well browned and tender, 25 to 30 minutes, stirring halfway through roasting time.

2. In small saucepan, whisk sugar, remaining 3 tablespoons soy sauce, oyster sauce, chili-garlic sauce, sesame oil, and sake together. Cook over medium heat until sugar has dissolved, about 1 minute; cover and set aside.

3. Meanwhile, bring 4 quarts water to boil in large pot. Add noodles and cook, stirring often, until tender. Reserve ½ cup cooking water, then drain noodles and return them to pot. Add sauce and roasted eggplant and toss to combine. Add reserved cooking water as needed to adjust consistency. Sprinkle individual portions with cilantro and sesame seeds and serve.

QUICK PREP TIP CUTTING UP EGGPLANT
Cutting up an awkwardly shaped vegetable— ike eggplant—can sometimes be a challenge. To cut an eggplant into tidy cubes, simply cut the eggplant crosswise into 1-inch-thick rounds, then cut the rounds into tidy 1-inch cubes.

Soba Noodles with Pork, Shiitakes, and Bok Choy

Serves 4

✔ **WHY THIS RECIPE WORKS:** Inspired by our Soba Noodles with Roasted Eggplant and Sesame (page 150), we looked to create another soba dish, this time featuring mild pork, crunchy baby bok choy, and meaty shiitake mushrooms. Vermouth can be substituted for the sake if necessary. A large head of bok choy (stems and leaves separated and sliced ½ inch thick) can be substituted for the baby bok choy; add the stems with the mushrooms and the leaves with the cooked pork. Do not substitute other types of noodles for the soba noodles here.

¼ cup soy sauce

3 tablespoons sugar

2 tablespoons oyster sauce

1 tablespoon Asian chili-garlic sauce

4 teaspoons sake (Japanese rice wine)

1 tablespoon sesame oil

1 pound boneless country-style pork ribs, trimmed and sliced crosswise into ⅛-inch-thick pieces

6 garlic cloves, minced

1 tablespoon grated fresh ginger

4 teaspoons vegetable oil

6 heads baby bok choy (4 ounces each), sliced crosswise ½ inch thick

10 ounces shiitake mushrooms, stemmed and quartered

8 ounces dried soba noodles

2 scallions, sliced thin on bias

1. Whisk soy sauce, sugar, oyster sauce, chili-garlic sauce, sake, and sesame oil together in medium bowl. Measure 3 tablespoons of mixture into separate bowl and stir in pork; cover and refrigerate for at least 15 minutes or up to 1 hour. In separate bowl, combine garlic, ginger, and 1 teaspoon vegetable oil.

2. Heat 1 teaspoon vegetable oil in 12-inch nonstick skillet over high heat until just smoking. Add half of pork in single layer and cook without stirring for 1 minute. Stir and continue to cook until browned, about 2 minutes; transfer to bowl. Repeat with 1 teaspoon vegetable oil and remaining pork; transfer to bowl.

3. Wipe now-empty skillet clean with paper towels, add remaining 1 teaspoon vegetable oil and heat over high heat until just smoking. Add bok choy and mushrooms and cook, stirring often, until vegetables are browned, 5 to 7 minutes. Clear center of skillet, add garlic-ginger mixture, and mash it into pan until fragrant, about 30 seconds; stir into vegetables. Stir in cooked pork with any accumulated juice. Stir in soy sauce mixture and simmer until sauce has thickened, about 1 minute. Remove from heat and cover to keep warm.

4. Meanwhile, bring 4 quarts water to boil in large pot. Add noodles and cook, stirring often, until tender. Reserve ½ cup cooking water, then drain noodles and return them to pot. Add pork mixture and toss to combine. Add reserved cooking water as needed to adjust consistency. Sprinkle individual portions with scallions and serve.

SMART SHOPPING OYSTER SAUCE
Oyster sauce is a rich, concentrated mixture of oyster extractives, soy sauce, brine, and assorted seasonings. The brown sauce is thick, salty, and strong. It is used sparingly to enhance the flavor of many dishes, including noodle dishes, stir-fries, and dipping sauces.

Pad Thai with Shrimp

Serves 4

✓ **WHY THIS RECIPE WORKS:** With its sweet-and-sour, salty-spicy sauce, plump, sweet shrimp, and tender rice noodles, pad thai is Thailand's most well-known noodle dish. But making it at home can be a chore, thanks to lengthy ingredient lists with hard-to-find items. We found we could achieve just the right balance of flavors in the sauce using a simple combination of fish sauce, lime juice, rice vinegar, and brown sugar. With such a flavorful base at the ready, we didn't even need to season the shrimp—we merely sautéed them in the pan until barely pink at the edges, then stirred them in later to finish cooking. To get the texture of the rice noodles just right, we first soaked them in hot water so they'd start to soften, then stir-fried them in the pan. Scrambled eggs, chopped peanuts, bean sprouts, and thinly sliced scallions completed our easy and authentic-tasting pad thai. Do not substitute other types of noodles for the rice noodles here.

8	ounces (¼-inch-wide) dried flat rice noodles
⅓	cup water
¼	cup lime juice (2 limes)
3	tablespoons fish sauce
3	tablespoons brown sugar
1	tablespoon rice vinegar
¼	cup vegetable oil
12	ounces medium shrimp (41 to 50 per pound), peeled, deveined, and tails removed
3	garlic cloves, minced
2	large eggs, lightly beaten
¼	teaspoon salt
6	tablespoons chopped unsalted roasted peanuts
6	ounces (3 cups) bean sprouts
5	scallions, sliced thin on bias
	Lime wedges
	Fresh cilantro leaves
	Sriracha sauce

1. Cover noodles with very hot tap water in large bowl and stir to separate. Let noodles soak until softened, pliable, and limp but not fully tender, about 20 minutes; drain. In separate bowl, whisk water, lime juice, fish sauce, brown sugar, rice vinegar, and 2 tablespoons oil together.

2. Pat shrimp dry with paper towels. Heat 1 tablespoon oil in 12-inch nonstick skillet over high heat until just smoking. Add shrimp in single layer and cook, without stirring, until beginning to brown, about 1 minute. Stir shrimp and continue to cook until spotty brown and just pink around edges, about 30 seconds; transfer to bowl.

3. Add remaining 1 tablespoon oil and garlic to now-empty skillet and cook over medium heat until fragrant, about 30 seconds. Stir in eggs and salt and cook, stirring vigorously until eggs are scrambled, about 20 seconds.

4. Add drained noodles and fish sauce mixture. Increase heat to high and cook, tossing gently, until noodles are evenly coated. Add cooked shrimp, ¼ cup peanuts, bean sprouts, and three-quarters of scallions. Continue to cook, tossing constantly, until noodles are tender, about 2 minutes. (If necessary, add 2 tablespoons water to skillet and continue to cook until noodles are tender.)

5. Transfer noodles to serving platter and sprinkle with remaining peanuts and remaining scallions. Serve with lime wedges, cilantro leaves, and Sriracha.

Spicy Basil Noodles with Crispy Tofu, Snap Peas, and Bell Peppers

Serves 4

✔ **WHY THIS RECIPE WORKS:** Spicy basil noodles are like a wake-up call for the sleepy palate. This brightly flavored Thai dish combines tender rice noodles with fragrant fresh basil and a spicy, aromatic sauce. We infused our dish with subtle heat by creating a paste of hot chiles, garlic, and shallots in the food processor. Cooking the mixture briefly deepened its flavor and mellowed the harshness of the raw aromatics. Fish sauce, brown sugar, lime juice, and chicken broth added sweet and savory flavors and gave our sauce a bit of body. A generous amount of basil gives this dish its trademark fresh flavor and color—we used a whopping 2 cups and stirred it in at the end to keep its freshness intact. Pan-fried tofu offered both creamy and crispy textures that paired well with the tender rice noodles, and stir-fried snap peas and red bell pepper strips added some crunch. To make this dish spicier, add the chile seeds. Do not substitute other types of noodles for the rice noodles here.

12 ounces (⅜-inch-wide) dried flat rice noodles

14 ounces extra-firm tofu, cut into 1-inch cubes

8 Thai, serrano, or jalapeño chiles, stemmed and seeded

6 garlic cloves, peeled

4 shallots, peeled

2 cups low-sodium chicken broth

¼ cup fish sauce

¼ cup brown sugar

3 tablespoons lime juice (2 limes)

½ cup cornstarch
Salt and pepper

7 tablespoons vegetable oil

6 ounces snap peas, strings removed

1 red bell pepper, stemmed, seeded, sliced into ¼-inch-wide strips, and halved crosswise

2 cups fresh Thai basil or sweet basil leaves

1. Cover noodles with very hot tap water in large bowl and stir to separate. Let noodles soak until softened, pliable, and limp but not fully tender, 35 to 40 minutes; drain. Spread tofu over paper towel–lined baking sheet, let drain for 20 minutes, then gently press dry with paper towels.

2. Pulse chiles, garlic, and shallots in food processor into smooth paste, about 30 pulses, scraping down bowl as needed. In bowl, whisk broth, fish sauce, sugar, and lime juice together.

3. Adjust oven rack to upper-middle position and heat oven to 200 degrees. Spread cornstarch into shallow dish or pie plate. Season tofu with salt and pepper, then dredge in cornstarch; transfer to plate. Heat 3 tablespoons oil in 12-inch nonstick skillet over medium-high heat until just smoking. Add tofu and cook, turning as needed, until all sides are crisp and browned, about 8 minutes; transfer to paper towel–lined plate and keep warm in oven.

4. Wipe now-empty skillet clean with paper towels, add 1 tablespoon oil, and heat over high heat until just smoking. Add snap peas and bell pepper and cook, stirring often, until vegetables are crisp-tender and beginning to brown, 3 to 5 minutes; transfer to bowl.

5. Add remaining 3 tablespoons oil to now-empty skillet and heat over medium-high heat until shimmering. Add processed chile mixture and cook until moisture evaporates and color deepens, 3 to 5 minutes. Add drained noodles and broth mixture and cook, tossing gently, until sauce has thickened and noodles are well coated and tender, 5 to 10 minutes.

6. Stir in cooked vegetables and basil and cook until basil wilts slightly, about 1 minute. Top individual portions with crispy tofu and serve.

Singapore Noodles with Shrimp

Serves 4

✔ **WHY THIS RECIPE WORKS:** This dish is Asian comfort food at its best: a big bowl of tender, moist noodles swathed in a savory sauce laced with fragrant curry. Thin rice noodles and curry powder are the defining elements, so we got these in order first. To prepare the noodles for stir-frying, we found it best to soak them in hot water, which worked to soften them enough for the pan; if we boiled them, they stuck together and turned gummy. As for the curry powder, a single tablespoon was enough to permeate our entire dish with its sweet and pungent flavor. Most versions of Singapore noodles include a protein; we rounded out our dish with tender, briny shrimp. Tossing them with a bit of the curry and some sugar ensured that they had great flavor and browned nicely in the hot skillet. Once they had browned, we set them aside and built our sauce in the same pan, then added back the noodles and shrimp to finish cooking. With minced cilantro for clean, citrusy notes and bean sprouts for crunch, this colorful dish is just as eye-catching as it is delicious. Do not substitute other types of noodles for the rice vermicelli here.

8	ounces dried rice vermicelli
1	pound extra-large shrimp (21 to 25 per pound), peeled, deveined, and tails removed
1	tablespoon curry powder
⅛	teaspoon sugar
8	teaspoons vegetable oil
6	shallots, sliced thin
2	red bell peppers, stemmed, seeded, and sliced into ¼-inch-wide strips
2	garlic cloves, minced
1	cup low-sodium chicken broth
⅓	cup soy sauce
1	tablespoon mirin
1	teaspoon Sriracha sauce
4	ounces (2 cups) bean sprouts
½	cup minced fresh cilantro

1. Cover noodles with very hot tap water in large bowl and stir to separate. Let noodles soak until softened, pliable, and limp but not fully tender, about 20 minutes; drain.

2. Meanwhile, pat shrimp dry with paper towels and toss with ½ teaspoon curry powder and sugar. Heat 4 teaspoons oil in 12-inch nonstick skillet over high heat until just smoking. Add shrimp in single layer and cook, without stirring, until beginning to brown, about 1 minute. Stir shrimp and continue to cook until spotty brown and just pink around edges, about 30 seconds; transfer to bowl.

3. Add remaining 4 teaspoons oil to now-empty skillet and heat over medium heat until shimmering. Add shallots, bell peppers, and remaining 2½ teaspoons curry powder and cook until vegetables are softened, 3 to 5 minutes. Stir in garlic and cook until fragrant, about 30 seconds.

4. Stir in drained noodles, shrimp with any accumulated juice, broth, soy sauce, mirin, and Sriracha and cook, tossing gently, until noodles are well coated, 2 to 3 minutes. Stir in bean sprouts and cilantro and serve.

SMART SHOPPING ASIAN CHILI SAUCES
Used both in cooking and as a condiment, these sauces come in a variety of styles. Sriracha (left) contains garlic and is made from chiles that are ground into a smooth paste. Chili-garlic sauce (middle) also contains garlic and is similar to Sriracha except that the chiles are coarsely ground. Sambal oelek (right) differs in that it is made purely from ground chiles without the addition of garlic or other spices, thus adding heat but not additional flavor. Once opened, these sauces will keep for several months in the refrigerator.

Coconut Rice Noodles with Shrimp and Pineapple

Serves 4

✔ **WHY THIS RECIPE WORKS:** We paired sweet, tropical coconut with bright, grassy green curry in this exotic yet easy Thai-influenced noodle dish. Making curry from scratch takes time and requires a laundry list of ingredients, so we reached for store-bought curry paste. To amp up its one-note flavor, we supplemented it with fresh chiles. Sweet, briny shrimp kept the tone of the dish light and bright, and pineapple reinforced the tropical notes of the coconut milk used in the sauce. For an easy one-pot dinner, we built our coconut-curry sauce in the pot, then poached the shrimp, pineapple, and snow peas (added for color and crunch) right in the sauce. Finally, we stirred in our softened rice noodles, along with a spritz of lime juice and a sprinkling of cilantro. To make this dish spicier, add the chile seeds. Do not substitute other types of noodles for the rice vermicelli here.

8   **ounces dried rice vermicelli**
2   **tablespoons vegetable oil**
2   **tablespoons green curry paste**
2   **Thai, serrano, or jalapeño chiles, stemmed, seeded, and minced**
3   **tablespoons fish sauce**
1   **tablespoon dark brown sugar**
2   **(14-ounce) cans coconut milk**
12   **ounces medium-large shrimp (31 to 40 per pound), peeled, deveined, and tails removed**
2   **cups pineapple, cut into ½-inch pieces**
6   **ounces snow peas, strings removed, halved crosswise on bias**
1   **tablespoon lime juice**
¼   **cup minced fresh cilantro**

1. Cover noodles with very hot tap water in large bowl and stir to separate. Let noodles soak until softened, pliable, and limp but not fully tender, about 20 minutes; drain.

2. Cook oil, curry paste, and chiles in Dutch oven over medium heat until paste begins to sizzle and no longer smells raw, about 2 minutes. Stir in fish sauce and sugar and cook for 1 minute. Stir in coconut milk and simmer until thickened, 5 to 8 minutes.

3. Gently stir in shrimp, pineapple, and snow peas and cook until shrimp are just opaque, about 3 minutes. Stir in drained noodles and cook, tossing gently, until shrimp are cooked through and noodles are well coated, 2 to 3 minutes. Off heat, stir in lime juice. Sprinkle with cilantro and serve.

SMART SHOPPING COCONUT MILK
Coconut milk is not the thin liquid found inside the coconut itself; that is called coconut water. Coconut milk is made by steeping equal parts shredded coconut meat and either warm milk or water. The meat is pressed or mashed to release as much liquid as possible, the mixture is strained, and the result is coconut milk. We tasted seven nationally available brands (five regular and two light) in coconut rice, a Thai-style chicken soup, chicken curry, and coconut pudding. In the savory recipes, tasters preferred **Chaokoh**, which boasted an incredibly smooth texture. When it came to the sweet recipes, tasters liked Ka-Me coconut milk best.

Vietnamese Rice Noodle Salad with Pork

Serves 6

✓ **WHY THIS RECIPE WORKS:** Naturally light and fresh-tasting, Vietnamese *bun* is a multilayered noodle salad that starts with lettuce on the bottom and ends with grilled meat or seafood on top. Shredded lettuce, pickled carrots, chile peppers, fresh herbs, and vermicelli rice noodles inhabit the space in between. For our own version, we started with thinly sliced pork tenderloin. Marinating it with brown sugar and fish sauce infused it with salty-sweet flavor, and broiling gave us golden medallions with crispy edges. Letting our carrots, cucumber, and fresh chiles rest in a tangy, spicy dressing allowed them to soak up bright flavor in just minutes—no fussy pickling required. After tossing the softened noodles and vegetables together, we topped servings with crispy slices of pork. To make this dish spicier, add the chile seeds. Do not substitute other types of noodles for the rice vermicelli here. For the nutritional information for this recipe, see page 306.

PORK

2	tablespoons fish sauce
2	tablespoons dark brown sugar
1	tablespoon vegetable oil
1	(1-pound) pork tenderloin, trimmed and sliced crosswise into ¼-inch-thick medallions

DRESSING

⅔	cup fish sauce
½	cup warm water
6	tablespoons lime juice (3 limes)
5	tablespoons granulated sugar
3	Thai, serrano, or jalapeño chiles, stemmed, seeded, and minced
2	garlic cloves, minced

SALAD

3	large carrots, peeled and shredded
1	large cucumber, peeled, halved lengthwise, seeded, and cut into 2-inch matchsticks
¼	cup chopped unsalted roasted peanuts
1	Thai, serrano, or jalapeño chile, stemmed, seeded, and minced
8	ounces dried rice vermicelli
½	small head red or green leaf lettuce (4 ounces), sliced thin
½	cup fresh Thai basil or sweet basil leaves
½	cup fresh cilantro or mint leaves

1. FOR THE PORK: Whisk fish sauce, brown sugar, and oil together in medium bowl until sugar dissolves. Stir in pork, cover, and refrigerate for at least 30 minutes or up to 24 hours.

2. FOR THE DRESSING: Whisk all ingredients together in bowl until sugar dissolves.

3. FOR THE SALAD: Toss carrots, cucumber, peanuts, and chile with ¼ cup dressing in bowl and let marinate until needed.

4. Bring 4 quarts water to boil in large pot. Remove from heat, add noodles, and let sit, stirring occasionally, until noodles are tender, about 10 minutes. Drain noodles and transfer to large bowl. Layer carrot-cucumber mixture, lettuce, basil, and cilantro on top of noodles (do not toss); set aside.

5. Adjust oven rack 6 inches from broiler element and heat broiler. Line broiler pan bottom with aluminum foil and top with broiler pan top. Spread marinated pork over prepared pan and broil until golden on both sides with crisp edges, about 10 minutes, flipping pork halfway through broiling time.

6. Pour half of remaining dressing over noodle mixture and toss to combine. Top individual portions with broiled pork. Serve with remaining dressing.

SMART SHOPPING FISH SAUCE
Fish sauce is a salty, amber-colored liquid made from fermented fish. It is used as both an ingredient and a condiment in certain Asian cuisines, most commonly in the foods of Southeast Asia. Fish sauce has a very concentrated flavor and, when used in very small amounts, lends dishes a salty complexity that is impossible to replicate. Color correlates with flavor in fish sauce; the lighter the sauce, the lighter the flavor. Fish sauce will keep indefinitely without refrigeration.

Drunken Noodles with Chicken

Serves 4

WHY THIS RECIPE WORKS: This supposed hangover cure (sorry—there's not actually any alcohol in it) features wide rice noodles in a spicy, potent sauce flavored with lots of basil. For our version, we selected the widest noodles we could find and soaked them in hot water until they were pliable but not fully limp. Then we added them to our hot skillet with a combination of soy sauce (for savory depth), lime juice (for its sweet-tart notes), dark brown sugar (preferred over light brown sugar for its richer flavor), and chili-garlic sauce (which contributed both heat and spicy flavor). Tossing the noodles in the sauce over the heat ensured that they would absorb its flavors and finish cooking, while also giving the sauce a chance to thicken. Thin slices of chicken, which we quickly stir-fried, made our noodle dish hearty and filling. Do not substitute other types of noodles for the rice noodles here.

12	ounces (⅜-inch-wide) dried flat rice noodles
12	ounces boneless, skinless chicken breasts, trimmed and sliced thin (see page 26)
1	tablespoon plus ½ cup soy sauce
¾	cup dark brown sugar
⅓	cup lime juice (3 limes), plus lime wedges for serving
¼	cup Asian chili-garlic sauce
¼	cup vegetable oil
½	head napa cabbage, cored and cut into 1-inch pieces (6 cups)
1½	cups coarsely chopped fresh Thai basil or cilantro
4	scallions, sliced thin on bias

1. Cover noodles with very hot tap water in large bowl and stir to separate. Let noodles soak until softened, pliable, and limp but not fully tender, 35 to 40 minutes; drain.

2. Meanwhile, toss chicken with 1 tablespoon soy sauce in bowl, cover, and refrigerate for at least 10 minutes or up to 1 hour. In separate bowl, whisk remaining ½ cup soy sauce, brown sugar, lime juice, and chili-garlic sauce together; set aside.

3. Heat 2 teaspoons oil in 12-inch nonstick skillet over high heat until just smoking. Add chicken in single layer and cook without stirring for 1 minute. Stir and continue to cook until nearly cooked through, about 2 minutes; transfer to bowl.

4. Add 1 teaspoon oil to now-empty skillet and heat over high heat until just smoking. Add cabbage and cook, stirring often, until spotty brown, 3 to 5 minutes; transfer to bowl with chicken.

5. Wipe now-empty skillet clean with paper towels, add remaining 3 tablespoons oil, and heat over medium-high heat until shimmering. Add drained rice noodles and soy sauce mixture and cook, tossing gently, until sauce has thickened and noodles are well coated and tender, 5 to 10 minutes. Stir in chicken-vegetable mixture and basil and cook until chicken is warmed through, about 1 minute. Sprinkle with scallions and serve with lime wedges.

SMART SHOPPING SOY SAUCE
At its most basic, soy sauce is a fermented liquid made from soybeans and wheat. Soybeans contribute a strong, pungent taste, while wheat lends sweetness. Soy sauce should add flavor and complexity to your recipes, not just make them salty. We use it not only in numerous Asian noodle recipes, but also to enhance meaty flavor in pasta sauces, soups, stews, and braises. Our taste test winner is **Lee Kum Kee Tabletop Soy Sauce**, which has a robust flavor that holds up well throughout cooking.

Potstickers with Scallion Dipping Sauce

Makes 24 dumplings, serving 4 to 6

WHY THIS RECIPE WORKS: These crispy potstickers are filled with tender ground pork and crunchy cabbage, and spiked with garlic, ginger, and soy sauce. Convenient, store-bought gyoza-style wrappers offered a nice, chewy texture. Serving these potstickers with a sweet and savory dipping sauce puts them over the top.

SAUCE

- ¼ **cup soy sauce**
- 2 **tablespoons rice vinegar**
- 2 **tablespoons mirin or sweet sherry**
- 2 **tablespoons water**
- 1 **teaspoon chili oil (optional)**
- ½ **teaspoon toasted sesame oil**
- 1 **scallion, minced**

POTSTICKERS

- 3 **cups minced napa cabbage**
- ¾ **teaspoon salt**
- 12 **ounces ground pork**
- 4 **scallions, minced**
- 2 **large egg whites, lightly beaten**
- 4 **teaspoons soy sauce**
- 1½ **teaspoons grated fresh ginger**
- 1 **garlic clove, minced**
- ⅛ **teaspoon pepper**
- 24 **round gyoza wrappers**
- 4 **teaspoons vegetable oil**
- 1 **cup water, plus extra for brushing**

1. FOR THE SAUCE: Combine all ingredients in bowl.

2. FOR THE POTSTICKERS: Toss cabbage with salt in colander and let drain for 20 minutes; press gently to squeeze out moisture. Combine cabbage, pork, scallions, egg whites, soy sauce, ginger, garlic, and pepper in bowl. Cover and refrigerate until chilled, at least 30 minutes or up to 24 hours.

3. Working with 4 wrappers at a time (cover others with moist paper towel), fill, brush edges with water, seal, and shape dumplings using generous 1 tablespoon chilled filling per wrapper; transfer to baking sheet and cover with damp kitchen towel. (Dumplings can be frozen for up to 1 month; if frozen, do not thaw before cooking.)

4. Brush 12-inch nonstick skillet with 2 teaspoons vegetable oil. Arrange half of dumplings, flat side down, in skillet (some may overlap). Cook over medium-high heat, without moving, until golden brown on bottom, about 5 minutes.

5. Reduce heat to low, add ½ cup water, and cover. Cook until most water is absorbed and wrappers are slightly translucent, about 10 minutes. Uncover, increase heat to medium-high, and cook, without stirring, until dumpling bottoms are well browned and crisp, 3 to 4 minutes.

6. Slide dumplings onto paper towel–lined plate, let drain briefly, and serve with sauce. Let skillet cool slightly and wipe clean with paper towels. Repeat with remaining vegetable oil, dumplings, and water.

QUICK PREP TIP MAKING POTSTICKERS
To make a potsticker, place generous tablespoon of filling in center of gyoza wrapper. Moisten edge, then fold it in half to make half-moon. (For square wrappers, fold diagonally into triangle; for rectangular wrappers, fold in half lengthwise.) Using your forefinger and thumb, pinch dumpling closed, pressing out air pockets. Lay dumpling on counter and press gently to flatten one side for even browning.

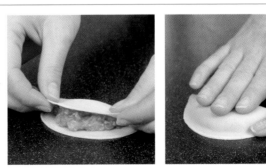

Steamed Chinese Dumplings (Shu Mai)

Makes 40 dumplings, serving 6 to 8

✓ **WHY THIS RECIPE WORKS:** Our shu mai boast a tender skin and a moist, flavorful filling of pork and shrimp, rounded out with dried shiitake mushrooms, minced cilantro, fresh ginger, and water chestnuts. Egg roll skins, cut into rounds with a biscuit cutter, worked well for the wrappers. Do not trim the excess fat from the ribs, as the fat contributes flavor and moistness. For the nutritional information for this recipe, see page 306.

½ teaspoon unflavored gelatin

2 tablespoons soy sauce

1 pound boneless country-style pork ribs, cut into 1-inch pieces

8 ounces shrimp, peeled, deveined, tails removed, and halved lengthwise

¼ cup chopped canned water chestnuts

4 dried shiitake mushroom caps, soaked in hot water for 30 minutes, squeezed dry, and cut into ¼-inch pieces

2 tablespoons cornstarch

2 tablespoons minced fresh cilantro

1 tablespoon toasted sesame oil

1 tablespoon Chinese rice wine or dry sherry

1 tablespoon rice vinegar

2 teaspoons sugar

2 teaspoons grated fresh ginger

½ teaspoon salt

½ teaspoon pepper

1 pound (5½-inch) square egg roll wrappers

¼ cup finely grated carrot (optional)
Chili oil

1. Sprinkle gelatin over soy sauce and let sit until gelatin softens, about 5 minutes.

2. Meanwhile, pulse half of pork in food processor until coarsely ground and pieces measure about ⅛ inch, about 10 pulses; transfer to large bowl. Add shrimp and remaining pork to food processor and pulse until pieces measure about ¼ inch, about 5 pulses; transfer to bowl. Stir in gelatin mixture, water chestnuts, mushrooms, cornstarch, cilantro, sesame oil, wine, vinegar, sugar, ginger, salt, and pepper until well combined.

3. Line large baking sheet with parchment paper. Working with stack of 6 or 7 wrappers, cut two 3-inch rounds from each wrapper using 3-inch biscuit cutter; you will have 40 to 42 rounds total. Cover rounds with moist paper towels to prevent drying.

4. Working with 6 rounds at a time, fill, brush edges with water, and shape dumplings using generous 1 tablespoon filling per round. Transfer to prepared baking sheet and cover with damp kitchen towel. Top dumplings with pinch grated carrot, if using. (Dumplings, without grated carrot, can be frozen for up to 3 months; do not thaw before cooking, and increase cooking time by 5 minutes.)

5. Cut sheet of parchment paper to be slightly smaller than diameter of steamer basket and place in basket. Poke 20 small steam holes in parchment and lightly coat with vegetable oil spray. Arrange batches of dumplings on parchment; do not let them touch. Cover, set steamer basket over simmering water, and cook until no longer pink, 8 to 10 minutes. Serve immediately with chili oil.

QUICK PREP TIP MAKING SHU MAI
To make shu mai, lay wrappers on clean counter, place generous tablespoon of filling in center of each wrapper, and brush edges with water. Pinch edges of wrapper to make eight equidistant folds, rotating dumpling as needed. Press folds flat and squeeze gently at top to create "waist." Then, holding shu mai, gently but firmly pack down filling with butter knife.

PASTA ALLA NORMA

Italy's Greatest Hits

Classic Spaghetti Marinara

Serves 4 to 6

✔ **WHY THIS RECIPE WORKS:** For the best, most robustly flavored marinara sauce, we started by picking the right tomatoes. Canned whole tomatoes provide great flavor and texture year-round; using our hands to remove the hard core and seeds was easy. For a sauce with intense tomato flavor, we sautéed the tomatoes until they glazed the bottom of the pan, then we added the reserved juice from the canned tomatoes. Using a skillet instead of a saucepan provided more surface area and encouraged faster evaporation and flavor concentration. Red wine added depth and complexity. Adding a portion of uncooked tomatoes, along with chopped basil and a drizzle of olive oil, just before serving gave our sauce a bright, fresh finish. If you prefer a chunkier sauce, give it just 3 or 4 pulses in the food processor in step 4. Nearly any shape of pasta pairs well with this sauce, so feel free to substitute another pasta for the spaghetti. For the nutritional information for this recipe, see page 307.

2 **(28-ounce) cans whole peeled tomatoes**
3 **tablespoons extra-virgin olive oil**
1 **onion, chopped fine**
2 **garlic cloves, minced**
2 **teaspoons minced fresh oregano or ½ teaspoon dried**
⅓ **cup dry red wine**
3 **tablespoons chopped fresh basil**
Salt and pepper
Sugar
1 **pound spaghetti**
Grated Parmesan cheese

1. Drain tomatoes in fine-mesh strainer set over large bowl. Open tomatoes with hands and remove and discard seeds and fibrous cores; let tomatoes drain, about 5 minutes. Measure out and reserve ¾ cup tomatoes separately. Reserve 2½ cups drained tomato juice; discard remaining tomato juice.

2. Heat 2 tablespoons oil in 12-inch skillet over medium heat until shimmering. Add onion and cook until softened and lightly browned, 5 to 7 minutes. Stir in garlic and oregano and cook until fragrant, about 30 seconds.

3. Stir in remaining drained tomatoes and increase heat to medium-high. Cook, stirring often, until liquid has evaporated and tomatoes begin to brown and stick to pan, 10 to 12 minutes. Stir in wine and cook until thick and syrupy, about 1 minute. Stir in reserved tomato juice, scraping up any browned bits. Bring to simmer and cook, stirring occasionally, until sauce is thick, 8 to 10 minutes.

4. Transfer sauce to food processor, add reserved ¾ cup tomatoes, and pulse until slightly chunky, about 8 pulses. Return sauce to now-empty skillet, stir in basil and remaining 1 tablespoon oil, and season with salt, pepper, and sugar to taste.

5. Meanwhile, bring 4 quarts water to boil in large pot. Add pasta and 1 tablespoon salt and cook, stirring often, until al dente. Reserve ½ cup cooking water, then drain pasta and return it to pot. Add sauce and toss to combine. Season with salt and pepper to taste and add reserved cooking water as needed to adjust consistency. Serve with Parmesan.

Pasta all'Amatriciana

Serves 4 to 6

✔ **WHY THIS RECIPE WORKS:** Like most Roman cooking, pasta all'amatriciana is bold and brash. Though the ingredients are few—tomatoes, bacon, and onion are the cornerstones—the flavors are big and potent. For a recipe that would do this classic sauce justice, we started with pancetta, which gave the sauce more meaty, salty notes than bacon. Diced tomatoes, onion, and red pepper flakes provided acidity, sweetness, and a hint of heat. Adding the cooked pancetta at the end kept it crisp. This dish is traditionally made with bucatini, also called perciatelli, which are thin, extra-long tubes (like drinking straws), but any strand pasta will work fine. When buying pancetta, ask the butcher to slice it ¼ inch thick; if using bacon, buy slab bacon and cut it into ¼-inch-thick slices yourself.

2　tablespoons extra-virgin olive oil

6　ounces pancetta, sliced ¼ inch thick and cut into 1-inch strips

1　onion, chopped fine

½　teaspoon red pepper flakes

1　(28-ounce) can diced tomatoes
　　Salt

1　pound bucatini

1½　ounces Pecorino Romano cheese, grated (¾ cup)

1. Cook oil and pancetta in 12-inch skillet over medium heat until pancetta is well browned and crisp, about 8 minutes. Using slotted spoon, transfer pancetta to paper towel–lined plate.

2. Pour off all but 2 tablespoons fat left in skillet, add onion, and cook over medium heat until softened, about 5 minutes. Stir in pepper flakes and cook until fragrant, about 30 seconds. Stir in tomatoes, bring to simmer, and cook until slightly thickened, about 10 minutes. Season with salt to taste.

3. Meanwhile, bring 4 quarts water to boil in large pot. Add pasta and 1 tablespoon salt and cook, stirring often, until al dente. Reserve ½ cup cooking water, then drain pasta and return it to pot. Add sauce, crisped pancetta, and Pecorino and toss to combine. Season with salt to taste and add reserved cooking water as needed to adjust consistency. Serve.

SMART SHOPPING YELLOW VERSUS WHITE ONIONS

In our recipes, unless otherwise specified we always use yellow onions, the kind that comes in 5-pound bags at the supermarket. But wondering if there was any difference between these onions and white onions (color aside, of course), we decided to hold a blind taste test to find out. We tried them raw in pico de gallo, cooked in a simple tomato sauce, and caramelized. More than half a dozen tasters could not tell the difference between the two types; the others tasted only minor variations in sweetness and pungency. Our conclusion? Since we go through onions quickly we find it easiest to buy a big bag of yellow onions, but you can use white and yellow onions interchangeably in any recipe calling for "onions."

Spaghetti Puttanesca

Serves 4 to 6

WHY THIS RECIPE WORKS: Gutsy and brazen, puttanesca is punctuated by the zesty flavors of garlic, anchovies, olives, and capers. We wanted to harmonize the bold flavors in this Neapolitan dish, while not letting any single one take center stage. Blooming the garlic, anchovies, and red pepper flakes in hot olive oil helped to develop and blend their flavors. After adding diced tomatoes, we simmered the sauce for less than 10 minutes to preserve the tomatoes' sweetness and meaty texture. Saving the olives and capers until the end kept them from disintegrating in the sauce. For a bit more richness, we drizzled olive oil over each bowl of pasta. This dish is fairly spicy; to make it milder, reduce the amount of red pepper flakes. For the nutritional information for this recipe, see page 307.

2   **tablespoons extra-virgin olive oil, plus extra for serving**

8   **anchovy fillets, rinsed and minced**

4   **garlic cloves, minced**

1   **teaspoon red pepper flakes**

1   **(28-ounce) can diced tomatoes, drained with ½ cup juice reserved**

½   **cup pitted kalamata olives, chopped coarse**

¼   **cup minced fresh parsley**

3   **tablespoons capers, rinsed**

1   **pound spaghetti**

    Salt and pepper

1. Cook oil, anchovies, garlic, and pepper flakes together in 12-inch skillet over medium heat, stirring often, until garlic turns golden but not brown, about 3 minutes. Stir in tomatoes and cook until slightly thickened, about 8 minutes. Stir in olives, parsley, and capers.

2. Meanwhile, bring 4 quarts water to boil in large pot. Add pasta and 1 tablespoon salt and cook, stirring often, until al dente. Reserve ½ cup cooking water, then drain pasta and return it to pot. Add sauce and ¼ cup reserved tomato juice and toss to combine. Season with salt and pepper to taste and add remaining ¼ cup reserved tomato juice or reserved cooking water as needed to adjust consistency. Drizzle individual portions with extra olive oil to taste and serve.

SMART SHOPPING **ANCHOVY FILLETS VERSUS PASTE**

Since most recipes call for only a small amount of anchovies, we wondered whether a tube of anchovy paste might be a more convenient option. Made from pulverized anchovies, vinegar, salt, and water, anchovy paste promises all the flavor of oil-packed anchovies without the mess. When we tested the paste and jarred or canned anchovies side by side in recipes calling for an anchovy or two, we found little difference, though a few astute tasters felt that the paste had a "saltier" and "slightly more fishy" flavor. You can substitute ¼ teaspoon of the paste for each fillet. However, when a recipe calls for more than a couple of anchovies, stick with jarred or canned as the paste's more intense flavor will be overwhelming. Our favorite brand of anchovies is **Ortiz Oil-Packed Anchovies.**

Spaghetti alla Carbonara

Serves 4 to 6

✔ **WHY THIS RECIPE WORKS:** Spaghetti draped in a velvety sauce of cheese and eggs and punctuated by bits of crispy bacon—is there anything more indulgent than carbonara? Though the method is pretty straightforward—make a raw sauce with eggs and cheese, cook the bacon, cook the pasta, then toss until all is creamy and combined—we had to nail down the details. First up, determining the right number of eggs: Three whole eggs gave our carbonara superior texture and richness. Next, the cheese: Opting for two kinds—Pecorino Romano and Parmesan—gave us creaminess with a sharp, tangy bite. For the bacon, we liked the standard domestic variety, which contributed the perfect crunch, a bit of sweetness, and some smoky flavor. Pouring the bacon and egg-and-cheese mixture (which also included minced raw garlic so our dish would retain some of its bite) over the hot pasta ensured evenly covered strands of spaghetti.

¼ cup extra-virgin olive oil

8 slices bacon, cut into ¼-inch pieces

½ cup dry white wine

3 large eggs

1½ ounces Parmesan cheese, grated (¾ cup)

¼ cup finely grated Pecorino Romano cheese

2 garlic cloves, minced

1 pound spaghetti

Salt and pepper

1. Adjust oven rack to lower-middle position, set large ovensafe serving bowl on rack, and heat oven to 200 degrees.

2. Heat oil in 12-inch skillet over medium heat until shimmering. Add bacon and cook until crisp, about 8 minutes. Stir in wine, bring to simmer, and cook until slightly reduced, 6 to 8 minutes. Remove from heat and cover to keep warm. In separate bowl, whisk eggs, Parmesan, Pecorino, and garlic together.

3. Meanwhile, bring 4 quarts water to boil in large pot. Add pasta and 1 tablespoon salt and cook, stirring often, until al dente. Reserve ⅓ cup cooking water, then drain pasta and transfer it to warmed serving bowl.

4. Immediately pour bacon mixture and egg mixture over hot pasta and toss to combine. Season with salt and pepper to taste and add reserved cooking water as needed to adjust consistency. Serve immediately.

SMART SHOPPING BACON

Premium bacon can cost double, even triple, the price of ordinary bacon. Is it worth it? To find out, we bought six artisanal mail-order bacons and two high-end grocery store bacons. The results? We were amazed that two of the four highest-rated bacons were not premium mail-order bacons, but supermarket brands. **Applegate Farms Uncured Sunday Bacon** and **Farmland/Carando Apple Cider Cured Bacon, Applewood Smoked**, were a step up from the usual mass-produced bacon, straddling the gap between artisanal and more mainstream supermarket styles. Although these bacons didn't receive quite the raves of the two top-ranked premium bacons, tasters praised them both for good meaty flavor and mild smokiness.

Penne alla Vodka

Serves 4 to 6

✔ **WHY THIS RECIPE WORKS:** In penne alla vodka, splashes of vodka and cream turn a simple tomato sauce into luxurious restaurant fare. For a sauce that was not too thin nor too chunky and that would cling to the penne, we combined both processed and hand-chopped tomatoes. A heavy hand with the vodka added zing, but to prevent the finished dish from tasting overly boozy, we added the vodka early on to allow the alcohol to mostly (but not completely) cook off, preventing a harsh alcohol flavor. Just half a cup of heavy cream kept the brightness of the tomatoes intact and gave us a velvety but not over-the-top sauce. Allowing the penne to finish cooking in the sauce encouraged cohesiveness. Red pepper flakes give this dish some kick; for more heat, add additional red pepper flakes. For the nutritional information for this recipe, see page 307.

1 **(28-ounce) can whole peeled tomatoes, drained with juice reserved**
2 **tablespoons olive oil**
¼ **cup finely chopped onion**
1 **tablespoon tomato paste**
2 **garlic cloves, minced**
¼ **teaspoon red pepper flakes, or to taste**
   Salt and pepper
⅓ **cup vodka**
½ **cup heavy cream**
1 **pound penne**
2 **tablespoons chopped fresh basil**
   Grated Parmesan cheese

1. Pulse half of tomatoes in food processor until smooth, about 12 pulses. Cut remaining tomatoes into ½-inch pieces, discarding cores. Combine pureed and diced tomatoes in liquid measuring cup and add reserved juice to equal 2 cups; discard extra juice.

2. Heat oil in large saucepan over medium heat until shimmering. Add onion and tomato paste and cook, stirring occasionally, until onion is softened and lightly browned, 5 to 7 minutes. Stir in garlic and pepper flakes and cook until fragrant, about 30 seconds.

3. Stir in tomato mixture and ½ teaspoon salt. Off heat, add vodka. Return sauce to medium-high heat and simmer, stirring often, until alcohol flavor is cooked off, 8 to 10 minutes. Stir in cream and cook until heated through, about 1 minute.

4. Meanwhile, bring 4 quarts water to boil in large pot. Add pasta and 1 tablespoon salt and cook, stirring often, until al dente. Reserve ½ cup cooking water, then drain pasta and return it to pot. Add sauce and cook over medium heat, tossing to combine, until pasta absorbs some sauce, 1 to 2 minutes. Stir in basil, season with salt and pepper to taste, and add reserved cooking water as needed to adjust consistency. Serve with Parmesan.

SMART SHOPPING VODKA
Does the quality of the vodka matter when it's getting mixed into a pasta dish and not starring in a vodka martini? We tested six brands of vodka in our penne alla vodka to find out. The penne made with **Grey Goose**, the most expensive contender in the tasting, won, with tasters noting a "fresher," "cleaner" flavor. Why the difference? Cheap vodkas are distilled only once to remove harsh tastes, while "premium" and "super-premium" brands are filtered three or more times—and you can taste the difference, even in a pasta sauce. While we think you don't necessarily need to cook with Grey Goose, don't ruin your sauce with the harsh-tasting, bottom-of-the-line stuff.

ALL ABOUT Matching Pasta Shapes and Sauces

Pairing a pasta shape with the right sauce might be an art form in Italy, but we think there's only one basic rule to follow: Thick, chunky sauces go with short pastas, and thin, smooth, or light sauces with strand pasta. (Of course, there are a few exceptions—but that's where the art comes in.) Although we specify pasta shapes for every recipe in this book, you should feel free to substitute other pasta shapes as long as you're following this one basic rule. Here are the most common pastas we use, along with what their names really mean, plus some measuring tips.

Short Pastas

Short tubular or molded pasta shapes do an excellent job of trapping and holding on to chunky sauces in dishes such as our Rustic Long-Simmered Pork Ragu (page 182) and Pasta alla Norma (page 183). Sauces with very large chunks are best with rigatoni or other large tubes. Sauces with small chunks make more sense with fusilli or penne.

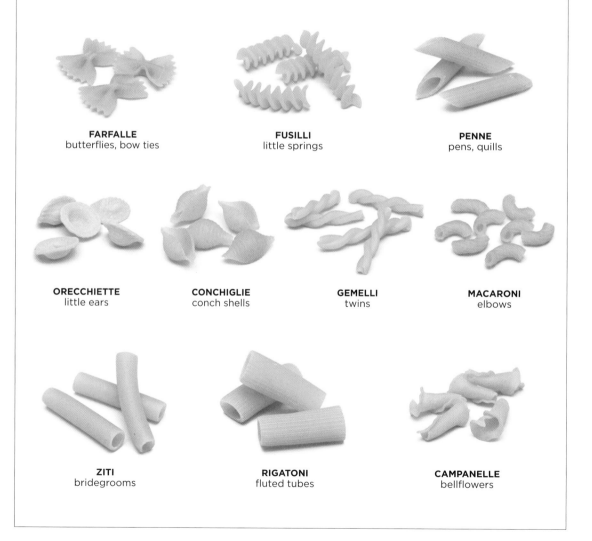

FARFALLE
butterflies, bow ties

FUSILLI
little springs

PENNE
pens, quills

ORECCHIETTE
little ears

CONCHIGLIE
conch shells

GEMELLI
twins

MACARONI
elbows

ZITI
bridegrooms

RIGATONI
fluted tubes

CAMPANELLE
bellflowers

Strand Pastas

Long strands are best with smooth sauces or sauces with very small chunks. In general, wider noodles, such as pappardelle and fettuccine, can support slightly chunkier sauces, like our Classic Bolognese (page 181).

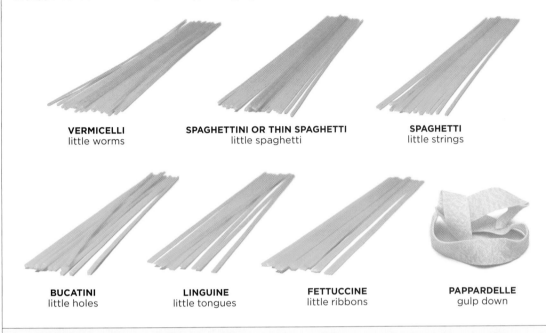

VERMICELLI
little worms

SPAGHETTINI OR THIN SPAGHETTI
little spaghetti

SPAGHETTI
little strings

BUCATINI
little holes

LINGUINE
little tongues

FETTUCCINE
little ribbons

PAPPARDELLE
gulp down

Measuring Less Than a Pound of Pasta

It's easy enough to measure out a pound of pasta, as most packages are sold in this quantity. But in this book we've included some recipes, most notably "Skillet Pastas" and "Pasta for Two" dishes (chapters 2 and 10, respectively), that call for less than 1 pound of pasta. Obviously, you can weigh out partial pounds of pasta using a scale or judge by how full the box is, but we think it's easier to measure shaped pasta using a dry measuring cup, and strand pasta by determining the diameter.

PASTA TYPE*	8 OUNCES	12 OUNCES
Elbow Macaroni and Small Shells	2 cups	3 cups
Orecchiette	2¼ cups	3⅓ cups
Penne, Ziti, and Campanelle	2½ cups	3¾ cups
Rigatoni, Fusilli, Medium Shells, Wagon Wheels, Wide Egg Noodles	3 cups	4½ cups
Farfalle	3¼ cups	4¾ cups

*These amounts do not apply to whole-wheat pasta.

When 8 ounces of uncooked strand pasta are bunched together into a tight circle, the diameter measures about 1¼ inches. When 12 ounces of uncooked pasta are bunched together, the diameter measures about 1¾ inches.

←------------ 1¼" ------------→

←------------- 1¾" -------------→

Spaghetti with Pecorino Romano and Black Pepper (Cacio e Pepe)

Serves 4 to 6

✓ **WHY THIS RECIPE WORKS:** With just three main ingredients—cheese, pepper, and pasta—this Roman dish is as delicious as it is easy. But time and again, our attempts at making it ended up with cheese that formed clumps and stuck to the tongs when tossed with the hot pasta. For a smooth, intensely cheesy sauce that stayed creamy, we whisked together some of the pasta cooking water with the grated Romano; the cooking water provided starch that kept the cheese's proteins from fusing together. Cutting the amount of cooking water in half upped the starch level even more. A couple spoonfuls of heavy cream further ensured a smooth sauce. If desired, half-and-half can be substituted for the heavy cream. Do not adjust the amount of water for cooking the pasta, as the amount used is critical to the success of the recipe. Make sure to stir the pasta frequently while cooking so that it doesn't stick to the pot. Using imported Pecorino Romano is crucial here for flavor. For the nutritional information for this recipe, see page 307.

6	ounces Pecorino Romano cheese, 4 ounces grated fine (2 cups) and 2 ounces grated coarse (1 cup)
1	pound spaghetti
	Salt
2	tablespoons heavy cream
2	teaspoons extra-virgin olive oil
1½	teaspoons pepper

1. Place finely grated Pecorino in medium bowl. Set colander in large bowl.

2. Bring 2 quarts water to boil in large pot. Add pasta and 1½ teaspoons salt and cook, stirring often, until al dente. Drain pasta into prepared colander, reserving cooking water. Measure 1½ cups cooking water into liquid measuring cup, discarding extra.

3. Transfer drained pasta to now-empty large bowl. Slowly whisk 1 cup reserved cooking water into finely grated Pecorino until smooth, then whisk in heavy cream, oil, and pepper. Gradually pour cheese mixture over pasta and toss to combine. Let pasta rest for 1 to 2 minutes, tossing frequently and adding remaining cooking water as needed to adjust consistency. Serve with coarsely grated Pecorino.

SMART SHOPPING BLACK PEPPER

In recipes calling for ground pepper, we greatly prefer grinding our own to using the preground variety, which has a faded aroma and flavor. All peppercorns are not the same, but when a recipe calls for a small dose any freshly ground pepper will be fine. But if you're cooking a dish that highlights the pepper, choosing a superior peppercorn can make a difference. We tested several varieties, and tasters gave top marks to highly aromatic peppercorns with complex flavor, and they preferred moderate heat rather than an overpowering, strong heat. Our favorite is **Kalustyan's Indian Tellicherry Black Peppercorns**, which is sold by a Manhattan emporium online, but a close second is supermarket brand **Morton & Bassett Organic Whole Black Peppercorns**.

Fettuccine Alfredo

Serves 4

✔ **WHY THIS RECIPE WORKS:** Classic Alfredo sauce should be transcendent, boasting fresh cream flavor and a silky, elegant texture. Using a light hand with two of the richer ingredients—the Parmesan and butter—was a good starting point, giving our sauce distinctive flavor without being overwhelming; restraint with the requisite ground nutmeg was important, too. The real challenge was managing the heavy cream, which is usually reduced by half, making for an overly thick sauce. We found it better to reduce only a portion of the cream, then add a splash of fresh cream at the end for clean flavor and silky texture. Also, fresh fettuccine was essential, as dried noodles didn't hold on to the sauce. Undercooking the pasta, then letting it finish cooking in the sauce, ensured that the finished sauce had the perfect consistency, neither too thick nor too thin. Finally, we found that serving Alfredo immediately in freshly warmed bowls is crucial, or else the dish congeals within a minute or so. Not only is it easy to use hot pasta water to warm the bowls, but the extra drips of water left inside the bowls help to keep the sauce fluid. Note that this dish is very rich, and therefore the portion size is quite small; serve it with a substantial salad or simply prepared fish or chicken.

1½ cups heavy cream
2 tablespoons unsalted butter
   Salt and pepper
1 (9-ounce) package fresh
   fettuccine
1½ ounces Parmesan cheese, grated
   (¾ cup)
⅛ teaspoon ground nutmeg

1. Bring 1 cup cream and butter to simmer in large saucepan. Reduce heat to low and simmer gently until mixture measures ⅔ cup, 12 to 15 minutes. Off heat, stir in remaining ½ cup cream, ½ teaspoon salt, and ½ teaspoon pepper. Cover and set aside.

2. Meanwhile, bring 4½ quarts water to boil in large pot. Ladle ½ cup boiling water into each individual serving bowl; set aside to warm. Return pot of water to boil, add pasta and 1 tablespoon salt, and cook, stirring often, until just shy of al dente. Reserve ¼ cup pasta cooking water, then drain pasta.

3. Return cream mixture to simmer. Reduce heat to low, add drained pasta, Parmesan, and nutmeg. Cook, tossing to combine, until cheese is melted, sauce coats pasta, and pasta is al dente, 1 to 2 minutes. Add reserved cooking water as needed to adjust consistency (sauce may look thin but will gradually thicken as pasta is served). Drain water from warmed serving bowls and serve immediately.

SMART SHOPPING **NUTMEG GRATER**
Freshly grated nutmeg might take a few extra minutes, but it's well worth the extra effort in dishes where there are no other spices to compete with it. Pitting three nutmeg mills against one another, we looked for one that worked efficiently while keeping fingers out of harm's way. The **Microplane Classic Black Spice Grater** ($7) was our favorite. It has a slender, tightly curled, 5-inch-long grating surface that provides a good margin of safety for your fingertips. It produced mounds of nutmeg in no time flat and can also be used for grating nuts and chocolate.

Pasta ai Quattro Formaggi

Serves 4 to 6

✔ **WHY THIS RECIPE WORKS:** Pasta ai quattro formaggi is the Italian take on mac and cheese. Made with four cheeses and heavy cream, this creamy casserole boasts great flavor and richness, tender pasta, and a crisp bread-crumb topping. The cheese was first up for consideration; for the best flavor and texture, we used Italian fontina, Gorgonzola, Pecorino Romano, and Parmesan cheeses. Heating the cheese and cream together made a greasy, curdled mess, so instead we built a basic white sauce (a béchamel) by cooking butter with flour and then adding cream. Combining the hot sauce and pasta with the cheese—and not cooking the cheese in the sauce—preserved the fresh flavor of the cheeses. Knowing the pasta would spend some time in the oven, we drained it before it was al dente so it wouldn't turn to mush when baked. Topped with bread crumbs and more Parmesan, and baked briefly in a very hot oven, our Italian-style mac and cheese was just what we wanted: creamy, rich, and undeniably flavorful.

3   **slices hearty white sandwich bread, torn into quarters**

1   **ounce Parmesan cheese, grated (½ cup)**

    Salt and pepper

4   **ounces fontina cheese, shredded (1 cup)**

3   **ounces Gorgonzola cheese, crumbled (¾ cup)**

1   **ounce Pecorino Romano cheese, grated (½ cup)**

1   **tablespoon unsalted butter**

2   **teaspoons all-purpose flour**

1½   **cups heavy cream**

1   **pound penne**

1. Adjust oven rack to middle position and heat oven to 500 degrees. Pulse bread in food processor to coarse crumbs, about 10 pulses. Transfer crumbs to small bowl and stir in ¼ cup Parmesan, ¼ teaspoon salt, and ⅛ teaspoon pepper. In large bowl, combine remaining ¼ cup Parmesan, fontina, Gorgonzola, and Pecorino.

2. Melt butter in small saucepan over medium heat. Whisk in flour until no lumps remain, about 30 seconds. Slowly whisk in cream, bring to simmer, and cook, stirring occasionally, for 1 minute. Off heat, stir in ¼ teaspoon salt and ¼ teaspoon pepper.

3. Meanwhile, bring 4 quarts water to boil in large pot. Add pasta and 1 tablespoon salt and cook, stirring often, until just shy of al dente. Drain pasta, then add to bowl of cheese. Immediately pour hot cream mixture over top, cover bowl, and let stand 3 minutes.

4. Stir pasta with rubber spatula, scraping up cheeses from bottom of bowl, until cheese has melted and mixture is thoroughly combined. Transfer to 13 by 9-inch baking dish, then sprinkle evenly with bread-crumb mixture, pressing down lightly. Bake until topping is golden brown, about 7 minutes. Serve.

ON THE SIDE LEMONY SPINACH SALAD
Whisk ⅓ cup extra-virgin olive oil, 3 tablespoons lemon juice, and 1 minced garlic clove together in bowl. Toss with 8 ounces (8 cups) baby spinach and season with salt and pepper to taste. Sprinkle with shaved Parmesan before serving. Serves 6.

Orecchiette with Escarole and White Beans

Serves 4 to 6

WHY THIS RECIPE WORKS: Rustic Italian peasant cuisine combines simple ingredients but takes them to a new level. We decided to pay homage to the classic pairing of fresh, spicy escarole with creamy canned white beans, and threw in a generous amount of sautéed garlic, too. We cooked the escarole briefly with the garlic to wilt it and infuse it with the garlic's aroma, then steamed it, covered, to ensure that it was completely tender. All we needed to do with the beans was stir them in at the end so they could heat through. A little pancetta rounded out the flavors and added a necessary, meaty backbone plus some crunch, and finishing with a couple pats of butter enriched the dish. Bacon can be substituted for the pancetta and canned chickpeas for the white beans, if necessary.

¼ cup olive oil

4 ounces thinly sliced pancetta, chopped fine

6 garlic cloves, minced

2 teaspoons minced fresh oregano or ½ teaspoon dried
   Pinch red pepper flakes

2 heads escarole (2 pounds), trimmed and sliced ½ inch thick

1 cup low-sodium chicken broth

1 (15-ounce) can cannellini beans, rinsed
   Salt and pepper

1 pound orecchiette

2 tablespoons unsalted butter
   Grated Parmesan cheese

1. Cook oil and pancetta in 12-inch skillet over medium heat until pancetta is well browned and crisp, about 8 minutes. Using slotted spoon, transfer pancetta to paper towel–lined plate.

2. Add garlic, oregano, and pepper flakes to fat left in skillet and cook over medium heat until fragrant, about 30 seconds. Add escarole, one handful at a time, and cook until completely wilted, about 5 minutes. Stir in broth and bring to simmer. Cover, reduce heat to medium-low, and simmer gently for 5 minutes. Stir in beans, cover, and simmer gently until flavors meld, about 5 minutes. Season with salt and pepper to taste.

3. Meanwhile, bring 4 quarts water to boil in large pot. Add pasta and 1 tablespoon salt and cook, stirring often, until al dente. Reserve ½ cup cooking water, then drain pasta and return it to pot. Add escarole mixture, crisped pancetta, and butter and toss to combine. Season with salt and pepper to taste and add reserved cooking water as needed to adjust consistency. Serve with Parmesan.

SMART SHOPPING ESCAROLE
Escarole is a leafy green that looks much like green leaf lettuce. Its bitter flavor makes it a great choice for salads. But unlike lettuce, escarole stands up well to cooking. Though commonly used in salads and side dishes, it makes a great addition to this simple pasta dish with beans and pancetta. Make sure to slice the escarole before washing it well. Use a salad spinner to wash it, as the fine, feathery leaves tend to hold a lot of soil.

Classic Bolognese with Pappardelle

Serves 8 to 10

✔ **WHY THIS RECIPE WORKS:** For a hearty, meaty Bolognese that would make anyone from Bologna proud, we tested scores of traditional recipes. Ultimately, we fell head over heels for a version that omits the usual dairy but uses half a dozen different types of meat in order to achieve this dish's traditional sweet, rich, meaty flavor. We started with the common trio of ground beef, pork, and veal, then added pancetta, mortadella, and chicken livers to further deepen the meaty flavor. To replicate the homemade beef *brodo* (or broth) often called for, we used store-bought broth (a mix of chicken and beef for the best savory, meaty flavor) thickened with gelatin. If you can't find ground veal, you can substitute an additional 12 ounces of ground beef. And though we think the chicken livers are essential to the authentic flavor of the dish, they can be omitted if desired. Eight teaspoons of gelatin is equivalent to one (1-ounce) box. Given that this sauce requires some work but freezes very well, we scaled it up to make enough for 2 pounds of pasta; you can either feed a crowd or save some for another meal. The sauce can be refrigerated for up to 3 days or frozen for up to 1 month.

1	cup low-sodium chicken broth
1	cup beef broth
8	teaspoons unflavored gelatin
1	onion, chopped coarse
1	large carrot, peeled and chopped coarse
1	celery rib, chopped coarse
4	ounces pancetta, chopped
4	ounces mortadella, chopped
6	ounces chicken livers
3	tablespoons extra-virgin olive oil
12	ounces 85 percent lean ground beef
12	ounces ground veal
12	ounces ground pork
3	tablespoons minced fresh sage
1	(6-ounce) can tomato paste
2	cups red wine
	Salt and pepper
2	pounds pappardelle
	Grated Parmesan cheese

1. Combine chicken broth and beef broth in bowl, sprinkle gelatin over top, and set aside. Pulse onion, carrot, and celery in food processor until finely chopped, about 10 pulses, scraping down bowl as needed; transfer to another bowl. Pulse pancetta and mortadella in now-empty food processor until finely chopped, about 25 pulses; transfer to separate bowl. Process chicken livers in now-empty food processor until pureed, about 5 seconds; transfer to separate bowl, cover, and refrigerate.

2. Heat oil in large Dutch oven over medium-high heat until shimmering. Add beef, veal, and pork and cook, stirring occasionally, until all liquid has evaporated and meat begins to sizzle, 10 to 15 minutes. Add processed pancetta mixture and sage; cook, stirring often, until pancetta is translucent, 5 to 7 minutes. Add processed vegetables and cook, stirring often, until softened, 5 to 7 minutes. Add tomato paste and cook, stirring constantly, until browned and fragrant, about 3 minutes.

3. Stir in wine, scraping up any browned bits, and simmer until sauce has thickened, about 5 minutes. Stir in broth mixture, bring to simmer, then reduce heat to low and cook at bare simmer until thickened (wooden spoon should leave trail when dragged through sauce), about 1½ hours.

4. Stir in processed chicken livers, bring to boil, then remove from heat. Season with salt and pepper to taste.

5. Meanwhile, bring 8 quarts water to boil in 12-quart pot. Add pasta and 2 tablespoons salt and cook, stirring often, until al dente. Reserve 1½ cups cooking water, then drain pasta and return it to pot. Add sauce and toss to combine. Season with salt and pepper to taste and add reserved cooking water as needed to adjust consistency. Serve with Parmesan.

Rustic Long-Simmered Pork Ragu

Serves 4 to 6

✓ **WHY THIS RECIPE WORKS:** A simple, long-simmered meat sauce is a common supper in the Italian countryside. At its core, the sauce is a can of tomatoes cooked low and slow with a stray piece of pork and an onion. Although it's a casual recipe at heart, not any cut of pork will do. We tried all manner of chops, but they turned dry during the long cooking time, so we turned to a fattier cut—country-style pork ribs. Country-style ribs turned meltingly tender and gave the tomato sauce a truly meaty, rich flavor. Browning them first ensured there was rich fond left behind on the bottom of the pan to infuse the sauce with deep flavor. Unlike other styles of pork ribs, country-style ribs are quite inexpensive and easy to buy in small quantities, making them the perfect choice for this simple, homey dish. To prevent the sauce from becoming greasy, be sure to trim all external fat from the ribs. For the nutritional information for this recipe, see page 307.

1½	pounds country-style pork ribs, trimmed
	Salt and pepper
1	tablespoon olive oil
1	onion, chopped fine
½	cup dry red wine
1	(28-ounce) can whole peeled tomatoes, drained with juice reserved, tomatoes chopped fine
1	pound rigatoni
	Grated Pecorino Romano or Parmesan cheese

1. Pat ribs dry with paper towels and season with salt and pepper. Heat oil in 12-inch skillet over medium-high heat until just smoking. Brown ribs well on all sides, 8 to 10 minutes; transfer to plate.

2. Pour off all but 1 teaspoon fat left in skillet, add onion, and cook over medium heat until softened, about 5 minutes. Stir in wine, scraping up any browned bits, and simmer until nearly evaporated, about 2 minutes.

3. Stir in tomatoes and reserved tomato juice. Nestle browned ribs along with any accumulated juice into sauce and bring to gentle simmer. Reduce heat to low, cover, and simmer gently, turning ribs occasionally, until meat is very tender and falling off bones, 1½ hours.

4. Transfer ribs to plate, let cool slightly, then shred meat into bite-size pieces, discarding fat and bones. Return shredded meat to sauce, bring to simmer, and cook until heated through and slightly thickened, about 5 minutes.

5. Meanwhile, bring 4 quarts water to boil in large pot. Add pasta and 1 tablespoon salt and cook, stirring often, until al dente. Reserve ½ cup cooking water, then drain pasta and return it to pot. Add sauce and toss to combine. Season with salt and pepper to taste and add reserved cooking water as needed to adjust consistency. Serve with Pecorino.

Pasta alla Norma

Serves 4 to 6

✔ **WHY THIS RECIPE WORKS:** With its lively combination of tender eggplant, robust tomato sauce, al dente pasta, and salty, milky *ricotta salata,* pasta alla Norma sings with each bite—appropriate, given that it was named for the title character of an opera. For our version, we microwaved salted eggplant on coffee filters (we've found paper towels with designs have dyes in them that aren't foodsafe) to draw out its moisture. A secret ingredient, anchovies, gave our tomato sauce a deep, savory flavor without any fishiness; capers and chopped kalamatas provided potency. Finally, shards of ricotta salata, a slightly aged ricotta, added a salty tang. If you can't find ricotta salata you can substitute French feta, Pecorino Romano, or Cotija (a firm, crumbly Mexican cheese). We prefer to use kosher salt in this recipe because it clings best to the eggplant in step 1; if using table salt, reduce salt amounts by half. To prevent the eggplant from breaking up into small pieces, do not stir it frequently when sautéing in step 2. To give this dish a little extra kick, add additional pepper flakes. For the nutritional information for this recipe, see page 307.

1½	pounds eggplant, cut into ½-inch pieces
	Kosher salt and pepper
3½	tablespoons extra-virgin olive oil, plus extra for serving
4	garlic cloves, minced
2	anchovy fillets, rinsed and minced
¼	teaspoon red pepper flakes, or to taste
1	(28-ounce) can crushed tomatoes
½	cup pitted kalamata olives, chopped coarse
6	tablespoons minced fresh parsley
2	tablespoons capers, rinsed
1	pound rigatoni
	Shredded ricotta salata

1. Line large plate with double layer of coffee filters and lightly spray with vegetable oil spray. Toss eggplant with 1 teaspoon salt, then spread out over coffee filters. Microwave eggplant, uncovered, until dry to touch and slightly shriveled, about 10 minutes, tossing halfway through cooking. Let cool slightly.

2. Transfer eggplant to large bowl, drizzle with 1 tablespoon oil, and toss gently to coat. Heat 1 tablespoon oil in 12-inch nonstick skillet over medium-high heat until shimmering. Add eggplant and cook, stirring occasionally, until well browned and fully tender, about 10 minutes; transfer to clean plate.

3. Let skillet cool slightly, about 3 minutes. Add 1 tablespoon oil, garlic, anchovies, and pepper flakes to now-empty skillet and cook over medium heat, stirring often, until garlic is lightly golden and fragrant, about 1 minute. Stir in tomatoes, increase heat to medium-high, and simmer, stirring occasionally, until slightly thickened, 8 to 10 minutes. Add eggplant and cook, stirring occasionally, until eggplant is heated through and flavors meld, 3 to 5 minutes. Stir in olives, parsley, capers, and remaining ½ tablespoon oil and season with salt to taste.

4. Meanwhile, bring 4 quarts water to boil in large pot. Add pasta and 2 tablespoons salt and cook, stirring often, until al dente. Reserve ½ cup cooking water, then drain pasta and return it to pot. Add sauce and toss to combine. Season with salt and pepper to taste and add reserved cooking water as needed to adjust consistency. Serve with ricotta salata and extra olive oil.

SMART SHOPPING **GLOBE VERSUS ITALIAN EGGPLANT**
You may be tempted to buy Italian eggplant when making an Italian pasta dish, but we suggest you stick with the classic globe eggplant instead (they look the same, but the Italian eggplant is about half the size). Globe eggplants contain fewer seeds than the smaller varieties, plus they retain their shape after cooking.

Spaghetti with Mushroom and Tomato Sauce

Serves 4 to 6

✔ **WHY THIS RECIPE WORKS:** Based on a Tuscan specialty known as *spaghetti alla boscaiola,* or "woodsman's pasta," this dish swaps in hearty mushrooms for the long-simmered meat typically found in traditional ragus. Portobellos give the sauce a meaty texture, while dried porcini infuse it with an ultra-concentrated smoky mushroom flavor. To amp up the meaty mushroom notes even further, we added the liquid we'd used to rehydrate the dried porcini; using chicken broth for this step provided more deep, savory notes. Whole tomatoes, crushed by hand, gave our sauce the right thickness, and woodsy rosemary continued the rustic nature of the dish. Pancetta imparted backbone to the sauce, but bacon can be substituted for the pancetta if necessary. For the nutritional information for this recipe, see page 307.

1 cup low-sodium chicken broth
1 ounce dried porcini mushrooms, rinsed
4 ounces pancetta, cut into ½-inch pieces
8 ounces portobello mushrooms, stemmed, gills removed, and cut into ½-inch pieces
3 tablespoons extra-virgin olive oil
4 garlic cloves, sliced thin
1 tablespoon tomato paste
2 teaspoons minced fresh rosemary
1 (14.5-ounce) can whole peeled tomatoes, drained with juice reserved, tomatoes coarsely crushed
   Salt and pepper
1 pound spaghetti
   Grated Pecorino Romano cheese

1. Microwave broth and porcini in covered bowl until steaming, about 1 minute. Let sit until softened, about 5 minutes. Drain mushrooms through fine-mesh strainer lined with coffee filter; reserve broth and finely chop porcini.

2. Cook pancetta in 12-inch skillet over medium heat until crisp, 5 to 7 minutes. Add chopped porcini, portobellos, oil, garlic, tomato paste, and rosemary. Cook, stirring often, until portobellos are softened and lightly browned and tomato paste starts to brown, 5 to 7 minutes. Stir in reserved mushroom broth, crushed tomatoes, and reserved tomato juice. Bring to simmer and cook until thickened, 15 to 20 minutes. Season with salt and pepper to taste.

3. Meanwhile, bring 4 quarts water to boil in large pot. Add pasta and 1 tablespoon salt and cook, stirring often, until al dente. Reserve ½ cup cooking water, then drain pasta and return it to pot. Add sauce and toss to combine. Season with salt and pepper to taste and add reserved cooking water as needed to adjust consistency. Serve with Pecorino.

QUICK PREP TIP **REMOVING PORTOBELLO GILLS**
The black gills on the underside of a portobello mushroom cap can make a sauce taste particularly muddy and look dark (especially if using lots of them). To avoid this, simply scrape the gills off the mushroom using a soupspoon before cooking.

Shrimp Fra Diavolo with Linguine

Serves 4 to 6

✓ **WHY THIS RECIPE WORKS:** For our diavolo, we flambéed the shrimp for sweetness and packed in as much garlic and pepper flakes as we could. Before flambéing, roll up long sleeves, tie back long hair, and turn off the exhaust fan and lit burners. This dish is fairly spicy; to make it milder, reduce the amount of pepper flakes.

1	pound medium-large shrimp (31 to 40 per pound), peeled and deveined
6	tablespoons extra-virgin olive oil
	Salt
1	teaspoon red pepper flakes, or to taste
¼	cup cognac or brandy
12	garlic cloves, minced
1	(28-ounce) can diced tomatoes, drained
1	cup dry white wine
½	teaspoon sugar
1	pound linguine
¼	cup minced fresh parsley

1. Toss shrimp with 1 tablespoon oil, ¾ teaspoon salt, and ½ teaspoon pepper flakes. Heat 1 tablespoon oil in 12-inch skillet over high heat until just smoking. Add shrimp in even layer and cook, without stirring, until bottoms of shrimp turn spotty brown, about 30 seconds. Off heat, flip shrimp, add cognac, and let warm through, about 5 seconds. Wave lit match over pan until cognac ignites, then shake pan to distribute flames. When flames subside, transfer shrimp to bowl.

2. Let skillet cool slightly, about 3 minutes. Add 3 tablespoons oil and three-quarters of garlic to now-empty skillet and cook over low heat, stirring constantly, until garlic foams and is sticky and straw-colored, about 10 minutes. Stir in tomatoes, wine, sugar, ¾ teaspoon salt, and remaining ½ teaspoon pepper flakes. Increase heat to medium-high and simmer until thickened, about 8 minutes.

3. Meanwhile, bring 4 quarts water to boil in large pot. Add pasta and 1 tablespoon salt and cook, stirring often, until al dente. Reserve ½ cup cooking water, then drain pasta and return it to pot.

4. Stir shrimp along with any accumulated juice, remaining garlic, and parsley into sauce and bring to quick simmer until shrimp are heated through, about 1 minute. Off heat, stir in remaining 1 tablespoon oil. Add several large spoonfuls of sauce (without shrimp) to pasta and toss to combine. Season with salt to taste and add reserved cooking water as needed to adjust consistency. Divide pasta among individual bowls. Top each bowl with remaining sauce and shrimp and serve.

QUICK PREP TIP HOW TO FLAMBÉ
Flambéing the shrimp in this dish adds a depth of flavor that you just can't get otherwise. Here's how to do it. Off the heat, add the cognac to the pan. After it has warmed through, wave a lit match over the shrimp and let the cognac ignite. Once it's ignited, gently shake the pan back and forth until the flames subside and finally extinguish themselves.

Linguine with Fresh Clam Sauce

Serves 4 to 6

✔ **WHY THIS RECIPE WORKS:** When it comes to clam sauce, most folks are accustomed to an ultra-buttery, ultra-garlicky sauce featuring canned chopped clams. We wanted the real deal—a fresher, lighter sauce that tasted of sweet, briny clams and used (wow!) fresh clams to get there. We steamed four pounds of littlenecks with aromatics and white wine until they released their liquid and popped open. With tender clams and a flavorful, from-scratch clam broth at the ready, all we had to do was add a couple chopped tomatoes for brightness and a hefty dose of butter for richness. When shopping for clams, choose the smallest ones you can find. Be sure to scrub the clams thoroughly of grit and sand before cooking. Note that the clams can be very briny, so be sure to taste the final dish before seasoning with additional salt.

2	tablespoons extra-virgin olive oil
2	shallots, minced
3	garlic cloves, minced
½	teaspoon red pepper flakes
4	pounds littleneck or cherrystone clams, scrubbed
½	cup dry white wine
1	bay leaf
2	tomatoes, cored and chopped fine
6	tablespoons unsalted butter, cut into ¼-inch pieces
¼	cup fresh parsley leaves
1	tablespoon minced fresh oregano or 1 teaspoon dried
	Salt and pepper
1	pound linguine

1. Heat oil in large Dutch oven over medium-high heat until shimmering. Add shallots and cook until softened, about 2 minutes. Stir in garlic and pepper flakes and cook until fragrant, about 15 seconds. Stir in clams, wine, and bay leaf. Cover and simmer, shaking pan occasionally, until clams begin to open, about 6 minutes.

2. Uncover and continue to simmer until all clams have opened and sauce is slightly reduced, about 2 minutes; discard any clams that refuse to open and remove bay leaf. (If clams release sand into sauce, remove clams and strain sauce; return sauce and clams to clean pot and continue.) Gently stir in tomatoes, butter, parsley, and oregano. Continue to cook until butter has melted and tomatoes are heated through, about 1 minute. Off heat, season with pepper to taste.

3. Meanwhile, bring 4 quarts water to boil in large pot. Add pasta and 1 tablespoon salt and cook, stirring often, until al dente. Reserve ½ cup cooking water, then drain pasta and return it to pot. Add clam mixture and toss to combine. Season with pepper to taste and add reserved cooking water as needed to adjust consistency. Serve.

SMART SHOPPING PARSLEY
You've probably noticed that your neighborhood grocer offers two different varieties of this recognizable herb (though there are actually more than 30 varieties out there): curly-leaf and flat-leaf (also called Italian). Curly-leaf parsley is more popular, but in the test kitchen flat-leaf is by far the favorite. We find flat-leaf to have a sweet, bright flavor that's much preferable to the bitter, grassy tones of curly-leaf parsley. Flat-leaf parsley is also much more fragrant than its curly cousin.

ZITI WITH FIRE-ROASTED TOMATOES, PEPPERONI, AND SMOKED MOZZARELLA

Pasta Plus Five

Spaghetti with Garlic, Olive Oil, and Marinated Artichokes

Serves 4 to 6

✔ **WHY THIS RECIPE WORKS:** Called *aglio e olio* in the old country, spaghetti with garlic and olive oil relies on a hefty hand with the garlic—we used a whopping 12 cloves. Cooking the garlic slowly over low heat turned it golden, nutty-tasting, and subtly sweet. To add more punch to this simple dish, we called on a staple of the antipasto platter—marinated artichokes—which gave our garlicky sauce a flavorful backbone and no need for other dried herbs or aromatics. For some textural contrast, we browned the artichokes until crisp around the edges, which took just minutes. Stirring a bit of raw garlic into the sauce, along with more olive oil, before tossing it with the browned artichokes and cooked pasta ensured a hit of potent garlic flavor in each bite. To make this dish a bit spicy, consider adding a pinch of red pepper flakes to the skillet with the garlic.

7	tablespoons extra-virgin olive oil
12	garlic cloves, minced
	Salt and pepper
3	cups drained marinated artichokes (14 ounces), patted dry
1	pound spaghetti
1	ounce Parmesan cheese, grated (½ cup), plus extra for serving
3	tablespoons minced fresh parsley

1. Cook 3 tablespoons oil, 3 tablespoons garlic, and ½ teaspoon salt in 10-inch nonstick skillet over low heat, stirring often, until garlic foams and is sticky and straw-colored, about 10 minutes. Transfer to bowl and stir in 3 tablespoons oil and remaining garlic.

2. Heat remaining 1 tablespoon oil in now-empty skillet over high heat until shimmering. Add artichokes and cook until edges are crisp and browned, about 6 minutes.

3. Meanwhile, bring 4 quarts water to boil in large pot. Add pasta and 1 tablespoon salt and cook, stirring often, until al dente. Reserve ½ cup cooking water, then drain pasta and return it to pot. Stir 2 tablespoons reserved cooking water into garlic mixture to loosen it. Add garlic mixture, artichokes, Parmesan, and parsley to pasta and toss to combine. Season with salt and pepper to taste and add remaining reserved cooking water as needed to adjust consistency. Serve with extra Parmesan.

QUICK PREP TIP SLOW-COOKING GARLIC
The secret to this dish is slow-cooking the garlic until it turns golden, nutty-tasting, and sweet. Cooking the garlic with a portion of the oil and salt over low heat draws out and tempers its harsh raw flavor. When the garlic foams and becomes sticky and straw-colored, which takes about 10 minutes, it should be removed from the heat.

Campanelle with Porcini Cream Sauce

Serves 4 to 6

✔ **WHY THIS RECIPE WORKS:** Dried porcini deliver concentrated, robust flavor in this simple recipe. To eke out the most flavor from the mushrooms, we used a two-step approach: First, we sautéed the porcini, which we'd softened in the microwave with water, with chopped onions for a rich foundation. Second, we saved the liquor leftover from rehydrating the dried mushrooms and used it as the base of the sauce—this way, none of the hearty porcini flavor went down the drain. Heavy cream enriched the sauce, while grated Parmesan thickened it and added a salty tang that enhanced the meaty, savory flavor of the porcini.

2 cups water

2 ounces dried porcini mushrooms, rinsed

3 tablespoons unsalted butter

2 onions, chopped fine
Salt and pepper

½ cup heavy cream

1 pound campanelle

2 ounces Parmesan cheese, grated (1 cup), plus extra for serving

1. Microwave water and porcini in covered bowl until steaming, about 1 minute. Let sit until softened, about 5 minutes. Drain mushrooms through fine-mesh strainer lined with coffee filter; reserve liquid and chop mushrooms into ¾-inch pieces.

2. Melt butter in large saucepan over medium heat. Add onions and ¼ teaspoon salt and cook until softened and lightly browned, 10 to 12 minutes. Stir in porcini and cook until fragrant, about 2 minutes. Stir in strained porcini liquid, scraping up any browned bits, and simmer until thickened, about 10 minutes. Stir in cream and simmer until thickened, about 2 minutes.

3. Meanwhile, bring 4 quarts water to boil in large pot. Add pasta and 1 tablespoon salt and cook, stirring often, until al dente. Reserve ½ cup cooking water, then drain pasta and return it to pot. Add sauce and Parmesan and toss to combine. Season with salt and pepper to taste and add reserved cooking water as needed to adjust consistency. Serve with extra Parmesan.

QUICK PREP TIP
REHYDRATING DRIED PORCINI
Rinse porcini thoroughly under running water, then place in bowl and cover with water (or add water as specified in recipe). Cover bowl and microwave until steaming, about 1 minute. Let sit until mushrooms are softened, about 5 minutes. Drain through fine-mesh strainer lined with coffee filter; reserve liquid and chop mushrooms as directed.

PENNE WITH FIRE-ROASTED TOMATO AND ROASTED RED PEPPER SAUCE

Spaghetti with Quickest Tomato Sauce

Serves 4 to 6

✔ **WHY THIS RECIPE WORKS:** With just a handful of ingredients, you can create a sauce with robust tomato flavor—and it takes only 20 minutes. The secret is using the right mix of tomato products; crushed tomatoes gave us the slightly thickened texture we wanted, while diced tomatoes offered big bites of tomato. Serve with grated Parmesan. For the nutritional information for this recipe, see page 307.

3	tablespoons extra-virgin olive oil
3	garlic cloves, minced
1	(28-ounce) can crushed tomatoes
1	(14.5-ounce) can diced tomatoes
1	pound spaghetti
	Salt and pepper
3	tablespoons chopped fresh basil

1. Cook oil and garlic in medium saucepan over medium heat, stirring often, until fragrant but not browned, about 2 minutes. Stir in crushed and diced tomatoes and simmer until slightly thickened, 15 to 20 minutes.

2. Meanwhile, bring 4 quarts water to boil in large pot. Add pasta and 1 tablespoon salt and cook, stirring often, until al dente. Reserve ½ cup cooking water, then drain pasta and return it to pot. Add sauce and basil and toss to combine. Season with salt and pepper to taste and add reserved cooking water as needed to adjust consistency. Serve.

Penne with Fire-Roasted Tomato and Roasted Red Pepper Sauce

Serves 4 to 6

✔ **WHY THIS RECIPE WORKS:** For an easy tomato sauce with a kick, we reached for a can of fire-roasted tomatoes. Roasted red peppers added sweet character and a bit of charred flavor. Pulsing the tomatoes and roasted peppers in the food processor gave the sauce a nice thickness. To balance the acidity and bring some richness to the sauce, we stirred in a good amount of heavy cream. If necessary, you can substitute regular canned whole tomatoes for the fire-roasted tomatoes.

1	(28-ounce) can fire-roasted whole tomatoes
3	cups jarred roasted red peppers, rinsed, patted dry, and chopped
3	tablespoons extra-virgin olive oil
3	garlic cloves, minced
¾	cup heavy cream
	Salt and pepper
1	pound penne

1. Pulse tomatoes and red peppers together in food processor until coarsely ground, about 12 pulses. Cook oil and garlic in medium saucepan over medium heat, stirring often, until fragrant but not browned, about 2 minutes. Stir in processed tomato mixture and simmer until slightly thickened, 15 to 20 minutes. Stir in heavy cream and simmer for 3 minutes. Off heat, season with salt and pepper to taste.

2. Meanwhile, bring 4 quarts water to boil in large pot. Add pasta and 1 tablespoon salt and cook, stirring often, until al dente. Reserve ½ cup cooking water, then drain pasta and return it to pot. Add sauce and toss to combine. Season with salt and pepper to taste and add reserved cooking water as needed to adjust consistency. Serve.

Ultimate Stovetop Macaroni and Cheese

Serves 4

✓ **WHY THIS RECIPE WORKS:** Just about as fast as the blue-box version, but with much more flavor, this creamy mac and cheese goes from stovetop to table in about 15 minutes—no oven stint necessary. After cooking the macaroni, we returned it to the pot and stirred in a simple sauce of evaporated milk, eggs, and dry mustard, plus a generous amount of shredded cheddar and butter, over low heat. Evaporated milk was the secret to a silky-smooth sauce—both milk and half-and-half curdled a bit when stirred in. Cheddar delivered ultra-cheesy flavor, though you can substitute Monterey Jack or Colby cheese if necessary.

8	ounces (2 cups) elbow macaroni
	Salt and pepper
2	large eggs
1	(12-ounce) can evaporated milk
1	teaspoon dry mustard, dissolved in 1 teaspoon water
4	tablespoons unsalted butter
12	ounces sharp cheddar cheese, shredded (3 cups)

1. Bring 4 quarts water to boil in large pot. Add pasta and 1 tablespoon salt and cook, stirring often, until al dente. Meanwhile, whisk eggs, half of evaporated milk, mustard mixture, ½ teaspoon salt, and ¼ teaspoon pepper together in bowl.

2. Drain pasta and return it to pot. Add butter and cook over low heat until melted. Stir in egg mixture and half of cheese. Cook, gradually stirring in remaining milk and cheese, until mixture is hot and creamy, about 5 minutes. Season with salt and pepper to taste. Serve.

Spicy Tomato and Chile Macaroni and Cheese

Serves 4

✓ **WHY THIS RECIPE WORKS:** We gave our stovetop mac and cheese a Tex-Mex spin with spicy, tangy Ro-Tel tomatoes (a blend of tomatoes, green chiles, and spices). Swapping the cheddar for pepper Jack cheese amped up the heat on this boldly flavored variation of a comfort classic. This dish is quite spicy; to make it more mild, substitute Monterey Jack, cheddar, or Colby cheese for the pepper Jack cheese.

8	ounces (2 cups) elbow macaroni
	Salt and pepper
2	large eggs
1	(12-ounce) can evaporated milk
2	(10-ounce) cans Ro-Tel tomatoes, drained
4	tablespoons unsalted butter
12	ounces pepper Jack cheese, shredded (3 cups)

1. Bring 4 quarts water to boil in large pot. Add pasta and 1 tablespoon salt and cook, stirring often, until al dente. Meanwhile, whisk eggs, half of evaporated milk, ½ teaspoon salt, and ¼ teaspoon pepper together in bowl.

2. Drain pasta and return it to pot. Add tomatoes and butter and cook over low heat until butter is melted. Stir in egg mixture and half of cheese. Cook, gradually stirring in remaining milk and cheese, until mixture is hot and creamy, about 5 minutes. Season with salt and pepper to taste. Serve.

Farfalle with Sautéed Mushrooms and Truffle Oil

Serves 4 to 6

✓ **WHY THIS RECIPE WORKS:** Perfectly sautéed mushrooms and rich, earthy truffle oil come together in this indulgent dish. For mushrooms with the ideal texture, we cooked them covered to start, which drew out their moisture, then removed the lid so they could brown. To deglaze the pan and loosen the flavorful fond (the browned bits left behind from sautéing the mushrooms), we added water from our already-boiling pot of pasta cooking water. The hot water, plus a generous amount of butter, formed an ultra-rich sauce that coated each piece of pasta perfectly. To keep the flavor of the truffle oil pure and intense, we stirred it in at the end, off the heat—cooking it would have muted its flavor. We prefer the flavor of white truffle oil to black truffle oil. You can substitute white mushrooms for the cremini mushrooms if necessary.

2   **tablespoons unsalted butter, plus 4 tablespoons cut into ¼-inch pieces and chilled**

1½   **pounds cremini mushrooms, trimmed and sliced ¼ inch thick**
  Salt and pepper

4   **garlic cloves, minced**

1   **pound farfalle**

2   **ounces Parmesan cheese, grated (1 cup), plus extra for serving**

4   **teaspoons white truffle oil, plus extra to taste**

1. Bring 4 quarts water to boil in large pot for pasta. Melt 2 tablespoons butter in 12-inch skillet over medium heat. Add mushrooms and ½ teaspoon salt, cover, and cook until mushrooms have released their liquid, about 8 minutes. Uncover and continue to cook until mushrooms are dry and well browned, 10 to 15 minutes.

2. Stir in garlic and cook until fragrant, about 30 seconds. Add ¾ cup boiling pasta water, scraping up any browned bits, and bring to simmer. Stir in chilled butter until melted, then remove from heat.

3. Meanwhile, add pasta and 1 tablespoon salt to boiling water and cook, stirring often, until al dente. Reserve ½ cup cooking water, then drain pasta and return it to pot. Add mushroom mixture, Parmesan, and truffle oil and toss to combine. Season with salt, pepper, and extra truffle oil to taste and add reserved cooking water as needed to adjust consistency. Serve with extra Parmesan.

SMART SHOPPING WHITE MUSHROOMS VERSUS CREMINI MUSHROOMS

Despite their different appearance, white button and cremini mushrooms (and portobellos) actually belong to the same mushroom species. Cremini are a brown-hued variety, while portobellos are cremini that have been allowed to grow large. We think of cremini as a recent introduction to the marketplace, but all button mushrooms were actually brown until 1926, when a mushroom farmer in Pennsylvania found a cluster of white buttons growing in his beds, which he cloned and began selling as a new variety. But does the loss of color mean a loss of flavor? To find out, we sautéed white button and cremini mushrooms and tasted them side by side in risotto and atop pizza. The flavor of the cremini was noticeably deeper and more complex. This difference in taste was also apparent, though less obvious, when we compared both types of mushroom sprinkled raw over salads. The lesson? If bolder mushroom flavor is what you're after, it's worth shelling out a little extra for cremini.

WHITE MUSHROOMS   CREMINI MUSHROOMS

Farfalle with Fennel, Cream, and Herbs

Serves 4 to 6

✔ **WHY THIS RECIPE WORKS:** This ultra-creamy, intensely flavored dish starts with sautéing thinly sliced fennel in butter until deeply caramelized and meltingly tender. Scallions provided a double dose of flavor—the minced whites, which we sautéed with our fennel, gave the sauce an aromatic backbone, while the thinly sliced greens added a bright, crisp touch and pop of color when stirred in at the end. Applying the same two-for-one philosophy to our fennel, we reserved the fronds, minced them, and stirred them in with the scallion greens for a delicate, herbal finish. Heavy cream worked to thicken the sauce and turned our simple pasta dish into a luxurious, rich main course. When shopping, look for fennel that has the fronds still attached; the fronds add significant flavor to the final dish.

3	tablespoons unsalted butter
2	fennel bulbs, fronds chopped, stalks discarded, bulbs halved, cored, and sliced thin (see page 248)
	Salt and pepper
8	scallions, white parts minced, green parts sliced thin
2	cups heavy cream
1	pound farfalle
¼	cup minced fresh tarragon or mint

1. Melt butter in 12-inch nonstick skillet over medium heat. Add sliced fennel bulbs and ½ teaspoon salt and cook until soft and golden, about 20 minutes. Stir in scallion whites and cook until fragrant, about 30 seconds. Stir in cream and simmer until thickened, about 8 minutes.

2. Meanwhile, bring 4 quarts water to boil in large pot. Add pasta and 1 tablespoon salt and cook, stirring often, until al dente. Reserve ½ cup cooking water, then drain pasta and return it to pot. Add sauce, fennel fronds, scallion greens, and tarragon and toss to combine. Season with salt and pepper to taste and add reserved cooking water as needed to adjust consistency. Serve.

QUICK PREP TIP SEPARATING SCALLION WHITES AND GREENS
To get the most out of the scallions in our Farfalle with Fennel, Cream, and Herbs, we found it best to separate the more pungent, oniony white part from the more delicate, herblike green part. The scallion whites can then be sautéed to soften their texture and temper their raw bite, leaving the more subtle greens to be added to the dish at the very end.

Spaghetti with Fried Eggs and Bread Crumbs

Serves 4

✔ **WHY THIS RECIPE WORKS:** This rustic Italian specialty of garlicky spaghetti topped with fried eggs and crunchy bread crumbs shows how simple really can be spectacular. The key is adding the eggs to the skillet all at once, rather than cracking them in one by one, to ensure that they finish cooking at the same time. Covering the skillet during cooking helped the surface of the eggs set so that we didn't have to flip them. But our perfectly fried eggs couldn't wait for the pasta—if they sat around for even a minute, the yolks firmed up, so we made sure to prepare the bread crumbs, garlic, and pasta before tackling the eggs.

2   slices hearty white sandwich bread, torn into quarters

10 tablespoons extra-virgin olive oil
     Salt and pepper

4   garlic cloves, minced

1   pound spaghetti

1   ounce Parmesan cheese, grated (½ cup), plus extra for serving

4   large eggs, cracked into 2 small bowls (2 eggs per bowl)

1. Adjust oven rack to middle position and heat oven to 375 degrees. Pulse bread in food processor to coarse crumbs, about 10 pulses. Toss crumbs with 2 tablespoons oil, season with salt and pepper, and spread over rimmed baking sheet. Bake, stirring often, until golden, 8 to 10 minutes.

2. Cook 3 tablespoons oil, garlic, and ¼ teaspoon salt in 12-inch nonstick skillet over low heat, stirring often, until garlic foams and is sticky and straw-colored, 8 to 10 minutes; transfer to bowl.

3. Meanwhile, bring 4 quarts water to boil in large pot. Add pasta and 1 tablespoon salt and cook, stirring often, until al dente. Reserve 1 cup cooking water, then drain pasta and return it to pot. Add garlic mixture, 3 tablespoons oil, Parmesan, and ½ cup reserved cooking water and toss to combine; cover and set aside while cooking eggs.

4. About 5 minutes before pasta is ready, wipe now-empty skillet clean with paper towels and place over low heat for 5 minutes. Add remaining 2 tablespoons oil, swirl to coat pan, then quickly add eggs. Season with salt and pepper, cover, and cook until whites are set but yolks are still runny, 2 to 3 minutes.

5. Season pasta with salt and pepper to taste and add reserved cooking water as needed to adjust consistency. Top individual portions with bread crumbs and fried egg and serve with extra Parmesan.

QUICK PREP TIP **MAKING FRIED EGGS**
Crack four eggs into two bowls. When ready to fry the eggs, slide them simultaneously into the hot skillet. This ensures that the eggs will all cook at the same rate.

Penne with Zucchini, Cherry Tomatoes, and Boursin Cheese

Serves 4 to 6

✔ **WHY THIS RECIPE WORKS:** We wanted to create a brightly flavored dish with tender vegetables and a tangy, creamy sauce—with just a handful of ingredients. Zucchini and tomatoes provided the perfect mix of quick-cooking, fresh-flavored vegetables. The tomatoes required no prep—we simply quartered them and stirred them in just before serving to heat through. The zucchini, however, needed some cooking to draw out excess moisture. Broiling proved optimal, as it also encouraged the development of some flavorful char on the vegetable's surface. We found it best to remove the zucchini from the oven before it was fully tender, since it continued to cook on the roasting pan. Finally, we had the sauce to consider. In a major coup, we discovered a single ingredient that could provide both the creamy texture and tangy flavor we were after, plus some herbal and aromatic notes: garlic-and-herb-rich Boursin cheese. The zucchini should be slightly undercooked after broiling in step 1; it will continue to soften as it waits for the pasta.

¼ cup extra-virgin olive oil

1½ pounds zucchini, quartered lengthwise and sliced ¾ inch thick
Salt and pepper

1 pound penne

1 pound cherry tomatoes, quartered

1 (5.2-ounce) package Boursin Garlic and Fine Herbs cheese, crumbled

½ cup chopped fresh basil

1. Adjust oven rack 4 inches from broiler element and heat broiler. Line rimmed baking sheet with aluminum foil and brush with 1 tablespoon oil. Toss zucchini in large bowl with 1 tablespoon oil, season with salt and pepper, and spread evenly onto prepared baking sheet. Broil zucchini, stirring occasionally, until lightly charred around edges but still firm in center, about 10 minutes; let cool slightly on baking sheet.

2. Meanwhile, bring 4 quarts water to boil in large pot. Add pasta and 1 tablespoon salt and cook, stirring often, until al dente. Reserve 1 cup cooking water, then drain pasta and return it to pot.

3. Add tomatoes, Boursin, and ¼ cup reserved cooking water to pasta and toss to combine. Gently stir in zucchini, basil, and remaining 2 tablespoons oil. Season with salt and pepper to taste and add remaining cooking water as needed to adjust consistency. Serve.

SMART SHOPPING BOURSIN CHEESE
Boursin is a soft, spreadable cheese that comes in several varieties and is available widely. The Garlic and Fine Herbs variety is a key ingredient in our Penne with Zucchini, Cherry Tomatoes, and Boursin Cheese, as it adds a creamy texture, cheesy tang, and a big hit of aromatic garlic and herb flavor.

Campanelle with Roasted Garlic, Chicken Sausage, and Arugula

Serves 4 to 6

✔ **WHY THIS RECIPE WORKS:** Roasted garlic adds sweet, intense flavor to this simple pasta dinner. To speed up the time required to deliver richly flavored, perfectly tender garlic, we turned out a few new tricks. First, we found we could roast the garlic more quickly when the cloves were separated, rather than bunched together in a compact head. Removing the skins also made the cloves easier to handle after being roasted. Combining the peeled garlic cloves, oil, and seasonings in a small baking dish made it a snap to both roast and mash them into a paste. We also found we could crank the oven all the way up to 425 degrees and cut the roasting time to just 20 minutes. Covering the dish with aluminum foil was essential, otherwise the exposed parts of the garlic cloves turned tough and overly brown during roasting. The mashed garlic paste ensured evenly distributed garlic and gave us a head start on the sauce—crumbled goat cheese turned it into a full-fledged thick and creamy coating for our campanelle. Lightly browned chicken sausage and a few handfuls of baby arugula made this flavorful dish filling, too. Chicken sausage is available in a wide variety of flavors; feel free to choose a flavor that you think will pair well with the other flavors in this dish.

⅓ cup plus 1 tablespoon olive oil
16 garlic cloves, peeled
Salt and pepper
12 ounces cooked chicken sausage, sliced ½ inch thick on bias
1 pound campanelle
5 ounces (5 cups) baby arugula
4 ounces goat cheese, crumbled (1 cup)

1. Adjust oven rack to upper-middle position and heat oven to 425 degrees. Combine ⅓ cup oil, garlic, ½ teaspoon salt, and ½ teaspoon pepper in 8-inch square baking dish and cover with aluminum foil. Bake, stirring occasionally, until garlic is caramelized and soft, about 20 minutes. Let cool slightly, then mash garlic and oil into paste with fork.

2. Heat remaining 1 tablespoon oil in 12-inch skillet over medium-high until shimmering. Add sausage and cook until lightly browned, about 4 minutes. Off heat, stir in garlic mixture.

3. Meanwhile, bring 4 quarts water to boil in large pot. Add pasta and 1 tablespoon salt and cook, stirring often, until al dente. Reserve 1½ cups cooking water, then drain pasta and return it to pot. Add sausage mixture, arugula, cheese, and ½ cup reserved cooking water and toss to combine. Season with salt and pepper to taste and add remaining cooking water as needed to adjust consistency. Serve.

SMART SHOPPING PREPEELED VERSUS FRESH GARLIC
Many supermarkets carry jars or deli containers of prepeeled garlic cloves, but how do they compare to fresh garlic bought by the head? We tasted both kinds of garlic in various recipes, both raw and cooked, and, in all cases, results were mixed. However, we did notice a difference in shelf life: A whole head of garlic stored in a cool, dry place will last for at least a few weeks, while prepeeled garlic in a jar (which must be kept refrigerated) lasts for only about two weeks before turning yellowish and developing an overly pungent aroma, even if kept unopened in its original packaging. (In fact, in several instances we found containers of garlic that had started to develop this odor and color on the supermarket shelf.) But if you go through a lot of garlic, prepeeled cloves can be a fine alternative. Just make sure they look firm and white and have a matte finish when you purchase them.

Orecchiette with Roasted Garlic and Chicken

Serves 4 to 6

✔ **WHY THIS RECIPE WORKS:** For another effortless dinner using our super-speedy roasted garlic, we added tender chicken and slightly spicy broccoli rabe. You can use leftover cooked chicken or store-bought rotisserie chicken here, or you can quickly cook chicken following the instructions on page 80.

⅓ cup olive oil
16 garlic cloves, peeled
　 Salt and pepper
2 cups shredded cooked chicken
1 pound broccoli rabe, trimmed (see page 23) and cut into 1½-inch pieces
1 pound orecchiette
2 ounces Parmesan cheese, grated (1 cup), plus extra for serving

1. Adjust oven rack to upper-middle position and heat oven to 425 degrees. Combine oil, garlic, ½ teaspoon salt, and ½ teaspoon pepper in 8-inch square baking dish and cover with aluminum foil. Bake, stirring occasionally, until garlic is caramelized and soft, about 20 minutes. Let cool slightly, then mash garlic and oil into paste with fork. Stir in chicken; cover until needed.

2. Meanwhile, bring 4 quarts water to boil in large pot. Add broccoli rabe and 1 tablespoon salt and cook until crisp-tender, 1 to 3 minutes; transfer to paper towel–lined plate.

3. Return pot of water to boil, add pasta, and cook, stirring often, until al dente. Reserve ½ cup cooking water, then drain pasta and return it to pot. Add chicken mixture, broccoli rabe, and Parmesan and toss to combine. Season with salt and pepper to taste and add reserved cooking water as needed to adjust consistency. Serve with extra Parmesan.

Campanelle with Roasted Garlic, Shrimp, and Feta

Serves 4 to 6

✔ **WHY THIS RECIPE WORKS:** Combining shrimp and feta with our easy roasted garlic gave us a pasta supper with a definitively Greek bent. If your shrimp are larger or smaller, alter the cooking time in step 1 accordingly.

⅓ cup olive oil
16 garlic cloves, peeled
　 Salt and pepper
1 pound medium-large shrimp (31 to 40 per pound), peeled, deveined, and tails removed
1 pound campanelle
4 ounces feta cheese, crumbled (1 cup)
1 cup chopped fresh basil

1. Adjust oven rack to upper-middle position and heat oven to 425 degrees. Combine oil, garlic, ½ teaspoon salt, and ½ teaspoon pepper in 8-inch square baking dish and cover with aluminum foil. Bake, stirring occasionally, until garlic is caramelized and soft, about 20 minutes. Let cool slightly, then mash garlic and oil into paste with fork. Stir in shrimp and continue to bake until shrimp are cooked through, about 10 minutes.

2. Meanwhile, bring 4 quarts water to boil in large pot. Add pasta and 1 tablespoon salt and cook, stirring often, until al dente. Reserve ½ cup cooking water, then drain pasta and return it to pot. Add shrimp mixture, feta, and basil; toss to combine. Season with salt and pepper to taste and add reserved cooking water as needed to adjust consistency. Serve.

BLT Pasta

Serves 4 to 6

✔ **WHY THIS RECIPE WORKS:** What's better than a BLT? BLT pasta! Our recipe took the familiar elements and turned them into a simple sauce. We started with the bacon, which we cooked until crisp and then stirred in at the end. Using the rendered fat to sauté the tomatoes added smoky flavor to the dish. Halved cherry tomatoes cut back on prep time; cooking them briefly brought out their sweetness and allowed them to soften slightly. Baby arugula made the perfect stand-in for the usual iceberg lettuce—the arugula offered a welcome spicy bite, and it wilted nicely when added to the hot pasta just before serving.

12	slices bacon, chopped
2	garlic cloves, minced
12	ounces cherry tomatoes, halved
1	pound orecchiette
	Salt and pepper
5	ounces (5 cups) baby arugula
2	ounces Parmesan cheese, grated (1 cup), plus extra for serving

1. Cook bacon in 12-inch nonstick skillet over medium-high heat until crisp, about 5 minutes; transfer to paper towel–lined plate. Pour off all but 2 tablespoons fat left in skillet, add garlic and tomatoes, and cook over medium-high heat until tomatoes are slightly softened, about 2 minutes.

2. Meanwhile, bring 4 quarts water to boil in large pot. Add pasta and 1 tablespoon salt and cook, stirring often, until al dente. Reserve 1½ cups cooking water, then drain pasta and return it to pot. Add bacon, garlic-tomato mixture, arugula, Parmesan, and 1 cup reserved cooking water and toss to combine. Season with salt and pepper to taste and add reserved cooking water as needed to adjust consistency. Serve with extra Parmesan.

Farfalle with Bacon, Toasted Corn, Cherry Tomatoes, and Basil

Serves 4 to 6

✔ **WHY THIS RECIPE WORKS:** This recipe makes the most of ripe, in-season corn and cherry tomatoes. Toasting the corn gives it a nutty flavor. Adding the halved tomatoes to the pan for a few minutes ensured that they softened slightly. This dish depends on the flavor of fresh corn; do not substitute frozen corn.

8	slices bacon, chopped
4	ears corn, kernels cut from cobs (see page 11)
	Salt and pepper
1	pound cherry tomatoes, halved
1	pound farfalle
2	ounces Parmesan cheese, grated (1 cup), plus extra for serving
½	cup chopped fresh basil

1. Cook bacon in 12-inch nonstick skillet over medium-high heat until crisp, about 5 minutes; transfer to paper towel–lined plate. Pour off all but 2 tablespoons fat left in skillet, add corn and ¼ teaspoon salt, and cook until spotty brown, about 10 minutes. Stir in tomatoes and cook until slightly softened, about 3 minutes.

2. Meanwhile, bring 4 quarts water to boil in large pot. Add pasta and 1 tablespoon salt and cook, stirring often, until al dente. Reserve ½ cup cooking water, then drain pasta and return it to pot. Add bacon, corn mixture, Parmesan, and basil and toss to combine. Season with salt and pepper to taste and add reserved cooking water as needed to adjust consistency. Serve with extra Parmesan.

BLT PASTA

Ziti with Stuffed Cherry Peppers, Pepperoni, and Tomato Sauce

Serves 4 to 6

✓ **WHY THIS RECIPE WORKS:** A classic antipasto ingredient—stuffed peppers—brings big flavor to this dish. Filled with provolone and prosciutto, the peppers provided spicy, savory, and salty notes—and all we had to do was chop them up. Pepperoni reinforced the peppery heat. Look for stuffed cherry peppers at the olive bar in the supermarket or next to the jarred pickles; one (12-ounce) jar of peppers will yield plenty for this recipe.

6 ounces sliced deli pepperoni, chopped fine

2 onions, chopped fine

8 oil-packed hot stuffed cherry peppers, rinsed, patted dry, and chopped fine

3 garlic cloves, minced

1 (15-ounce) can tomato sauce

1 pound ziti

Salt and pepper

1. Cook pepperoni in 12-inch skillet over medium-high heat until rendered and crisp, about 5 minutes. Stir in onions and cook until softened and lightly browned, 8 to 10 minutes. Stir in cherry peppers and garlic and cook until fragrant, about 1 minute. Stir in tomato sauce and simmer until thickened, about 10 minutes.

2. Meanwhile, bring 4 quarts water to boil in large pot. Add pasta and 1 tablespoon salt and cook, stirring often, until al dente. Reserve ½ cup cooking water, then drain pasta and return it to pot. Add sauce and toss to combine. Season with salt and pepper to taste and add reserved cooking water as needed to adjust consistency. Serve.

Ziti with Fire-Roasted Tomatoes, Pepperoni, and Smoked Mozzarella

Serves 4 to 6

✓ **WHY THIS RECIPE WORKS:** This smoky, spicy dish relies on pepperoni for heat and smoked mozzarella and fire-roasted canned tomatoes for a hint of char. Freezing the cheese was key to ensuring that it softened properly when mixed with the hot pasta; don't skip this step, or the mozzarella will form a gummy wad when tossed with the pasta. Regular canned whole tomatoes can be substituted for the fire-roasted tomatoes.

3 (14.5-ounce) cans fire-roasted diced tomatoes

6 ounces sliced deli pepperoni, chopped fine

3 garlic cloves, minced

6 ounces smoked mozzarella, cut into ½-inch cubes

1 pound ziti

Salt and pepper

¼ cup chopped fresh basil

1. Pulse tomatoes in food processor until coarsely ground, about 12 pulses. Cook pepperoni in 12-inch skillet over medium-high heat until rendered and crisp, about 5 minutes. Stir in garlic and cook until fragrant, about 30 seconds. Stir in processed tomatoes and simmer until slightly thickened, 15 to 20 minutes.

2. Meanwhile, place mozzarella on plate and freeze until slightly firm, about 10 minutes. Bring 4 quarts water to boil in large pot. Add pasta and 1 tablespoon salt and cook, stirring often, until al dente. Reserve ½ cup cooking water, then drain pasta and return it to pot. Add sauce, frozen mozzarella, and basil and toss gently to combine. Season with salt and pepper to taste and add reserved cooking water as needed to adjust consistency. Serve.

ALL ABOUT Canned Tomatoes

We love using fresh tomatoes, but good-quality tomatoes are available only a few months out of the year. Enter canned tomatoes, which are packed at the height of ripeness and deliver better flavor than their off-season counterparts. In this book, we use a variety of canned tomato products. Here are the most common ones we call for, the types of recipes we use them in, and the brands that we prefer.

Whole Tomatoes

Whole tomatoes are best reserved for recipes with a short simmering time, such as our Classic Spaghetti Marinara (page 166). We found that whole tomatoes packed in juice rather than in puree had a livelier, fresher flavor. Our top-rated brand is **Muir Glen Organic Whole Peeled Tomatoes**, which offers bold acidity, an appealing sweetness, and a firm texture. We also like Hunt's Whole Plum Tomatoes, which finished a close second and is our Best Buy (it costs $1 less per can).

Crushed Tomatoes

Crushed tomatoes work well in smoother sauces, such as in our Pasta alla Norma (page 183), offering both great flavor and body. We also employ crushed tomatoes in casseroles where we want long-simmered flavor without having to cook the sauce separately for a long time, such as our Baked Ziti (page 92). We prefer chunky and fresh-tasting **Tuttorosso Crushed Tomatoes** in Thick Puree with Basil. Muir Glen Organic Crushed Tomatoes with Basil came in a close second in our testing.

Diced Tomatoes

Diced tomatoes are best for rustic tomato sauces with a chunky texture, such as our Spaghetti Puttanesca (see page 168) and Pasta with Weekday Meat Sauce (see page 33). Diced tomatoes may also be processed with their juice in a food processor and used in place of crushed tomatoes when called for in a recipe. They are available both packed in juice and in puree; we favor diced tomatoes packed in juice because they have a fresher flavor. Overall, our preferred brand is **Hunt's Diced Tomatoes**, which tasters liked most for its fresh flavor and good balance of sweet and tart notes.

Tomato Puree and Tomato Sauce

Tomato puree and tomato sauce are both cooked and strained to remove the tomato seeds, making them much smoother and thicker than other canned tomato products. We found that tomato puree works well when we need a thick sauce, as in our Ultimate Chili Mac (page 77) and Classic Lasagna with Hearty Meat Sauce (page 90). We prefer tomato sauce when we need a slightly thinner sauce, but still want the same smooth texture and long-simmered tomato flavor, as in our No-Prep Baked Spaghetti (page 68). We found **Hunt's Tomato Puree** to be the best, with its thick consistency and tomatoey flavor.

Tomato Paste

Because it's naturally full of glutamates, which stimulate taste buds, tomato paste brings out subtle depths and savory notes. We use it in a variety of recipes, including both long-simmered sauces, such as our Classic Bolognese with Pappardelle (page 181), and quicker-cooking dishes, such as Ziti with Fennel and Italian Sausage (page 210), to lend a deeper, well-rounded tomato flavor and color. Our preferred brand is **Goya Tomato Paste**, for its bright, robust tomato flavor. Tasters liked its sweetness, yet found it well-balanced.

Gemelli with Caramelized Onions, Kale, and Bacon

Serves 4 to 6

✔ **WHY THIS RECIPE WORKS:** Glossy caramelized onions, braised kale, and crisped bacon give this pasta dish a sweet, savory, and deeply addictive flavor profile. Caramelized onions usually take hours to make—not ours. We jump-started the process by cooking the onions covered so they'd release their moisture, then we removed the lid and sautéed them for 20 minutes to let the liquid evaporate and give the onions a chance to become deeply browned and meltingly tender. For the kale, we simply added it to the pan with the onions. The pasta cooking water did double duty—after bringing the pot to a boil, we added a scoop of the hot water to the pan to braise the kale. Grated Parmesan cheese brought the sauce together and reinforced the meaty, salty notes of the bacon. Twisty gemelli paired especially well with this sauce—the kale and caramelized onions clung to its curves, promising rich, flavorful bites with every forkful. Don't dry the kale completely after washing; a little extra water clinging to the leaves will help them wilt when cooking in step 2.

8 slices bacon, cut into ½-inch pieces

3 onions, halved and sliced thin
 Salt and pepper

4 garlic cloves, minced

1 pound kale, stemmed and chopped into 1-inch pieces

1 pound gemelli

2 ounces Parmesan cheese, grated (1 cup), plus extra for serving

1. Bring 4 quarts water to boil in large pot for pasta. Cook bacon in 12-inch nonstick skillet over medium-high heat until crisp, about 5 minutes; transfer to paper towel–lined plate. Add onions and ½ teaspoon salt to fat left in pan, cover, and cook over medium-high heat until soft, 5 to 8 minutes. Remove lid, reduce heat to medium, and continue to cook onions, stirring often, until well browned, 20 to 25 minutes.

2. Stir in garlic and cook until fragrant, about 30 seconds. Stir in half of kale and cook until it begins to wilt, about 2 minutes. Add remaining kale and 1½ cups boiling pasta water (skillet will be very full). Cover and simmer, tossing occasionally, until kale is tender, about 15 minutes.

3. Meanwhile, add pasta and 1 tablespoon salt to boiling water and cook, stirring often, until al dente. Reserve ½ cup cooking water, then drain pasta and return it to pot. Add kale mixture, bacon, and Parmesan and toss to combine. Season with salt and pepper to taste and add reserved cooking water as needed to adjust consistency. Serve with extra Parmesan.

QUICK PREP TIP
PREPPING HEARTY GREENS

To prepare kale, Swiss chard, or collard greens, cut away leafy green portion from either side of stalk or stem using chef's knife. Stack several leaves on top of one another, and either slice leaves crosswise or chop them into pieces (as directed in recipe). Wash and dry leaves after they are cut, using a salad spinner.

Shells with Blue Cheese, Radicchio, and Walnuts

Serves 4 to 6

✔ **WHY THIS RECIPE WORKS:** Blue cheese, simmered with cream, gives this simple dish a luxurious, potently flavored sauce in just 10 minutes. Slightly bitter radicchio played off the richness of the sauce, and walnuts added crunch. Use either a mild blue cheese (like Stella) or a slightly sweet blue cheese (like Gorgonzola dolce).

2 cups heavy cream

3 garlic cloves, minced

1 head radicchio (10 ounces), cored and cut into ½-inch pieces

2 ounces blue cheese, crumbled (½ cup)

1 pound medium pasta shells
  Salt and pepper

1 cup walnuts, toasted and chopped

1. Simmer cream and garlic together in 12-inch skillet over medium-high heat, whisking often, until thickened, about 5 to 7 minutes. Stir in radicchio and ¼ cup blue cheese and cook until radicchio is wilted and cheese is melted, 3 to 5 minutes; cover and set aside.

2. Meanwhile, bring 4 quarts water to boil in large pot. Add pasta and 1 tablespoon salt and cook, stirring often, until al dente. Reserve 1½ cups cooking water, then drain pasta and return it to pot. Add cream mixture and ½ cup reserved cooking water and toss to combine. Season with salt and pepper to taste and add remaining cooking water as needed to adjust consistency. Sprinkle individual portions with nuts and remaining ¼ cup blue cheese before serving.

Rotini with Brussels Sprouts and Blue Cheese

Serves 4 to 6

✔ **WHY THIS RECIPE WORKS:** After one bite, you'll be hooked on this bold, rich dish featuring thinly sliced Brussels sprouts, sweet cream, and tangy blue cheese. Small, firm Brussels sprouts (about 1 inch in diameter) work best here. Slicing the Brussels sprouts in a food processor can help to cut down on their prep time.

6 slices bacon, chopped

1 pound Brussels sprouts, trimmed and sliced thin (see page 102)
  Salt and pepper

1 cup heavy cream

4 ounces blue cheese, crumbled (1 cup)

1 pound rotini

¼ cup pine nuts, toasted

1. Cook bacon in 12-inch skillet over medium-high heat until crisp, about 5 minutes; transfer to paper towel–lined plate. Pour off all but 2 tablespoons fat left in skillet, add Brussels sprouts, ½ teaspoon salt, and ¼ teaspoon pepper, and cook over medium-high heat until they begin to soften, about 5 minutes. Stir in cream, cover, and simmer until sprouts are tender, about 3 minutes. Off heat, stir in blue cheese.

2. Meanwhile, bring 4 quarts water to boil in large pot. Add pasta and 1 tablespoon salt and cook, stirring often, until al dente. Reserve ½ cup cooking water, then drain pasta and return it to pot. Add sprouts mixture and bacon and toss to combine. Season with salt and pepper to taste and add reserved cooking water as needed to adjust consistency. Sprinkle individual portions with pine nuts before serving.

Brats with Beer and Mustard on Egg Noodles

Serves 4 to 6

✓ **WHY THIS RECIPE WORKS:** Not known to shy away from rich, hearty dishes, Midwesterners have a special appreciation for bratwurst and beer—a pairing brought to its glory in a popular tailgating dish that adds onions to the mix to create a saucy topping for the brats. We decided to swap the hot dog buns for pasta, and incorporate the trio of brats, beer, and onions to create a hearty new dish perfect for football season. For big flavor from the outset, we browned our sausages and then built the sauce using the flavorful bits left behind in the pan. Thinly sliced onions and mustard flavored the sauce, and picked up the rich, meaty flavor of the sausage when they mingled with the fond in the skillet. A bottle of beer formed the bulk of the sauce, which we used to cook the brats through and instill them with complex flavor. As for the pasta, egg noodles seemed just right for this casual supper.

2	tablespoons vegetable oil
1	pound bratwurst
2	onions, halved and sliced thin
	Salt and pepper
1	(12-ounce) bottle mild beer
⅓	cup Dijon mustard
12	ounces (7¾ cups) egg noodles

1. Heat 1 tablespoon oil in 12-inch skillet over medium heat until shimmering. Add sausage and cook until well browned, about 5 minutes; transfer to plate.

2. Add remaining 1 tablespoon oil, onions, and ⅛ teaspoon salt to now-empty skillet and cook, stirring frequently, until softened and lightly browned, about 15 minutes. Whisk in beer and mustard until smooth. Nestle sausages, along with any accumulated juice, into pan, cover, and simmer gently until sausages are cooked through, about 10 minutes.

3. Transfer sausages to cutting board, let cool slightly, then slice ½ inch thick on bias. Return sausage to skillet and season with salt and pepper to taste.

4. Meanwhile, bring 4 quarts water to boil in large pot. Add pasta and 1 tablespoon salt and cook, stirring often, until al dente. Reserve ½ cup cooking water, then drain pasta and return it to pot. Add sausage mixture and toss to combine. Season with pepper to taste and add reserved cooking water as needed to adjust consistency. Serve.

SMART SHOPPING BEER FOR COOKING
Cooking intensifies the flavor of beer, so if you start with a dark or bitter brew, it will overwhelm the flavor of the final dish. We recommend using a light or medium beer, like a domestic lager, which will add just the right amount of depth of flavor without being all you taste in the finished dish.

Fusilli with Giardiniera and Sausage

Serves 4 to 6

✔ **WHY THIS RECIPE WORKS:** This easy recipe derives its big flavor from a surprising yet easy-to-find convenience product: pickled Italian vegetables, also known as giardiniera. In this clever dish, we called upon the giardiniera to do double duty: The vegetables themselves added crunch and flavor—and saved us from having to prep a number of ingredients—while the brine added bright, tangy notes to the sauce. Browned Italian sausage, sautéed onions, chopped giardiniera vegetables, and canned tomato sauce gave us a boldly flavored sauce in shockingly little time. Chopped basil added a fresh finishing touch. Look for giardiniera either at the olive bar in the supermarket or next to the jarred pickles; one (16-ounce) jar of giardiniera will yield enough for this recipe. For the nutritional information for this recipe, see page 307.

1 **pound sweet Italian sausage, casings removed**

2 **onions, chopped fine**

1 **(15-ounce) can tomato sauce**

3 **cups giardiniera pickled vegetables, drained with 6 tablespoons brine reserved, and chopped coarse**

1 **pound fusilli**
Salt and pepper

½ **cup chopped fresh basil**

1. Cook sausage in 12-inch nonstick skillet over medium-high heat, breaking up meat with wooden spoon, until no longer pink, about 4 minutes. Stir in onions and cook until softened and lightly browned, 10 to 12 minutes. Stir in tomato sauce, giardiniera, and 4 tablespoons brine and simmer until thickened, about 10 minutes.

2. Meanwhile, bring 4 quarts water to boil in large pot. Add pasta and 1 tablespoon salt and cook, stirring often, until al dente. Reserve ½ cup cooking water, then drain pasta and return it to pot. Add sausage mixture, basil, and 1 tablespoon brine and toss to combine. Season with salt, pepper, and remaining 1 tablespoon brine to taste and add reserved cooking water as needed to adjust consistency. Serve.

SMART SHOPPING **GIARDINIERA**

In Italy, giardiniera refers to pickled vegetables that are typically eaten as an antipasto. But here in the United States, it's most recognized as a combination of pickled cauliflower, carrots, celery, and sweet and hot peppers that is served alongside sandwiches or other lunch fare. We've seen several brands available in the pickle aisle of our local supermarket, but on a recent trip to Chicago we were impressed by the city's particular devotion to this spicy condiment. Figuring a local variety might exceed what we could find elsewhere, we tracked down three regional Chicago brands of jarred giardiniera (Scala's Hot, Dell'Alpe, and Il Primo) and tasted them against five national brands. While tasters were impressed by the "spicy complexity" and "pleasant bitterness" of Scala's Hot from Chicago, overall we wanted a larger variety of vegetables—the Chicago giardinieras are mostly peppers. We agreed: No need to travel to Chicago for the best—our favorite giardiniera was the national brand **Pastene**.

Ziti with Italian Sausage, Broccoli, and Sun-Dried Tomatoes

Serves 4 to 6

✔ **WHY THIS RECIPE WORKS:** To jazz up chicken, broccoli, and ziti, we swapped mild chicken for spiced Italian sausage and added sun-dried tomatoes. For the nutritional information for this recipe, see page 307.

1	pound sweet or hot Italian sausage, casings removed
1	cup low-sodium chicken broth
¾	cup oil-packed sun-dried tomatoes, rinsed, patted dry, and sliced thin
12	ounces broccoli florets
	Salt and pepper
1	pound ziti
2	ounces Parmesan cheese, grated (1 cup), plus extra for serving

1. Cook sausage in 12-inch skillet over medium-high heat, breaking up meat, until no longer pink, about 4 minutes. Stir in broth and sun-dried tomatoes; simmer until tomatoes soften, about 2 minutes.

2. Meanwhile, bring 4 quarts water to boil in large pot. Add broccoli and 1 tablespoon salt and cook until crisp-tender, about 2 minutes; transfer to paper towel–lined plate.

3. Return water to boil, add pasta, and cook, stirring often, until pasta is al dente. Reserve ½ cup cooking water, then drain pasta and return it to pot. Add sausage mixture, broccoli, and Parmesan; toss to combine. Season with salt and pepper to taste; add reserved cooking water as needed to adjust consistency. Serve.

Ziti with Fennel and Italian Sausage

Serves 4 to 6

✔ **WHY THIS RECIPE WORKS:** This deceptively easy supper gets its deep flavor from browned Italian sausage, caramelized onions and fennel, and a full can of tomato paste. Starchy pasta cooking water and grated Pecorino Romano gave the sauce an ultra-rich texture. For the nutritional information for this recipe, see page 307.

1	pound sweet or hot Italian sausage, casings removed
2	onions, halved and sliced thin
1	fennel bulb, fronds chopped, stalks discarded, bulb halved, cored, and sliced into ½-inch pieces (see page 248)
1	(6-ounce) can tomato paste
1	pound ziti
	Salt and pepper
1	ounce Pecorino Romano cheese, grated (½ cup), plus extra for serving

1. Bring 4 quarts water to boil in large pot for pasta. Cook sausage in large Dutch oven over medium-high heat, breaking up meat with wooden spoon, until no longer pink, about 4 minutes. Stir in onions and fennel, cover, and cook until softened, about 5 minutes. Uncover, reduce heat to medium, and continue to cook until vegetables are golden, 10 to 12 minutes. Add tomato paste and cook until darkened, about 3 minutes. Stir in 2 cups boiling pasta water and simmer until thickened, about 5 minutes.

2. Meanwhile, add pasta and 1 tablespoon salt to boiling water and cook, stirring often, until al dente. Reserve 1½ cups cooking water, then drain pasta and return it to pot. Add sausage mixture, Pecorino, and 1 cup reserved cooking water and toss to combine. Season with salt and pepper to taste and add remaining cooking water as needed to adjust consistency. Sprinkle individual portions with fennel fronds and extra Pecorino before serving.

Pasta with Shrimp, Andouille Sausage, and Bell Pepper

Serves 4 to 6

✔ **WHY THIS RECIPE WORKS:** For a supper boasting the best flavors of the Bayou, we combined sweet, tender shrimp with smoky, spicy andouille sausage. Building the sauce around the browned sausage ensured that its flavors permeated the dish—no extra aromatics or dried spices needed. Chopped red bell peppers added sweetness and texture, while a can of crushed tomatoes offered up rich flavor in short order and delivered a thick, clingy sauce. Rather than sautéing the shrimp separately, we poached it right in the flavorful sauce, which ensured moist, tender shrimp and kept the method easy and streamlined. Minced parsley gave our deeply flavored sauce some freshness and upped its complexity. If your shrimp are larger or smaller, be sure to alter the cooking time in step 1 accordingly. If your andouille seems very dry and crumbly when cooking in step 1, add 1 tablespoon olive oil to the pan. For the nutritional information for this recipe, see page 307.

1	pound andouille sausage, sliced ½ inch thick on bias
2	red bell peppers, stemmed, seeded, and cut into ½-inch pieces
1	(28-ounce) can crushed tomatoes
1	pound extra-large shrimp (21 to 25 per pound), peeled, deveined, and tails removed
1	pound ziti
	Salt and pepper
¼	cup minced fresh parsley

1. Cook sausage in 12-inch nonstick skillet over medium-high heat until well browned and fat is rendered, about 5 minutes. Add peppers and cook until just softened, about 3 minutes. Stir in tomatoes and simmer until thickened, about 10 minutes. Stir in shrimp, cover, and simmer gently until shrimp are cooked through, about 5 minutes.

2. Meanwhile, bring 4 quarts water to boil in large pot. Add pasta and 1 tablespoon salt and cook, stirring often, until al dente. Reserve ½ cup cooking water, then drain pasta and return it to pot. Add shrimp mixture and parsley and toss to combine. Season with salt and pepper to taste and add reserved cooking water as needed to adjust consistency. Serve.

SMART SHOPPING ANDOUILLE

Traditional andouille (pronounced an-DOO-ee) sausage from Louisiana is made from ground pork, salt, and garlic—and seasoned with plenty of black pepper—then slowly smoked over pecan wood and sugarcane for up to 14 hours. Used in a wide range of Cajun dishes, such as gumbo, jambalaya, and red beans and rice, it bolsters any dish with intense smoky, spicy, earthy flavor. We tasted four brands, looking for the right combination of smokiness and heat with a traditionally chewy but dry texture. Not surprisingly, a sausage straight from Louisiana, **Jacob's World Famous Andouille**, won the day.

Farfalle with Salmon and Leeks

Serves 4 to 6

✔ **WHY THIS RECIPE WORKS:** For this refined, company-worthy dish, we wanted moist, buttery salmon, ultra-tender leeks, and al dente pasta, all tossed together in a velvety cream sauce. For perfectly tender leeks, we sautéed them in butter until softened. Shallow-poaching the salmon right in the pan with the leeks—we used white wine for the cooking liquid—kept the fish moist and the procedure streamlined. Cream, added directly to the pan, thickened nicely and absorbed the subtle oniony flavor of the leeks. To prevent the salmon from breaking apart into tiny shreds, we set it aside while the cream simmered, then stirred it into the pasta with the sauce so the fillets would separate into fork-friendly bites. Be careful to handle the salmon gently after it's cooked, or else it will break apart into very fine pieces.

2	tablespoons unsalted butter
2	pounds leeks, white and light green parts only, quartered lengthwise, sliced crosswise into ½-inch pieces, and washed thoroughly
	Salt and pepper
2	(6-ounce) skinless salmon fillets, 1¼ inches thick
1	cup dry white wine
¾	cup heavy cream
1	pound farfalle

1. Melt butter in 12-inch nonstick skillet over medium-high heat. Add leeks and ¼ teaspoon salt and cook until tender, about 7 minutes. Season salmon with salt and pepper and nestle into skillet. Add wine, cover, and cook until salmon is just cooked through, about 6 minutes.

2. Transfer salmon to plate and cover to keep warm. Stir cream into skillet and simmer until thickened, about 2 minutes; remove from heat and cover.

3. Meanwhile, bring 4 quarts water to boil in large pot. Add pasta and 1 tablespoon salt and cook, stirring often, until al dente. Reserve ½ cup cooking water, then drain pasta and return it to pot. Add sauce and salmon, along with any accumulated juice, and toss gently to combine, breaking salmon into bite-size pieces. Season with salt and pepper to taste and add reserved cooking water as needed to adjust consistency. Serve.

SMART SHOPPING WILD SALMON VERSUS FARMED SALMON
In season, we've always preferred the more pronounced flavor of wild-caught salmon to farmed Atlantic salmon, traditionally the main farm-raised variety in this country. But with more wild and farmed species now available, we decided to reevaluate. We tasted three kinds of wild Pacific salmon and two farmed. While we love the generally stronger flavor of wild-caught fish, if you're going to spend the extra money, make sure it looks and smells fresh, and realize that high quality is available only from late spring through the end of summer.

Mediterranean Penne with Tuna and Niçoise Olives

Serves 4 to 6

✔ **WHY THIS RECIPE WORKS:** For a zesty, Mediterranean-inspired pasta dish, we combined meaty chunks of tuna and piquant niçoise olives in a simple yet speedy sauce. After some testing, we found it better to use oil-packed rather than water-packed tuna, because it has a more tender texture and richer flavor. Also, we found we could be extra thrifty and use the packing oil for sautéing the aromatics (several cloves of garlic provided a potent flavor base). Canned tomatoes, plus a cup and a half of their juice, gave us a chunky, fresh-tasting sauce. Finally, we turned to one more boldly flavored ingredient—capers—to give our dish just a little more punch. Serve with grated Parmesan cheese and extra olive oil. If necessary, you can substitute olive oil for the reserved oil from the cans of tuna.

2	**(5-ounce) cans oil-packed solid white tuna, drained with ½ cup oil reserved, tuna flaked**
6	**garlic cloves, minced**
3	**(14.5-ounce) cans diced tomatoes, drained with 1½ cups juice reserved**
¾	**cup pitted niçoise olives, chopped**
¼	**cup capers, rinsed and minced**
1	**pound penne**
	Salt and pepper

1. Cook reserved tuna oil and garlic together in large saucepan over medium heat until fragrant, 1 to 2 minutes. Stir in tomatoes and reserved juice and simmer until tomatoes soften and sauce thickens, about 15 minutes. Stir in tuna, olives, and capers and simmer until well combined, about 5 minutes.

2. Meanwhile, bring 4 quarts water to boil in large pot. Add pasta and 1 tablespoon salt and cook, stirring often, until al dente. Reserve ½ cup cooking water, then drain pasta and return it to pot. Add sauce and toss to combine. Season with salt and pepper to taste and add reserved cooking water as needed to adjust consistency. Serve.

QUICK PREP TIP PITTING OLIVES

To pit a lot of olives at once, we like to use this easy trick: Place the olives between two clean paper towels (or kitchen towels), then gently pound them with a mallet. Be careful not to pound too hard or you will smash the olives and crack the pits into pieces. Once all of the olives have been cracked open, use your fingers to remove the pit from each olive.

Fettuccine with Shrimp, Tarragon, and Cream

Serves 4 to 6

✔ **WHY THIS RECIPE WORKS:** Elegant yet easy, this rich, creamy dish features the complementary flavors of tender, briny shrimp and sweet, aniselike tarragon. Searing the shrimp in butter infuses it with rich flavor and couldn't be faster. After setting the shrimp aside (we'd stir it in at the end to warm through), we simmered heavy cream in the pan until slightly thickened. Then we added the cream and a couple tablespoons of minced tarragon to the cooked fettuccine; heating the mixture for just a minute ensured that the pasta absorbed the sauce, and it kept the tarragon flavor from becoming muted. Note that it is important to cook the pasta until it is not quite al dente because it will continue to cook after being tossed with the sauce. We prefer to use fresh fettuccine in this dish; however, you can use substitute 12 ounces of dried fettuccine if necessary.

1¼ pounds medium-large shrimp (31 to 40 per pound), peeled, deveined, and tails removed
Salt and pepper
2 tablespoons unsalted butter
2 garlic cloves, minced
2 cups heavy cream
2 (9-ounce) packages fresh fettuccine
2 tablespoons minced fresh tarragon

1. Pat shrimp dry with paper towels and season with salt and pepper. Melt butter in 12-inch skillet over medium-high heat until just beginning to brown, about 2 minutes. Add shrimp and cook, stirring occasionally, until just pink at edges, about 1½ minutes. Stir in garlic and cook until fragrant, about 30 seconds; transfer to bowl and cover.

2. Add cream to now-empty skillet and simmer over medium-high heat until slightly thickened and measures 1½ cups, about 8 minutes; cover and remove from heat.

3. Meanwhile, bring 4 quarts water to boil in large pot. Add pasta and 1 tablespoon salt and cook, stirring often, until nearly al dente. Reserve ½ cup cooking water, then drain pasta and return it to pot. Add cream and tarragon and cook over low heat until sauce clings lightly to pasta, about 1 minute. Off heat, stir in shrimp along with any accumulated juice. Season with salt and pepper to taste and add reserved cooking water as needed to adjust consistency. Serve.

SMART SHOPPING SHRIMP SIZES
Shrimp are sold by size (small, medium, large, and so on) as well as by the number needed to make 1 pound, usually given in a range. Choosing shrimp by the numerical rating is more accurate than choosing them by the size label, which varies from store to store. Here's how the two sizing systems generally compare.

SIZE	COUNT PER POUND
Colossal	under 12
Extra-Jumbo	under 15
Jumbo	16 to 20
Extra-Large	21 to 25
Large	26 to 30
Medium-Large	31 to 40
Medium	41 to 50
Small	51 to 60
Extra-Small	61 to 70

Linguine with Clams and Chorizo

Serves 4 to 6

✓ **WHY THIS RECIPE WORKS:** This gutsy, bold dish gives classic clam sauce a decidedly Spanish feel by adding spicy chorizo. For our version, we started by sautéing the chorizo, then added clams and white wine to the pot and let the clams steam; the wine contributed much-needed brightness. A generous amount of butter, stirred in after the clams had released their juice, gave the sauce a rich, velvety texture. Chopped parsley provided the perfect fresh finishing touch. If your chorizo seems very dry and crumbly when cooking in step 1, add 1 tablespoon olive oil to the pan. When shopping for clams, choose the smallest ones you can find. Be sure to scrub the clams thoroughly of grit and sand before cooking. Note that the clams can be very briny, so be sure to taste the final dish before seasoning with additional salt.

8	ounces chorizo sausage, sliced ½ inch thick on bias
4	pounds littleneck or cherrystone clams, scrubbed
½	cup dry white wine
6	tablespoons unsalted butter, cut into ¼-inch pieces
½	cup chopped fresh parsley
	Salt and pepper
1	pound linguine

1. Cook chorizo in large Dutch oven over medium heat, stirring often, until well browned, about 6 minutes. Stir in clams and wine. Cover and simmer, shaking pan occasionally, until clams begin to open, about 6 minutes.

2. Uncover and continue to simmer until all clams have opened and sauce is slightly reduced, about 2 minutes. Discard any clams that refuse to open. (If clams release sand into sauce, remove clams and strain sauce; return sauce and clams to clean pot and continue.) Gently stir in butter and parsley. Off heat, season with pepper to taste.

3. Meanwhile, bring 4 quarts water to boil in large pot. Add pasta and 1 tablespoon salt and cook, stirring often, until al dente. Reserve ½ cup cooking water, then drain pasta and return it to pot. Add clam mixture and toss to combine. Season with salt and pepper to taste and add reserved cooking water as needed to adjust consistency. Serve.

SMART SHOPPING CHORIZO

When shopping for chorizo, you may come across several different styles, including Spanish, Colombian/Argentinean, and Mexican. Though they all will work in this recipe, they will have distinctly different flavors and textures. The dry-cured Spanish chorizo has a coarsely ground texture and a bright red color and smoky flavor from the inclusion of smoked paprika; depending on the paprika, the chorizo can be sweet (dulce) or hot (picante). Colombian/Argentinean chorizo can be either raw or cooked and is very coarsely ground and seasoned with garlic and herbs (think Italian sausage). Mexican chorizo is raw and made from either pork or beef, is very finely ground, and has a spicy tanginess due to the inclusion of chili powder and vinegar.

SPANISH

COLOMBIAN/ARGENTINEAN

MEXICAN

HEARTY VEGETABLE LASAGNA

Pasta for Company

Spring Vegetable Pasta

Serves 8

✔ **WHY THIS RECIPE WORKS:** A fresher, brighter take on classic pasta primavera, this spring vegetable pasta dish provides the ultimate marriage of tender pasta, luscious sauce, and fresh-tasting spring vegetables. We started with asparagus and green peas, adding chives for bite and garlic and leeks for aromatic depth and sweetness. For a deeply flavored sauce, we toasted the pasta before cooking it right in the sauce (much like a risotto). Not only did this one-pot method streamline the procedure, but the sauce flavored the pasta and the pasta starch helped thicken the broth into a creamy sauce without using cream or butter, which otherwise would have overpowered the delicate flavors of the vegetables. Doctoring store-bought vegetable broth with extra flavor was crucial for a fresh-tasting sauce; luckily, this was easy to do using the vegetable trimmings. Campanelle is our pasta of choice for this dish, although both farfalle and penne are acceptable substitutes. You will need at least a 6-quart Dutch oven for this recipe.

2½	pounds leeks, white and light green parts halved lengthwise, sliced ½ inch thick, and washed thoroughly; dark green parts chopped coarse and washed thoroughly
1½	pounds asparagus, trimmed, tough ends reserved and chopped coarse; spears sliced ½ inch thick on bias
3	cups frozen peas, thawed
6	garlic cloves, minced
6	cups vegetable broth
1½	cups water, plus extra as needed
9	tablespoons extra-virgin olive oil
	Salt and pepper
¼	teaspoon red pepper flakes
1½	pounds campanelle
1½	cups dry white wine
3	tablespoons minced fresh mint
3	tablespoons minced fresh chives
¾	teaspoon grated lemon zest plus 3 tablespoons juice
1½	ounces Parmesan cheese, grated (¾ cup), plus extra for serving

1. Place dark green leek parts, asparagus ends, 1½ cups peas, one-half of garlic, vegetable broth, and water in large saucepan. Bring to simmer and cook gently for 10 minutes. Strain through fine-mesh strainer into 8-cup liquid measuring cup, pressing on solids to extract as much liquid as possible. (You should have 8 cups broth; add water as needed to measure 8 cups.) Return broth to saucepan, cover, and keep warm over low heat.

2. Meanwhile, heat 3 tablespoons oil in large Dutch oven over medium heat until shimmering. Add white and light green leek parts and pinch salt, cover, and cook, stirring occasionally, until leeks begin to brown, about 5 minutes. Stir in asparagus and cook until asparagus is crisp-tender, 4 to 6 minutes. Stir in remaining garlic, pepper flakes, and pinch pepper and cook until fragrant, about 30 seconds. Stir in remaining 1½ cups peas and cook for 1 minute. Transfer vegetables to plate. Clean pot and wipe dry.

3. Heat remaining 6 tablespoons oil in now-empty pot over medium heat until shimmering. Add pasta and cook, stirring often, until just beginning to brown, 5 to 7 minutes. Stir in wine and cook, stirring constantly, until absorbed, about 2 minutes.

4. Add warm broth, increase heat to medium-high, and bring to boil. Cook, stirring frequently, until most of liquid is absorbed and pasta is al dente, 12 to 14 minutes. Meanwhile, combine mint, chives, and lemon zest in bowl.

5. Off heat, stir in cooked vegetables, half of mint mixture, lemon juice, and Parmesan. Season with salt and pepper to taste. Serve with remaining mint mixture and extra Parmesan.

Hearty Vegetable Lasagna

Serves 12

✔ **WHY THIS RECIPE WORKS:** For a hearty vegetable lasagna with bold flavor, we started with a summery mix of zucchini, yellow squash, and eggplant. Salting and microwaving the eggplant and sautéing the vegetables worked to cut down on excess moisture and deepen their flavor. Spinach and olives added textural contrast and flavor without much work. We dialed up the usual cheese filling by switching out mild-mannered ricotta for tangy cottage cheese mixed with heavy cream for richness and Parmesan and garlic for added flavor. Our quick no-cook tomato sauce brought enough moisture to the lasagna to ensure that the no-boil noodles softened properly while baking. We prefer kosher salt for salting the eggplant in step 1; if using table salt, reduce all salt amounts in the recipe by half. Do not use fat-free mozzarella cheese here. Food-safe, undyed paper towels can be substituted for the coffee filters in step 1. You will need a 15 by 10-inch casserole dish, or shallow 4-quart casserole dish, for this recipe. Note that you will need two boxes of no-boil lasagna noodles for this recipe. The lasagna cannot be assembled ahead of time, but both of the sauces and the cooked vegetables (prepared through step 5) can be refrigerated separately for up to 1 day.

VEGETABLE FILLING

2	pounds eggplant, peeled and cut into ½-inch pieces
	Kosher salt and pepper
1½	pounds zucchini, cut into ½-inch pieces
1½	pounds yellow squash, cut into ½-inch pieces
6	tablespoons plus 1 teaspoon extra-virgin olive oil
6	garlic cloves, minced
4½	teaspoons minced fresh thyme
1	pound (16 cups) baby spinach

1. FOR THE VEGETABLE FILLING: Adjust oven rack to middle position and heat oven to 450 degrees. Line large plate with double layer of coffee filters and coat lightly with vegetable oil spray. Toss eggplant with 1 teaspoon salt, then spread evenly over coffee filter–lined plate. Microwave, uncovered, until eggplant is dry to touch and slightly shriveled, about 15 minutes, tossing halfway through cooking. Let cool slightly.

2. Combine cooled eggplant, zucchini, squash, ½ teaspoon salt, and ½ teaspoon pepper in bowl. In small bowl, combine 2 tablespoons oil, garlic, and thyme. Heat 2 tablespoons oil in 12-inch nonstick skillet over medium-high heat until shimmering. Add half of vegetables and cook until spotty brown, about 10 minutes. Clear center of skillet, add one-half of garlic mixture, and cook, mashing mixture into pan, until fragrant, about 30 seconds. Stir garlic mixture into vegetables; transfer to large bowl. Repeat with 2 tablespoons oil, remaining vegetables, and remaining garlic mixture.

3. Heat remaining 1 teaspoon oil in now-empty skillet over medium-high heat until shimmering. Add spinach, one handful at a time, and cook, stirring frequently, until wilted, about 3 minutes. Transfer spinach to paper towel–lined plate, let drain for 2 minutes, then stir into cooked vegetables.

TOMATO SAUCE

1½	(28-ounce) cans crushed tomatoes (4½ cups)
⅓	cup chopped fresh basil
3	tablespoons extra-virgin olive oil
3	garlic cloves, minced
1	teaspoon kosher salt
¼	teaspoon red pepper flakes

CREAM SAUCE

12	ounces (1½ cups) whole-milk cottage cheese
1½	cups heavy cream
6	ounces Parmesan cheese, grated (3 cups)
3	garlic cloves, minced
1½	teaspoons cornstarch
¾	teaspoon pepper
½	teaspoon kosher salt

18	no-boil lasagna noodles
¾	cup pitted kalamata olives, minced
1	pound mozzarella cheese, shredded (4 cups)
3	tablespoons chopped fresh basil

4. FOR THE TOMATO SAUCE: Whisk all ingredients together in bowl.

5. FOR THE CREAM SAUCE: Whisk all ingredients together in bowl.

6. To assemble lasagna, grease 15 by 10-inch baking dish. Spread 1½ cups tomato sauce evenly over bottom of dish. Lay 6 noodles in dish (noodles will overlap). Spread half of vegetable mixture over noodles, followed by half of olives. Spoon one-half of cream sauce over top and sprinkle with 1 cup mozzarella. Repeat layering with 6 noodles, 1½ cups tomato sauce, remaining vegetables, remaining olives, remaining cream sauce, and 1 cup mozzarella. For final layer, lay remaining 6 noodles on top, cover completely with remaining tomato sauce, and sprinkle with remaining 2 cups mozzarella.

7. Cover dish tightly with aluminum foil that has been sprayed with vegetable oil spray and set on foil-lined baking sheet. Bake until edges are bubbling, about 1¼ hours. Let cool for 30 minutes. Sprinkle with basil and serve.

ON THE SIDE CAESAR SALAD FOR A CROWD

For croutons, whisk ⅓ cup olive oil, ¼ cup grated Parmesan cheese, 2 minced garlic cloves, and ¼ teaspoon salt together in bowl. Place 10 ounces ciabatta bread, cut into ¾-inch cubes (8 cups), in large bowl; sprinkle with ⅓ cup water and squeeze bread to absorb, then toss with oil mixture. Bake in 450-degree oven until golden, about 15 minutes; let cool. For salad, whisk 1½ teaspoons garlic paste (see page 237) with ¼ cup lemon juice in large bowl; let stand for 10 minutes. Whisk in 1 teaspoon Worcestershire sauce, 8 anchovy fillets, patted dry and mashed to paste, and 4 large egg yolks. Whisking constantly, slowly add ½ cup canola oil and 3 tablespoons extra-virgin olive oil. Whisk in 1 cup finely grated Parmesan and season with pepper to taste. Toss with 6 romaine lettuce hearts, sliced ¾ inch thick, and garnish with shaved Parmesan and croutons. Serves 12.

Creamy Lobster Fettuccine with Fennel

Serves 8 to 10

✔ **WHY THIS RECIPE WORKS:** Dotted with tender chunks of lobster and infused with the sweet, anise notes of fennel and tarragon, this creamy pasta dish is luxurious and elegant—and can also be incredibly easy to make. You can use either cooked lobster meat or live lobsters and steam and shell them following the instructions below. Be sure to use dried fettuccine in this recipe; fresh fettuccine will not work. When adding the fettuccine in step 2, stir gently to avoid breaking the noodles; after a minute or two they will soften enough to allow for easier stirring. Be ready to serve the pasta as soon as it is finished; the sauce will turn thick and clumpy if held for too long. Warm serving bowls (warmed in a 200-degree oven) will help extend the serving time for the pasta. You will need at least a 6-quart Dutch oven for this recipe.

3	tablespoons olive oil
1	onion, chopped fine
1	fennel bulb, stalks discarded, bulb halved, cored, and chopped fine (see page 248)
	Salt and pepper
1	tablespoon minced fresh thyme
3	garlic cloves, minced
¼	teaspoon cayenne pepper
¾	cup dry sherry
4	cups low-sodium chicken broth
4	cups water
2	cups heavy cream
2	pounds fettuccine
2	pounds cooked lobster meat, cut into ⅓-inch pieces
3	tablespoons minced fresh tarragon
1	tablespoon lemon juice
	Grated Parmesan cheese

1. Heat oil in large Dutch oven over medium heat until shimmering. Add onion, fennel, and ½ teaspoon salt and cook until softened, 5 to 7 minutes. Stir in thyme, garlic, and cayenne and cook until fragrant, about 30 seconds. Stir in sherry and simmer until it has nearly evaporated, about 4 minutes.

2. Stir in broth, water, cream, and pasta. Increase heat to medium-high and cook at vigorous simmer, stirring often, until pasta is tender and sauce has thickened, 12 to 15 minutes.

3. Reduce heat to low and add lobster and tarragon. Cook, gently tossing to combine, until lobster is just warmed through, about 3 minutes. Off heat, stir in lemon juice and season with salt and pepper to taste. Serve in warm bowls with Parmesan.

QUICK PREP TIP HOW TO COOK LOBSTER

To steam lobster, fit a large Dutch oven with a steamer basket and fill with water until it just touches the bottom of the basket; bring to boil over high heat. Add the lobsters, cover, and steam according to the times in the chart below, making sure to check the pot periodically and add water as needed. Let the lobsters cool slightly before shelling them. The cooked lobster meat can be refrigerated in an airtight container for up to two days.

LOBSTER	STEAMING TIME	MEAT YIELD
Soft-Shell		
1 lb.	8 to 9 minutes	about 3 oz.
1¼ lbs.	11 to 12 minutes	3½ to 4 oz.
1½ lbs.	13 to 14 minutes	5½ to 6 oz.
1¾–2 lbs.	17 to 18 minutes	6¼ to 6½ oz.
Hard-Shell		
1 lb.	10 to 11 minutes	4 to 4½ oz.
1¼ lbs.	13 to 14 minutes	5½ to 6 oz.
1½ lbs.	15 to 16 minutes	7½ to 8 oz.
1¾–2 lbs.	about 19 minutes	8½ to 9 oz.

Mussels Marinara with Linguine

Serves 8 to 10

✔ **WHY THIS RECIPE WORKS:** For a simple yet sensational Mussels Marinara, we started by instilling our sauce with bold, bright, tomatoey flavor. In lieu of canned diced tomatoes or tomato sauce, we turned to canned crushed tomatoes; just 20 minutes of cooking rid them of their raw flavor and gave us a seriously clingy sauce with just the right thickness. A good amount of red pepper flakes provided an underlying heat, and two anchovy fillets amped up the savory notes. Clam juice reinforced the briny flavor of the mussels, and white wine provided acidity. Cooking our mussels in the sauce infused our shellfish with bright flavor, and in turn the sauce absorbed their briny liquor. After just a few minutes, our mussels had popped open and the richly flavored sauce was ready to be tossed with a pot of steaming linguine. See page 205 for more information on our favorite brand of crushed tomatoes. Sometimes mussels have a scrubby weed protruding from the shell; if so, you will need to remove it (a technique known as debearding) by firmly pulling it out. You will need at least a 6-quart Dutch oven and a 12-quart stockpot for this recipe.

¼ cup extra-virgin olive oil
2 onions, chopped fine
9 garlic cloves, minced
2 anchovy fillets, rinsed and minced
½ teaspoon red pepper flakes
1 cup dry white wine
3 (28-ounce) cans crushed tomatoes
2 (8-ounce) bottles clam juice
4 pounds mussels, scrubbed and debearded
2 pounds linguine
Salt and pepper
½ cup minced fresh parsley

1. Heat oil in large Dutch oven over medium heat until shimmering. Add onions and cook until softened, 8 to 10 minutes. Stir in garlic, anchovy, and pepper flakes and cook until fragrant, about 30 seconds. Stir in wine and simmer, scraping up any browned bits, until nearly evaporated, about 5 minutes. Stir in tomatoes and clam juice and simmer until slightly thickened, about 20 minutes.

2. Add mussels, cover, and cook until mussels have opened, about 5 minutes. Using slotted spoon, transfer mussels to bowl, discarding any that have not opened, and cover to keep warm.

3. Meanwhile, bring 8 quarts water to boil in 12-quart pot. Add pasta and 2 tablespoons salt and cook, stirring often, until al dente. Reserve 1 cup cooking water, then drain pasta and return it to pot. Add sauce and parsley and toss to combine. Season with salt and pepper to taste and add reserved cooking water as needed to adjust consistency. Serve, garnishing individual portions with mussels.

ON THE SIDE EASY GARLIC ROLLS
Mix ¼ cup olive oil, 1 large minced garlic clove, ½ teaspoon salt, and ¼ teaspoon pepper in bowl. Cut 2 pounds pizza dough into 10 pieces, roll loosely into balls, and arrange on parchment paper–lined baking sheet. Brush rolls with 1 beaten egg and bake in 375-degree oven until golden, 30 to 35 minutes, brushing rolls with garlic oil halfway through baking time. Let cool slightly before serving. Makes 10.

Rigatoni with Genovese Ragu

Serves 8 to 10

✔ **WHY THIS RECIPE WORKS:** Rumored to have been brought down the boot by a Neapolitan cook, Genovese sauce is like ragu in character: rich, hearty, and immensely satisfying. But unlike ragu, Genovese relies on lots of onions, not tomatoes, for its underlying sweetness; the onions are braised with beef until both are incredibly tender and the resulting sauce is rich and velvety. For our version, we cooked a hefty amount of sliced onions in the fat rendered from browned short ribs. Once the onions were wilted and golden, we added the ribs back to the pot and simmered the sauce for two hours—enough time for the meat to become fall-off-the-bone tender and the onions silky and sweet. Though we kept the tomatoes out of our recipe, we found that a small amount of tomato paste added undeniable depth of flavor. To prevent the sauce from becoming greasy, trim as much fat as possible from the ribs. You will need at least a 6-quart Dutch oven and a 12-quart stockpot for this recipe.

4	**pounds beef short ribs, trimmed**
	Salt and pepper
1	**tablespoon vegetable oil**
4	**ounces pancetta, cut into ¼-inch pieces**
2	**carrots, peeled and cut into ¼-inch pieces**
2	**celery ribs, cut into ¼-inch pieces**
4	**pounds onions, halved and sliced thin**
2	**tablespoons tomato paste**
1	**tablespoon minced fresh marjoram or thyme**
1	**cup dry white wine**
2	**pounds rigatoni**
	Grated Pecorino Romano cheese

1. Pat ribs dry with paper towels and season with salt and pepper. Heat oil in large Dutch oven over medium-high heat until just smoking. Brown half of ribs well on all sides, 8 to 10 minutes; transfer to plate. Repeat with remaining ribs using fat left in pot; transfer to plate.

2. Pour off all but 1 tablespoon fat left in pot, add pancetta, and cook over medium heat until pancetta is lightly browned, about 6 minutes. Stir in carrots and celery and cook until just softened, 5 to 7 minutes.

3. Stir in onions and ¼ teaspoon salt. Increase heat to high, cover, and cook, stirring occasionally, until onions are wilted and release their moisture, about 10 minutes. Uncover, reduce heat to medium-high, and continue to cook, stirring often, until onions are golden brown, 8 to 10 minutes.

4. Stir in tomato paste and marjoram and cook until fragrant, about 1 minute. Add wine and simmer for 2 minutes. Nestle beef, with any accumulated juice, into pot and bring to gentle simmer. Reduce heat to low, cover, and simmer gently, turning ribs occasionally, until meat is very tender and falling off bones, about 2 hours.

5. Transfer ribs to plate, let cool slightly, then shred meat into bite-size pieces, discarding fat and bones. Meanwhile, return sauce to simmer and cook, stirring often, until slightly thickened and creamy, 12 to 15 minutes. Stir in shredded meat and season with salt and pepper to taste.

6. Meanwhile, bring 8 quarts water to boil in 12-quart pot. Add pasta and 2 tablespoons salt and cook, stirring often, until al dente. Reserve 1½ cups cooking water, then drain pasta and return it to pot. Add sauce and ½ cup cooking water; toss to combine. Season with salt and pepper to taste and add remaining reserved cooking water as needed to adjust consistency. Serve with Pecorino.

Hearty Italian Meat Sauce (Sunday Gravy)

Serves 8 to 10

✔ **WHY THIS RECIPE WORKS:** This ultra-hearty Italian-American tomato sauce typically calls for six cuts of meat and half a day at the stove. We wanted a full-flavored meal on the table in less time than that and set our limit at four hours, with no more than an hour of hands-on cooking. To start, we limited ourselves to pork sausage and baby back ribs, and replaced the time-consuming braciole (stuffed, rolled Italian beef) with standout meatballs. For flavorful yet streamlined meatballs, we started with meatloaf mix, then incorporated a panade (or binder) of bread and buttermilk for tenderness and subtle tang. Browning the meatballs, then adding them to the sauce later on, ensured a seamless procedure, but left the sauce needing more depth, which we added by browning the onions and cooking the tomato paste until it was nearly blackened. Cooking our sauce in the oven rather than on the stovetop meant we could leave our sauce unattended for most of the cooking time. Meatloaf mix is a prepackaged mix of ground beef, pork, and veal; if it's unavailable, use 1 pound each of ground pork and 85 percent lean ground beef. You can substitute 6 tablespoons plain yogurt mixed with 2 tablespoons milk for the buttermilk. The sauce and meatballs can be prepared through step 5, cooled, and refrigerated in the Dutch oven for up to 2 days. To reheat, drizzle ½ cup water over the sauce (do not stir it in) and heat on the lower-middle rack of a 325-degree oven for 1 hour. You will need at least a 6-quart Dutch oven for this recipe.

SAUCE

2	tablespoons olive oil
2¼	pounds baby back ribs, cut into 2-rib sections
	Salt and pepper
1	pound hot Italian sausage
2	onions, chopped fine
1¼	teaspoons dried oregano
3	tablespoons tomato paste
4	garlic cloves, minced
2	(28-ounce) cans crushed tomatoes
⅔	cup beef broth

1. FOR THE SAUCE: Adjust oven rack to lower-middle position and heat oven to 325 degrees. Heat oil in large Dutch oven over medium-high heat until just smoking. Pat ribs dry with paper towels and season with salt and pepper. Working in two batches, brown ribs well on both sides, 5 to 7 minutes; transfer to plate. Add sausage to pot and brown well on all sides, 5 to 7 minutes; transfer to plate.

2. Add onions and oregano to fat left in pot and cook over medium heat, stirring often, until softened and lightly browned, 5 to 7 minutes. Stir in tomato paste and cook until very dark, about 3 minutes. Stir in garlic and cook until fragrant, about 30 seconds. Stir in crushed tomatoes and broth, scraping up any browned bits. Nestle browned ribs and sausage into pot. Bring to simmer, cover, and transfer to oven. Cook until ribs are tender, about 2½ hours.

QUICK PREP TIP
COOKING TOMATO PASTE
Cooking the tomato paste until nearly blackened concentrates its sweetness and adds body and complexity to the sauce.

MEATBALLS AND PASTA

- **2** slices hearty white sandwich bread, crusts removed and bread torn into small pieces
- **½** cup buttermilk
- **1** pound meatloaf mix
- **2** ounces thinly sliced prosciutto, chopped fine
- **1** ounce Pecorino Romano cheese, grated (½ cup)
- **¼** cup minced fresh parsley
- **2** garlic cloves, minced
- **1** large egg yolk
  Salt and pepper
- **¼** teaspoon red pepper flakes
- **½** cup olive oil
- **1½** pounds spaghetti or linguine
- **¼** cup chopped fresh basil
  Grated Parmesan cheese

3. FOR THE MEATBALLS AND PASTA: Meanwhile, mash bread and buttermilk to paste in large bowl; let stand for 10 minutes. Mix in meatloaf mix, prosciutto, Pecorino, parsley, garlic, egg yolk, ½ teaspoon salt, and pepper flakes with hands. Lightly shape mixture into 1½-inch round meatballs (about ¼ cup each; about 12 meatballs total); transfer to plate, cover, and refrigerate until needed.

4. During final ½ hour of sauce simmering time, heat oil in 12-inch nonstick skillet over medium-high heat until shimmering. Brown meatballs well on all sides, 5 to 7 minutes; transfer to paper towel–lined plate.

5. Remove sauce from oven and skim fat from surface using large spoon. Gently add meatballs to sauce. Cover, return pot to oven, and continue to cook until meatballs are just cooked through, about 15 minutes.

6. Meanwhile, bring 6 quarts water to boil in large pot. Add pasta and 2 tablespoons salt and cook, stirring often, until al dente. Reserve ½ cup cooking water, then drain pasta and return it to pot.

7. Using tongs, transfer meatballs, ribs, and sausage to serving platter; cut each sausage in half. Stir basil into sauce and season with salt and pepper to taste. Add 1 cup sauce and reserved cooking water to pasta and toss to combine. Serve with remaining sauce, platter of meat, and Parmesan.

ON THE SIDE **ITALIAN-STYLE SALAD WITH FENNEL AND ARTICHOKES**

In large bowl, gently toss 1 chopped head romaine lettuce, 4 ounces (4 cups) baby arugula, 1 thinly sliced fennel bulb, ½ cup fresh parsley leaves, and ⅓ cup coarsely chopped kalamata olives together. Whisk 3 tablespoons white balsamic vinegar or white wine vinegar, 1 minced garlic clove, ¼ teaspoon salt, and ⅛ teaspoon pepper together in medium bowl; slowly whisk in 6 tablespoons extra-virgin olive oil. Drizzle all but 1 tablespoon of dressing over salad and toss to coat. Toss 1 (14-ounce) can artichoke hearts, rinsed, patted dry, and quartered, with remaining 1 tablespoon dressing. Serve, garnishing individual portions with artichokes and shaved Asiago cheese. Serves 8 to 10.

Spaghetti and Meatballs for a Crowd

Serves 12

✔ **WHY THIS RECIPE WORKS:** This recipe delivers incredibly tender, rich-tasting meatballs in flavorful, full-bodied tomato gravy in 90 minutes. For the ultimate meatballs, we started with ground chuck and ground pork, amped up with savory, salty prosciutto. Gelatin helped to plump and soften the meatballs, while a panade of panko (Japanese bread crumbs, a more convenient choice than homemade bread crumbs) soaked in buttermilk kept them moist. As for cooking the meatballs, we roasted them in the oven first and then braised them in the sauce to keep our recipe moving and give us a window of time to prep our sauce. Finishing the meatballs in the sauce beefed up its flavor and allowed the meatballs to cook through. To make sure the sauce didn't overreduce, we swapped some of the crushed tomatoes for tomato juice. You can substitute 1 cup plain yogurt mixed with ½ cup milk for the buttermilk. You will need at least a 6-quart Dutch oven and a 12-quart stockpot for this recipe.

MEATBALLS

- 2¼ cups panko bread crumbs
- 1½ cups buttermilk
- 1½ teaspoons unflavored gelatin
- 3 tablespoons water
- 3 large eggs, lightly beaten
- 2 pounds 85 percent lean ground beef
- 1 pound ground pork
- 6 ounces thinly sliced prosciutto, chopped fine
- 3 ounces Parmesan cheese, grated (1½ cups)
- 6 tablespoons minced fresh parsley
- 3 garlic cloves, minced
  Salt and pepper

SAUCE AND PASTA

- 3 tablespoons extra-virgin olive oil
- 1½ cups grated onion
- 6 garlic cloves, minced
- ½ teaspoon red pepper flakes
- 1 teaspoon dried oregano
- 6 cups tomato juice
- 3 (28-ounce) cans crushed tomatoes
- 6 tablespoons dry white wine
  Salt and pepper
- 3 pounds spaghetti
  Sugar
- ½ cup chopped fresh basil
- 3 tablespoons minced fresh parsley
  Grated Parmesan cheese

1. FOR THE MEATBALLS: Spray two wire racks with vegetable oil spray and set in aluminum foil–lined rimmed baking sheets. Adjust oven racks to lower-middle and upper-middle positions and heat oven to 450 degrees. Combine panko and buttermilk in large bowl and let sit, mashing occasionally with fork, until smooth paste forms, about 10 minutes. Sprinkle gelatin over water and let sit until gelatin softens, about 5 minutes.

2. Using hands, gently mix gelatin mixture, eggs, beef, pork, prosciutto, Parmesan, parsley, garlic, 1½ teaspoons salt, and ½ teaspoon pepper into bread-crumb mixture until thoroughly combined. Lightly shape mixture into 40 meatballs (about ¼ cup each). Place meatballs on prepared wire racks, spaced evenly apart. Roast until browned, about 30 minutes, switching and rotating baking sheets halfway through roasting time.

3. FOR THE SAUCE AND PASTA: Meanwhile, heat oil in large Dutch oven over medium heat until shimmering. Add onion; cook until softened and lightly browned, 6 to 8 minutes. Stir in garlic, pepper flakes, and oregano and cook until fragrant, about 30 seconds. Stir in tomato juice, crushed tomatoes, wine, and 1½ teaspoons salt and simmer until slightly thickened, about 15 minutes.

4. Gently add meatballs to sauce. Reduce oven temperature to 300 degrees. Cover pot, place in oven, and cook until meatballs are firm and sauce has thickened, about 1 hour.

5. Bring 10 quarts water to boil in 12-quart pot. Add pasta and 2 tablespoons salt and cook, stirring often, until al dente. Reserve ½ cup cooking water, then drain pasta and return it to pot. Season sauce with salt, pepper, and sugar to taste; stir in basil and parsley. Toss pasta with 1½ cups sauce until lightly coated, adding reserved cooking water as needed to adjust consistency. Serve pasta with meatballs, remaining sauce, and Parmesan.

Pappardelle with Rabbit Ragu

Serves 8 to 10

✓ **WHY THIS RECIPE WORKS:** A nod to hearty, rustic old-world cooking that relied on the hunter's catch, rabbit ragu is guaranteed to elicit oohs and aahs at the dining table. For our own rich and intensely flavored ragu, we started by browning bone-in rabbit pieces, then set them aside while we built the sauce. Sautéed dried porcini mushrooms and tomato paste provided a flavorful backbone that stood up to the gaminess of the dark meat. Red wine and canned tomatoes contributed acidity, while pancetta added further complexity. After stirring in chicken broth to give our sauce volume and more depth, we added the meat back to the pot, then moved it all to the oven to cook through in its gentle, even heat. Once the meat was tender, we shredded it and stirred it back into the sauce, which we'd reduced further on the stovetop to concentrate its intense flavor. Tossed with wide pappardelle, our robust, rich ragu was a company-worthy dish that paid homage to classic Italian cookery. You will need at least a 6-quart Dutch oven and a 12-quart pot for this recipe.

1	**(3-pound) whole rabbit, cut into 7 pieces**
	Salt and pepper
3	**tablespoons olive oil**
4	**ounces pancetta, cut into ¼-inch pieces**
2	**onions, chopped fine**
2	**carrots, peeled and cut into ¼-inch pieces**
¾	**ounce dried porcini, rinsed and minced**
1	**(6-ounce) can tomato paste**
6	**garlic cloves, minced**
1	**cup red wine**
4	**cups low-sodium chicken broth**
2	**(28-ounce) cans diced tomatoes**
3	**bay leaves**
½	**teaspoon sugar**
2	**pounds pappardelle**
	Grated Parmesan cheese

1. Adjust oven rack to middle position and heat oven to 325 degrees. Pat rabbit dry with paper towels and season with salt and pepper. Heat 1 tablespoon oil in large Dutch oven over medium-high heat until just smoking. Brown half of rabbit lightly on both sides, about 6 minutes; transfer to bowl. Repeat with 1 tablespoon oil and remaining rabbit; transfer to bowl.

2. Add remaining 1 tablespoon oil and pancetta to now-empty pot and cook over medium heat until pancetta is lightly browned, about 6 minutes. Stir in onions, carrots, and porcini, increase heat to medium-high, and cook until vegetables are just softened, 6 to 10 minutes. Stir in tomato paste and cook until darkened and fragrant, about 3 minutes. Stir in garlic and cook until fragrant, about 30 seconds.

3. Stir in wine, scraping up any browned bits, and simmer until sauce has thickened, about 2 minutes. Stir in broth, tomatoes, and bay leaves. Nestle browned rabbit and any accumulated juice into pot and bring to simmer. Partially cover pot (leaving about 1 inch of pot open), transfer to oven, and cook until rabbit is very tender and falling off bones, 1½ to 2 hours.

4. Remove pot from oven and remove bay leaves. Transfer rabbit to cutting board, let cool slightly, then shred meat, discarding bones. Meanwhile, bring sauce to simmer over medium-high heat and cook until thickened, 10 to 15 minutes. Stir in shredded meat and sugar. Season with salt and pepper to taste.

5. Meanwhile, bring 8 quarts water to boil in 12-quart pot. Add pasta and 2 tablespoons salt and cook, stirring often, until al dente. Reserve 1 cup cooking water, then drain pasta and return it to pot. Add sauce and toss to combine. Season with salt and pepper to taste and add reserved cooking water as needed to adjust consistency. Serve with Parmesan.

1. Using chef's knife, start by cutting hindquarters from loin.

2. Then cut hindquarters into two pieces by slicing through spine.

3. Trim and discard thin flap that hangs between rib cage and loin.

4. Remove loin from forequarters by cutting through spine at point where rib cage is attached.

5. Then cut loin into two pieces by slicing it in half crosswise.

6. Finally, separate two forequarters from neck by cutting through rib cage on either side of neck.

ON THE SIDE EASY SPINACH AND ARUGULA SALAD WITH SWEET-BALSAMIC VINAIGRETTE

In large bowl, toss 10 ounces (10 cups) baby spinach and 8 ounces (8 cups) baby arugula. In small bowl, whisk ½ cup extra-virgin olive oil, 2 tablespoons strawberry (or other) jam, 2 tablespoons balsamic vinegar, ½ teaspoon salt, and ¼ teaspoon pepper together. Drizzle dressing over salad and toss to coat. Serves 12.

MINI MEAT LASAGNA

Pasta for Two

Spaghetti with Garlic, Olive Oil, and Artichokes

Serves 2

✔ **WHY THIS RECIPE WORKS:** When it comes to weeknight fare for two, we've got ease and speed on our minds. For a simple yet satisfying pantry supper, we combined fresh garlic, artichoke hearts, and spaghetti in an effortless, olive oil–based sauce. Canned and marinated artichoke hearts tasted watery and had flavors that seemed out of place here, so we used a package of frozen artichoke hearts. As for the garlic, we found we could achieve a deep, mellow flavor when we cooked it slowly over low heat. We also added a small amount of garlic, minced to a paste, right at the end for a bright, potent kick of flavor. Red pepper flakes, lemon juice, and parsley rounded out the dish. To thaw the artichokes, microwave them in a covered bowl for about 3 minutes. See page 173 for tips on how to measure out long strands of pasta without using a scale.

3	tablespoons extra-virgin olive oil
6	garlic cloves, 5 minced and 1 minced to a paste
⅛	teaspoon red pepper flakes
	Salt and pepper
9	ounces frozen artichoke hearts, thawed and patted dry
8	ounces spaghetti
2	tablespoons minced fresh parsley
1	teaspoon lemon juice
	Grated Parmesan cheese

1. Cook 1 tablespoon oil, minced garlic, pepper flakes, and ¼ teaspoon salt in 10-inch nonstick skillet over low heat, stirring often, until garlic is sticky and golden, about 10 minutes; transfer to bowl. In separate bowl, combine 1 tablespoon oil and garlic paste.

2. Add remaining 1 tablespoon oil to now-empty skillet and heat over medium-high heat until shimmering. Add artichokes and ⅛ teaspoon salt and cook until lightly browned, 4 to 6 minutes; set aside.

3. Meanwhile, bring 4 quarts water to boil in large pot. Add pasta and 1 tablespoon salt and cook, stirring often, until al dente. Reserve ½ cup cooking water, then drain pasta and return it to pot. Add cooked garlic mixture, raw garlic mixture, sautéed artichokes, parsley, and lemon juice. Season with salt and pepper to taste and add reserved cooking water as needed to adjust consistency. Serve with Parmesan.

QUICK PREP TIP MINCING GARLIC TO A PASTE
Mashing garlic to a paste can be helpful when adding raw garlic to a dish. The flavor of the garlic mellows substantially, and it can be more easily incorporated. To make garlic paste, mince the garlic and then sprinkle it with a pinch of salt. Scrape the blade of a chef's knife across the garlic, mashing the garlic into a cutting board. After a few scrapes, the garlic will turn into a sticky paste.

Shells with Ricotta, Roasted Red Peppers, and Goat Cheese

Serves 2

✔ **WHY THIS RECIPE WORKS:** Pasta with a creamy, slightly sweetened ricotta sauce is a naturally quick and convenient meal for two, but such a simple sauce can require expert execution. Lots of recipes simply stir the ricotta into the hot pasta, but this method just delivers grainy cheese that doesn't even coat the pasta. We had better luck when we combined the ricotta with a little butter for richness and goat cheese for tangy flavor; some of the hot pasta cooking water helped to smooth out the sauce. Once added to the hot pasta, it coated each piece perfectly. We liked bite-size shells for the way they held on to the ricotta sauce. Roasted red peppers added color and sweetness, while crisped prosciutto brought some crunch to the dish. Other pasta shapes can be substituted for the shells; however, their cup measurements may vary (see page 173).

4	ounces (½ cup) whole-milk or part-skim ricotta cheese
2	ounces goat cheese, crumbled (½ cup)
1	tablespoon unsalted butter, cut into 4 pieces
1	tablespoon balsamic vinegar
	Salt and pepper
1½	teaspoons olive oil
2	ounces thinly sliced prosciutto, cut into ¼-inch strips
1	small onion, chopped fine
1	garlic clove, minced
8	ounces (2 cups) small shells
1	cup jarred roasted red peppers, rinsed, patted dry, and chopped
2	tablespoons chopped fresh basil

1. Mix ricotta, goat cheese, butter, vinegar, ⅛ teaspoon salt, and ¼ teaspoon pepper together in bowl. Cook oil and prosciutto in 8-inch nonstick skillet over medium heat until prosciutto is browned and crisp, about 5 minutes. Using slotted spoon, transfer prosciutto to paper towel–lined plate.

2. Add onion to fat left in skillet and cook over medium heat until softened and lightly browned, 5 to 7 minutes. Stir in garlic and cook until fragrant, about 30 seconds; transfer to bowl with ricotta mixture.

3. Meanwhile, bring 4 quarts water to boil in large pot. Add pasta and 1 tablespoon salt and cook, stirring often, until al dente. Reserve ½ cup cooking water, then drain pasta and return it to pot.

4. Whisk ¼ cup reserved pasta cooking water into ricotta mixture until smooth. Add ricotta mixture and roasted red peppers to pasta and toss to combine. Season with salt and pepper to taste and add remaining reserved cooking water as needed to adjust consistency. Sprinkle individual portions with crisped prosciutto and basil before serving.

SMART SHOPPING ROASTED RED PEPPERS
We tasted eight brands of roasted red peppers, both straight out of the jars and in roasted red pepper soup, to find the best one. Overall, tasters preferred firmer, smokier, sweeter-tasting peppers packed in simple brines made of salt and water. Peppers packed in brines that contained garlic, vinegar, olive oil, and grape must—characteristic of most of the European brands—rated second. Our winner? Tasters preferred the domestically produced **Dunbars Sweet Roasted Peppers**, which lists only red bell peppers, water, salt, and citric acid in its ingredient list.

Campanelle with Sautéed Mushrooms, Peas, and Camembert

Serves 2

✔ **WHY THIS RECIPE WORKS:** To up the ante on a simple pasta and mushrooms dinner for two, we decided to add creamy, earthy Camembert to the mix. Starting with the mushrooms, a one-two punch of shiitakes and cremini delivered hearty mushroom flavor. Sautéing the mushrooms first, then setting them aside while we built the sauce, ensured that they retained a toothsome, slightly chewy texture. Once the mushrooms were done, we added chicken broth to the pan and scraped up the flavorful browned mushroom bits left behind. Besides being convenient, frozen peas also added color and freshness to the sauce, and a little cream gave it a velvety consistency. As for the Camembert, we simply cut the cheese into small pieces. Adding it just before serving allowed the residual heat to soften but not completely melt it. Other pasta shapes can be substituted for the campanelle; however, their cup measurements may vary (see page 173).

1	tablespoon olive oil
1	tablespoon unsalted butter
3	shallots, minced
4	ounces shiitake mushrooms, stemmed and sliced ¼ inch thick
6	ounces cremini mushrooms, trimmed and sliced ¼ inch thick
	Salt and pepper
2	garlic cloves, minced
⅔	cup low-sodium chicken broth
½	cup frozen peas, thawed
¼	cup heavy cream
8	ounces (2½ cups) campanelle
3	ounces Camembert, rind left intact, cut into ½-inch pieces
1	tablespoon minced fresh chives
1½	teaspoons lemon juice

1. Heat oil and butter in 10-inch skillet over medium heat until butter melts. Add shallots and cook until softened, about 3 minutes. Increase heat to medium-high, stir in shiitakes, and cook for 1 minute. Stir in cremini and ¼ teaspoon salt and cook until golden, about 6 minutes. Stir in garlic and cook until fragrant, about 30 seconds. Transfer mushrooms to bowl and cover to keep warm.

2. Add broth and peas to now-empty skillet and bring to boil, scraping up any browned bits. Stir in cream, bring to simmer, and cook until sauce has thickened slightly and reduced to ⅔ cup, about 4 minutes.

3. Meanwhile, bring 4 quarts water to boil in large pot. Add pasta and 1 tablespoon salt and cook, stirring often, until al dente. Reserve ½ cup cooking water, then drain pasta and return it to pot. Add mushrooms, sauce, Camembert, chives, and lemon juice and toss to combine. Season with salt and pepper to taste and add reserved cooking water as needed to adjust consistency. Serve.

SMART SHOPPING **FROZEN PEAS**

We've always been big fans of frozen peas. Individually frozen right after being shucked from the pod, they are often sweeter and fresher-tasting than the shuck-'em-yourself "fresh" peas that may have spent days in storage. We've seen two varieties in the freezer aisle: regular frozen peas and bags labeled "petite peas" (or sometimes "petit pois" or "baby sweet peas"). To find out if there's a difference, we tasted each type with butter. Tasters unanimously favored the smaller peas for their sweeter flavor and creamier texture. Regular peas were by no means unacceptable but had tougher skins and mealier interiors. Since both varieties are available for the same price, we're going with the petite peas from now on.

Pesto Pasta Salad with Chicken and Vegetables

Serves 2

✔ **WHY THIS RECIPE WORKS:** For a scaled-down pesto pasta salad, we made a simple sauce with basil, olive oil, Parmesan, lemon juice, a shallot, and garlic. To quickly deepen the flavor of the garlic, we toasted it first in a skillet. Our pesto tasted great, but to take it to the next level, we stirred in a bit of mayonnaise, which added creaminess and a hint of tang. Farfalle was our choice for pasta that would hold on to the piquant sauce; after draining it, we tossed it with a spoonful of olive oil and spread it onto a baking sheet so it could cool and wouldn't clump together later on. With bites of cooked chicken, shredded carrot, cherry tomatoes, and bell pepper pieces stirred in, our pesto pasta salad was complete. Other pasta shapes can be substituted for the farfalle; however, their cup measurements may vary (see page 173). You can either use leftover chicken in this dish, or quickly cook a chicken breast following the instructions on page 80.

4	ounces (1⅔ cups) farfalle
	Salt and pepper
1	tablespoon olive oil
1½	cups lightly packed basil leaves
2	garlic cloves, toasted (see page 257) and minced
¼	cup grated Parmesan cheese
3	tablespoons mayonnaise
1	small shallot, minced
1	tablespoon lemon juice
1	cup shredded cooked chicken breast
1	carrot, peeled and shredded
½	red bell pepper, stemmed, seeded, and cut into ½-inch pieces
6	ounces cherry tomatoes, quartered

1. Bring 4 quarts water to boil in large pot. Add pasta and 1 tablespoon salt and cook, stirring often, until tender. Reserve ½ cup cooking water, then drain pasta. Toss pasta with 1 teaspoon oil, then spread out onto rimmed baking sheet. Let cool to room temperature, about 30 minutes.

2. Place basil in heavy-duty gallon-size zipper-lock bag and pound with rolling pin until leaves are lightly bruised. Process bruised basil, toasted garlic, Parmesan, mayonnaise, shallot, lemon juice, remaining 2 teaspoons oil, and ¼ teaspoon salt in food processor until smooth, about 30 seconds. Transfer mixture to bowl and season with salt and pepper to taste.

3. In large bowl, toss cooled pasta, chicken, carrot, and bell pepper with pesto, adjusting consistency with reserved pasta cooking water as needed. Fold in tomatoes, season with salt and pepper to taste, and serve.

SMART SHOPPING BONELESS, SKINLESS CHICKEN BREASTS

To find out which brand of boneless, skinless chicken breasts tastes best, we gathered six popular brands, broiled them without seasoning, and tasted them all side by side. Among the contenders were one kosher bird, two "natural," and one "free-range"; the remaining two were just "chicken." Our tasters liked two above the rest. The tie for first place went to **Empire Kosher** (left) and the all-natural **Bell & Evans** (right), both of which were praised for their good flavor and texture.

Rotini with Garden Vegetable Sauce

Serves 2

✓ **WHY THIS RECIPE WORKS:** Though pasta with fresh summer vegetables sounds like an easy meal, it's actually more difficult than you'd think. The trick is figuring out how to cook the vegetables so they retain their fresh flavor and texture. We gathered a variety of veggies—zucchini, cherry tomatoes, carrot, and bell pepper—and started sautéing. Cooking them together, though easy, didn't work—the flavors became too homogeneous. Rather, we had better luck when we cooked the vegetables in two batches. First, we sautéed the zucchini and tomatoes, then set them aside until the end so they didn't become waterlogged in the sauce. Then we added the carrot, bell pepper, and onion to the pan; with chicken broth and a little tomato paste, we had our sauce. Baby arugula and chopped basil, added at the end, ensured that our dinner tasted—and looked—like it was fresh from the garden. Other pasta shapes can be substituted for rotini; however, their cup measurements may vary (see page 173). For the nutritional information for this recipe, see page 307.

1	tablespoon extra-virgin olive oil
½	zucchini or yellow squash (4 ounces), halved lengthwise and sliced ¼ inch thick
3	ounces cherry tomatoes, halved
1	carrot, peeled and shredded
1	small onion, sliced thin
½	red bell pepper, stemmed, seeded, and cut into ¼-inch pieces
	Salt and pepper
1½	tablespoons tomato paste
2	garlic cloves, minced
	Pinch red pepper flakes
¾	cup low-sodium chicken broth
4	ounces (1½ cups) rotini
1½	ounces (1½ cups) baby arugula
2	tablespoons chopped fresh basil
	Grated Parmesan cheese

1. Heat 1 teaspoon oil in 10-inch nonstick skillet over medium-high heat until shimmering. Add zucchini and cook, stirring often, until well browned, about 3 minutes. Stir in cherry tomatoes and cook until slightly wilted, about 1 minute; transfer to bowl.

2. Add 1 teaspoon oil to now-empty skillet and heat over medium heat until shimmering. Add carrot, onion, bell pepper, and ½ teaspoon salt, cover, and cook until vegetables have softened, 5 to 7 minutes. Uncover, stir in tomato paste, and cook until it begins to brown, about 1 minute. Stir in garlic and pepper flakes and cook until fragrant, about 30 seconds. Stir in broth, scraping up any browned bits. Bring to simmer and cook until slightly thickened, about 1 minute. Off heat, season with salt and pepper to taste.

3. Meanwhile, bring 4 quarts water to boil in large pot. Add pasta and 1 tablespoon salt and cook, stirring often, until al dente. Reserve ½ cup cooking water, then drain pasta and return it to pot. Add cooked vegetables, sauce, arugula, basil, and remaining 1 teaspoon oil and gently toss to combine. Season with salt and pepper to taste and add reserved cooking water as needed to adjust consistency. Serve with Parmesan.

ON THE SIDE EASY GARLIC FLATBREAD
Microwave 1 tablespoon unsalted butter and 1 minced garlic clove together in bowl until melted and fragrant, 30 seconds. Place one (8-inch) store-bought naan bread on rimmed baking sheet, brush with garlic butter, and season with salt and pepper. Bake in 400-degree oven until hot and crisp, 5 to 8 minutes. Serves 2.

Tortellini with Spring Vegetables

Serves 2

✔ **WHY THIS RECIPE WORKS:** Dried tortellini from the supermarket is the ultimate in convenience—a single package provides plenty for two, plus it cooks quickly and offers the supple texture of fresh, made-that-day pasta from an Italian market. But many recipes hide the flavor and texture of the tortellini with a heavy, cream-laden sauce or a pile of vegetables. We decided to fix that, and paired cheese tortellini with a handful of spring vegetables, including fennel, peas, and spinach, in a lighter sauce. After slicing the fennel thin, we sautéed it, then built the sauce around it in the same pan; the peas and spinach simply needed to be stirred in at the end of cooking to warm through and wilt. Cutting the heavy cream with chicken broth ensured that the sauce was velvety but not too heavy. To cook our tortellini, we found it easy to simmer them right in the skillet after building the sauce—no extra pot needed. If necessary, add hot water, 1 tablespoon at a time, to adjust the consistency of the sauce before serving. For more information on buying tortellini, see page 124.

1	ounce thinly sliced prosciutto, cut into ¼-inch pieces
1	tablespoon unsalted butter
1	small fennel bulb, stalks discarded, bulb halved, cored, and sliced thin (see page 248)
2	garlic cloves, minced
1¾	cups water
½	low-sodium chicken broth
6	ounces dried cheese tortellini
3	ounces (3 cups) baby spinach
½	cup frozen peas
¼	cup heavy cream
¼	cup grated Parmesan cheese, plus extra for serving
2	teaspoons lemon juice
	Salt and pepper

1. Cook prosciutto in 12-inch nonstick skillet over medium heat until browned and crisp, about 5 minutes. Using slotted spoon, transfer prosciutto to paper towel–lined plate.

2. Melt butter in now-empty skillet over medium heat. Add fennel and cook until browned, 6 to 9 minutes. Stir in garlic and cook until fragrant, about 30 seconds. Stir in water, broth, and tortellini and bring to rapid simmer. Cook, stirring often, until tortellini is tender and sauce is thickened, 6 to 9 minutes.

3. Turn heat to low, stir in spinach, peas, and cream and cook until spinach is wilted and tortellini is coated with sauce, 2 to 3 minutes. Off heat, stir in Parmesan and lemon juice and season with salt and pepper to taste. Sprinkle individual portions with crisped prosciutto and serve with extra Parmesan.

SMART SHOPPING LEMON JUICE SUBSTITUTES
Nothing beats fresh-squeezed lemon juice, but can you swap in a convenience product if only using a little splash? To find out, we tested six packaged lemon juice products in two serious lemon recipes: lemonade and lemon curd. Not surprisingly, none came close to beating the tart, clean, bright flavor of fresh-squeezed lemon juice, but both **True Lemon** (left) crystallized lemon juice and **ReaLemon** (right) lemon juice from concentrate were deemed acceptable in a pinch. Both can be found at grocery stores nationwide (True Lemon in the baking aisle, and ReaLemon in the bottled juice aisle).

Pasta with Quick Chicken Bolognese

Serves 2

✔ **WHY THIS RECIPE WORKS:** Traditional Bolognese gets its big flavor and tender texture from braising ground beef, pork, and veal with milk, wine, and tomatoes for upwards of three hours—but this just doesn't make sense if you want to make a small batch of Bolognese to feed two. Switching to ground chicken for the meat cuts back on both the shopping list and the simmering time; chicken is leaner and takes less time to become tender, but that leanness translates to a less flavorful sauce. To compensate, we added pancetta, dried porcini, and tomato paste for flavor, along with a little butter for richness. White wine, which we reduced to concentrate its sweetness, contributed deep flavor. For a finely textured sauce, be sure to mince the vegetables and break the chicken into small pieces as it cooks in step 3. Other pasta shapes can be substituted for rigatoni; however, their cup measurements may vary (see page 173).

1	**(14.5-ounce) can diced tomatoes**
⅔	**cup sweet white wine, such as Gewürztraminer, Riesling, or white Zinfandel**
2	**tablespoons unsalted butter**
2	**ounces pancetta, cut into ¼-inch pieces**
3	**tablespoons minced carrot**
1	**large shallot, minced**
⅛	**ounce dried porcini mushrooms, rinsed and minced**
	Salt and pepper
1	**garlic clove, minced**
½	**teaspoon sugar**
8	**ounces ground chicken**
¾	**cup whole milk**
1	**tablespoon tomato paste**
8	**ounces (3 cups) rigatoni**
	Grated Parmesan cheese

1. Pulse tomatoes in food processor until finely chopped, about 6 pulses; set aside. Simmer wine in 10-inch nonstick skillet over medium-low heat until it has reduced to about 1 tablespoon, about 12 minutes; transfer to small bowl.

2. Melt butter in now-empty skillet over medium heat. Add pancetta and cook until browned, about 5 minutes. Stir in carrot, shallot, porcini, and ⅛ teaspoon salt and cook until vegetables are softened, about 4 minutes. Stir in garlic and sugar and cook until fragrant, about 30 seconds.

3. Add chicken and cook, breaking up meat with wooden spoon, for 1 minute (chicken will still be pink). Stir in milk, bring to simmer, and cook, breaking up meat into small pieces, until most of liquid has evaporated and meat begins to sizzle, about 10 minutes.

4. Stir in tomato paste and cook for 1 minute. Stir in processed tomatoes, ⅛ teaspoon salt, and ⅛ teaspoon pepper. Bring to simmer and cook until sauce has thickened, about 7 minutes. Stir in reduced wine and continue to cook until flavors meld, about 5 minutes.

5. Meanwhile, bring 4 quarts water to boil in large pot. Add pasta and 1 tablespoon salt and cook, stirring often, until al dente. Reserve ½ cup cooking water, then drain pasta and return it to pot. Add sauce and toss to combine. Season with salt and pepper to taste and add reserved cooking water as needed to adjust consistency. Serve with Parmesan.

Mini Meat Lasagna

Serves 2

☑ **WHY THIS RECIPE WORKS:** Nothing satisfies like a big square of cheesy, meaty, homemade lasagna. But this timeless classic usually feeds a crowd and takes some time to put together. For a petite lasagna better suited for a couple, we scaled down from the standard large baking dish to a loaf pan. Using no-boil lasagna noodles made lasagna assembly go quickly, plus the noodles fit perfectly into the loaf pan. For a thick, rich, and complexly flavored meat sauce without the all-day simmer, we turned to meatloaf mix—a mix of ground beef, pork, and veal sold in a single package—and added a splash of cream for richness. Using two types of canned tomatoes (diced and sauce) gave us a sauce that perfectly coated the noodles. We covered the lasagna with aluminum foil to prevent it from drying out in the oven, then removed the foil for the last few minutes of baking to achieve the same browned, cheesy top layer found on full-size lasagna. If you cannot find meatloaf mix, substitute equal parts 80 percent lean ground beef and sweet Italian sausage, casings removed. Do not substitute fat-free ricotta here.

1   tablespoon olive oil

1   small onion, chopped fine
     Salt and pepper

2   garlic cloves, minced

8   ounces meatloaf mix

2   tablespoons heavy cream

1   (14.5-ounce) can diced tomatoes, drained with ¼ cup juice reserved

1   (8-ounce) can tomato sauce

4   ounces (½ cup) whole-milk or part-skim ricotta cheese

1   ounce Parmesan cheese, grated (½ cup), plus 2 tablespoons

3   tablespoons chopped fresh basil

1   large egg, lightly beaten

4   no-boil lasagna noodles

4   ounces whole-milk mozzarella cheese, shredded (1 cup)

1. Heat oil in large saucepan over medium heat until shimmering. Add onion and ⅛ teaspoon salt and cook until softened and lightly browned, 5 to 7 minutes. Stir in garlic and cook until fragrant, about 30 seconds. Stir in meatloaf mix and cook, breaking up meat with wooden spoon, until it is no longer pink, about 2 minutes.

2. Stir in cream, bring to simmer, and cook until liquid evaporates, about 2 minutes. Stir in drained tomatoes, reserved tomato juice, and tomato sauce. Bring to simmer and cook until flavors meld, about 2 minutes. Season with salt and pepper to taste.

3. Adjust oven rack to middle position and heat oven to 400 degrees. Combine ricotta, ½ cup Parmesan, basil, egg, ⅛ teaspoon salt, and ⅛ teaspoon pepper in bowl.

4. Spread ½ cup sauce over bottom of 9 by 5-inch loaf pan, avoiding large chunks of meat. Place 1 noodle in pan and spread ⅓ of ricotta mixture over top. Sprinkle evenly with ¼ cup mozzarella and spoon ½ cup sauce evenly over top.

5. Repeat layering process of noodle, ricotta mixture, mozzarella, and sauce twice more. Place remaining noodle on top, cover with remaining 1 cup sauce, and sprinkle with remaining ¼ cup mozzarella and remaining 2 tablespoons Parmesan.

6. Cover dish tightly with aluminum foil that has been sprayed with vegetable oil spray. Bake until sauce bubbles lightly around edges, 25 to 30 minutes. Remove foil and continue to bake until hot throughout and cheese is browned in spots, about 10 minutes longer. Let cool for 15 minutes before serving.

Whole-Wheat Spaghetti with Fennel and Italian Sausage

Serves 2

✔ **WHY THIS RECIPE WORKS:** Whole-wheat pasta has such a distinctive and hearty flavor that it can easily dominate any dish. We wanted a simple pasta dish for two that would provide the right complement to the hearty flavor and firm texture of whole-wheat spaghetti. We found that a boldly flavored sauce made with sausage and chunks of sautéed fennel provided a nice counterpoint to the pasta's texture. Starch from the pasta cooking water thickened the sauce nicely and helped it cling to the spaghetti. A sprinkling of freshly grated Pecorino Romano added a salty tang, while pine nuts contributed crunch. For more information on buying whole-wheat pasta, see page 97. See page 173 for tips on how to measure out long strands of pasta without using a scale.

2	tablespoons extra-virgin olive oil
3	garlic cloves, minced
¼	teaspoon red pepper flakes
	Salt and pepper
4	ounces sweet Italian sausage, casings removed
1	small fennel bulb, stalks discarded, bulb halved, cored, and sliced thin
¼	cup pine nuts, toasted and chopped coarse
¼	cup chopped fresh basil
1	tablespoon lemon juice
6	ounces whole-wheat spaghetti
	Grated Pecorino Romano cheese

1. Combine oil, garlic, pepper flakes, and ¼ teaspoon salt in bowl; set aside. Cook sausage in 12-inch nonstick skillet over medium-high heat, breaking up meat with wooden spoon, until browned and crisp, 5 to 7 minutes. Using slotted spoon, transfer sausage to paper towel–lined plate.

2. Add fennel and ⅛ teaspoon salt to fat left in skillet and cook over medium-high heat, stirring often, until softened, 5 to 7 minutes. Clear center of skillet, add oil-garlic mixture, and cook, mashing mixture into pan, until fragrant, about 20 seconds. Off heat, stir in sausage, pine nuts, basil, and lemon juice.

3. Meanwhile, bring 4 quarts water to boil in large pot. Add pasta and 1 tablespoon salt and cook, stirring often, until al dente. Reserve ½ cup cooking water, then drain pasta and return it to pot.

4. Add sauce and ⅓ cup reserved cooking water and toss to combine. Season with salt and pepper to taste and add reserved cooking water as needed to adjust consistency. Sprinkle individual portions with Pecorino before serving.

QUICK PREP TIP PREPARING FENNEL
After cutting off stems, feathery fronds, and thin slice from base of fennel bulb, remove any tough or blemished layers and cut bulb in half vertically through base. Use small knife to remove pyramid-shaped core, and then slice each half into thin strips.

Sesame Noodles with Shredded Chicken and Vegetables

Serves 2

✔ **WHY THIS RECIPE WORKS:** It's nearly impossible to find good sesame noodles unless you live near Chinatown—so we decided to make our own. Hard-to-find Asian sesame paste is the main ingredient in authentic recipes; we found that chunky peanut butter and toasted sesame seeds made great stand-ins. Pulverizing the peanut butter and sesame seeds in the blender gave us a nutty, fresh-tasting sauce with complex flavor. Rice vinegar, soy sauce, brown sugar, ginger, and garlic rounded out the flavors. Bell pepper strips, sliced cucumber, shredded carrot, and thinly sliced scallions added color and crunch. Both fresh Chinese noodles (found in the produce section at the supermarket) and dried spaghetti work here. This recipe is a great way to use up leftover cooked chicken; otherwise, follow the instructions on page 80 to quickly cook and shred chicken. See page 173 for tips on how to measure out long strands of pasta without using a scale.

SAUCE

- 2½ tablespoons soy sauce
- 2 tablespoons chunky peanut butter
- 1½ tablespoons sesame seeds, toasted
- 1 tablespoon rice vinegar
- 1 tablespoon light brown sugar
- 1½ teaspoons grated fresh ginger
- 1 garlic clove, minced
- ½ teaspoon hot sauce
- 2 tablespoons hot water, plus extra as needed

CHICKEN AND NOODLES

- 8 ounces fresh Chinese noodles or 6 ounces dried spaghetti
- 1 tablespoon salt
- 1 tablespoon toasted sesame oil
- 1 cup shredded cooked chicken
- ½ red bell pepper, stemmed, seeded, and cut into ¼-inch-wide strips
- ½ cucumber, peeled, halved lengthwise, seeded, and sliced ¼ inch thick
- 1 carrot, peeled and shredded
- 2 scallions, sliced thin
- 1 tablespoon minced fresh cilantro (optional)
- 1 tablespoon sesame seeds, toasted

1. FOR THE SAUCE: Process all ingredients except hot water in blender until smooth, about 30 seconds. With blender running, add hot water, 1 tablespoon at a time, until sauce has consistency of heavy cream.

2. FOR THE CHICKEN AND NOODLES: Bring 4 quarts water to boil in large pot. Add noodles and salt and cook, stirring often, until tender. Drain noodles, rinse with cold water, drain again, then toss with oil.

3. Transfer noodles to large bowl, add sauce, shredded chicken, red pepper, cucumber, carrot, scallions, and cilantro (if using) and toss to combine. Sprinkle with sesame seeds and serve.

SMART SHOPPING A BETTER BLENDER

A blender has one basic job, which is to blend food into a uniform consistency, regardless if it's pasta sauce or a smoothie. We found two features to be the most important in a blender: The blades should be tapered or serrated, and the jar should also be tapered to keep food close to the blade edges. After testing 10 models by crushing ice, pureeing soup, and making smoothies, we had our winner. The **KitchenAid 5-Speed Blender** ($119.95; left) impressed us with its brute strength and efficiency, while the **Kalorik BL Blender** ($45; right) performed nearly as well and was also the quietest of the bunch, making it our Best Buy.

Spaghetti with Lemon, Basil, and Shrimp

Serves 2

✔ **WHY THIS RECIPE WORKS:** Frozen shrimp are a secret weapon for smaller households—they can be stashed in the freezer, ready to be pressed into service for dinner at a moment's notice (and that's about how long it takes to cook them). Paired with pasta in a simple sauce of lemon juice and olive oil thickened with a little Parmesan, they make for an easy yet elegant meal. Because there aren't many other ingredients involved, the sweet, briny flavor of the shrimp can take center stage. The only trick is to use high-quality extra-virgin olive oil and fresh-squeezed lemon juice for the best flavor possible. Poaching the shrimp right in the pasta cooking water saves time and cuts down on dishes. Be sure not to overcook the shrimp in step 2 or else they will taste rubbery and dry; remember that residual heat will continue to cook the shrimp after you remove them from the cooking water. See page 173 for tips on how to measure out long strands of pasta without using a scale.

3 tablespoons extra-virgin olive oil

1 teaspoon grated lemon zest plus 2½ tablespoons juice

1 garlic clove, minced to a paste (see page 237)
Salt and pepper

1 ounce Parmesan cheese, grated (½ cup)

8 ounces extra-large shrimp (21 to 25 per pound), peeled, deveined, and tails removed

6 ounces spaghetti

2 tablespoons shredded fresh basil

1 tablespoon unsalted butter, softened

1. Whisk oil, lemon zest, lemon juice, garlic, and ¼ teaspoon salt together in bowl, then stir in Parmesan cheese until thick and creamy; set aside.

2. Bring 4 quarts water to boil in large pot over high heat. Add shrimp and 1 tablespoon salt and cook until pink and curled, about 1 minute. Using slotted spoon, transfer shrimp to bowl, season with salt and pepper to taste, and cover to keep warm.

3. Return pot of water to boil, add pasta, and cook, stirring often, until al dente. Reserve ½ cup cooking water, then drain pasta and return it to pot. Stir in oil-garlic mixture, cooked shrimp, basil, and butter and toss to combine. Season with salt and pepper to taste and add reserved cooking water as needed to adjust consistency. Serve.

ON THE SIDE BABY SPINACH SALAD WITH FRISÉE AND STRAWBERRIES
Combine 3 ounces (3 cups) baby spinach, ½ head frisée, thinly sliced, 1 cup strawberries, hulled and sliced thin, and 1 tablespoon chopped fresh basil in large bowl. In separate bowl, whisk 4 teaspoons balsamic vinegar, 1 minced small shallot, ½ teaspoon mayonnaise, and ½ teaspoon Dijon mustard together; slowly whisk in 6½ teaspoons extra-virgin olive oil and season with salt and pepper to taste. Toss salad with dressing and serve. Serves 2.

Skillet Shrimp and Orzo Casserole

Serves 2

✔ **WHY THIS RECIPE WORKS:** For a bright, fresh-tasting orzo and shrimp casserole that paid tribute to this classic Greek duo, we started by cooking the pasta. Sautéing it briefly in oil until browned worked to deepen its flavor. Then we added our cooking liquid to the pan—chicken broth and tomato juice provided a savory backbone with some brightness—and simmered the orzo briefly before stirring in the shrimp. We moved the pan to the oven to finish; this way both the pasta and shrimp would be perfectly done at the same time. For a briny, salty punch, we sprinkled crumbled feta over the top before baking. Saffron contributed its typical sunny hue and flavor, while scallions, peas, and tomatoes rounded out the dish. Though the saffron is optional, it is worth including if you have some on hand. If using smaller or larger shrimp, the oven cooking time may vary accordingly. For the nutritional information for this recipe, see page 307.

8 ounces extra-large shrimp (21 to 25 per pound), peeled, deveined, and tails removed
Salt and pepper
1 tablespoon olive oil
1 small red onion, chopped fine
½ red bell pepper, stemmed, seeded, and cut into ½-inch pieces
3 garlic cloves, minced
1 teaspoon minced fresh oregano or ¼ teaspoon dried
1 cup orzo (6 ounces)
Pinch saffron threads, crumbled (optional)
1½ cups low-sodium chicken broth
½ cup drained canned diced tomatoes, with ¼ cup juice reserved
⅓ cup frozen peas
1 ounce feta cheese, crumbled (¼ cup)
2 scallions, sliced thin
Lemon wedges

1. Adjust oven rack to middle position and heat oven to 400 degrees. Pat shrimp dry with paper towels and season with salt and pepper; cover and refrigerate until needed.

2. Heat oil in 10-inch ovensafe skillet over medium heat until shimmering. Add onion, bell pepper, and ¼ teaspoon salt and cook until vegetables are softened, about 5 minutes. Stir in garlic and oregano and cook until fragrant, about 30 seconds. Stir in orzo and saffron (if using) and cook, stirring often, until orzo is lightly browned, about 4 minutes.

3. Stir in broth and reserved tomato juice, bring to simmer, and cook, stirring occasionally, until orzo is al dente, 10 to 12 minutes. Stir in shrimp, tomatoes, and peas, then sprinkle feta evenly over top. Transfer skillet to oven and bake until shrimp are cooked through and cheese is lightly browned, about 20 minutes. Sprinkle with scallions and serve with lemon wedges.

QUICK PREP TIP DEVEINING SHRIMP

To devein shrimp, hold the shrimp firmly in one hand, then use a paring knife to cut down the back side of the shrimp, about ⅛- to ¼-inch deep, to expose the vein. Using the tip of the knife, gently remove the vein. Wipe the knife against a paper towel to remove the vein and discard.

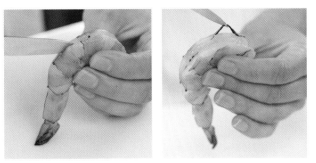

KALE AND SUNFLOWER SEED PESTO

Pestos and No-Cook Sauces

Classic Basil Pesto

Serves 4 to 6

✓ **WHY THIS RECIPE WORKS:** The ultimate no-cook sauce, basil pesto balances the grassy, perfumed flavor of fresh basil against the spicy bite of raw garlic and the rich, fruity notes of extra-virgin olive oil. To bring out the basil's flavor, we gently pounded it with a mallet before tossing it in the food processor—this helped to release its flavorful oils. To tame the raw, spicy garlic flavor, we toasted our cloves in a small skillet; toasting the nuts as well deepened their flavor. Basil usually turns a darker green shade in homemade pesto, but we found that adding a little fresh parsley boosted its vibrant green hue. Processing everything at once in the food processor gave us a pesto that retained some texture, but we found we needed to thin it with some reserved pasta cooking water so it would coat every piece of pasta evenly. For sharper flavor, use Pecorino Romano cheese in place of the Parmesan.

2	**cups packed fresh basil leaves**
2	**tablespoons fresh parsley leaves (optional)**
7	**tablespoons extra-virgin olive oil**
¼	**cup grated Parmesan or Pecorino Romano cheese, plus extra for serving**
¼	**cup pine nuts, toasted**
3	**garlic cloves, toasted (see page 257) and minced Salt and pepper**
1	**pound pasta**

1. Place basil and parsley, if using, in large zipper-lock bag and pound lightly with meat pounder or rolling pin until leaves are bruised. Process bruised herbs, oil, Parmesan, pine nuts, garlic, and ½ teaspoon salt in food processor until smooth, 30 to 60 seconds, scraping down bowl as needed. Transfer to medium bowl and season with salt and pepper to taste.

2. Meanwhile, bring 4 quarts water to boil in large pot. Add pasta and 1 tablespoon salt and cook, stirring often, until al dente. Reserve ¾ cup cooking water, then drain pasta and return it to pot.

3. Stir several tablespoons of reserved pasta water into pesto to loosen it, then add it to pasta and toss to combine. Season with salt and pepper to taste and add remaining reserved cooking water as needed to adjust consistency. Serve with extra Parmesan.

SMART SHOPPING EXTRA-VIRGIN OLIVE OIL
Extra-virgin olive oil has a uniquely fruity flavor that makes it a great choice when making a vinaigrette or a pesto, but the available options can be overwhelming. Many things can impact the quality and flavor of olive oil, but the type of olives, the harvest (earlier means greener, more peppery; later, more golden and mild), and processing are the most important factors. The best-quality oil comes from olives picked at their peak and processed as soon as possible, without heat or chemicals (which can coax more oil from the olives but at the expense of flavor). Our favorite oils were produced from a blend of olives and, thus, were well rounded. Our favorite is **Columela Extra Virgin Olive Oil** from Spain.

Low-Fat Basil Pesto

Serves 4 to 6

✓ WHY THIS RECIPE WORKS: For a low-fat version of our basil pesto, we started by cutting back on the olive oil and getting rid of the nuts altogether. To guarantee the same emulsified texture of a traditional pesto, we kept a couple spoonfuls of olive oil, which we reinforced with part-skim ricotta cheese. This duo helped the ingredients come together in the food processor and provided a slightly creamy texture. To ensure that our pesto still offered deep, complex flavor, we increased the amount of basil, grated Parmesan, and garlic, and tossed in a whole shallot, too. Do not use nonfat ricotta here or the pesto will be dry and gummy. For the nutritional information for this recipe, see page 307.

3 cups packed fresh basil leaves

1 ounce Parmesan cheese, grated (½ cup), plus extra for serving

¼ cup part-skim ricotta cheese

2 tablespoons extra-virgin olive oil

1 shallot, chopped coarse

4 garlic cloves, toasted and minced

Salt and pepper

1 pound pasta

1. Place basil in large zipper-lock bag and pound lightly with meat pounder or rolling pin until leaves are bruised. Process bruised basil, Parmesan, ricotta, oil, shallot, garlic, and ½ teaspoon salt in food processor until smooth, 30 to 60 seconds, scraping down bowl as needed. Transfer to medium bowl and season with salt and pepper to taste.

2. Meanwhile, bring 4 quarts water to boil in large pot. Add pasta and 1 tablespoon salt and cook, stirring often, until al dente. Reserve ¾ cup cooking water, then drain pasta and return it to pot.

3. Stir several tablespoons of reserved pasta water into pesto to loosen it, then add it to pasta and toss to combine. Season with salt and pepper to taste and add remaining reserved cooking water as needed to adjust consistency. Serve with extra Parmesan.

QUICK PREP TIP TOASTING GARLIC
To temper the raw bite of fresh garlic, toast the unpeeled cloves in a small skillet over medium heat, shaking the pan occasionally, until the color of the cloves deepens slightly, about 7 minutes. Transfer the garlic to a plate, let cool, then peel the cloves and mince.

Roasted Red Pepper Pesto

Serves 4 to 6

✔ **WHY THIS RECIPE WORKS:** Smoky, sweet, and boldly flavored, roasted red peppers make the perfect starring ingredient for a new take on traditional pesto. To start, we roasted our own peppers, then combined them with olive oil, Parmesan, a shallot, and toasted garlic (toasting the garlic mellows its flavor) in the food processor. Parsley and thyme provided a mild herbal background that balanced the flavor of our piquant, brightly colored sauce. Using freshly roasted red peppers makes the flavor of this pesto really sparkle, but you can substitute 1½ cups jarred roasted red peppers, rinsed and patted dry, if necessary (see page 238 for more information on buying jarred peppers).

2	**red bell peppers, roasted, peeled, and chopped coarse**
7	**tablespoons extra-virgin olive oil**
¼	**cup grated Parmesan cheese, plus extra for serving**
¼	**cup packed fresh parsley leaves**
1	**tablespoon fresh thyme leaves**
1	**small shallot, chopped coarse**
3	**garlic cloves, toasted (see page 257) and minced**
	Salt and pepper
1	**pound pasta**

1. Process roasted peppers, oil, Parmesan, parsley, thyme, shallot, garlic, and ½ teaspoon salt in food processor until smooth, 30 to 60 seconds, scraping down bowl as needed. Transfer to medium bowl and season with salt and pepper to taste.

2. Meanwhile, bring 4 quarts water to boil in large pot. Add pasta and 1 tablespoon salt and cook, stirring often, until al dente. Reserve ¾ cup cooking water, then drain pasta and return it to pot.

3. Stir several tablespoons of reserved pasta water into pesto to loosen it, then add it to pasta and toss to combine. Season with salt and pepper to taste and add remaining reserved cooking water as needed to adjust consistency. Serve with extra Parmesan.

QUICK PREP TIP ROASTING RED PEPPERS
Adjust oven rack 3 inches from broiler element and heat broiler. (If necessary, set upside-down rimmed baking sheet on oven rack.) To prep peppers, cut off tops and bottoms, discard seeds and core, then slice through one side and flatten. Spread flattened peppers, pepper tops (stem discarded), and pepper bottoms onto aluminum foil–lined baking sheet; broil until skin is charred and puffed but flesh is still firm, 8 to 10 minutes, rotating sheet halfway through cooking. Transfer peppers to bowl, cover with plastic wrap, and let steam until skin peels off easily, 10 to 15 minutes. Peel and discard skin.

ALL ABOUT Fresh Herbs

Herbs add a flavorful backbone to many of our pasta sauces, but when it comes to our pestos and no-cook sauces, they do more than just provide background notes. Here are a few things we have discovered about herbs that will help you make the most of them in any recipe, no matter if it's a quick pesto or a long-simmered red sauce.

Who Has the Thyme?

Picking minuscule leaves off fresh thyme can really pluck at your nerves. In the test kitchen, we rely on some tricks to make this job go faster. If the thyme has very thin, pliable stems, just chop the stems and leaves together, discarding the tough bottom portions as you go. If the stems are thicker and woodier, run your thumb and forefinger down the stem to release the leaves and smaller offshoots. The tender tips can be left intact and chopped along with the leaves once the woodier stems have been sheared clean and discarded.

Easy Herb Washing

The most efficient way to gently wash and dry herbs is to use a salad spinner. Simply remove any ties or rubber bands from the bunch of herbs and gently swish the loose sprigs of herbs around in cold water. Lift the basket out of the dirty water, letting the water drain off, pour off the water in the spinner, and gently spin the herbs to dry.

Keeping Herbs Fresh Longer

To get the most out of fresh herbs, we start by gently rinsing and drying them before loosely rolling them in a few sheets of paper towels. Then we put the roll of herbs in a zipper-lock bag and place it in the crisper drawer of our refrigerator. (Note that basil should not be washed until you are ready to use it.) Stored in this manner, the herbs stay fresh and ready to use for up to a week.

Refreshing Tired Herbs

If your bunch of parsley, cilantro, or mint is looking a little weary, there's an easy way to refresh it (and, in the process, wash it). First, lop off the stems from your herb, then submerge the leaves in a bowl of ice water and swish them around to loosen any dirt and grit. Let them stand for 5 to 10 minutes, until they perk up and regain their lost vitality. If the herbs are utterly limp and lifeless, however, they are probably beyond resurrection.

Shredding Basil

Shredded basil is an attractive alternative to the rustic look of chopped basil; we tend to call for shredded basil in dishes that are a bit more refined, such as our Spaghetti with Lemon, Basil, and Scallops (page 34) and Fusilli with Asparagus, Peas, and Arugula (page 96). To shred basil, start by stacking three or four clean, dry leaves on top of one another, then roll the leaves up like a cigar. Using a chef's knife, slice through the rolled leaves thinly.

Low-Fat Roasted Red Pepper Pesto

Serves 4 to 6

✔ **WHY THIS RECIPE WORKS:** For a leaner roasted red pepper pesto, we swapped in part-skim ricotta cheese for much of the olive oil—the ricotta gave us the consistency we were after, but it was kinder on the waistline. Doubling up on the Parmesan added more savory, salty notes without upping the fat and calories too much, and increasing the number of garlic cloves from 3 to 4 enhanced the overall flavor of the pesto. Do not use nonfat ricotta here or the pesto will be dry and gummy. We strongly prefer the flavor of freshly roasted peppers here, but you can substitute 1½ cups jarred roasted red peppers, rinsed and patted dry, if necessary (see page 238 for more information on buying jarred peppers). For the nutritional information for this recipe, see page 307.

2   **red bell peppers, roasted, peeled, and chopped coarse (see page 258)**
1   **ounce Parmesan cheese, grated (½ cup), plus extra for serving**
¼   **cup part-skim ricotta cheese**
¼   **cup packed fresh parsley leaves**
1   **tablespoon fresh thyme leaves**
1   **shallot, chopped coarse**
4   **garlic cloves, toasted (see page 257) and minced**
2   **tablespoons extra-virgin olive oil**
     Salt and pepper
1   **pound pasta**

1. Process roasted peppers, Parmesan, ricotta, parsley, thyme, shallot, garlic, oil, and ½ teaspoon salt in food processor until smooth, 30 to 60 seconds, scraping down bowl as needed. Transfer to medium bowl and season with salt and pepper to taste.

2. Meanwhile, bring 4 quarts water to boil in large pot. Add pasta and 1 tablespoon salt and cook, stirring often, until al dente. Reserve ¾ cup cooking water, then drain pasta and return it to pot.

3. Stir several tablespoons of reserved pasta water into pesto to loosen it, then add it to pasta and toss to combine. Season with salt and pepper to taste and add remaining reserved cooking water as needed to adjust consistency. Serve with extra Parmesan.

SMART SHOPPING FOOD PROCESSOR
At the bare minimum, a food processor should be able to chop, grate, and slice vegetables, grind dry ingredients, cut fat into flour for pastry—and, not to mention, make a decent pesto. If it can't whiz through these tasks, it's wasting counter space. The cheaper models we tested failed most of these basic tests. Vegetables were torn into mangled slices, soup leaked from the workbowl, and attempts to make pizza dough resulted in seriously strained motors and the acrid smell of smoke. We checked out more-expensive options and realized, just after a few tests, that more money does indeed buy a better food processor. Our top pick is the **KitchenAid Professional KFP750 12-Cup Food Processor** ($179.99). It has sturdy, sharp blades and a weighty motor that did not slow under a heavy load of dough. The KitchenAid chopped and sliced as cleanly and evenly as a skilled chef with a knife in hand. As a bonus, it ran more quietly than the other models we tested.

Mushroom Pesto with Parsley

Serves 4 to 6

✔ **WHY THIS RECIPE WORKS:** For a hearty, satisfying pesto that could be prepared even in the dead of winter, we started by roasting white mushrooms to concentrate their earthy, meaty notes. Processing them with dried porcini and woodsy fresh thyme amplified their savory flavor even more. A bit of water kept our rich pesto from becoming too thick. If desired, cremini mushrooms can be substituted for the white mushrooms.

10	ounces white mushrooms, trimmed and sliced ¼ inch thick
9	tablespoons extra-virgin olive oil
	Salt and pepper
¼	cup water
¼	cup grated Parmesan cheese, plus extra for serving
¼	cup packed fresh parsley leaves
1	tablespoon fresh thyme leaves
1	small shallot, chopped coarse
3	garlic cloves, toasted (see page 257) and minced
½	ounce dried porcini mushrooms, rehydrated (see page 191) and minced
1	pound pasta

1. Adjust oven rack to lowest position and heat oven to 450 degrees. Toss white mushrooms with 2 tablespoons oil, ¼ teaspoon salt, and ¼ teaspoon pepper and spread evenly over aluminum foil–lined rimmed baking sheet. Roast, stirring occasionally, until browned, about 25 minutes.

2. Process roasted mushrooms, remaining 7 tablespoons oil, water, Parmesan, parsley, thyme, shallot, garlic, and rehydrated porcini in food processor until smooth, 30 to 60 seconds, scraping down bowl as needed. Transfer to medium bowl and season with salt and pepper to taste.

3. Meanwhile, bring 4 quarts water to boil in large pot. Add pasta and 1 tablespoon salt and cook, stirring often, until al dente. Reserve ¾ cup cooking water, then drain pasta and return it to pot.

4. Stir several tablespoons of reserved pasta water into pesto to loosen it, then add it to pasta and toss to combine. Season with salt and pepper to taste and add remaining reserved cooking water as needed to adjust consistency. Serve with extra Parmesan.

QUICK PREP TIP MUSHROOMS: WASH OR BRUSH?

Culinary wisdom holds that raw mushrooms must never touch water, lest they soak up the liquid and become soggy. Many sources call for cleaning dirty mushrooms with a soft-bristled brush or a damp cloth. These fussy techniques may be worth the effort if you plan to eat the mushrooms raw, but we wondered whether mushrooms destined for the sauté pan or the oven could be simply rinsed and patted dry. To test this, we submerged 6 ounces of white mushrooms in a bowl of water for 5 minutes. We drained and weighed the mushrooms and found that they had soaked up only about 1½ teaspoons of water, not nearly enough to affect their texture. So when we plan to cook mushrooms we don't bother with the brush. Instead, we place the mushrooms in a salad spinner, rinse the dirt and grit away with cold water, and spin to remove excess moisture.

Low-Fat Mushroom Pesto

Serves 4 to 6

✔ **WHY THIS RECIPE WORKS:** To lighten our Mushroom Pesto with Parsley (page 262), we traded some of the olive oil for part-skim ricotta cheese. Roasting the mushrooms in the oven drove off too much moisture for this lean sauce, so we used a skillet to quickly cook the mushrooms instead. If desired, cremini mushrooms can be substituted for the white mushrooms. For the nutritional information for this recipe, see page 307.

10	ounces white mushrooms, trimmed and sliced ¼ inch thick
1	shallot, minced
2	tablespoons extra-virgin olive oil
½	ounce dried porcini mushrooms, rehydrated (see page 191) and minced
	Salt and pepper
4	garlic cloves, minced
1	tablespoon fresh thyme leaves
¼	cup water
1	ounce Parmesan cheese, grated (½ cup), plus extra for serving
¼	cup part-skim ricotta cheese
¼	cup packed fresh parsley leaves
1	pound pasta

1. Combine white mushrooms, shallot, 1 tablespoon oil, rehydrated porcini, and ½ teaspoon salt in 12-inch nonstick skillet. Cover and cook over medium-low heat until mushrooms release their juice, about 7 minutes. Uncover and stir in garlic and thyme. Increase heat to medium-high and cook until liquid has evaporated and mushrooms are browned, about 5 minutes. Off heat, stir in water and scrape up any browned bits.

2. Process mushroom mixture, Parmesan, ricotta, parsley, and remaining 1 tablespoon oil in food processor until smooth, 30 to 60 seconds, scraping down bowl as needed. Transfer to medium bowl and season with salt and pepper to taste.

3. Meanwhile, bring 4 quarts water to boil in large pot. Add pasta and 1 tablespoon salt and cook, stirring often, until al dente. Reserve ¾ cup cooking water, then drain pasta and return it to pot.

4. Stir several tablespoons of reserved pasta water into pesto to loosen it, then add it to pasta and toss to combine. Season with salt and pepper to taste and add remaining reserved cooking water as needed to adjust consistency. Serve with extra Parmesan.

QUICK TIP STORING PESTO

All of our pestos, with the exception of our Tomato and Almond Pesto (Pesto alla Trapanese; page 271), can be refrigerated for up to three days. To store pesto, you can either cover it with a sheet of plastic wrap pressed flush against the surface, or you can pour a thin film of oil on top of the pesto and cover the entire container.

Green Olive and Orange Pesto

Serves 4 to 6

✔ **WHY THIS RECIPE WORKS:** For an olive pesto with a bold citrus presence, we balanced the briny notes of green olives with sweet and bright orange zest and juice. Using high-quality green olives is crucial to the success of this pesto. Look for fresh green olives in the refrigerated section of the supermarket (packed in brine) or at the salad bar.

1½ **cups packed fresh parsley leaves**
1½ **ounces Parmesan cheese, grated (¾ cup), plus extra for serving**
½ **cup pitted green olives**
½ **cup slivered almonds, toasted**
2 **garlic cloves, toasted (see page 257) and minced**
½ **teaspoon grated orange zest plus 2 tablespoons juice**
Salt and pepper
½ **cup extra-virgin olive oil**
1 **pound pasta**

1. Pulse parsley, Parmesan, olives, almonds, garlic, orange zest, orange juice, and ½ teaspoon pepper in food processor until finely ground, 20 to 30 pulses, scraping down bowl as needed. With processor running, slowly add oil until incorporated. Transfer to medium bowl and season with salt and pepper to taste.

2. Meanwhile, bring 4 quarts water to boil in large pot. Add pasta and 1 tablespoon salt and cook, stirring often, until al dente. Reserve ¾ cup cooking water, then drain pasta and return it to pot.

3. Stir several tablespoons of reserved pasta water into pesto to loosen it, then add it to pasta and toss to combine. Season with salt and pepper to taste and add remaining reserved cooking water as needed to adjust consistency. Serve with extra Parmesan.

Kalamata Olive Pesto

Serves 4 to 6

✔ **WHY THIS RECIPE WORKS:** This pesto looks the way it tastes—ultra-rich and intense. High-quality ingredients make a difference here; look for kalamata olives in the supermarket's refrigerated section or at the salad bar.

1½ **cups pitted kalamata olives**
1 **ounce Parmesan cheese, grated (½ cup), plus extra for serving**
6 **tablespoons extra-virgin olive oil**
8 **large fresh basil leaves**
¼ **cup packed fresh parsley leaves**
1 **shallot, chopped coarse**
3 **garlic cloves, toasted (see page 257) and minced**
1 **tablespoon lemon juice**
1 **anchovy fillet, rinsed and minced (optional)**
Salt and pepper
1 **pound pasta**

1. Process olives, Parmesan, oil, basil, parsley, shallot, garlic, lemon juice, and anchovy, if using, in food processor until smooth, 30 to 60 seconds, scraping down bowl as needed. Transfer to medium bowl and season with salt and pepper to taste.

2. Meanwhile, bring 4 quarts water to boil in large pot. Add pasta and 1 tablespoon salt and cook, stirring often, until al dente. Reserve ¾ cup cooking water, then drain pasta and return it to pot.

3. Stir several tablespoons of reserved pasta water into pesto to loosen it, then add it to pasta and toss to combine. Season with salt and pepper to taste and add remaining reserved cooking water as needed to adjust consistency. Serve with extra Parmesan.

GREEN OLIVE AND ORANGE PESTO

Sun-Dried Tomato Pesto

Serves 4 to 6

✓ **WHY THIS RECIPE WORKS:** Sun-dried tomatoes make for a rich, sweet, and pantry-friendly pesto that you can make any time of year. As with most pestos, the key is to use the best-quality ingredients you can find, which in this case means good sun-dried tomatoes. We prefer sun-dried tomatoes that are packed in oil, rather than those that are packaged dried.

1	cup oil-packed sun-dried tomatoes, rinsed, patted dry, and chopped
½	cup extra-virgin olive oil
1	ounce Parmesan cheese, grated (½ cup), plus extra for serving
¼	cup walnuts, toasted
3	garlic cloves, toasted (see page 257) and minced
	Salt and pepper
1	pound pasta

1. Process tomatoes, oil, Parmesan, walnuts, and garlic in food processor until smooth, 30 to 60 seconds, scraping down bowl as needed. Transfer to medium bowl and season with salt and pepper to taste.

2. Meanwhile, bring 4 quarts water to boil in large pot. Add pasta and 1 tablespoon salt and cook, stirring often, until al dente. Reserve ¾ cup cooking water, then drain pasta and return it to pot.

3. Stir several tablespoons of reserved pasta water into pesto to loosen it, then add it to pasta and toss to combine. Season with salt and pepper to taste and add remaining reserved cooking water as needed to adjust consistency. Serve with extra Parmesan.

Sun-Dried Tomato Pesto with Arugula and Goat Cheese

Serves 4 to 6

✓ **WHY THIS RECIPE WORKS:** Here we matched sun-dried tomatoes with equally assertive baby arugula and creamy goat cheese. Using oil-packed sun-dried tomatoes here is key; dried tomatoes will taste tough and chewy.

1	cup oil-packed sun-dried tomatoes, rinsed, patted dry, and chopped
1	ounce Parmesan cheese, grated (½ cup)
6	tablespoons extra-virgin olive oil
¼	cup walnuts, toasted
1	small garlic clove, minced
	Salt and pepper
1	pound pasta
10	ounces (10 cups) baby arugula, chopped coarse
3	ounces goat cheese, crumbled (¾ cup)

1. Process tomatoes, Parmesan, oil, walnuts, and garlic in food processor until smooth, 30 to 60 seconds, scraping down bowl as needed. Transfer to medium bowl and season with salt and pepper to taste.

2. Meanwhile, bring 4 quarts water to boil in large pot. Add pasta and 1 tablespoon salt and cook, stirring often, until al dente. Reserve ¾ cup cooking water, then drain pasta and return it to pot.

3. Stir several tablespoons of reserved pasta water into pesto to loosen it, then add it to pasta and toss to combine. Stir in arugula until wilted, about 1 minute. Season with salt and pepper to taste and add remaining reserved cooking water as needed to adjust consistency. Sprinkle individual portions with goat cheese and serve.

Parsley and Toasted Nut Pesto

Serves 4 to 6

✔ **WHY THIS RECIPE WORKS:** Though basil is the go-to herb when making a green pesto, parsley makes a surprisingly delicious substitute. To stand up to the grassy, heartier flavor of parsley, we found it necessary to ramp up the nut flavor. Pecans have a more pronounced flavor than pine nuts, and using a full cup made for an ultra-rich pesto. You can substitute walnuts, blanched almonds, skinned hazelnuts, or any combination thereof for the pecans.

1	cup pecans, toasted
7	tablespoons extra-virgin olive oil
¼	cup packed fresh parsley leaves
¼	cup grated Parmesan cheese, plus extra for serving
3	garlic cloves, toasted (see page 257) and minced
	Salt and pepper
1	pound pasta

1. Process pecans, oil, parsley, Parmesan, and garlic in food processor until smooth, 30 to 60 seconds, scraping down bowl as needed. Transfer to medium bowl and season with salt and pepper to taste.

2. Meanwhile, bring 4 quarts water to boil in large pot. Add pasta and 1 tablespoon salt and cook, stirring often, until al dente. Reserve ¾ cup cooking water, then drain pasta and return it to pot.

3. Stir several tablespoons of reserved pasta water into pesto to loosen it, then add it to pasta and toss to combine. Season with salt and pepper to taste and add remaining reserved cooking water as needed to adjust consistency. Serve with extra Parmesan.

Parsley, Arugula, and Ricotta Pesto

Serves 4 to 6

✔ **WHY THIS RECIPE WORKS:** Peppery arugula shares the stage with parsley in this boldly flavored pesto. To balance their flavors, we added two mild yet rich ingredients: pine nuts and ricotta cheese. Part-skim ricotta can be substituted here; do not use nonfat ricotta here or the pesto will be dry and gummy.

1	cup packed fresh parsley leaves
1	cup baby arugula
7	tablespoons extra-virgin olive oil
¼	cup pine nuts, toasted
2	tablespoons grated Parmesan cheese, plus extra for serving
3	garlic cloves, toasted (see page 257) and minced
	Salt and pepper
⅓	cup whole-milk ricotta cheese
1	pound pasta

1. Process parsley, arugula, oil, pine nuts, Parmesan, garlic, and ½ teaspoon salt in food processor until smooth, 30 to 60 seconds, scraping down bowl as needed. Transfer to medium bowl, stir in ricotta, and season with salt and pepper to taste.

2. Meanwhile, bring 4 quarts water to boil in large pot. Add pasta and 1 tablespoon salt and cook, stirring often, until al dente. Reserve ¾ cup cooking water, then drain pasta and return it to pot.

3. Stir several tablespoons of reserved pasta water into pesto to loosen it, then add it to pasta and toss to combine. Season with salt and pepper to taste and add remaining reserved cooking water as needed to adjust consistency. Serve with extra Parmesan.

Oregano, Lemon, and Feta Pesto

Serves 4 to 6

✓ **WHY THIS RECIPE WORKS:** For a pesto with a definitively Greek bent, we added fresh oregano, crumbled feta, and lemon zest and juice to the traditional ingredients. Fresh oregano is crucial here; do not substitute dried oregano.

1¾   **cups packed fresh basil leaves**
7   **tablespoons extra-virgin olive oil**
¼   **cup packed fresh oregano leaves**
¼   **cup pine nuts, toasted**
1   **ounce feta cheese, crumbled (¼ cup)**
3   **garlic cloves, toasted (see page 257) and minced**
½   **teaspoon grated lemon zest plus 2 tablespoons juice**
    Salt and pepper
1   **pound pasta**

1. Process basil, oil, oregano, pine nuts, feta, garlic, lemon zest, lemon juice, and ½ teaspoon salt in food processor until smooth, 30 to 60 seconds, scraping down bowl as needed. Transfer to medium bowl and season with salt and pepper to taste.

2. Meanwhile, bring 4 quarts water to boil in large pot. Add pasta and 1 tablespoon salt and cook, stirring often, until al dente. Reserve ¾ cup cooking water, then drain pasta and return it to pot.

3. Stir several tablespoons of reserved pasta water into pesto to loosen it, then add it to pasta and toss to combine. Season with salt and pepper to taste and add remaining reserved cooking water as needed to adjust consistency. Serve.

Cilantro-Lime Pesto

Serves 4 to 6

✓ **WHY THIS RECIPE WORKS:** Citrusy cilantro, delicate pistachios, and sweet, tart lime come together in this bright, summery pesto, and Pecorino Romano gives it a salty edge. This pesto tastes great on pasta, but it also works well as a sauce for chicken and fish, too.

2   **cups packed fresh cilantro leaves**
7   **tablespoons extra-virgin olive oil**
¼   **cup shelled pistachios, toasted**
¼   **cup grated Pecorino Romano cheese, plus extra for serving**
3   **garlic cloves, toasted (see page 257) and minced**
½   **teaspoon grated lime zest plus 1 tablespoon juice**
    Salt and pepper
1   **pound pasta**

1. Process cilantro, oil, pistachios, Pecorino, garlic, lime zest, lime juice, and ½ teaspoon salt in food processor until smooth, 30 to 60 seconds, scraping down bowl as needed. Transfer to medium bowl and season with salt and pepper to taste.

2. Meanwhile, bring 4 quarts water to boil in large pot. Add pasta and 1 tablespoon salt and cook, stirring often, until al dente. Reserve ¾ cup cooking water, then drain pasta and return it to pot.

3. Stir several tablespoons of reserved pasta water into pesto to loosen it, then add it to pasta and toss to combine. Season with salt and pepper to taste and add remaining reserved cooking water as needed to adjust consistency. Serve with extra Pecorino.

Kale and Sunflower Seed Pesto

Serves 4 to 6

✔ **WHY THIS RECIPE WORKS:** Kale, with its earthy, slightly bitter flavor, steps in as the starring ingredient in this hearty pesto. Sunflower seeds, with their strong flavor, match well with the potent kale.

2	cups packed chopped kale leaves
1	cup packed fresh basil leaves
1½	ounces Parmesan cheese, grated (¾ cup), plus extra for serving
½	cup raw sunflower seeds, toasted
2	garlic cloves, toasted (see page 257) and minced
1	teaspoon red pepper flakes (optional)
	Salt and pepper
½	cup extra-virgin olive oil
1	pound pasta

1. Pulse kale, basil, Parmesan, sunflower seeds, garlic, pepper flakes, if using, and ½ teaspoon pepper in food processor until finely ground, 20 to 30 pulses, scraping down bowl as needed. With processor running, slowly add oil until incorporated. Transfer to medium bowl and season with salt and pepper to taste.

2. Meanwhile, bring 4 quarts water to boil in large pot. Add pasta and 1 tablespoon salt and cook, stirring often, until al dente. Reserve ¾ cup cooking water, then drain pasta and return it to pot.

3. Stir several tablespoons of reserved pasta water into pesto to loosen it, then add it to pasta and toss to combine. Season with salt and pepper to taste and add remaining reserved cooking water as needed to adjust consistency. Serve with extra Parmesan.

Fennel-Tarragon Pesto

Serves 4 to 6

✔ **WHY THIS RECIPE WORKS:** Fennel and tarragon instill this pesto with a delicate, springtime flavor. Blanching the fennel and garlic works to soften the fennel and tame the garlic's raw, harsh notes.

2	garlic cloves, peeled
1	fennel bulb, stalks discarded, bulb halved, cored, and cut into ¼-inch pieces (see page 248)
1½	ounces Parmesan cheese, grated (¾ cup), plus extra for serving
½	cup packed fresh parsley leaves
½	cup packed fresh tarragon leaves
1	tablespoon lemon juice
	Salt and pepper
	Pinch sugar
6	tablespoons extra-virgin olive oil
1	pound pasta

1. Bring 4 quarts water to boil in large pot. Add garlic and cook for 1 minute; transfer to paper towel, let cool, and mince. Add fennel to boiling water; cook until softened, 2 to 3 minutes. Transfer to colander, rinse under cold water, and let drain.

2. Pulse cooked fennel and garlic, Parmesan, parsley, tarragon, lemon juice, ¾ teaspoon salt, and sugar in food processor until finely ground, 20 to 30 pulses, scraping down bowl as needed. With processor running, slowly add oil until incorporated. Transfer to medium bowl and season with salt and pepper to taste.

3. Return pot of water to boil. Add pasta and 1 tablespoon salt and cook, stirring often, until al dente. Reserve ¾ cup cooking water, then drain pasta and return it to pot.

4. Stir several tablespoons of reserved pasta water into pesto to loosen it, then add it to pasta and toss to combine. Season with salt and pepper to taste and add remaining reserved cooking water as needed to adjust consistency. Serve with extra Parmesan.

TOMATO AND ALMOND PESTO (PESTO ALLA TRAPANESE)

Tomato and Almond Pesto (Pesto alla Trapanese)

Serves 4 to 6

✔ **WHY THIS RECIPE WORKS:** Fresh tomatoes and almonds take center stage in this vibrant Sicilian pesto. A single pepperoncini added a nice, spicy kick; however, you can substitute ½ teaspoon red wine vinegar and ¼ teaspoon red pepper flakes for the pepperoncini if necessary.

12	ounces cherry or grape tomatoes
½	cup packed fresh basil leaves
¼	cup slivered almonds, toasted
1	small pepperoncini (hot pepper in vinegar), stemmed, seeded, and minced
1	garlic clove, minced
	Salt
	Pinch red pepper flakes (optional)
⅓	cup extra-virgin olive oil
1	pound linguine or spaghetti
1	ounce Parmesan cheese, grated (½ cup), plus extra for serving

1. Process tomatoes, basil, almonds, pepperoncini, garlic, 1 teaspoon salt, and pepper flakes, if using, in food processor until smooth, 30 to 60 seconds, scraping down bowl as needed. With processor running, slowly add oil until incorporated. Transfer to medium bowl and season with salt to taste.

2. Meanwhile, bring 4 quarts water to boil in large pot. Add pasta and 1 tablespoon salt and cook, stirring often, until al dente. Reserve ½ cup cooking water, then drain pasta and return it to pot. Add pesto and Parmesan and toss to combine. Season with salt to taste and add reserved cooking water as needed to adjust consistency. Serve with extra Parmesan.

Romesco Pesto

Serves 4 to 6

✔ **WHY THIS RECIPE WORKS:** Inspired by traditional Spanish romesco sauce, we created our own sweet, tangy version to dress pasta. We kept the familiar romesco ingredients—roasted red peppers, almonds, and garlic—and added parsley and Parmesan to round out the flavors.

2	cups packed fresh parsley leaves
½	cup jarred roasted red peppers, rinsed, patted dry, and chopped coarse
7	tablespoons extra-virgin olive oil
¼	cup slivered almonds, toasted
¼	cup grated Parmesan cheese, plus extra for serving
3	garlic cloves, toasted (see page 257) and minced
2	teaspoons red wine vinegar
	Salt and pepper
1	pound pasta

1. Process parsley, roasted red peppers, oil, almonds, Parmesan, garlic, vinegar, and ½ teaspoon salt in food processor until smooth, 30 to 60 seconds, scraping down bowl as needed. Transfer to medium bowl and season with salt and pepper to taste.

2. Meanwhile, bring 4 quarts water to boil in large pot. Add pasta and 1 tablespoon salt and cook, stirring often, until al dente. Reserve ¾ cup cooking water, then drain pasta and return it to pot.

3. Stir several tablespoons of reserved pasta water into pesto to loosen it, then add it to pasta and toss to combine. Season with salt and pepper to taste and add remaining reserved cooking water as needed to adjust consistency. Serve with extra Parmesan.

No-Cook Fresh Tomato Sauce

Serves 4 to 6

✓ **WHY THIS RECIPE WORKS:** Ultra-ripe, in-season tomatoes need little adornment in this super-easy no-cook sauce. All we did was simply marinate our tomatoes in a little olive oil with garlic, shallot, sugar, and lemon juice until they released their juice and softened slightly. Then we tossed them with hot pasta, which absorbed their moisture and flavor. For the pasta, we liked penne, rotini, or campanelle—which were just as fork-friendly as our tender bites of tomato. The success of this dish depends on using ripe, flavorful tomatoes. Be sure to include both the seeds and inner tomato gel in the sauce, as they are responsible for much of its flavor and moisture. For the nutritional information for this recipe, see page 307.

¼ cup extra-virgin olive oil, plus extra for serving

2 teaspoons lemon juice, plus extra as needed

1 shallot, minced

1 garlic clove, minced
   Salt and pepper
   Sugar

2 pounds very ripe, in-season tomatoes, cored and cut into ½-inch pieces

1 pound short pasta, such as penne, rotini, or campanelle

3 tablespoons chopped fresh basil
   Grated Parmesan cheese

1. Stir oil, lemon juice, shallot, garlic, 1 teaspoon salt, ¼ teaspoon pepper, and pinch sugar together in large bowl. Stir in tomatoes and let marinate until very soft and flavorful, at least 30 minutes and up to 3 hours.

2. Bring 4 quarts water to boil in large pot. Add pasta and 1 tablespoon salt and cook, stirring often, until al dente. Reserve ½ cup cooking water, then drain pasta and return it to pot. Add tomato mixture and basil and toss to combine. Season with salt, pepper, sugar, and extra lemon juice to taste and add reserved cooking water as needed to adjust consistency. Serve with extra olive oil and Parmesan.

ON THE SIDE FOOLPROOF GREEN SALAD
Whisk 1 tablespoon vinegar (red wine, white wine, or champagne), 1½ teaspoons minced shallot, ½ teaspoon mayonnaise, ½ teaspoon Dijon mustard, ⅛ teaspoon salt, and pinch pepper together in small bowl until mixture is smooth and looks milky. Very slowly drizzle in 3 tablespoons extra-virgin olive oil while whisking constantly until emulsified. Toss with 10 cups lightly packed greens. Serves 4 to 6.

No-Cook Fresh Tomato Sauce with Olives and Capers

Serves 4 to 6

✔ **WHY THIS RECIPE WORKS:** This zesty variation on our No-Cook Fresh Tomato Sauce (page 272) adds the briny, bright flavors of puttanesca but keeps things just as easy. Kalamatas provide their trademark bold, pungent flavor, an anchovy adds depth without contributing a distinctive fishy flavor, and capers offer up noticeable piquancy. Rinsing the capers prevented our sauce from tasting too salty. A small amount of red pepper flakes contributes subtle heat, and lemon juice adds brightness. Marinating the tomatoes with the olives, capers, anchovy, and red pepper flakes ensures that their flavors permeate the entire dish. The success of this dish depends on using ripe, flavorful tomatoes. Be sure to include both the seeds and inner tomato gel in the sauce, as they are responsible for much of its flavor and moisture. For the nutritional information for this recipe, see page 307.

½ cup pitted kalamata olives, chopped coarse

¼ cup extra-virgin olive oil, plus extra for serving

1 shallot, minced

1 tablespoon capers, rinsed and chopped coarse

1 anchovy fillet, rinsed and minced

1 tablespoon lemon juice, plus extra as needed

1 garlic clove, minced
   Salt and pepper

¼ teaspoon red pepper flakes
   Sugar

2 pounds very ripe, in-season tomatoes, cored and cut into ½-inch pieces

1 pound short pasta, such as penne, rotini, or campanelle

3 tablespoons chopped fresh basil or parsley
   Grated Parmesan cheese

1. Stir olives, oil, shallot, capers, anchovy, lemon juice, garlic, 1 teaspoon salt, ¼ teaspoon pepper, pepper flakes, and pinch sugar together in large bowl. Stir in tomatoes and let marinate until very soft and flavorful, at least 30 minutes and up to 3 hours.

2. Bring 4 quarts water to boil in large pot. Add pasta and 1 tablespoon salt and cook, stirring often, until al dente. Reserve ½ cup cooking water, then drain pasta and return it to pot. Add tomato mixture and basil and toss to combine. Season with salt, pepper, sugar, and extra lemon juice to taste and add reserved cooking water as needed to adjust consistency. Serve with extra olive oil and Parmesan.

FARM STAND TOMATO SAUCE

Sauces from
the Slow Cooker

Big-Batch Marinara Sauce

Makes 9 cups Enough to sauce 3 pounds of pasta

✔ **WHY THIS RECIPE WORKS:** Using our slow cooker to make a super-size batch of marinara sauce seemed perfect—the low and slow cooking environment of this handy countertop appliance would reduce our tomatoes to the perfect rich, full-bodied marinara, so we wouldn't have to struggle with a pot filled to the brim on the stovetop. But after a few tests, it was clear this wouldn't be a walk in the park. Since the slow cooker doesn't allow for evaporation and reduction, the biggest hurdle was choosing the right tomato products, as many of our tests produced sauces that were either too watery or too thick. Our solution was a combination of four different tomato products (paste, crushed, diced, and sauce). The concentrated products (tomato paste and tomato sauce) provided lots of strong, complex flavor without unwanted water—so no need for evaporation. For more layers of flavor, we sautéed our aromatics with two anchovies (commonly used in the test kitchen to add deep, savory flavor to a variety of dishes); raw aromatics, not surprisingly, tasted raw in the sauce. Then we deglazed the pan with red wine before stirring everything together with 2 tablespoons of soy sauce—the anchovies and soy sauce added much-needed meaty flavor to the sauce. For the nutritional information for this recipe, see page 307.

2	tablespoons extra-virgin olive oil
2	onions, chopped fine
6	garlic cloves, minced
2	tablespoons tomato paste
2	tablespoons minced fresh oregano or 2 teaspoons dried
2	anchovy fillets, rinsed and minced
	Pinch red pepper flakes
1	cup dry red wine
1	(28-ounce) can crushed tomatoes
1	(28-ounce) can diced tomatoes, drained
1	(28-ounce) can tomato sauce
2	tablespoons soy sauce
½	cup chopped fresh basil
2	teaspoons sugar, plus extra as needed
	Salt and pepper

1. Heat oil in 12-inch skillet over medium-high heat until shimmering. Add onions, garlic, tomato paste, oregano, anchovies, and pepper flakes and cook until onions are softened and lightly browned, 8 to 10 minutes. Stir in wine, scraping up any browned bits, and simmer until thickened, about 5 minutes; transfer to slow cooker.

2. Stir crushed tomatoes, diced tomatoes, tomato sauce, and soy sauce into slow cooker. Cover and cook until sauce is deeply flavored, 9 to 11 hours on low or 5 to 7 hours on high.

3. Before serving, stir in basil and sugar and season with salt, pepper, and additional sugar to taste.

Fire-Roasted Tomato Sauce

Makes 9 cups Enough to sauce 3 pounds of pasta

WHY THIS RECIPE WORKS: Taking inspiration from canned fire-roasted tomatoes, we set out to develop an easy tomato sauce with a kick. Working with our Big-Batch Marinara Sauce (page 276) as a starting point, we swapped two of our tomato products (diced and crushed tomatoes) for fire-roasted versions, giving our sauce a mild smokiness with no extra work. To further enhance the smoky flavor, after we cooked our aromatics to rid them of their raw flavor, we sautéed the drained diced tomatoes, browning them and intensifying and deepening their flavor. For a final dose of smoky flavor, we stirred in ¼ teaspoon of liquid smoke—which packs quite a smoky punch. For the nutritional information for this recipe, see page 307.

2	tablespoons extra-virgin olive oil
2	onions, chopped fine
8	garlic cloves, minced
2	tablespoons tomato paste
2	tablespoons minced fresh oregano or 2 teaspoons dried
	Pinch red pepper flakes
1	(28-ounce) can fire-roasted diced tomatoes, drained
1	cup dry red wine
1	(28-ounce) can fire-roasted crushed tomatoes
1	(28-ounce) can tomato sauce
¼	teaspoon liquid smoke
½	cup minced fresh parsley
	Salt and pepper

1. Heat oil in 12-inch skillet over medium-high heat until shimmering. Add onions, garlic, tomato paste, oregano, and pepper flakes and cook until onions are softened and lightly browned, 8 to 10 minutes.

2. Stir in diced tomatoes and cook until dry and lightly browned, 8 to 10 minutes. Stir in wine, scraping up any browned bits, and simmer until thickened, about 5 minutes; transfer to slow cooker.

3. Stir crushed tomatoes, tomato sauce, and liquid smoke into slow cooker. Cover and cook until sauce is deeply flavored, 9 to 11 hours on low or 5 to 7 hours on high.

4. Before serving, stir in parsley and season with salt and pepper to taste.

SMART SHOPPING LIQUID SMOKE
We were among the many people who assume that there must be some kind of synthetic chemical chicanery going on in the making of "liquid smoke" flavoring, but that's not the case. Liquid smoke is made by channeling smoke from smoldering wood chips through a condenser, which quickly cools the vapors, causing them to liquefy (just like the drops that form when you breathe on a piece of cold glass). The water-soluble flavor compounds in the smoke are trapped within this liquid, while the nonsoluble, carcinogenic tars and resins are removed by a series of filters, resulting in a clean, smoke-flavored liquid. When buying liquid smoke, be sure to avoid brands with additives such as salt, vinegar, and molasses. Our top-rated brand, **Wright's Liquid Smoke**, contains nothing but smoke and water.

ALL ABOUT Using the Slow Cooker for Pasta Sauces

The slow cooker provides the perfect low and slow cooking environment to intensify the flavors in our slow-cooked pasta sauces. Plus, it's incredibly convenient; you can prep everything, get it in the slow cooker, and, several hours later, have dinner waiting for you—all you have to do is cook the pasta. Here's some information on our favorite slow cooker, along with a few tips that will guarantee slow-cooking success.

Getting to Know Your Slow Cooker

We've worked with a lot of slow cookers in the test kitchen and know that some can run hot (and fast) while others run cool (and slow). Since our slow-cooker recipes come with a large time range, knowing how your slow cooker runs will be helpful in determining which end of the range will yield the best results. (For our tests, we used our winning slow cooker.) One quick way to determine how hot or cool your cooker runs is to perform a simple test. Place 4 quarts room-temperature water in your slow cooker, cover it, and cook on either high or low for six hours; at the end, the water should register between 195 and 205 degrees. If your cooker runs hotter or cooler, be ready to check the food for doneness earlier or later than indicated. Also, some cookers run hot or cool on just one of the settings, so consider checking both if you find you are having problems.

Using Tapioca

One drawback of the slow cooker is that it doesn't allow for evaporation, so getting the right consistency in a sauce or stew can be a problem. That's when adding a thickener can help. Our Farm Stand Tomato Sauce (page 280) uses 7 pounds of fresh tomatoes for full, ripe tomato flavor—but those tomatoes also contribute a lot of liquid that doesn't have the chance to cook off. So we added tapioca, which required no precooking or advance prep and thickened the sauce nicely. Tapioca also worked well to thicken our Creamy Chicken and Mushroom Sauce (page 289).

Buying a Slow Cooker

Looking for the best slow cooker on the market, we recently tested seven models to find out which one would deliver a perfectly cooked supper every time. In general, we prefer slow cookers that are oval-shaped, which are more versatile than round models, and have a capacity of 6 quarts or more, so they can hold a big batch of pasta sauce or a large roast. We also like cookers with programmable timers, warming modes, clear glass lids (so we can monitor the food as it cooks), and inserts that have handles and are dishwasher-safe. Our favorite model is the **Crock-Pot Touchscreen Slow Cooker** ($129.99), which cooked food perfectly in our tests. It had the best control panel (with a timer that counted up to 20 hours even on high). The Crock-Pot Touchscreen was simple to set and clearly indicated that the cooker was programmed.

Using Your Microwave

Surprisingly, we found that the fastest appliance in the kitchen was incredibly useful when paired with the slowest. When it came to preparing aromatics for the slow cooker (adding them raw resulted in raw-tasting sauces), we found there were instances where we could simply microwave our onions and garlic to soften them and develop their flavor instead of sautéing them in a skillet. The microwave also came in handy for other uses, such as parcooking the meatballs to render out fat that would otherwise make for a greasy sauce in our Meatballs and Marinara (page 285).

Farm Stand Tomato Sauce

Makes 9 cups Enough to sauce 3 pounds of pasta

✔ **WHY THIS RECIPE WORKS:** The beauty of this recipe is that you can put a bounty of peeled and cored fresh whole tomatoes into a slow cooker with a few other ingredients, walk away for up to 11 hours, and after a brief stovetop simmer to eliminate extra liquid, you end up with a brightly flavored tomato sauce—enough to serve a crowd (or plenty to freeze for later). The trick to making this fresh tomato sauce in a slow cooker is to add a hefty amount of tomato paste to deepen its flavor, along with tapioca for thickening. A potato masher came in handy at the end to get the right chunky texture, while a quick stovetop simmer eliminated the liquid released by the tomatoes during the long cooking time. For more information on peeling fresh tomatoes, see page 13. For the nutritional information for this recipe, see page 307.

7	pounds tomatoes (about 14 large)
2	onions, chopped fine
¼	cup tomato paste
2	tablespoons extra-virgin olive oil, plus extra as needed
6	garlic cloves, minced
1	tablespoon minced fresh oregano or 1 teaspoon dried
½	cup dry red wine
¼	cup Minute tapioca
2	bay leaves
¼	cup chopped fresh basil
	Salt and pepper

1. Bring 4 quarts water to boil in large pot. Using paring knife, cut out tomatoes' stem and core, then score small X in bottom of each. Working with several tomatoes at a time, add to boiling water and cook until skins begin to loosen, 15 to 45 seconds. Remove tomatoes from water, let cool, then remove loosened tomato skins with paring knife; transfer to slow cooker. (Do not seed or chop tomatoes.)

2. Microwave onions, tomato paste, oil, garlic, and oregano in bowl, stirring occasionally, until onions are softened, about 5 minutes; transfer to slow cooker. Stir wine, tapioca, and bay leaves into slow cooker. Cover and cook until tomatoes are very soft and beginning to disintegrate, 9 to 11 hours on low or 5 to 7 hours on high.

3. Discard bay leaves. Mash tomatoes with potato masher until mostly smooth. Transfer sauce to large Dutch oven and simmer over medium-high heat until thickened, about 20 minutes. Before serving, stir in basil and season with salt, pepper, and additional olive oil to taste.

QUICK PREP TIP FREEZING PASTA SAUCES
One of the greatest things about making a large batch of pasta sauce is that you can freeze it in smaller batches for easy last-minute dinners in the future. We've found that the best way to freeze pasta sauce is to spoon it into zipper-lock freezer bags, then lay the bags flat in the freezer to save space. To reheat the sauce, simply cut away the bag, place the frozen block of sauce in a large pot with several tablespoons of water, and reheat gently over medium-low heat, stirring occasionally, until hot. Alternatively, you can microwave the frozen sauce in a covered bowl, stirring occasionally, until hot. Before serving, stir in any additional fresh herbs if desired, and season with salt and pepper.

Weeknight Meat Sauce

Makes 12 cups Enough to sauce 3 pounds of pasta

✔ **WHY THIS RECIPE WORKS:** Kid-friendly and easy to make, our Weeknight Meat Sauce has all the flavor of the long-simmered traditional version but with a substantial amount of hands-off, walk-away time. To ensure that our ground beef was still tender and flavorful after hours in the slow cooker, it was necessary to mix it with a panade (a paste of bread and milk). The panade bound with the meat, keeping it moist throughout the long cooking time. Instead of browning the meat, then the aromatics, we got enough flavor from simply browning our aromatics and deglazing the pan with wine, which saved us time. You can substitute ground turkey for the ground beef in this recipe. For the nutritional information for this recipe, see page 307.

2	tablespoons extra-virgin olive oil
2	onions, chopped fine
6	garlic cloves, minced
2	tablespoons tomato paste
2	tablespoons minced fresh oregano or 2 teaspoons dried
	Pinch red pepper flakes
1	cup dry red wine
1	(28-ounce) can crushed tomatoes
1	(28-ounce) can diced tomatoes, drained
1	(28-ounce) can tomato sauce
2	slices hearty white sandwich bread, torn into quarters
¼	cup whole milk
2	pounds 85 percent lean ground beef
	Salt and pepper
½	cup chopped fresh basil

1. Heat oil in 12-inch skillet over medium-high heat until shimmering. Add onions, garlic, tomato paste, oregano, and pepper flakes and cook until onions are softened and lightly browned, 8 to 10 minutes. Stir in wine, scraping up any browned bits, and simmer until thickened, about 5 minutes; transfer to slow cooker. Stir crushed tomatoes, diced tomatoes, and tomato sauce into slow cooker.

2. Mash bread and milk into paste in large bowl using fork. Mix in ground beef, ½ teaspoon salt, and ½ teaspoon pepper using hands. Stir beef mixture into slow cooker, breaking up any large pieces. Cover and cook until beef is tender, 9 to 11 hours on low or 5 to 7 hours on high.

3. Let sauce settle for 5 minutes, then remove fat from surface using large spoon. Break up any remaining large pieces of beef with spoon. Before serving, stir in basil and season with salt and pepper to taste.

ON THE SIDE GARLIC BREAD
Toast 10 unpeeled garlic cloves in small skillet over medium heat, shaking pan occasionally, until fragrant, about 8 minutes. Let garlic cool, then peel and mince. Using fork, mash garlic with 2 tablespoons unsalted butter, 2 tablespoons grated Parmesan cheese, and ½ teaspoon salt in bowl. Cut 1 large loaf Italian bread in half lengthwise, spread both pieces with butter mixture, then season with salt and pepper. Lay bread, buttered side up, on baking sheet. Bake in 500-degree oven until surface of bread is golden brown and toasted, 8 to 10 minutes. Slice and serve warm. Serves 6 to 8. (This recipe can be doubled.)

Spicy Sausage Ragu with Red Peppers

Makes 12 cups Enough to sauce 3 pounds of pasta

✔ **WHY THIS RECIPE WORKS:** Spicy Italian sausages and sweet bell peppers are a classic pairing that we thought would translate perfectly into a bright, slightly sweet, and deeply flavored slow-cooker pasta sauce. We liked the flavorful heat that hot Italian sausages imparted, and browning them in a skillet for a few minutes gave the sauce an even richer flavor. Since we already had our skillet out, we sautéed our aromatics (onions, garlic, oregano, and red pepper flakes) and deglazed the pan with red wine. Tomato paste, crushed tomatoes, diced tomatoes, and tomato sauce were the perfect combination of tomato products with which to build our sauce—neither too watery nor too thick. As for the bell peppers, we simply softened them in the microwave and then stirred them into the sauce just before serving so they wouldn't become overcooked and mushy. For the nutritional information for this recipe, see page 307.

2	tablespoons extra-virgin olive oil
2	pounds hot Italian sausage, casings removed
2	onions, chopped fine
6	garlic cloves, minced
2	tablespoons tomato paste
2	tablespoons minced fresh oregano or 2 teaspoons dried
1	teaspoon red pepper flakes
1	cup dry red wine
1	(28-ounce) can crushed tomatoes
1	(28-ounce) can diced tomatoes, drained
1	(28-ounce) can tomato sauce
2	red bell peppers, stemmed, seeded, and cut into ½-inch pieces
½	cup minced fresh parsley
	Salt and pepper

1. Heat 1 tablespoon oil in 12-inch skillet over medium-high heat until just smoking. Add sausage and brown well, breaking up large pieces with wooden spoon, about 5 minutes; transfer to slow cooker. Pour off all but 2 tablespoons fat left in skillet.

2. Add onions, garlic, tomato paste, oregano, and pepper flakes to fat in skillet and cook over medium-high heat until onions are softened and lightly browned, 8 to 10 minutes. Stir in wine, scraping up any browned bits, and simmer until thickened, about 5 minutes; transfer to slow cooker.

3. Stir crushed tomatoes, diced tomatoes, and tomato sauce into slow cooker. Cover and cook until sauce is deeply flavored, 9 to 11 hours on low or 5 to 7 hours on high.

4. Let sauce settle for 5 minutes, then remove fat from surface using large spoon. Microwave bell peppers with remaining 1 tablespoon oil in bowl, stirring occasionally, until tender, about 5 minutes. Stir softened bell peppers into sauce and let sit until heated through, about 5 minutes. Before serving, stir in parsley and season with salt and pepper to taste.

ON THE SIDE SOFT AND CHEESY BREADSTICKS
Roll out 1 pound pizza dough on lightly floured counter into 12 by 6-inch rectangle. Cut dough crosswise into 1-inch-wide strips and lay on well-oiled rimmed baking sheet. Brush with 1½ tablespoons olive oil, sprinkle with ¼ cup grated Parmesan cheese, and season with salt and pepper. Bake in 400-degree oven until golden, about 20 minutes. Serve warm. Makes 12. (This recipe can be doubled.)

Meatballs and Marinara

Makes 18 meatballs and 5½ cups sauce Enough to sauce 1½ pounds of pasta

✔ **WHY THIS RECIPE WORKS:** Our slow-cooker version of meatballs and marinara involves some advance work, but once everything is in the slow cooker, you've bought yourself hours of freedom with the promise of a great dinner waiting in the wings. To build a sauce with long-simmered flavor, we started by sautéing onions, tomato paste, and garlic, and then we deglazed the pan with red wine. Crushed tomatoes, water, and a little soy sauce (for meaty depth of flavor) were all we needed to add to this base. And for the meatballs, a combination of ground beef and Italian sausage, along with some of the sautéed aromatics, Parmesan, and parsley, were a solid start for our meatballs, but they were still a bit dry. Adding a panade—a paste of bread and milk—provided the moisture they needed. Microwaving the meatballs before adding them to the slow cooker helped render just enough fat to ensure that our sauce wasn't greasy.

2 tablespoons extra-virgin olive oil
2 onions, chopped fine
¼ cup tomato paste
8 garlic cloves, minced
2 tablespoons minced fresh oregano or 2 teaspoons dried
¼ teaspoon red pepper flakes
½ cup dry red wine
2 (28-ounce) cans crushed tomatoes
½ cup water
2 tablespoons soy sauce
2 slices hearty white sandwich bread, torn into quarters
⅓ cup whole milk
1¼ pounds 85 percent lean ground beef
4 ounces Italian sausage, casings removed
1 ounce Parmesan cheese, grated (½ cup), plus extra for serving
¼ cup minced fresh parsley
2 large egg yolks
Salt and pepper
2 tablespoons chopped fresh basil
1 teaspoon sugar, plus extra as needed

1. Heat oil in 12-inch skillet over medium-high heat until shimmering. Add onions, tomato paste, garlic, oregano, and pepper flakes and cook until onions are softened and lightly browned, 8 to 10 minutes.

2. Transfer half of onion mixture to large bowl; set aside. Stir wine into skillet with remaining onion mixture and scrape up any browned bits; transfer to slow cooker. Stir tomatoes, water, and soy sauce into slow cooker.

3. Add bread and milk to bowl with onion mixture and mash to paste with fork. Mix in ground beef, sausage, Parmesan, parsley, egg yolks, ¾ teaspoon salt, and ½ teaspoon pepper using hands. Pinch off and roll mixture into 1½-inch meatballs (about 18 meatballs total).

4. Microwave meatballs on large plate until fat renders and meatballs are firm, 5 to 7 minutes. Nestle meatballs into slow cooker, discarding rendered fat. Cover and cook until meatballs are tender, 4 to 6 hours on low.

5. Let meatballs and sauce settle for 5 minutes, then remove fat from surface using large spoon. Gently stir in basil and sugar, season with salt, pepper, and additional sugar to taste, and serve with extra Parmesan.

Shredded Pork Ragu

Makes 12 cups Enough to sauce 3 pounds of pasta

✔ **WHY THIS RECIPE WORKS:** For a rustic, simple, peasant-style meat sauce that would make our Italian grandmothers proud, we turned to a humble cut of pork, country-style ribs, which turned meltingly tender during a long spell in the slow cooker. Once the pork was fully cooked, it was easy to break into shreds using a spoon. To prevent the sauce from turning out watery, we relied on a trio of tomato products: tomato paste, diced tomatoes, and tomato puree. A dose of soy sauce further enhanced the sauce's meaty flavor, while a hefty 12 cloves of garlic really packed in the old-country flavor. For the nutritional information for this recipe, see page 307.

2	onions, chopped fine
12	garlic cloves, minced
¼	cup tomato paste
2	tablespoons extra-virgin olive oil
2	tablespoons minced fresh oregano or 2 teaspoons dried
¼	teaspoon red pepper flakes
1	(28-ounce) can diced tomatoes, drained
1	(28-ounce) can tomato puree
¾	cup dry red wine
⅓	cup soy sauce
2	bay leaves
3	pounds boneless country-style pork ribs, trimmed and cut into 1½-inch chunks
	Salt and pepper
¼	cup minced fresh parsley

1. Microwave onions, garlic, tomato paste, oil, oregano, and pepper flakes in bowl, stirring occasionally, until onions are softened, about 5 minutes; transfer to slow cooker.

2. Stir diced tomatoes, tomato puree, wine, soy sauce, and bay leaves into slow cooker. Season pork with salt and pepper and nestle into slow cooker. Cover and cook until pork is tender, 9 to 11 hours on low or 5 to 7 hours on high.

3. Let sauce settle for 5 minutes, then remove fat from surface using large spoon. Discard bay leaves. Break up pieces of pork with spoon. Before serving, stir in parsley and season with salt and pepper to taste.

SMART SHOPPING COUNTRY-STYLE PORK RIBS
Country-style pork ribs are the perfect choice for a long-simmered pasta sauce because they have enough marbled fat to stay moist and tender during the longer simmering time, they add a hearty flavor to the sauce, and they naturally begin to shred into smaller pieces when thoroughly cooked. And unlike buying a large pork shoulder roast (which has a similar marbling and shredded texture when cooked), you can easily buy the country-style ribs in much smaller and more exact amounts. When buying country-style ribs, look for those that have striations of fat throughout the meat, and avoid those that look very lean.

Short Ribs and Red Wine Sauce

Makes 12 cups Enough to sauce 3 pounds of pasta

WHY THIS RECIPE WORKS: The classic pairing of short ribs and red wine sauce struck us as the perfect basis for an elegant slow-cooked pasta dinner for company. Here boneless short ribs are cooked until tender and easy to shred in a rich red wine–based sauce (bone-in ribs gave up too much fat and resulted in a greasy sauce). To build our sauce we first sautéed aromatics (onions, carrots, celery, garlic, and tomato paste), then deglazed the pan with a healthy dose of red wine, reducing it down to concentrate its flavor and evaporate any unwanted liquid. To further complement the rich flavor of the meat and wine, we stirred diced tomatoes and tomato puree into the slow cooker, which gave our sauce just the right body and flavor. When the sauce was ready, we simply shredded the meat and stirred in some parsley before serving it over our favorite pasta.

2	tablespoons extra-virgin olive oil
2	onions, chopped fine
2	carrots, peeled and cut into ¼-inch pieces
1	celery rib, minced
¼	cup tomato paste
6	garlic cloves, minced
1½	cups dry red wine
1	(28-ounce) can diced tomatoes, drained
1	(28-ounce) can tomato puree
2	bay leaves
3	pounds boneless beef short ribs, trimmed and cut into 1½-inch chunks
	Salt and pepper
½	cup minced fresh parsley

1. Heat oil in 12-inch skillet over medium-high heat until shimmering. Add onions, carrots, celery, tomato paste, and garlic and cook until vegetables are softened and lightly browned, 8 to 10 minutes. Stir in wine, scraping up any browned bits, and simmer until thickened, about 6 minutes; transfer to slow cooker.

2. Stir diced tomatoes, tomato puree, and bay leaves into slow cooker. Season beef with salt and pepper and nestle into slow cooker. Cover and cook until beef is tender, 9 to 11 hours on low or 5 to 7 hours on high.

3. Let sauce settle for 5 minutes, then remove fat from surface using large spoon. Discard bay leaves. Break up pieces of beef with spoon. Before serving, stir in parsley and season with salt and pepper to taste.

SMART SHOPPING BONELESS BEEF SHORT RIBS
Short ribs are just that: fatty ribs (cut from any location along the length of the cow's ribs) that are shorter than the more common larger beef ribs. Short ribs are available both bone-in and boneless. Although we expected that bone-in short ribs would exude more fat than their boneless counterparts, we were shocked by the dramatic difference—a quarter-cup versus about 1½ cups (six times as much)! So, to prevent the sauce from tasting overly greasy, be sure to use boneless ribs.

BONELESS = MANAGEABLE FAT

BONE-IN = LOTS OF FAT

Creamy Chicken and Mushroom Sauce

Makes 5 cups Enough to sauce 1½ pounds of pasta

WHY THIS RECIPE WORKS: For an earthy, full-flavored pasta dish with tender, shredded chicken and an abundance of mushrooms, we turned to everyday white mushrooms and meaty boneless chicken thighs. To keep things easy, we microwaved the aromatics and then added them, along with chicken thighs and the sliced mushrooms (no browning necessary), to the slow cooker. Our first tests were lacking deep mushroom flavor so we microwaved dried porcini mushrooms along with the aromatics, which added plenty of deep, earthy flavor and aroma. Chicken broth, white wine, and the liquid released by the mushrooms combined to create a flavorful sauce, into which we stirred cream and Parmesan cheese at the end for added richness, along with a bit of parsley to liven it up a touch.

1	onion, chopped fine
6	garlic cloves, minced
½	ounce dried porcini mushrooms, rinsed and minced
1	tablespoon extra-virgin olive oil
1	tablespoon tomato paste
1	tablespoon minced fresh thyme or 1 teaspoon dried
1	pound white mushrooms, trimmed and sliced thin
1½	cups low-sodium chicken broth
½	cup dry white wine
2	tablespoons Minute tapioca
1½	pounds boneless, skinless chicken thighs, trimmed
	Salt and pepper
¼	cup heavy cream
1	ounce Parmesan cheese, grated (½ cup)
3	tablespoons minced fresh parsley

1. Microwave onion, garlic, porcini, oil, tomato paste, and thyme in bowl, stirring occasionally, until onion is softened, about 5 minutes; transfer to slow cooker.

2. Stir white mushrooms, broth, wine, and tapioca into slow cooker. Season chicken with salt and pepper and nestle into slow cooker. Cover and cook until chicken is tender, 4 to 6 hours on low.

3. Transfer chicken to cutting board, let cool slightly, then shred into bite-size pieces. Let sauce settle for 5 minutes, then remove fat from surface using large spoon. Stir shredded chicken and cream into sauce and let sit until heated through, about 5 minutes. Stir in Parmesan. Before serving, stir in parsley and season with salt and pepper to taste.

QUICK PREP TIP SHREDDING MEAT
To shred poultry (and other types of meat) into bite-size pieces, simply hold a fork in each hand (tines facing down), insert forks into cooked meat, and gently pull meat apart.

GAZPACHO PASTA SALAD

Fresh Pasta Salads

Gazpacho Pasta Salad

Serves 8 to 10

✔ **WHY THIS RECIPE WORKS:** Looking for a lighter, fresher alternative to the traditional creamy pasta salad, we took our inspiration from gazpacho with its fresh mix of tomatoes and crisp vegetables. Here we added rotini to the mix and swapped the farmers' market tomatoes for canned diced tomatoes and consistently sweet cherry tomatoes, making this salad an option year-round. Combining the diced tomatoes with basil, olive oil, red wine vinegar, garlic, and red pepper flakes gave us a bright and zesty sauce. Rinsing the cooked pasta in cold water washed away excess starches that would have made the individual pieces stick together. Cucumber slices and chunks of bell pepper contributed great crunch and flavor, and letting the cooked pasta and vegetables briefly marinate in the dressing ensured that all the flavors came together. Crumbled feta cheese, black olives, parsley, and scallions made the perfect last-minute garnishes. Cooking the pasta until it is completely tender and leaving it slightly wet after rinsing are important for the texture of the finished salad. The salad can be prepared through step 3 and refrigerated in an airtight container for up to 1 day; before continuing, add warm water and additional olive oil as needed to refresh its texture. For the nutritional information for this recipe, see page 307.

1	**pound rotini**
	Salt and pepper
1	**(14.5-ounce) can diced tomatoes**
¼	**cup fresh basil leaves**
1	**tablespoon red wine vinegar**
2	**garlic cloves, minced**
¼–½	**teaspoon red pepper flakes**
1	**cucumber, peeled, halved lengthwise, seeded, and sliced thin**
1	**red bell pepper, stemmed, seeded, and cut into ½-inch pieces**
1	**yellow bell pepper, stemmed, seeded, and cut into ½-inch pieces**
12	**ounces cherry tomatoes, halved**
¼	**cup extra-virgin olive oil**
2	**ounces feta cheese, crumbled (½ cup)**
½	**cup pitted black olives, quartered**
¼	**cup minced fresh parsley**
3	**scallions, sliced thin**

1. Bring 4 quarts water to boil in large pot. Add pasta and 1 tablespoon salt and cook, stirring often, until tender. Drain pasta, rinse with cold water, and drain again, leaving pasta slightly wet.

2. Meanwhile, process diced tomatoes, basil, vinegar, garlic, pepper flakes, and ½ teaspoon salt in blender until smooth.

3. Toss pasta, sauce, cucumber, bell peppers, cherry tomatoes, and oil together in large bowl to combine. Cover and let sit for 15 minutes.

4. Before serving, stir in feta, olives, parsley, and scallions and season with salt and pepper to taste.

QUICK PREP TIP
SEEDING A CUCUMBER
To seed a cucumber, first peel it, then cut it in half lengthwise. Run small spoon inside each cucumber half to scoop out seeds and surrounding liquid.

Summer Garden Pasta Salad with Asiago

Serves 8 to 10

✔ **WHY THIS RECIPE WORKS:** When it's hot and humid out, there's nothing better than a simply dressed pasta salad full of crisp, in-season vegetables for an effortless but flavorful complement to supper. With whimsical farfalle as the centerpiece, we created a bold vinaigrette of extra-virgin olive oil, red wine vinegar, lemon juice, shallot, Dijon mustard, oregano, and garlic powder (which we preferred over fresh garlic for the way it dissolved in the vinaigrette). Quartered cherry tomatoes, shredded carrots, and sliced yellow bell pepper introduced a variety of textures and bright flavors. Letting the vegetables and pasta rest in the vinaigrette for a few minutes allowed them to take on its potent flavor. A healthy dose of basil, grated Asiago cheese, and capers tossed in at the end helped add piquant notes to our summery pasta salad. Cooking the pasta until it is completely tender and leaving it slightly wet after rinsing are important for the texture of the finished salad. The salad can be prepared through step 3 and refrigerated in an airtight container for up to 1 day; before continuing, add warm water and additional olive oil as needed to refresh its texture. For the nutritional information for this recipe, see page 307.

1	pound farfalle
	Salt and pepper
6	tablespoons extra-virgin olive oil
3	tablespoons red wine vinegar
3	tablespoons lemon juice
1	shallot, minced
1	tablespoon Dijon mustard
1	tablespoon minced fresh oregano or ½ teaspoon dried
¼	teaspoon garlic powder
12	ounces cherry tomatoes, quartered
2	carrots, peeled and shredded
1	yellow bell pepper, stemmed, seeded, and cut into ¼-inch strips
3	ounces Asiago cheese, grated (1½ cups)
½	cup chopped fresh basil
3	tablespoon capers, rinsed

1. Bring 4 quarts water to boil in large pot. Add pasta and 1 tablespoon salt and cook, stirring often, until tender. Drain pasta, rinse with cold water, and drain again, leaving pasta slightly wet.

2. Meanwhile, whisk oil, vinegar, lemon juice, shallot, mustard, oregano, garlic powder, 1 teaspoon salt, and ¼ teaspoon pepper together in large bowl.

3. Add pasta, tomatoes, carrots, and bell pepper to vinaigrette and toss to combine. Cover and let sit for 15 minutes.

4. Before serving, stir in Asiago, basil, and capers and season with salt and pepper to taste.

SMART SHOPPING DIJON MUSTARD

While common yellow mustard is made from mild yellow mustard seeds, Dijon mustard is made from spicier brown or sometimes black mustard seeds. Although many people swear by the Dijon mustard manufactured in France, we wondered if our tasters would find American varieties as worthwhile. We conducted two taste tests comparing eight popular brands, including one Dijon mustard made in France, one made in Canada, and six from the United States. Our tasters were looking for a Dijon with a smooth texture, a clean aftertaste without any off-flavors, and a nose-tingling heat. The winner, which happened to be domestically produced, was **Grey Poupon Dijon Mustard**, which tasters praised for its good balance of flavors and its high level of heat.

Tortellini Salad with Asparagus and Fresh Basil Vinaigrette

Serves 8 to 10

✔ **WHY THIS RECIPE WORKS:** For a super-easy pasta salad that would impress any picnic crowd, we paired convenient, store-bought cheese tortellini with asparagus and a dressing inspired by the classic pesto flavors. First, we blanched the asparagus in the same water we later used to cook the tortellini, which instilled the pasta with the asparagus' delicate flavor. Once the tortellini was cooked, we marinated it, with bright, juicy cherry tomatoes, in a bold dressing made of extra-virgin olive oil, basil, lemon juice, shallot, and garlic. To finish the salad and complete our deconstructed pesto, we tossed in some grated Parmesan and toasted pine nuts, along with the blanched asparagus, just before serving. Cooking the tortellini until it is completely tender and leaving it slightly wet after rinsing are important for the texture of the finished salad. The salad and asparagus can be prepared through step 4 and refrigerated in separate airtight containers for up to 1 day; before continuing, add warm water and additional olive oil as needed to refresh the salad's texture. For more information on buying tortellini, see page 124.

1	pound asparagus, trimmed and cut into 1-inch pieces
	Salt and pepper
1	pound dried cheese tortellini
6	tablespoons extra-virgin olive oil
½	cup chopped fresh basil
3	tablespoons lemon juice
1	shallot, minced
1	garlic clove, minced
12	ounces cherry tomatoes, halved
1	ounce Parmesan cheese, grated (½ cup)
¼	cup pine nuts, toasted

1. Bring 4 quarts water to boil in large pot. Fill large bowl with ice water. Add asparagus and 1 tablespoon salt to boiling water and cook until asparagus is crisp-tender, about 2 minutes. Using slotted spoon, transfer asparagus to ice water and let cool, about 2 minutes; drain and pat dry.

2. Return pot of water to boil. Add tortellini and cook, stirring often, until tender. Reserve ¼ cup cooking water. Drain tortellini, rinse with cold water, and drain again, leaving tortellini slightly wet.

3. Meanwhile, whisk olive oil, basil, lemon juice, shallot, garlic, ½ teaspoon salt, and ½ teaspoon pepper together in large bowl.

4. Add tortellini and tomatoes to vinaigrette and toss to combine, adding remaining reserved cooking water as needed to adjust consistency. Cover and let sit for 15 minutes.

5. Before serving, stir in asparagus, Parmesan, and pine nuts and season with salt and pepper to taste.

SMART SHOPPING GARLIC SUBSTITUTE
We find garlic indispensable in the test kitchen, but we've noticed myriad garlic products in the supermarket that seem like a convenient substitution for fresh: garlic powder, made from garlic cloves that are dehydrated and ground; dehydrated minced garlic, which is minced while fresh and then dehydrated; and garlic salt, which is typically 3 parts salt to 1 part garlic powder. When garlic is the predominant flavor in a recipe, we have found that nothing comes close to using fresh cloves, but in recipes where garlic is a background flavor and the recipe calls for only a clove or two, in a pinch you can use garlic powder. Substitute ¼ teaspoon of garlic powder for each clove of fresh garlic. We don't recommend dehydrated garlic (it takes a while to rehydrate and is quite mild) or garlic salt (our tasters disapproved of its "super-salty," "chemical" taste).

Fusilli Salad with Salami, Provolone, and Sun-Dried Tomato Vinaigrette

Serves 8 to 10

✔ **WHY THIS RECIPE WORKS:** Pasta salad from the deli counter might be convenient, but that's about all it has going for it—the heavy dose of mayo, flabby pasta, and dull, overcooked vegetables translates into one sad side dish. For a bold, fresh-tasting pasta salad, we decided to incorporate traditional antipasto flavors. We lost the mayonnaise in favor of an olive oil–based vinaigrette accented with sunny and tangy sun-dried tomatoes, red wine vinegar, garlic, and basil. Marinating the cooked pasta in the dressing flavored it through and through. Thickly cut salami (or pepperoni) and provolone added a salty, savory bite and richness. Baby spinach, stirred in at the end, contributed color and freshness to our pasta salad, and a handful of sliced kalamata olives added a brininess that helped to punch up its flavor. Cooking the pasta until it is completely tender and leaving it slightly wet after rinsing are important for the texture of the finished salad. The salad can be prepared through step 3 and refrigerated in an airtight container for up to 1 day; before continuing, add warm water and additional olive oil as needed to refresh its texture.

1	pound fusilli
	Salt and pepper
1	cup oil-packed sun-dried tomatoes, rinsed, patted dry, and minced
6	tablespoons extra-virgin olive oil
¼	cup red wine vinegar
2	tablespoons chopped fresh basil or parsley
1	garlic clove, minced
8	ounces thickly sliced salami or pepperoni, cut into matchsticks
8	ounces thickly sliced provolone, cut into matchsticks
1½	ounces (1½ cups) baby spinach
½	cup pitted kalamata olives, sliced

1. Bring 4 quarts water to boil in large pot. Add pasta and 1 tablespoon salt and cook, stirring often, until tender. Drain pasta, rinse with cold water, and drain again, leaving pasta slightly wet.

2. Meanwhile, whisk sun-dried tomatoes, oil, vinegar, basil, garlic, ½ teaspoon salt, and ½ teaspoon pepper together in large bowl.

3. Add pasta and salami to vinaigrette and toss to combine. Cover and let sit for 15 minutes.

4. Before serving, stir in provolone, spinach, and olives and season with salt and pepper to taste.

SMART SHOPPING RED WINE VINEGAR
Red wine vinegar has a sharp but clean flavor, making it the most versatile choice in salads. While acidity is the obvious key factor in vinegar, it is actually the inherent sweetness of the grapes used to produce the vinegar that makes its flavor appealing to the palate. After tasters sampled 10 red wine vinegars plain, in vinaigrette, and in pickled onions, it was clear that they found highly acidic vinegars too harsh; brands with moderate amounts of acidity scored higher. Tasters also preferred those brands that were blends—either blends of different grapes or blends of different vinegars (such as aged and nonaged)—as they offered more complex flavor. In the end, tasters ranked French import **Laurent du Clos Red Wine Vinegar** first. Made from a mix of red and white grapes, this vinegar won the day with its "good red wine flavor."

Pesto Pasta Salad with Chicken and Arugula

Serves 8 to 10

✔ **WHY THIS RECIPE WORKS:** Marrying pesto with hot pasta is no problem. But try to add pesto to cold pasta for a salad and you'll end up with a gummy, sticky mess with no dressing in sight. To ensure that our pesto stayed rich and creamy, even when partnered with room-temperature fusilli (which we preferred over other types of pasta for the way it trapped the pesto), we borrowed a common pasta salad ingredient: mayonnaise. Just a quarter-cup, added to our traditional basil pesto, kept the sauce creamy and luscious, so it coated the pasta perfectly. Leaving the pasta slightly wet after draining it helped, too. Marinating the pasta, shredded chicken, and cherry tomatoes (which added bright color and some acidity) in the pesto for 15 minutes allowed their flavors to meld. A final addition of baby arugula lent our pasta salad a pleasant spiciness. Cooking the pasta until it is completely tender and leaving it slightly wet after rinsing are important for the texture of the finished salad. You can either use leftover cooked chicken here, or quickly cook chicken following the instructions on page 80. The salad can be prepared through step 3 and refrigerated in an airtight container for up to 1 day; before continuing, add warm water and additional olive oil as needed to refresh its texture.

1	pound fusilli
	Salt and pepper
1	cup fresh basil leaves
½	cup pine nuts, toasted
½	cup extra-virgin olive oil
2	tablespoons lemon juice
1	garlic clove, minced
1	ounce Parmesan cheese, grated (½ cup)
¼	cup mayonnaise
12	ounces cherry tomatoes, halved
2	cups shredded cooked chicken
3	ounces (3 cups) baby arugula

1. Bring 4 quarts water to boil in large pot. Add pasta and 1 tablespoon salt and cook, stirring often, until tender. Drain pasta, rinse with cold water, and drain again, leaving pasta slightly wet.

2. Meanwhile, process basil, pine nuts, olive oil, lemon juice, and garlic in food processor until smooth, about 1 minute, scraping down bowl as needed. Add Parmesan and mayonnaise and pulse to incorporate, about 5 pulses.

3. Toss pasta, pesto, tomatoes, and chicken together in large bowl to combine. Cover and let sit for 15 minutes.

4. Before serving, stir in arugula and season with salt and pepper to taste.

SMART SHOPPING PINE NUTS

Also called *piñons* (Spanish) or *pignoli* (Italian), these diminutive nutlike seeds are harvested from pinecones. There are two main types of pine nuts: the delicately flavored, torpedo-shaped Mediterranean pine nuts and the more assertive corn kernel–shaped Chinese pine nuts (shown). The less-expensive Chinese variety is more widely available, but both can be used interchangeably. Pine nuts have a mild taste and a slightly waxy texture. Pine nuts need to be stored with care to prevent rancidity. They are best transferred to an airtight container as soon as their original packaging is opened. They will keep in the refrigerator for up to three months or in the freezer for up to nine months.

Pea and Pistachio Pesto Pasta Salad

Serves 8 to 10

LIGHTER OPTION

✔ **WHY THIS RECIPE WORKS:** For a light, fresh-tasting, no-cook sauce, we built a pesto starring creamy, milky ricotta cheese and sweet frozen peas (all they needed was a quick thaw). Mint, often partnered with peas, stood in for the basil, while delicately flavored pistachios took the role of the usual pine nuts. Lemon zest contributed bright, clean-tasting notes. Adding a bit of the pasta cooking water to the pesto helped to thin it out so it would coat each piece of pasta. For textural interest, we saved a portion of the pistachios and peas and stirred them in at the end. Cooking the pasta until it is completely tender and leaving it slightly wet after rinsing are important for the texture of the finished salad. The salad can be refrigerated in an airtight container for up to 1 day; before serving, add warm water and additional olive oil as needed to refresh its texture and season with salt and pepper. For the nutritional information for this recipe, see page 307.

1	**pound penne, fusilli, or campanelle**
	Salt and pepper
2	**ounces (¼ cup) whole-milk or part-skim ricotta cheese**
1¼	**cups frozen peas, thawed**
½	**cup unsalted pistachios, toasted and chopped**
¼	**cup grated Pecorino Romano cheese**
¼	**cup extra-virgin olive oil**
2	**tablespoons chopped fresh mint**
1	**garlic clove, minced**
1	**teaspoon grated lemon zest**

1. Bring 4 quarts water to boil in large pot. Add pasta and 1 tablespoon salt and cook, stirring often, until tender. Reserve ¾ cup cooking water. Drain pasta, rinse with cold water, and drain again, leaving pasta slightly wet.

2. Process ricotta and 2 tablespoons reserved cooking water in food processor until smooth, about 1 minute. Add ¾ cup peas, ¼ cup pistachios, Pecorino, oil, mint, garlic, lemon zest, ½ teaspoon salt, and ¼ teaspoon pepper and process until smooth, about 1 minute, scraping down bowl as needed.

3. Toss pasta, pesto, remaining ½ cup peas, and remaining ¼ cup pistachios in large bowl, adding remaining reserved cooking water as needed to adjust consistency. Cover and let sit for 15 minutes. Season with salt and pepper to taste and serve.

SMART SHOPPING MINT

When you're shopping for mint, what you'll most likely find at the supermarket is spearmint, even though it might be labeled just "mint." Spearmint has a light, sweet flavor and its leaves are bright green with pointed tips; its stalk is a light brown shade.

Roasted Red Pepper Shrimp and Pasta Salad

Serves 8 to 10

✔ **WHY THIS RECIPE WORKS:** In this elegant pasta salad studded with sweet, briny shrimp and delicate asparagus, we kept both prep work and pots to a minimum. Blanching the shrimp and asparagus at the same time in salted water streamlined our recipe. When they were done, we set them aside and used the flavorful water to cook the pasta. Combining feta cheese, jarred roasted red peppers, and lemon juice and zest gave us a tangy, boldly flavored dressing that livened up the dish, and adding mayonnaise kept it creamy. Juicy cherry tomatoes contributed a punch of color. Cooking the pasta until it is completely tender and leaving it slightly wet after rinsing are important for the texture of the finished salad. The salad can be refrigerated in an airtight container for up to 1 day; before serving, add warm water as needed to refresh its texture and season with additional mayonnaise, salt, and pepper.

2 **pounds extra-large shrimp (21 to 25 per pound), peeled, deveined, and tails removed**
1 **pound asparagus, trimmed and cut into 1-inch pieces**
   Salt and pepper
1 **pound rotini**
4 **ounces feta cheese, crumbled (1 cup)**
¾ **cup mayonnaise**
¾ **cup drained jarred roasted red peppers, rinsed, patted dry, and chopped**
2 **teaspoons grated lemon zest plus 3 tablespoons juice**
1 **garlic clove, minced**
12 **ounces cherry tomatoes, halved**
3 **tablespoons minced fresh parsley**

1. Bring 4 quarts water to boil in large pot. Fill large bowl with ice water. Add shrimp, asparagus, and 1 tablespoon salt and boil until shrimp are fully cooked and asparagus is crisp-tender, about 2 minutes. Using slotted spoon, transfer shrimp and asparagus to ice water and let cool, about 2 minutes; drain and pat dry.

2. Return pot of water to boil. Add pasta and cook, stirring often, until tender. Reserve ¼ cup cooking water. Drain pasta, rinse with cold water, and drain again, leaving pasta slightly wet.

3. Process feta and reserved cooking water in food processor until combined. Add mayonnaise, roasted peppers, lemon zest, lemon juice, garlic, ½ teaspoon salt, and ½ teaspoon pepper and process until smooth, about 1 minute, scraping down bowl as needed.

4. Toss pasta, shrimp, asparagus, sauce, tomatoes, and parsley together in large bowl to combine. Cover and let sit for 15 minutes. Season with salt and pepper to taste and serve.

QUICK PREP TIP THAWING SHRIMP
To defrost frozen shrimp, you can thaw them overnight in the refrigerator in a covered bowl. For a quicker thaw, place them in a colander under cold running water; they will be ready in a few minutes.

Cool and Creamy Macaroni Salad

Serves 8 to 10

✔ **WHY THIS RECIPE WORKS:** It's often the simplest dishes that cause the most trouble. Case in point: creamy macaroni salad, a backyard party staple. By the time the guests are gone, the pasta has soaked up all the dressing, and what's left behind in the bowl is usually dry and chalky. To ensure that our creamy macaroni salad lived up to its name, we cooked the pasta until just tender and left a little moisture on it—this way, the pasta could absorb the extra liquid, rather than the creamy dressing (leaving behind a dry, bland salad). Then we tossed the pasta with lemon juice, cayenne, and Dijon mustard, plus chopped onion, celery, and parsley. Garlic powder worked better than fresh garlic because it dissolved into the smooth dressing. Once the pasta had taken on the flavors of the dressing, we stirred in a good amount of mayonnaise. Cooking the pasta until it is completely tender and leaving it slightly wet after rinsing are important for the texture of the finished salad. The salad can be refrigerated in an airtight container for up to 2 days; before serving, add warm water as needed to refresh its texture and season with additional mayonnaise, salt, and pepper.

1	**pound elbow macaroni**
	Salt and pepper
¼	**cup finely chopped red onion**
1	**celery rib, minced**
¼	**cup minced fresh parsley**
2	**tablespoons lemon juice**
1	**tablespoon Dijon mustard**
⅛	**teaspoon garlic powder**
⅛	**teaspoon cayenne pepper**
1½	**cups mayonnaise**

1. Bring 4 quarts water to boil in large pot. Add pasta and 1 tablespoon salt and cook, stirring often, until tender. Drain pasta, rinse with cold water, and drain again, leaving pasta slightly wet.

2. Toss pasta, onion, celery, parsley, lemon juice, mustard, garlic powder, and cayenne together in large bowl to combine. Let sit until flavors are absorbed, about 2 minutes. Stir in mayonnaise, cover, and let sit for 10 minutes. Season with salt and pepper to taste and serve.

SMART SHOPPING MAYONNAISE

Mayonnaise is a key ingredient in our macaroni salads. So does it really matter which brand you buy? We sampled eight popular brands of mayonnaise, but tasters were hooked on one. They were unanimous in selecting **Hellmann's Real Mayonnaise** (also known as Best Foods west of the Rockies), the creamiest of the group, as their top pick. It "tasted like what mayonnaise should taste like," and was liked for its bright, well-seasoned, and balanced flavors. Many tasters even felt that it was as good, if not better, than most home-made mayonnaise.

Macaroni Salad with Cheddar and Chipotle

Serves 8 to 10

✓ **WHY THIS RECIPE WORKS:** For a punched-up, but still no-fuss, macaroni salad worthy of any picnic spread, we added sharp cheddar and smoky canned chipotle chiles to our Cool and Creamy Macaroni Salad (page 303). To prevent the salad from drying out, we drained the pasta briefly but made sure to leave a little water on it so it would absorb the moisture instead of the mayonnaise. Stirring the seasonings into the pasta first, before adding the mayonnaise, allowed the pasta to take on a deeper flavor before it was dressed by the richer mayo. Cooking the pasta until it is completely tender and leaving it slightly wet after rinsing are important for the texture of the finished salad. The salad can be refrigerated in an airtight container for up to 2 days; before serving, add warm water as needed to refresh its texture and season with additional mayonnaise, salt, and pepper.

1   pound elbow macaroni
     Salt and pepper
1   small red onion, chopped fine
1   celery rib, minced
6   ounces extra-sharp cheddar
     cheese, shredded (1½ cups)
¼   cup minced fresh parsley
2   tablespoons minced canned
     chipotle chile in adobo sauce
2   tablespoons lemon juice
1   tablespoon Dijon mustard
⅛   teaspoon garlic powder
⅛   teaspoon cayenne pepper
1½   cups mayonnaise

1. Bring 4 quarts water to boil in large pot. Add pasta and 1 tablespoon salt and cook, stirring often, until tender. Drain pasta, rinse with cold water, and drain again, leaving pasta slightly wet.

2. Toss pasta, onion, celery, cheddar, parsley, chipotle, lemon juice, mustard, garlic powder, and cayenne together in large bowl to combine. Let sit until flavors are absorbed, about 2 minutes. Stir in mayonnaise, cover, and let sit for 10 minutes. Season with salt and pepper to taste and serve.

SMART SHOPPING CHIPOTLE CHILES IN ADOBO SAUCE
Canned chipotle chiles are jalapeños that have been ripened until red and then smoked and dried. They are sold as is, ground to a powder, or packed in a tomato-based sauce. We prefer the latter since they are already reconstituted by the sauce, making them easier to use. Most recipes don't use an entire can, but these chiles will keep for 2 weeks in the refrigerator or they can be frozen. To freeze, puree the chiles and quick-freeze teaspoonfuls on a plastic wrap-covered plate. Once these "chipotle chips" are hard, peel them off the plastic and transfer them to a zipper-lock freezer bag. Then thaw what you need before use. They can be stored this way for up to 2 months.

Barbecue Macaroni Salad with Smoked Sausage

Serves 8 to 10

✓ **WHY THIS RECIPE WORKS:** Instead of tasting bright and tangy, barbecue macaroni salad tends to be saccharine-sweet and sticky. To take down the sweetness a notch, we combined bottled barbecue sauce (since we needed just half a cup, store-bought sauce worked fine) with mayonnaise. Now the tangy, sweet, smoky barbecue flavors were balanced by the neutral, creamy mayo. Sautéed smoked sausage added to the cookout feel of our salad and made it more substantial, and cider vinegar and hot sauce amped up the piquant flavors. Cooking the pasta until it is completely tender and leaving it slightly wet after rinsing are important for the texture of the finished salad. The salad can be refrigerated in an airtight container for up to 2 days; before serving, add warm water as needed to refresh its texture and season with additional mayonnaise, salt, and pepper.

1	teaspoon vegetable oil
8	ounces smoked sausage or kielbasa, cut into ½-inch chunks
1	pound elbow macaroni
	Salt and pepper
1	red bell pepper, stemmed, seeded, and chopped fine
1	celery rib, minced
4	scallions, sliced thin
2	tablespoons cider vinegar
1	teaspoon hot sauce
1	teaspoon chili powder
⅛	teaspoon garlic powder
	Pinch cayenne pepper
1	cup mayonnaise
½	cup barbecue sauce

1. Heat oil in 12-inch nonstick skillet over medium-high heat until shimmering. Add sausage and cook until browned, about 5 minutes. Transfer to paper towel–lined plate and let cool.

2. Meanwhile, bring 4 quarts water to boil in large pot. Add pasta and 1 tablespoon salt and cook, stirring often, until tender. Drain pasta, rinse with cold water, and drain again, leaving pasta slightly wet.

3. Toss pasta, browned sausage, bell pepper, celery, scallions, vinegar, hot sauce, chili powder, garlic powder, and cayenne together in large bowl to combine. Let sit until flavors are absorbed, about 2 minutes. Stir in mayonnaise and barbecue sauce, cover, and let sit for 10 minutes. Season with salt and pepper to taste and serve.

SMART SHOPPING BARBECUE SAUCE
Homemade barbecue sauce is pretty simple to make, but there may be times (such as when you need only a small amount) when you just want to open up a bottle of the store-bought variety. But which one? In just one local supermarket we found more than 30 varieties! To make sense of all these options, we conducted a blind taste test of leading national brands. We chose tomato-based sauces that were labeled "original" and tasted them as a dipping sauce for homemade chicken fingers. Although tasters' personal preferences varied, our winner was **Bull's-Eye Original Barbecue Sauce**, which tasters found "robust" and "spicy."

Lighter Option Recipes

Recipes with no more than 600 calories and 14 grams of fat per serving have been tagged as a Lighter Option throughout the book. If a recipe provided a range for the yield, we used the greater number of servings to determine if it met this criteria. We also used the greater number of servings to determine the nutritional values below.

	CAL	FAT	SAT FAT	CHOL	CARB	PROTEIN	FIBER	SODIUM
NEW CLASSICS								
Fusilli with Fresh Tomato Sauce page 10	390	11 g	1.5 g	0 mg	62 g	12 g	4 g	300 mg
Ziti with Roasted Tomato Sauce and Goat Cheese page 16	390	8 g	2.5 g	5 mg	68 g	14 g	5 g	440 mg
Penne with Pancetta, White Beans, and Rosemary page 21	560	14 g	5 g	25 mg	75 g	27 g	7 g	1210 mg
Penne with Sausage and Broccoli Rabe page 23	460	11 g	2.5 g	35 mg	66 g	23 g	3 g	760 mg
Pasta with Garlicky Tuscan Chicken page 25	570	13 g	3 g	80 mg	67 g	40 g	3 g	850 mg
Pasta with Chicken Cacciatore Sauce page 26	540	13 g	3 g	55 mg	70 g	34 g	6 g	1190 mg
Chicken Riggies page 27	580	12 g	4.5 g	85 mg	75 g	40 g	6 g	740 mg
SKILLET PASTAS								
Bachelor Spaghetti with Sausage, Peppers, and Onions page 38	490	14 g	4.5 g	35 mg	65 g	30 g	7 g	1360 mg
Skillet Pasta with Fresh Tomato Sauce page 40	460	9 g	1.5 g	0 mg	78 g	14 g	6 g	610 mg
Skillet Pasta Puttanesca page 41	510	14 g	2 g	5 mg	79 g	17 g	6 g	1490 mg
Skillet Spicy Chicken Abruzzo page 49	450	11 g	2 g	75 mg	53 g	33 g	4 g	1040 mg
Skillet Penne with Chicken Sausage, Sun-Dried Tomatoes, and Spinach page 53	400	12 g	2.5 g	50 mg	52 g	23 g	5 g	1360 mg
Skillet Wagon Wheel Pasta with Turkey Sausage page 58	410	12 g	3.5 g	35 mg	54 g	23 g	5 g	960 mg
Skillet Penne with Cherry Tomatoes, White Beans, and Olives page 60	420	14 g	2.5 g	5 mg	59 g	17 g	6 g	1130 mg
Skillet-Baked Shrimp and Orzo page 63	550	11 g	4 g	160 mg	81 g	34 g	7 g	1870 mg
CASSEROLES								
No-Prep Baked Spaghetti page 68	590	13 g	5 g	75 mg	80 g	39 g	7 g	1420 mg
Stuffed Shells with Meat Sauce page 82	480	13 g	6 g	50 mg	51 g	35 g	4 g	1940 mg
Roasted Eggplant and Zucchini Lasagna page 91	370	14 g	6 g	35 mg	41 g	23 g	8 g	1000 mg
WHOLE-WHEAT PASTA								
Fusilli with Asparagus, Peas, and Arugula page 96	490	11 g	3 g	5 mg	79 g	20 g	15 g	550 mg
Penne with Turkey Sausage, Fennel, and Spinach page 108	530	13 g	2 g	50 mg	71 g	27 g	14 g	1150 mg
Penne with Chicken, Caramelized Onions, and Red Peppers page 109	600	14 g	2.5 g	80 mg	71 g	39 g	13 g	930 mg
Spinach Lasagna page 112	390	13 g	6 g	30 mg	47 g	25 g	5 g	850 mg
ASIAN NOODLES AND DUMPLINGS								
Hot and Sour Ramen with Tofu, Shiitakes, and Spinach page 144	520	12 g	1 g	0 mg	87 g	21 g	11 g	1930 mg
Vietnamese Rice Noodle Salad with Pork page 158	390	7 g	1 g	50 mg	60 g	23 g	3 g	1540 mg
Steamed Chinese Dumplings (Shu Mai) page 163	290	6 g	1.5 g	85 mg	36 g	22 g	1 g	1030 mg

	CAL	FAT	SAT FAT	CHOL	CARB	PROTEIN	FIBER	SODIUM
ITALY'S GREATEST HITS								
Classic Spaghetti Marinara page 166	410	8 g	1.5 g	0 mg	69 g	13 g	5 g	530 mg
Spaghetti Puttanesca page 168	380	9 g	1.5 g	5 mg	63 g	13 g	4 g	810 mg
Penne alla Vodka page 170	450	13 g	6 g	25 mg	64 g	12 g	4 g	550 mg
Spaghetti with Pecorino Romano and Black Pepper (Cacio e Pepe) page 175	410	12 g	6 g	25 mg	58 g	18 g	3 g	590 mg
Rustic Long-Simmered Pork Ragu page 182	510	10 g	3 g	85 mg	64 g	35 g	4 g	610 mg
Pasta alla Norma page 183	450	12 g	2 g	0 mg	73 g	14 g	9 g	780 mg
Spaghetti with Mushroom and Tomato Sauce page 184	460	14 g	3.5 g	15 mg	65 g	18 g	4 g	690 mg
PASTA PLUS 5								
Spaghetti with Quickest Tomato Sauce page 193	400	8 g	1.5 g	0 mg	69 g	13 g	6 g	480 mg
Fusilli with Giardiniera and Sausage page 209	430	8 g	3 g	25 mg	68 g	25 g	4 g	1760 mg
Ziti with Italian Sausage, Broccoli, and Sun-Dried Tomatoes page 210	480	12 g	4.5 g	30 mg	64 g	29 g	5 g	940 mg
Ziti with Fennel and Italian Sausage page 210	460	9 g	3.5 g	25 mg	70 g	26 g	5 g	730 mg
Pasta with Shrimp, Andouille Sausage, and Bell Pepper page 211	540	13 g	4.5 g	140 mg	69 g	37 g	6 g	1290 mg
PASTA FOR TWO								
Rotini with Garden Vegetable Sauce page 243	350	9 g	1.5 g	0 mg	58 g	12 g	6 g	1140 mg
Skillet Shrimp and Orzo Casserole page 253	570	13 g	3.5 g	155 mg	81 g	33 g	6 g	1830 mg
PESTOS AND NO-COOK SAUCES								
Low-Fat Basil Pesto page 257	360	8 g	2 g	10 mg	59 g	14 g	3 g	470 mg
Low-Fat Roasted Red Pepper Pesto page 261	370	8 g	2 g	10 mg	61 g	14 g	3 g	490 mg
Low-Fat Mushroom Pesto page 263	380	8 g	2 g	10 mg	61 g	15 g	3 g	500 mg
No-Cook Fresh Tomato Sauce page 272	390	11 g	1.5 g	0 mg	63 g	12 g	4 g	500 mg
No-Cook Fresh Tomato Sauce with Olives and Capers page 273	420	13 g	2 g	0 mg	64 g	12 g	4 g	620 mg
SAUCES FROM THE SLOW COOKER*								
Big-Batch Marinara Sauce page 276	340	3 g	0.5 g	0 mg	66 g	12 g	5 g	650 mg
Fire-Roasted Tomato Sauce page 278	340	2.5 g	0.5 g	0 mg	66 g	12 g	4 g	510 mg
Farm Stand Tomato Sauce page 280	340	3 g	0.5 g	0 mg	68 g	12 g	5 g	115 mg
Weeknight Meat Sauce page 281	460	11 g	3.5 g	35 mg	67 g	22 g	5 g	600 mg
Spicy Sausage Ragu with Red Peppers page 282	420	7 g	2 g	15 mg	68 g	20 g	5 g	770 mg
Shredded Pork Ragu page 286	440	7 g	2 g	55 mg	65 g	28 g	4 g	930 mg
FRESH PASTA SALADS								
Gazpacho Pasta Salad page 292	280	9 g	2 g	5 mg	41 g	9 g	4 g	440 mg
Summer Garden Pasta Salad with Asiago page 293	300	12 g	3 g	10 mg	39 g	9 g	3 g	520 mg
Pea and Pistachio Pesto Pasta Salad page 299	280	10 g	2 g	5 mg	38 g	10 g	3 g	280 mg

*The nutritional values given for this chapter are based on 18 servings and 3 pounds of pasta.

Index

C

G

Garlic
Bread, 281
Flatbread, Easy, 243
Garlicky Tortellini with
     Shrimp and Arugula, *114,* 124
mincing to a paste, 237
Olive Oil, and Artichokes, Spaghetti with, *236, 237*
Olive Oil, and Marinated Artichokes, Spaghetti
     with, 190
Pasta with Garlicky Tuscan Chicken, *24,* 25
prepeeled versus fresh, 200
Roasted, and Chicken, Orecchiette with, 201
Roasted, Chicken Sausage,
     and Arugula, Campanelle with, 200
Roasted, Shrimp, and Feta, Campanelle with, 201
Roasted Broccoli, and Almonds, Pasta with, 20
Roasted Cauliflower, and Walnuts, Pasta with, *18, 19*
Rolls, Easy, 226
Shrimp Fra Diavolo with Linguine, 186
slow-cooking, 190
substitutes, taste tests on, 294
toasting, 257
Garlic presses, ratings of, 7
Gazpacho Pasta Salad, *290,* 292
Gemelli with Caramelized Onions,
     Kale, and Bacon, 206
Giardiniera
and Sausage, Fusilli with, 209
taste tests on, 209
Gnocchi
Cauliflower, and Gorgonzola Gratin, 129
Gratin, Tomato-Basil, 128
with Mushrooms and Cream Sauce, 126, *127*
Ricotta, Homemade, with
     Browned Butter and Sage, 130, *131*
taste tests on, 128
Graters, cheese, ratings of, 7
Green Olive and Orange Pesto, 264, *265*
Greens
Baby Spinach Salad with
     Frisée and Strawberries, 252
Beans, Pancetta, and Garlic Bread Crumbs,
     Spaghetti with, 103
Caesar Salad, 43

Greens *(cont.)*
Caesar Salad for a Crowd, 223
Creamy Baked Tortellini with
     Radicchio, Peas, and Bacon, *122,* 123
escarole, about, 179
Foolproof Green Salad, 272
Gemelli with Caramelized Onions,
     Kale, and Bacon, 206
hearty, preparing, 206
Kale and Sunflower Seed Pesto, *254,* 269
Orecchiette with Escarole and White Beans, 179
Romaine and Endive Salad with Pear, 99
Shells with Blue Cheese,
     Radicchio, and Walnuts, 207
Spaghetti with Lentils, Pancetta,
     and Escarole, 104, *105*
Tricolor Salad with Balsamic Vinaigrette, 92
see also Arugula; Spinach

H

Ham
Arugula Salad with Figs and Prosciutto, 12
and Peas, Skillet Macaroni and Cheese with, 57
Skillet Saltimbocca Spaghetti, 50, *51*
Hearty Italian Meat Sauce
     (Sunday Gravy), 228–29
Hearty Vegetable Lasagna, *218,* 222–23
Herbs
fresh, washing and storing, 259
Herbed Ricotta Bruschetta, 40
tired, refreshing, 259
see also specific herbs
Homemade Ricotta Gnocchi with
     Browned Butter and Sage, 130, *131*
Hot and Sour Ramen with
     Tofu, Shiitakes, and Spinach, 144

I

Ingredients, tastings of
anchovy fillets versus paste, 168
andouille sausage, 211
bacon, premium, 169
barbecue sauce, 305

M

Macaroni

Bacon-Cheeseburger Pasta Bake, 70, *71*

and Cheese, Baked, 76

and Cheese, Skillet, with Broccoli, 56

and Cheese, Skillet, with Ham and Peas, 57

and Cheese, Spicy Tomato and Chile, 194

and Cheese, Ultimate Stovetop, 194

Pastitsio, 84

Pizza Pasta Bake, 72

Salad, Barbecue, with Smoked Sausage, 305

Salad, Cool and Creamy, *302,* 303

Salad with Cheddar and Chipotle, 304

Skillet-Baked Tex-Mex, 54, *55*

taste tests on, 56

Ultimate Chili Mac, 77

Manicotti, Meaty, 86, *87*

Manicotti Puttanesca, 85

Mayonnaise, taste tests on, 303

Meat

Meaty Manicotti, 86, *87*

shredding, 289

see also Beef; Meatloaf mix; Pork; Rabbit; Veal

Meatballs

Hearty Italian Meat Sauce (Sunday Gravy), 228–29

and Marinara, *284,* 285

Spaghetti and, for a Crowd, 230, *231*

Turkey-Pesto, Spaghetti with, 30

Meatloaf mix

Classic Lasagna with Hearty Meat Sauce, 90

Hearty Italian Meat Sauce (Sunday Gravy), 228–29

Mini Meat Lasagna, *234,* 247

Ravioli with Meat Sauce, 118

Skillet Meaty Lasagna, 47

Mediterranean Penne
with Tuna and Niçoise Olives, 214

Mini Meat Lasagna, *234,* 247

Mint, about, 299

Miso, Pork, and Shiitakes,
Udon Noodles with, 145

Mozzarella

Baked Penne with Spinach,
Artichokes, and Chicken, 80

Baked Ziti, 92, *93*

Classic Lasagna with Hearty Meat Sauce, 90

Easiest-Ever Lasagna, 88

Hearty Vegetable Lasagna, *218,* 222–23

Manicotti Puttanesca, 85

Meaty Manicotti, 86, *87*

Mini Meat Lasagna, *234,* 247

Pasta Caprese, *8,* 12

Pizza Pasta Bake, 72

Roasted Eggplant and Zucchini Lasagna, 91

Skillet Pasta with Eggplant
and Roasted Red Peppers, *36,* 46

Smoked, Fire-Roasted Tomatoes,
and Pepperoni, Ziti with, *188,* 204

Spinach Lasagna, 112, *113*

Stuffed Shells with Meat Sauce, 82, *83*

taste tests on, 69

Mushroom(s)

Campanelle with Porcini Cream Sauce, 191

Chicken Riggies, 27

and Chicken Sauce, Creamy, 289

cleaning, 262

and Cream Sauce, Gnocchi with, 126, *127*

dried porcini, rehydrating, 191

Hot and Sour Ramen with
Tofu, Shiitakes, and Spinach, 144

Pasta with Chicken Cacciatore Sauce, 26

Pesto, Low-Fat, 263

Pesto with Parsley, 262

Pizza Pasta Bake, 72

Pork Lo Mein with Shiitakes
and Napa Cabbage, 136, *137*

portobello, removing gills from, 184

Ramen with Beef,
Shiitakes, and Spinach, *140,* 141

Sautéed, and Thyme, Campanelle with, 17

Sautéed, and Truffle Oil, Farfalle with, 195

Sautéed, Peas, and
Camembert, Campanelle with, 240